What Reviewers Are Saying

"Robin Bartlett's book brought to life Vietnam events in vivid detail that I had forgotten. I found it hard to put down and finished reading it in two days."—Dan "Doc" Cleary, Medic, A 1/5 Air Cav

"Vietnam Combat gives an excellent description of the areas where we patrolled, our living conditions and combat episodes. I felt like he was telling my story! If one wishes to understand the unvarnished experiences of a combat soldier in 1968, this book is a must-read!"—Arthur Kuhner, RTO, A 1/5 Air Cav

"...a first-rate memoir about preparing for and then surviving a tour of combat. Highly recommended for educators and students wanting to learn about the world of an airmobile infantryman during the height of the Vietnam War."—Dr. Erik B. Villard, author of *Army Combat Operations in the Vietnam War*

"Robin Bartlett's narrative immerses you into the action and you can feel the sweat dripping down your neck, smell the stench of dirty, unwashed uniforms, and hear the crack of rifles and the staccato pop of the M-60 machine guns. ... I strongly recommend Bartlett's book as it provides a compelling snapshot into a Platoon Leader's experience in the 1st Cavalry Division in Vietnam during the critical period from 1968 to 1969."—Lt Col David Siry, Director of the Center for Oral History at USMA, West Point

"Robin Bartlett's poignant memoir is more than a personal journey through his Vietnam experiences. It is an informative, emotional, and visceral examination of day-to-day life for a young platoon leader in grueling circumstances."—Kelly E. Crager, PhD, Head, Oral History Project, Vietnam Center and Archive, Texas Tech University

"Bartlett's first-hand, boots-in-the mud account is a rare and sobering look at both the character and nature of combat. To wit, violence inflicts many scars—many not visible—and many do not heal, with the tincture of time alone. With prior service as a 'Dog-faced Soldier' and past duty as the 1st Cavalry Division Psychiatrist serving in combat, I would submit that authentic connection makes the difference in taking care of soldiers in the field and in the clinical setting. From 'mad minutes' to Monarch butterflies, the manner in which Bartlett shares his memories can connect and heal."—Colonel Dennis Sarmiento, MD, Psychiatrist, US Army War College

"If you thought you knew about war by reading the post 9/11 stories from Iraq and Afghanistan, think again. 110-degree heat, 50 lb rucks, an unrelenting enemy using mines and booby traps, pure terror, and a cloudy mission; it's Operation Iraqi Freedom except four decades earlier. Some things never change in war: brave soldiers and bad politics. There are so many similarities between generations of warriors. Robin Bartlett does a great job taking us right to his battle position and walking on patrol. This was a war fought by twenty-somethings who matured in rice paddies and mortar pits while their peers were eating popcorn at a drive-in. Welcome Home to every one of you. Read this book not only for the history lesson it provides but to remember that what we all learned in the Global War on Terror was learned before."—Matt Eversmann, USA (Ret), co-author of *Walk in My Combat Boots* with James Patterson

"Ordinarily I would not choose to read about the gruesome Vietnam war or any other war, but this book is so compelling and beautifully written that I read every single word. … I recommend this extraordinary book to all because it is informative, moving, personal, and easy to follow. I have known Robin since we were children catching butterflies."—Mitzi, The Butterfly Lady

"What a story! I felt as if I was right there with them as the stories unfolded. I knew that part of the story would be ugly, and, sure enough, there were times when I could only read a few pages at a time before being overcome with emotion. Bartlett found the perfect way to relay the horrific experiences he and his comrades encountered while still expressing the incredible bonds they shared. That made my heart swell with pride. … We can never underestimate the day-to-day situations the Vietnam war put our military in. We plucked them out of their ordinary lives and put them in extraordinary circumstances. Those who came home were forever changed and marked by the losses of the ones who did not. We owe a debt to them that can never be repaid."—Patti Elliott, Proud Gold Star Mother of SPC Daniel Lucas Elliott, KIA 7/15/2011, Iraq

"Robin Bartlett's book is vastly different from most Vietnam war books. The author takes us on a tour of the daily tasks and thoughts of a soldier serving during the war rather than a top-down view. … It brought back memories of my time in Vietnam like no other Vietnam book I have read. I laughed, cried, and shuddered while reading it."—Ron Berman, Vietnam veteran, Board Member, peacetreesvietnam.org

"Bartlett's vivid description of life as a junior officer in combat rings 100% true. Red nylon mail bags with a piece of ice and warm beer cans, ambushes that don't quite go according to plan, and under-manned infantry companies in the field. ... The common dominator he stressed was the enormous burden carried daily by every infantry lieutenant attempting to balance mission accomplishment and taking care of his men. He makes a good case for this soul-wrenching burden that affected many long after they returned from war."—Col Dick Baumer, USA (Ret)

"It is difficult for those comfortably ensconced while reading Bartlett's tale to comprehend the wearing challenges he and his soldiers faced, day after day, in an environment where death or massive wounds were just around the next bend in the trail, or tangle of rainforest. Dedication, endurance, desperation; all are found in his saga, with time out for occasional humor."—Phil Gioia, author of *Danger Close!*

"As an intelligence officer at MACV Headquarters, I had a strategic view of the war. Robin Bartlett's superbly written book has brought me face-to-face with combat in Vietnam, a reality I only vaguely understood during my tour. Although this is the story of an infantry lieutenant's experience, in many ways it is the story of every infantryman who served in that war. It is a story of emotions ranging from sheer terror to irony, guilt, and even levity: sometimes all of them in the space of a day."—Lt Col James Carson USAR (Ret), author of *Chasing Mosby, Killing Booth*

"A bitter war. An interesting read. *Vietnam Combat* is the cathartic, detailed account of a young infantry lieutenant's courageous, personal, combat experiences in an increasingly unpopular war. The war's political mismanagement and disconcerting outcome left him embittered. Some fifty years later, he concludes his book's final chapter still burdened by that war, 'damaged' and 'unforgiving toward my military and political leaders.' His journey began faithfully fighting in a war for duty, honor, and country. The war's tragic end began his lifelong struggle with the aftermath of a war lost not on Vietnam's battlefields, but in Washington, DC. Even so, he remains proud to be a former soldier, a 'brother in arms' with fellow veterans."—Lt Col Ed Sherwood, USA (Ret), author of *Courage Under Fire*

"This gritty, realistic account of training for, deploying to, and fighting in Vietnam will stick with you. All gave some; Robin and his soldiers gave far more than most."—Lt Col (Ret) Daniel Gade, author of *Wounding Warriors*

"All in all, this is a great memoir by an officer in the Vietnam War and I highly recommend it to anyone interested in the war or the goings on within a combat infantry platoon. An engaging story from the very first page. Well written and exciting from beginning to end. Well done, Mr. Bartlett, welcome home!"—John Podlaski, award-winning author

"Having served as a US Army Lieutenant in Vietnam during the same general time frame as Robin Bartlett, his book brought back a lot of memories. Not only is it an account of his horrific combat experiences during the Vietnam War, but also recalls many non-combat 'battles' he had to fight. The book holds the reader's attention throughout."—Terry A. McCarl, Historian, 15th Medical Battalion Association and former historian, 1st Cavalry Division Association

"Robin Bartlett's book, *Vietnam Combat*, made me proud to have served this country with valor despite coming home with PTSD and exposed to Agent Orange. Sharing his experience in Vietnam is both nostalgic and therapeutic. It is not only historical, but it is important to all Americans that PATRIOTISM is still alive and well."—Takeshi "Tak" Furumoto, District Intelligence Officer, Operation Phoenix Advisor to National Vietnamese Police, President & CEO, Furumoto Realty Group

"I got a new perspective about being an officer of an infantry platoon. I specifically liked the section when he decided to walk point for the platoon. ... I would recommend this book for fellow Vietnam Veterans and for the general public."—Keith Goudy, President, Vietnam War History Foundation, Vietnam Veteran

VIETNAM COMBAT

Firefights and Writing History

By

ROBIN BARTLETT

CASEMATE

Philadelphia & Oxford

Published in the United States of America and Great Britain in 2023 by
CASEMATE PUBLISHERS
1950 Lawrence Road, Havertown, PA 19083, USA
and
The Old Music Hall, 106–108 Cowley Road, Oxford OX4 1JE, UK

Copyright 2023 © Robin Bartlett

Hardback Edition: ISBN 978-1-63624-242-2
Digital Edition: ISBN 978-1-63624-243-9

A CIP record for this book is available from the British Library

Printed and bound in the United Kingdom by TJ Books Ltd

Typeset in India by Lapiz Digital Services, Chennai.

For a complete list of Casemate titles, please contact:

CASEMATE PUBLISHERS (US)
Telephone (610) 853-9131
Fax (610) 853-9146
Email: casemate@casematepublishers.com
www.casematepublishers.com

CASEMATE PUBLISHERS (UK)
Telephone (01865) 241249
Email: casemate-uk@casematepublishers.co.uk
www.casematepublishers.co.uk

Front cover: View from assault helicopter. (Public domain)

DEDICATION

This book is dedicated to the more than 58,000 American soldiers killed during the Vietnam War and especially to those of the 82nd Airborne Division (All American) and the 1st Air Cavalry Division (The First Team).

I wish to thank the following people for their assistance in bringing this book to publication:

Dr. Clyde Ladell Payne, Claremont McKenna College, who started me on this journey.
Ruth Sheppard, Casemate Publishers, who believed in my story.
Sharon Goldinger, Book Shepherd, and Ann Bilodeau, friend, for critical reading and advice.
Patricia Gallo-Stenman and Daisy Lo Carpenter for proofreading and advice.
Louis Cannizzaro, LAC Communications, for developing my YouTube video of "The Trail."
My son, Dr. Jason Bartlett, for helping to organize photographs and captions.
My other sons, Brendan, and Matthew, but most importantly my wife, Barbara, for their love and support before, during and after.

And to all my veteran brothers and readers: thank you for walking the trail with me.

Robin Bartlett
Foggy Day 1-6, A 1/5 Air Cav and HHC Air Cav Division
Norwood, NJ

Contents

The Trail		xi
Preface: Dragging Chains		xiii
Introduction		xvii

1	My First Worst Day in Vietnam	1
2	Training for War	10
3	Ranger School: Learning to Lead, Preparing to Kill	19
4	Back at the 82nd	33
5	First Days in Country	39
6	Ambushing Gazelles	55
7	The Jungle Penetrator	60
8	FNGs in the Field and Base Camp	72
9	Face-to-Face	76
10	Pay Officer	87
11	Blown Ambush	90
12	Saturation Ambushing	96
13	Recon by Fire—Enemy Base Camp	101
14	Beyond Artillery Cover	107
15	LZ is Green	110
16	Autorotate	116
17	Stream Crossing	124
18	Letting It All Hang Out	128
19	Tracer Rounds	133
20	Surviving Leg Cramps	137
21	Ambush in the Rain	142
22	Escort to Laos	146
23	Tear Gas Attack	150
24	Night Firefight	155
25	Hard Luck Simons	164
26	Walking Point	172
27	You Fight It, We Write It	178

28	The Battle of the Parrot's Beak	185
29	Assistant Defense Counsel	198
30	Buying Art Supplies	203
31	Welcome Home	212
32	Butterfly Coincidences	220
33	Attributions	226
34	A Boots on the Ground Point of View	229

Glossary and Abbreviations of Military Terms	235
US and Enemy Weapons	245
Author's Military Awards, Decorations, Assignments and Timeline	249
Bibliography	251
Resources	253
Index	261

The Trail

The trail is only a meter wide and weaves its way through thick green and brown underbrush so overgrown that even a jack rabbit would have trouble threading its way. Large, thorny limbs form a matted barrier as you strain, push, shove, and bleed to get through. "Wait-a-minute" vines seem to take special pleasure in tripping you—spraining your ankle, causing you to swear. With each conquering, a new thicket presents itself, as though to say: "You made it through that one; now try me."

As the trail wears on, your sore muscles, aching feet, and back cry out for relief from a 60-pound pack filled with C-Rations, ammunition, canteens, and combat equipment. Ten-minute breaks ease the pain for a short while, and then you're numb again. Rest is a beautiful dream. You must conserve water, so you sip sweet mouthfuls, allowing it to run slowly down your cotton-dry throat. If you stop sweating, the dirt cakes on your arms and face and you can't spare the water to wash it off. It's time to push on, waddling like a pregnant woman.

The trail is a struggle between mind and body; the two fight every step, clawing a trough, your brain forcing you on. Your mind is filled with thoughts—home, cool beer, women—but ever alert for any noise, any false movement, anything out of the ordinary along the trail. There are so many things to remember. Keep alert, stay alive. You must kill him first, you must pull the trigger first, and you must be fast.

But the trail pulls you down. Eyes droop; sweat drips into them, the salt burning and stinging. Dirty hands rub the tears away and nails, bitten to the quick, scratch the mosquito bites from the night before. Alert. Alert. Keep your head up; breathe deep; don't think about home; don't think about anything except staying alive. Forget the pain, the aching muscles, the tired feet. Clear your mind, protect your life. Don't let the trail win.

The perspiration runs in big dirty drops off the stock of your M16 rifle. Your hands push the thorns aside; you work your body through but your pack catches. You pull. Thorns cut across your shoulders—DAMN! But keep following that little green trail—keep pushing, keep pushing, feet obeying a harsh command. But listen, stay alert… the jungle is quiet and only an occasional monkey screams out, making you jump and duck.

You follow the trail by feel—toes pointing forward, searching for vines and roots. Your eyes scan to the front, searching for movement; ears strain like radar listening for the click of a safety being released. Their weapons sound like popcorn exploding—listen for popcorn. Your knees are bent, limp, ready to drop face-flat in a split second as you walk the trail.

The trail is life: pain, frustration, wishes, agony, and death. You get to know it well and you learn quickly what life means and how precious it is and how much you took it for granted… before.

The trail changes many lives. It ends some too.

Robin Bartlett, *Army Digest*, April 1969.
https://youtu.be/XZq5mJ-qW9o or Google: "The Trail by Robin Bartlett".

Preface: Dragging Chains

The edges of the wounds we bear get softer, but they never go away.
They never heal. I don't think there's ever a resolution.

As early as 1678, Swiss military physicians used the term "nostalgia" to define a condition characterized by insomnia, anxiety, cardiac palpitations, stupor, and melancholy. At the time, German doctors called these symptoms *Heimweh* or homesickness while Spanish physicians called the condition *estar roto* or "to be broken." French doctors named it *maladie du pays* (disease of the country).

During the American Civil War, the condition was "Soldier's Heart" or "Irritable Heart." The malaise was marked by a rapid pulse, anxiety and trouble breathing. Stephen Crane's *The Red Badge of Courage* provides an excellent portrayal of the problem experienced by a Union Army recruit facing bombardment. In 1905, Russia coined the term *boy shok* or battle shock. In 1919, at the end of World War I, President Woodrow Wilson proclaimed November 11 as the first observance of Armistice Day, now known as Veterans Day. During World War I some soldiers were reported to have experienced "shell shock," a term established by British psychologist Charles Myers. The term was used to describe a reaction to the explosion of artillery shells. Common symptoms included panic and sleeplessness. "War neuroses" was a term used by military psychiatrists during World War I and II to describe the nervous and mental disorders soldiers experienced from intense wartime environments.

World War II saw the name change again, this time to "Combat Stress Reaction." This was yet another name given to describe the adverse effects resulting from battle stress. Typical symptoms include exhaustion, decrease in responsiveness, uncertainty, feeling disconnected and an inability to focus. Almost half of World War II military discharges were said to be the result of combat exhaustion. This symptom was made famous by General George Patton who, among others, believed such men were cowards. He was severely criticized for striking a man in a hospital unit suffering from the condition.

In 1952, Post Traumatic Stress Disorder (PTSD) made its first appearance in the American Psychiatric Association's Diagnostic and Statistical Manual of Mental Disorders (APA's DSM-1). The term used was "gross stress reaction." That term was dropped in the second edition of the book, but in 1980 PTSD came back into the vernacular. The entry was in direct response to research involving returning Vietnam War veterans as well as Holocaust survivors and other trauma sufferers such as police officers who had killed suspects or had been shot and women who had been attacked, sexually assaulted, or beaten. In 1989, the Veterans Administration created the National Center for PTSD. Between 1989 and 2013, the center reported treating more than a half-million veterans diagnosed with PTSD. According to a March 2023 National Vietnam Veterans Readjustment Study, about 15 percent of Vietnam veterans are currently diagnosed with PTSD.

My own experience with PTSD is discussed in Chapter 12, "Saturation Ambushing." The fact that I was raised in a military family familiar with the effects of PTSD may have helped with my adjustment upon return to The World. I also remained in the service for several years and continued to live in a military community, within a "Band of Brothers" that acknowledged the condition.

But the traumatic experiences that I endured should have been acknowledged and brought to light. They were not. For many years, I simply locked all those events up in the titanium trunk located in the back of my mind… until—one day—they started to leak out. Then, I sought and received help from a psychiatrist friend. Writing this book, too, is an effort for me to come to grips with events from 50-plus years ago.

I certainly have profited from my military training and experiences. That training made me fearless about facing challenges. But the training has also been a challenge in my civilian career. I frequently thought I knew more and had more life experience than the people who were my managers. Relearning lessons of sympathy, empathy, courtesy, compassion, love, and peace have not always come easy. I thank my wife for frequently kicking me in the butt to remind me.

There is a line from Charles Dickens's famous story *A Christmas Carol* that has always resonated with me. These words describe how I have often felt over the past 50 years:

> "I wear the chain I forged in life," replied the Ghost. "I made it link by link, and yard by yard; I girded it on of my own free will, and of my own free will I wore it."

We all wear the chains of life we forge day to day. We also tend to relive and remember our negative experiences more frequently than the positive ones. Perhaps that is to remind us not to repeat our mistakes. And while my experiences occurred over 50 years ago, those events are as fresh and as real in my mind today as the day they occurred. There is rarely a day that goes by that I don't recall some event that happened to me during those 365 days. I am sure they will be with me for the rest of my life. They are the chains I drag behind me.

Many people feel that the Vietnam War is a black stain on American history because it is the first war that "we lost." While I personally find the Vietnam War Memorial to be a wonderful tribute to those who made the ultimate sacrifice, its color and design reinforce our country's loss of the war. Even though I did not experience the negativism and discourtesy that many Vietnam vets did upon return to the US, that negative attitude became so apparent as the war wound down. It became clear that the American people wanted to put this war out of mind and memory—and behind them—as quickly as possible. This frequently meant ignoring the veterans who served there and "lost the war" as well. I am so pleased to see that attitude has dramatically changed for our vets currently returning from Afghanistan, Iraq, and Syria. We have welcomed these vets home in airports, in parades, in society, in memorial services, and in hospitals. It's a shame that Vietnam vets did not receive something similar. In fact, many met quite the opposite response after stepping back into the civilian world, furthering the common embarrassed and negative feelings so many of my brothers have about the war.

But we Vietnam vets are a tough breed, now in our late 60s and 70s. We plan to be here for a while longer, but many of us are still suffering from PTSD, homelessness, horrific memories, and stories that need to be told. The edges of the wounds we bear get softer, but they never go away. They never heal. For many there's never a resolution.

Ironically, even though he never served in the armed forces, one of the most famous quotes attributed to John Wayne is: "Courage is being scared to death but saddling up anyway." I think this sums up how so many of us feel about our Vietnam experience.

I hope you will take time to ask your Vietnam vet to tell you his or her story. Listen and ask questions. Many still need to unburden themselves. We only wish to be recognized and to share our own "Stories from the Trail." We need someone to care. We need your empathy.

Above all, please—always use the code words "Welcome home" rather than "Thank you for your service" when you speak with a Vietnam vet. These words are so meaningful to us. They will bring tears to our eyes and lumps to our throats.

Introduction

As I walk down the path leading to the apex of the chevron-shaped marble walls, I notice several things. It gets darker. It gets cooler. It gets quieter.

The year 1968 was the most significant in the history of the Vietnam War. It certainly was the most significant year in my life. The war was at its height. There were more American troops in country and more American and enemy casualties, both wounded in action (WIA) and killed in action (KIA) than in any other year. The panel for 1968 of the Vietnam Veterans War Memorial has more names on it than any other. It was also the year when the Viet Cong and North Vietnamese Army attempted to re-assert themselves in the hearts and minds of the South Vietnamese people. For the first time these enemies launched a large-scale coordinated attack on major cities in the south. The Tet Offensive of January 31, 1968 and Mini-Tet Offensives that followed in May and August of that year initially caught American troops by surprise. The offensives and significant losses of lives caused Americans at home to doubt President Johnson's administration's claims that we were "winning the war."

According to Dr. Erik Villard, military historian at the US Army Center for Military History, the Tet Offensive "was one of the most significant military, political and social events of the second half of the 20th Century." It was the largest enemy offensive launched by North Vietnam and is generally interpreted as the turning point in American public opinion from believing that American and South Vietnamese soldiers were winning, to recognizing we were in a stalemate. In a surprise series of attacks focused on 300 cities the NVA achieved initial success partly because of lack of preparation and partly because more than 50 percent of the ARVN troops were away from their units celebrating the holiday. While the NVA succeeded in penetrating major cities like Saigon, Hue and Quang Tri, the overall engagement was considered a military failure with the loss of as many as 40,000 ground troops out of a total of 120,000. The US suffered more Americans killed on January 31 than on any other day of the war with a total of 216 killed and 1,609 wounded. An additional 421 ARVN troops were killed, 2,123 wounded and 31 missing. The offensive, however, became a stunning propaganda victory for North Vietnam. It not only served to begin to change American public opinion but also placed a strain on relations between the

xviii • VIETNAM COMBAT

governments of South Vietnam and the United States. The battle, watched nightly on color TVs, also planted the seeds of doubt in American political and military leaders.

Soon war protests in American streets rose to new heights. Americans were tired of war and tired of losing their sons to questionable objectives. Patience and support for the war began to waver. Each night the evening news paraded the names and photographs of American soldiers who died that day. Walter Cronkite, "The Most Trusted Man in America," was a war correspondent who spent significant amounts of time embedded with American troops during the battle of Hue. His announcement on February 27 and the dramatic daily television coverage of the war are widely interpreted as a turning point in American support. Cronkite stated: "It seems now more certain than ever that the bloody experience of Vietnam is to end in a stalemate." Don Oberdorfer, professor at Johns Hopkins University, in his book *Tet! The Turning Point*, states that Tet "was the first true life big event in which television played a catalytic role in changing people's thinking and behavior on matters of national and international policy." The nation gradually became polarized with protests, marches, draft card- and flag-burning pervading city streets and college campuses. It was a year of tremendous dissent and unrest further traumatized with the assassinations of Dr. Martin Luther King and Robert F. Kennedy. Furthermore, there was an awakening among senior and junior American officers and non-commissioned officers that our civilian leaders had shamelessly lied to us about the purpose and objectives of the war.

American troops stationed in Vietnam in 1968 also knew this was a war we could not win. Yes, we could always out-bomb, out-shoot, and out-kill more of them than they could of us. Whenever we could locate, block, and hold a massed enemy force in a specific area we could always bring superior firepower to bear. But the enemy was adept at dispersing, breaking into small groups, evading, and finding their way back across the border into safe havens in Laos and Cambodia where American troops were not permitted to follow. Among many American soldiers and junior officers stationed in Vietnam, the desire to win was waning, replaced by a philosophy of self-protection. The common goal was "serve my 365 and return home in one piece."

Other events that colored American opinion were the shocking televised execution of a captured and handcuffed VC prisoner by a South Vietnamese General Nguyen Ngoc Loan, chief of the national police, in February 1968. The video of this execution exposed the brutality of the war and the callous way in which Viet Cong (VC) prisoners were commonly treated. Later in November 1969, the events of the My Lai massacre under the leadership of Lieutenant William Calley came to light. The officer ordered his soldiers to kill innocent men, women, children, and animals of a village without cause. A total massacre of the village was narrowly avoided by the quick action taken by a helicopter pilot who witnessed what was happening and ordered the platoon to stand down. This public event amplified the negativism directed toward returning American soldiers and soured the American public's opinion of our military. Soldiers returning home refused to wear their uniforms in public for fear of being spit upon or called "baby killers."

The 12 months I spent in Vietnam were the most challenging and difficult of my life. As a 22-year-old second lieutenant, I had recently completed the Infantry Officer Basic Course, Airborne, and Ranger training at Ft. Benning, Georgia. I was assigned to the 82nd Airborne Division in Ft. Bragg, North Carolina and knew I would receive orders for Vietnam within the next six to nine months. Imbued with this training and skills, my demeanor was one of blustery self-confidence. I had gone through the best training the army had to offer. I was in the best physical condition of my life, and I had been trained to lead a platoon in combat and overcome any enemy obstacle that confronted me. I walked tall and proudly in my spit-shined jump boots with Airborne wings and Ranger Tab on my uniform and paratrooper emblem on my hat. Soldiers in my unit saluted me and said, "Airborne, Sir," and I responded, "All the way." But silently, I felt deeply conflicted.

Within a few months of completing training and a brief assignment with the 82nd, I found myself on an airplane bound for Tan Son Nhut Airbase near Saigon on orders to join the 101st Airborne Division. My attitude and the attitude of many of the other officers and men I led had begun to change. The philosophy was "keep your head and butt down and don't take chances with your men." The belief that Vietnam was a lost cause had begun to creep into our minds and was reinforced by protests where the common cry was: "Hell no, we won't go!" A soldier headed for Vietnam only had to endure for 365 days of field duty and officers were required to spend only six months before transferring to a staff position. Yet the rumors persisted that platoon leaders had a survival rate of less than 90 days in country. Upon arrival, we all received a "short-timer calendar." It was the most valuable piece of paper every soldier carried. The image on the paper was that of a nude female body partitioned into 365 units and each day I religiously colored in another section, tracking the days until I could return to the World.

The years 1968–9 were to be the worst times to be a combat infantry platoon leader in that God-forsaken land, let alone a combat rifleman. Officers and soldiers alike commonly recognized those years as transitional. I saw the combat tactics of my unit change from aggressive "find the enemy, attack and kill him," to "locate the enemy, pull back and blow them away with superior firepower." Unnecessary risk-taking by leaders was met with grave concern by front-line soldiers. As a platoon leader I quickly learned that I commanded respect and support from my men by not taking unnecessary risks and by using "reconnaissance by (artillery) fire" before entering any danger zone. Gradually, I and many of my fellow junior officers came to realize that the strategy of not allowing American troops to pursue enemy units into Cambodia, Laos, and even North Vietnam was a prescription for failure. Despite this realization, the war persisted for another four years because no president wanted the stigma of being the first to lose an American war.

Short-timer calendar, one of many different types throughout war (See disclaimer)

Writing this book has also been a cathartic and healing experience for me. It was challenging to recall these stories and retell them to the best of my memory and writing ability. Some are humorous; some are horrific. As I wrote, I was amazed at how many details my mind retained. At times, the writing transported me back to a day and time more than 50 years ago, and I relived the incident as vividly as it occurred. I saw the colors. I felt the fear. There was sweat on my face and underarms. I even recalled the smells.

Many of these stories have been difficult to remember and write. Writing made me relive the events and actions I locked away at the back of my mind for so many years. I never wanted to relive them, but in time I learned I needed to heal from the experience. Killing enemy soldiers was the most frightening experience I ever had. Most kills were at a distance which made it a bit easier to cope with, but often the enemy was blown away at close range with Claymore mines, machine gun and M16 fire. The enemy rarely survived, and the bodies were always badly mutilated. After an ambush it became necessary to search the bodies for documents. It was not a task for the faint of heart and many of my men just could not bring themselves to do it. Thus, the job often fell to me and my platoon sergeant to search the pockets, helmets, and packs of the dead enemy soldiers. At first, I was repulsed, but in time I simply packed my emotions away in the back of my mind and did what needed to be done. Usually there was little of value to be found.

Much harder was the handling of KIAs from my platoon. This involved wrapping them in ponchos, filling out death cards, entering the coordinates where they died, signing my name, and tying the card to their boot. This was always a traumatic experience and never to be forgotten. These events changed me. They made me a different person. I became unemotional and cold-hearted. I compartmentalized all emotion and feelings. I refused to allow the experiences to affect me. I lost aspects of my personality during my months in combat: love, empathy, caring, and patience, to mention just a few. I have spent a good deal of time over the past 50-plus years dragging the chains of Vietnam behind me and trying to recapture the person I once was—before Vietnam. It has not been an easy road, but with the love and support of an amazing wife, three marvelous sons and close friends who have stayed with me through the years, I have made progress.

Remembering, writing, and sharing my stories from "The Trail" is part of my healing experience, as well as my continuing attempt to understand and cope with the impact 1968–9 had on my life. As many of my Vietnam veteran brothers know, the experience has changed us all indelibly. The war each of us experienced was colored by the terrain we humped, the amount of time we spent in the boonies, and the engagements we fought. All veterans have a different story to tell. This one is mine.

The Vietnam War Memorial has great meaning for me, and I have visited it many times. It's always a cathartic experience. As I walk down the path leading to the apex of the chevron-shaped marble walls, I notice several things: It gets darker. It gets cooler. It gets quieter. The experience always reminds me of the foxholes I dug and huddled in at night. It brings back memories of the seven months I spent as a platoon leader, the night ambushes, firefights, and the instant fear I experienced from hearing sounds of movement. Many of the names of the men I led are inscribed on The Wall. I do not remember all their names because we called each other by nicknames and call signs, but I always spend a few minutes visiting and touching the names I do recall. As I walk down the path leading to the memorial the memories and events often come flooding back. At first, that experience was exceedingly difficult for me to handle, but now, with time, I come away feeling better. It truly is "The Wall that Heals."

* * *

Author's note: While proofing and rewriting this manuscript, I remembered the 100+ letters I wrote home during my year in Vietnam that my mother had carefully saved. I think she had a premonition I might someday try to write this book. I had also sent a few letters to a college classmate who thoughtfully saved and returned them to me. I dusted the letters off, put them in chronological order and started reading what I wrote over 50 years ago. I've included snippets from these letters in appropriate chapters in an effort to add more of my personal feelings at the time and provide insight into the juxtaposition between what actually happened and what I wrote home about.

I took many of the photographs in this book. Others were taken by army buddies and unknown combat photographers assigned to the Public Information Office of the 1st Air Cav Division (Airmobile). Some of these photographs are highlighted in a short video found here: https://youtu.be/XZq5mJ-qW9o or Google: "The Trail by Robin Bartlett." Additional information is also available at www.RobinBartlettAuthor. com

These photographs and art pieces have survived two lost and founds. I first rescued many of the photographs and art pieces included in this book when the 1st Cav Division relocated from Camp Evans in I Corps to Phuoc Vinh in III Corps. They were in a pile to be burned. I obtained permission to "help myself." I kept the photographs and art pieces in three binders and ultimately decided to donate them to the Vietnam Art Museum located in Chicago. I was told that an exhibit would be arranged of the pieces, but after several months of not hearing anything, I contacted the museum to find out what had happened to my binders. I was informed that the museum was closed, and new management was being sought. I visited the museum to rescue my binders. I found two of them right away but even after an exhaustive search the third binder remained lost. After several hours of fruitless searching, I took a break at the manager's desk. There was a windowsill adjacent to the desk and there underneath some papers was my third binder! The photographs and art pieces had been rescued for a second time.

* * *

Disclaimer: The stories and events described in this book are true to the best of my recollection. Some events may have a different interpretation by other veterans who encountered similar situations. While these were actual occurrences that happened to me, I have changed the names of the soldiers for reasons of privacy.

Robin Bartlett
Foggy Day 1-6, A 1/5 Air Cav
www.RobinBartlettAuthor.com

CHAPTER I

My First Worst Day in Vietnam

It struck me at that moment that for the first time in history, the army was attempting to record the exact location for every soldier killed.

The diameter of an AK-47 round is 7.62mm with a shell casing of 39mm. The Kalashnikov 47 was the most common weapon carried by the Viet Cong (VC) guerilla soldiers and North Vietnamese Army (NVA) regular soldiers when I served as a combat infantry platoon leader with the 1st Air Cav Division in Vietnam from 1968–9. The round packs a tremendous punch and leaves the chamber of the weapon with extreme velocity. When one of these rounds strikes a body, it creates a small hole going in, but leaves an exceptionally large hole coming out the other side. The bullet is moving so fast it can often pass through the first body and injure anyone standing behind. If the bullet should hit bone within the body, it is designed to mushroom, deflect, and tumble, causing intense trauma.

Up until 1965, the US Army used the M14. They switched to the M16 primarily because of weight and firepower. The M14 weighs in at just under 14 lbs and carries a 20-round magazine. An M16 weighs just over seven. But the M16 has superior firepower with a high-velocity bullet and capability to fire off a 20-round magazine in 2.5 seconds with the selector switch set to full automatic. These factors made the weapon a favorite among GIs. (Even though the magazine would hold 20 rounds, my unit never loaded more than 18, so the magazine spring was not fully compressed, as this could possibly jam the weapon.) The M16 cartridge (.223mm) is only slightly larger than the common .22 round and was commonly referred to as a "pregnant .22."

Ammunition for the M16 was lighter too, and it was easy to strap two bandoliers (20 mags total) around your waist. This provided an extra layer of protection. If an enemy bullet struck one of your magazines it would still cause serious bodily injury, but the impact would be slowed, possibly making the wound survivable. The M16 provided American soldiers an ideal firearm for close combat. Most ambushes and skirmishes with the enemy that I encountered took place within 15–50m.

Early on in my field tour with the 1st Air Cav Division, my platoon received a replacement by the name of Sergeant Ron Roberts. He was a Fucking New Guy (FNG) and had been in country for about two weeks. He flew in one morning on the log bird (supply chopper) that brought water, C-Rats, and ammo. Roberts was 19 years old, fair-haired, short, and stocky, measuring in at about 5 foot 6 inches. It was obvious that he was a newbie because his face, neck and arms were white and without suntan lines. He was wearing both a jungle fatigue shirt and a T-shirt. No one wore underwear in Vietnam—it was just too damn hot. Roberts' skin was ashen. He looked like an immediate candidate for heat stroke. He saluted as he introduced himself. I returned the salute and told him to sit down and cool off. The man was agitated and nervous, this being his first day in the field. We chatted. I asked him where he was from and how long he had been in country. He told me he had recently completed Basic and Advanced Infantry Training and had gone through a six-week NCO training program that promoted him to Sergeant E-5 or squad leader. He was anxious to take over a squad and get into the fight just as soon as possible. Here was an overly aggressive and gung-ho soldier, but without any field experience. It was a liability for him to take on a leadership position until he had become both more acclimatized and experienced in the tactics and strategies that were the 1st Air Cav's hallmarks.

I told him to make the salute he gave me to be the last he made in the field. There was to be no saluting of officers, and in the future, I was to be addressed as One-Six and not Lieutenant or Sir. ("One" was for the first platoon and "six" for the platoon leader.) These measures were intended to give a slight measure of protection in case of enemy observation of our unit. Roberts was carrying way too much equipment, and clearly no one had shown him how to pare down to the essentials before humping the boonies, or how to pack them. I pointed out that many of the items he was carrying were superfluous weight, but he was reluctant to discard anything and argued he was willing to carry the extra load. I assigned Roberts to work with my most experienced squad leader, Specialist Johnson, and told "One-Three" (Squad leader/Third Squad) to get him squared away—convince him to peel off the extra clothing and lose the extra equipment. As he left, Roberts almost saluted me again, but caught himself and trotted off following Johnson.

Letter: 10 June 1968, A Company, 1/5 Cav, 1st Air Cav Division, LZ Jane, I Corps, Vietnam

For your information, everyone over here is referred to by their call sign numbers. This eliminates saying "sir" which is forbidden as well as saluting. The BN CO is General Motors 6, the S-3 is 3-6, A Company CO is Foggy Day 6, 1st platoon leader is 1-6 and the platoon sergeant is 1-5. So it goes, right on down the line to squad leader, fire team leader and almost everyone. My RTO is Foggy Day 1-6 Romeo.

It was our company and battalion's policy to have all FNG sergeants walk as regular soldiers within the platoon for several weeks before assigning them to leadership positions. Roberts was a sergeant E-5, a squad leader by rights, while my other squad leaders were SP4s, and Roberts had seniority over them. However, I was not about to allow an FNG sergeant to assume a squad leader position until he was thoroughly acclimatized, vetted, familiar with our tactics and strategy, and mentally prepared to assume responsibility for a squad. I explained this to Roberts, but it didn't sit well. He said he had seniority and wanted to know when he would be assigned as a squad leader. I reiterated that he should walk along, observe our procedures, and get to know the men in the squad and platoon. I would assign him as a squad leader when the time was right. When he continued to press me, I told him firmly, "I will assign you to the position when I see that you are comfortable and competent enough to lead a squad."

As we talked, it occurred to me that like many of the young men who were aggressively trained by the army, Roberts wanted to get into a fight, get his first kill and win a medal. As we talked, I explained to him that our tactical philosophy was to avoid close contact with the enemy, and to seek, locate, and contain a large enemy concentration and then bring to bear the incredible firepower of the 1st Air Cav Division. The 1st Air Cav was one of the most decorated divisions in the US Army and in Vietnam and was chosen to be the first fully "air mobile" division. This meant that the unit had more helicopters available to it than any other division and the capability of airlifting and assaulting a full battalion into a firefight within a few hours. The division also included a full complement of Aerial Rocket Artillery (ARA) or Cobra helicopter gunships plus traditional 105mm, 155mm and 8-inch artillery support. These artillery units too were capable of being airlifted using Sikorsky sky cranes, a heavy-lift helicopter. It was our policy not to avoid a fight with the enemy, but to make sure that we always employed superior and overwhelming force against them. My final words of advice to Roberts before he joined Johnson's squad were: "Watch, learn, and keep your mouth shut." This was the same advice my company commander (CO) had given me.

Roberts was new and needed to learn how my platoon operated. My platoon sergeant was also an "Instant NCO" (non-commissioned officer). Officers and NCOs who normally would have had several years of experience under their belts found themselves leading platoons within weeks of landing in country. The need for both officers and NCOs was so great, due to casualties resulting from the Tet Offensive of 1968, that the army started the "Instant NCO Program" to provide more small-unit leaders. Select soldiers underwent a 90-day training program at Ft. Benning, Georgia prior to coming to Vietnam and were promoted to E-5 or E-6 upon successful completion of the course. Typically, a sergeant E-6 in a regular army unit would have at least five or six years of experience to earn that rank. My platoon sergeant had six months training and was 19 years old.

My CO initially assigned me as the mortar platoon leader (the platoon that carried one 81mm mortar in the field) for the first three weeks with the company. This gave me time to get up to speed and develop confidence. I was grateful for the adjustment period and when I was assigned as the first platoon leader, I was prepared to assess terrain and conditions, implement the tactics, and lead my men.

For the first couple of days after Roberts arrived, I checked in regularly with Johnson to see how he was getting along. He'd been asking lots of questions and challenging tactics as well as Johnson's decisions. He'd refused to give up his heavy and unnecessary equipment and continued to carry a very heavy pack. Despite some misgivings, I trusted Johnson and felt it best to let him help Roberts make the necessary adjustments.

About two weeks into his tour, my company made a helicopter combat assault, called a Charlie Alpha (CA), into a suspected enemy position. We received word that battalion had intelligence that an enemy unit of unknown size had been sighted moving in dense jungle. A one-chopper landing zone (LZ) was nearby. Minimal intel plus a one-bird LZ was always a cause for great anxiety as additional helicopters would not land to support the assault until "LZ Green" was called by the first helicopter. After a quick briefing by the CO, my platoon was assigned to take the lead. It was Johnson's squad's turn to go with me. It was my responsibility to divide the unit into eight-man groups and spread them out in the landing area with enough space between helicopters so that the birds could land safely and pick up the troops. Each group was prepared to mark their pickup location with the same color smoke which is confirmed by the lead pilot before setting down. The platoon leader communicates with the lead bird as it approaches the LZ to provide information about the landing area layout, wind direction and confirm the color smoke being used. As the birds land, four men rush to load from each side of the helicopter. A bench seat across the back of each cabin holds four soldiers and the rest sit cross-legged in the bed of the chopper or in the open doors. The helicopter's crew consists of a pilot, co-pilot, a crew chief and two door gunners manning M60 machine guns on either side for a total of 13 men in each helicopter.

As we prepared for pickup, Roberts was insisting on being on the first bird with me, but Johnson wanted a more experienced man in the position. I was annoyed—this was no time for Roberts to pull rank. Busy making final arrangements for the choppers to land, I told Roberts bluntly that regardless of his rank he was to follow Johnson's instructions. If he was ordered to ride in the second or third bird, then that's what he would do. Roberts responded that he was anxious to "get into the fight." I told him, "You have plenty of time to get into the shit, now shut the fuck up and get back into your pickup group." I got a prompt, "Yes, Sir," and a near salute—which would have really pissed me off. After that I gave the order to pop smoke and four purple clouds swirled up simultaneously showing the wind direction. The choppers settled into their landing formation and my men and I rushed in and climbed aboard.

This assault, fortunately, went smoothly and we met no enemy resistance. I radioed the CO that the LZ was green, and my men fanned out in 360 degrees to secure the perimeter to await the arrival of the next chopper. Even so, it was a hairy time for me as you never knew what might be waiting once you hit the ground. Should enemy fire erupt with only the first bird landing, the seven men and I would have to defend ourselves and call for aerial and artillery support. Through the front window of the helicopter, past the pilots' heads, I could see and appreciated the 105mm artillery bombardment preparation as my lead bird was a couple of miles out from the LZ. Then, as we got closer to the LZ, a white phosphorus artillery round signaled the last shell had been fired. This gave approval to the Cobra helicopters to buzz in firing rockets and miniguns, sweeping the edges of the LZ and making sure that any enemy force had left the area or was dead or pinned down. It was unusual for any VC or NVA to be able to survive such an artillery and ARA assault. They learned to rapidly evacuate the area as the bombardment began or suffer the consequences. As the officer in charge of the landing and always riding in the first bird when it was my turn, I owed my life and the lives of my men to the artillery battery supporting us and the fearless Cobra pilots and the incredible firepower they brought to bear.

Once the entire company was on the ground and a perimeter had been set, my platoon sent out a patrol to search the area for any signs of the enemy but encountered none. Searching further into the sector of the new area of operation (AO), we did find blood trails, but no bodies. As we patrolled, we also evaluated sites for that evening's ambushes. Each platoon was responsible for putting out one ambush of about 10 men. Knowing that Charlie, as the Viet Cong were nicknamed, was always watching us we would make a fuss over several sites to try to confuse them as to which one we would ultimately choose for that night's ambush. It was sweltering (well over 100 degrees), and we returned to the command post (CP) at noon, ate our meal, drank water, and rested. Everyone was still on edge because of the combat assault and the intelligence briefing that indicated enemy had been sighted in the area. The blood trails confirmed this.

At about 2 PM, my CO brought all the platoon leaders to his CP and told us to send out a second set of patrols that afternoon and search each sector again. He was concerned that Charlie might try slipping back into the area after we had cleared it, and he didn't want the company to be caught by surprise. I returned to the platoon and told the first squad to get ready to go out on a search mission. At this point, Roberts again presented himself and requested to go out on patrol with the first squad. He told me that he wanted to observe another squad leader and learn as much as he could. He said it would be valuable experience.

I spoke with SP4 Terhune, the squad leader assigned to lead the patrol. He said he was OK with having Roberts accompany his unit, but only if Roberts clearly understood that Terhune was leading the squad and Roberts was to take orders from him. Roberts readily agreed and I gave the OK. After that, my platoon sergeant and I checked each man before they went out on the patrol to make sure they were carrying enough ammo and water and that their equipment wasn't making clanking noises.

My experience with the VC was that they were excellent soldiers and skilled in guerilla warfare. In the deepest jungles we often passed within a few feet of them, unaware they were hiding and observing our movements. One of their standard tactics was to return to an area immediately after we had searched it as we would be feeling confident there were no enemy present and let our guard down. Then they would ambush us when we least expected it. Occasionally we would backtrack on our own movements or stop, set up a quick ambush and wait to see if an enemy group was following us.

About an hour after the patrol left, we heard a series of rifle shots coming from the squad followed by machine-gun fire and a grenade explosion. Everyone scrambled into foxholes and grabbed their weapons. I immediately told the second squad to saddle up and be prepared to move out with me to support the squad in the firefight, but to hold until I received orders to move. The firefight lasted for about five minutes during which time the CO was on the radio to Terhune trying to get a situation report (sitrep). In rapid fire speech, Terhune relayed that they had encountered a single enemy sniper and there had been one KIA—a man killed in action. The squad leader reported that the enemy had retreated and gave a direction of suspected movement. Our forward observer (FO) dropped some artillery into the area beyond where the contact had occurred, but the squad leader could not see the rounds land in the dense jungle, so it was impossible and dangerous to try to adjust the fire by the sounds of where the shells landed. The CO ordered the squad to return and bring the KIA back to the CP. My heart sank when I heard that the KIA was Roberts.

When the squad returned four men were carrying Roberts, one man holding each arm and leg plus his weapon and equipment. A cloth had been placed over Roberts' face. I pulled back the cloth and saw a small hole in his forehead about the size of a dime, but most of the back of his skull and brains had been blown away. He was placed on the ground near where my platoon CP was located. For several minutes, I stood motionless not really knowing what to do. This was my first experience with a KIA and my mind was a blur.

Terhune came over, sat down, drank some water, and lit a cigarette. His hands were shaking as he told me the story. As the squad moved cautiously through the dense jungle, the point man heard a noise and alerted. The squad moved up even with the point man to provide support. They laid down a base of fire in the direction of the noise and had received return fire from what was thought to be a single enemy soldier. The squad leader directed four men to move to the right flank and come in at the side of where the suspected enemy was holed up. These men were in dense, hilly jungle, so it was impossible to see more than 20–30m in any direction.

The four men moved out while the rest of the squad continued to lay down a base of fire. Roberts was among the four men moving to the flank.

As the riflemen approached the suspected enemy position, Roberts suddenly stood up and charged forward. Everyone stopped firing as Roberts threw a grenade at the suspected enemy position. After the explosion, a single shot rang out and Roberts fell dead, shot in the head. The men crawled forward and pulled him back from where he had fallen and then regrouped. Eventually, the squad moved forward again and cleared the area where the enemy sniper had been hidden. There was no sign of the enemy and no blood trails to follow.

Roberts' body lay on the ground next to me. He had already started to bloat and smell due to the extreme heat. My medic came over with a preprinted 3x5 card. There was a hole punched through one corner that had a string tied to it. He reminded me of my responsibilities and that prompted me to act.

I had one of my men write out an inventory of Roberts' equipment. He had still been carrying far too much stuff. I went through his pockets to see if there was anything that might be incriminating, and I put all his personal items into a plastic bag and placed the bag on his chest. I conferred with my squad leader, looking at my map, to determine as closely as possible the exact coordinates where Roberts had been killed. It struck me at that moment that for the first time in history, the army was attempting to record the exact location for every soldier killed. I filled in the rest of the information on the card and tied it to Roberts' boot. I took one dog tag from around his neck and tied it to his boot lace. Then I had three men lift him so we could wrap a poncho around his body.

I realized that when the helicopter came in to pick up the body, the poncho would be blown about from the downdraft—always a dangerous thing. I took some cord from my pack and tied the poncho around his feet, waist and above his head, creating a cocoon. His boots protruded from the bottom of the poncho so that the toe tag and dog tag were visible. Then we all stood around his body and said a silent prayer.

I asked if anyone wanted to say something about Roberts, but as he had only been with us for a couple of weeks no one had gotten to know him very well. He had been so gung-ho, so aggressive, and wanted so desperately to assume a leadership position and get his first kill. It was understandable to me and my men how his death occurred. In his enthusiasm, Roberts had single-handedly charged the enemy and exposed himself to the enemy sniper's fire. While being somewhat of a heroic act, it was not an intelligent tactic to have followed and it cost Roberts his life. The supply chopper came in a few hours later to unload C-Rats (C-Rations), ammo, water and supplies and we loaded Roberts' body and his equipment on the departing bird.

We finished digging our foxholes for the night, put out Claymore mines and trip flares and established the first watch. We pulled on our shirts, buttoned our collars and sleeves against mosquitoes and lathered up with insect repellent.

As I went to sleep that night, I thought of what I had done to prepare Roberts' body for his long trip back home. As night fell, I recalled how I had tried to be as exact as possible to record the location where his death had occurred. I thought about tying up the poncho with the cord that I carried in my pack, our brief silent ceremony before loading him into the supply helicopter. I thought about my conversations with Roberts and how I had tried to get him acclimated and ready to assume a leadership position. At 22, it was truly the first worst day of my life.

I knew that Roberts' body would be transported back to An Khe, in Vietnam's central highlands, where the division morgue was located. It would be prepared for burial and placed in a metal casket, marked with his name, serial number, and draped with an American flag for the journey stateside. Within 36 hours of his death, a military survival assistance detail would be dispatched, usually a soldier of equal rank as the deceased along with a senior sergeant, to Roberts' home to inform the family of his death. They would stay with the family for many days to be of assistance and often attended the military burial as well.

Roberts was my first KIA, but he was not to be my last. Nothing prepared me to handle the deaths of my men. There was no training, no protocol and it was up to me to handle the situation. My men did not want to be involved nor did they want to touch the body. Perhaps this was simple superstition as I'm sure they were afraid this might happen to them—the next time. I had to wrap many men into ponchos in the months that ensued, and I followed the same routine each time. The task became a little easier and I tried to do it with efficiency and respect.

When I went through the officer orientation training program in Vietnam, we were advised not to make friends with our men or NCOs. The rationale was that I might have to give an order to a soldier that would cost him his life. I needed to obey the chain of command and never show favoritism. I needed to be able to react decisively and aggressively under fire and in a crisis regardless of who might be killed or wounded around me. For better or worse, my men depended on me for impartial orders and decision making. I made no friends and blocked the emotion and feelings for each WIA or KIA. I became as cold and unfeeling as I could manage and refused to allow the situation to have an impact on me.

I resolved to do what needed to be done as quickly, efficiently, and respectfully as possible. The days when I oversaw KIAs were always my worst days in Vietnam and Roberts, being the first, was certainly the worst of all. Here was a young man whose potential would never be fulfilled. His life ended far too soon. One might conclude that his enthusiasm and aggressiveness may have been responsible for his death, but that was how the army had trained him and the path he chose to follow. After the chopper had removed Roberts' body, I asked one of my men to take a photograph of me so that I would always remember how I felt on that day.

Here is what I wrote to a college classmate soon after this incident.

Letter: 9 August 1968, A Company 1/5 Cav, 1st Air Cav Division, out in the boonies, I Corps, Vietnam

You do know it takes a lot of shit for me to despair. Well, I am despairing. I have really had it. The main problem as I see it is that there is no mental commitment whatsoever to this war. There is but one desire and that is to kill by any means possible—without emotion, heroism, glory, patriotism, etc. I can't live a life like this. I refuse not to care, to live without emotion.

Anyway, I have made up my mind that if this is the army of today, I want no part of it. I plan to resign my commission at the earliest opportunity and just pray to God that I won't have to spend a second tour in this hell hole. I pray also that you won't have to come over here—you had better do some praying too.

* * *

After the war's end, a group of veterans from the Cav as well as other divisions volunteered to participate with Gold Star organizations such as Sons and Daughters in Touch (SDIT) and coordinate visits to Vietnam returning to the site where loved ones were killed. The mission of SDIT is "to locate, unite and support children of American Servicemen who were killed or remain missing in the Vietnam War." In March 2003, twenty combat veterans and nurses took a historic trip to Vietnam guiding fifty SDIT members. These sons and daughters stood as close as possible to the locations where their fathers had been lost. The coordinates for each KIA, where possible, had been duly recorded by the officer first responsible for processing the KIA. The group conducted memorial services for the fallen soldiers thus bringing a measure of closure to each family member. By the time each soldier's death had been memorialized the families and veterans had become fast friends. Before returning to the United States, the group conducted a final ceremony at Cam Ranh Bay, floating out into the ocean a wreath celebrating all the soldiers' lives. Local Vietnamese, aware of the ceremony, respectfully observed.

I often recall my actions surrounding events when men in my platoon were killed and I had to prepare them for their final trip home. Roberts' death was my first worst day in Vietnam. There would be more.

But let me start this story at the beginning.

CHAPTER 2

Training for War

*Two things were memorable about Jump School: the increasing number
of soldiers who showed up for church services on Sunday, and
the parachute-malfunction orientation lecture.*

Letter: Claremont McKenna College, California, October 13, 1968
*   ROTC started up again today with the first drill period. It was a lot of fun and
I fell right back into the groove from last year. It looks as if this year will be a good one
even though we had a poor turnout. I think I may go shooting this weekend if I can
get my homework done. I feel so out of practice and yearn for that old trigger squeeze.*

In June 1967, I graduated from college and was commissioned as a Regular Army
second lieutenant in the infantry. I was a Distinguished Military Graduate (DMG)
from the ROTC Program and had my choice of any combat arms branch I wanted.
For several reasons, but primarily because I came from three generations of army
officers, I volunteered for Airborne and Ranger training, and to be assigned to the
famous 82nd Airborne Division (All American). The Vietnam War was escalating,
and I was accepted for everything I volunteered for (no surprise as infantry officers
were in short supply). Two days after graduation, my car packed with clothes,
uniforms, and mementoes from college, I drove from California scheduled to report
to the 82nd at Ft. Bragg, North Carolina. Upon arrival, I would spend six weeks as a
"Leg" in the division (a Leg is a soldier who has not gone through Airborne training).
    After five days of hard driving, I arrived at Ft. Bragg and spent the first night in
a motel off post as I had no idea where the bachelor officers' quarters (BOQ) was
located. Furthermore, I had not even processed into the army. Staying in a cheap
motel for one night to get myself organized for the next day seemed like a clever idea.
    I pulled out my green uniform, polished and applied all my brass insignia and
carefully measured to make sure that my butter bars (second lieutenant insignia) and

crossed rifles were properly positioned. My 82nd Airborne patch was already sewn on the left shoulder of my uniform, proudly showing off the unit to which I was assigned. It was still early in the evening, so I decided to find the Officers' Club, enjoy a couple of drinks, and have a satisfying meal. I put on the uniform and headed out to the post. Receiving directions from the guard at the entry gate, I received a snappy salute and proceeded through. I thought I heard him mumble something like "Leg" as I drove past.

Once inside, I wandered up to the bar and ordered a bourbon and water. After a while, a major came in and sat next to me. We struck up a conversation and I told him this was my first official day in the army, that I was a brand-new second lieutenant, and had just arrived on post. After buying me a drink to celebrate my first official day, he questioned me about my background, education, ROTC training and what my plans were for the army. The liquor started to hit me. I hadn't eaten anything since breakfast. Feeling comfortable, I told the major how I expected to be an exceptional officer. I came from a military background and my brother, father and grandfather had all attended West Point and served as career officers. The major let me do all the talking. After finishing his drink, he stood up and laughing hysterically said, "Well, Lieutenant Bartlett, I think you still have a lot to learn about being an officer and leading troops, but the first thing you should learn is how to put your bars on straight." I looked at my shoulder and my face turned bright red discovering that I had put my bars on horizontally rather than perpendicular to the edge of my shoulder. I was so embarrassed I rushed to the men's room, made the repair to my uniform, and left without having anything to eat. What an auspicious beginning!

The next day was spent processing into the army. There was a mound of forms to complete: personnel forms, insurance, medical, security, education, and more. It took me several hours to finish them all. Finally, I was escorted to the brigade headquarters where I met a captain, the brigade S-1 (an S-1 is the personnel officer of a unit). Seeing how uncomfortable I was in my dress uniform, given the temperatures in the high nineties, the captain suggested I change into my fatigues, which I promptly did.

The captain asked if I had a place to stay that night. I told him I was in a motel off post. He checked to see if any rooms were available at the BOQ but there were none. When the captain heard I was staying in a motel, he offered me the spare room in a house he was sharing with another officer. I told him I'd think about it.

Finally, I was escorted to my battalion headquarters by the brigade executive officer (XO) who was a major, but thankfully not the one from the previous night. I knew the protocol for walking next to a senior officer which was to always "put the rank to the right." This meant that a junior officer always walked on the left of a senior officer. I started out correctly, but then got confused and crossed over to the other side. The major was nice enough and corrected me to move back to his left. Again, I was totally embarrassed and felt that I now had two strikes against me with senior officers. And to think that I thought I would be a "superior officer" because of my military upbringing and family tradition… what a joke!

There was another round of paperwork at the battalion headquarters, and I was assigned to a line company. By this time, it was getting late in the day. I was told to return the next day to be introduced to my company commander. Realizing that I had no place to stay that night I called the captain who had taken pity on me at brigade headquarters to take advantage of his offer. This house was to become my home for the next six weeks until I received orders transferring me to Ft. Benning, Georgia to attend Airborne, Infantry Officer Basic Training Course, and Ranger training.

I made my way to the company headquarters the next morning and was introduced to my company commander (CO) and given a desk. The CO said he wanted me to stay with him at the company headquarters rather than take over a platoon because I had no training as an officer, had not been to Airborne school and was not ready to lead a platoon of Airborne-qualified troops. This made good sense, and for the next six weeks I read military manuals and worked on "special projects" for the CO.

Letter: 30 June 1967, A Company, 1/325 Infantry, 82nd Airborne Division, Ft. Bragg, NC (Letter to college classmate)

I have had some other good jobs too. One is called a report of survey. This is to establish pecuniary liability for the loss or damage of equipment. Mine is only $220.85, but some go as high as $2,000. It is a real leg job—you have to get statements and write up the whole thing.

My first project was to prepare a "Report of Survey" for the S-4 (officer responsible for supply and logistics). My job was to account for clothing and equipment of a soldier who had gone absent without leave (AWOL). All his possessions had been lost or confiscated during his absence. I dutifully read the military manual on how to prepare a "Report of Survey" and went to work investigating the story, interviewing several soldiers, recording their sworn testimony, and obtaining signatures. My report concluded that the equipment had been stored in a locked footlocker that had been broken into during his absence and the soldier should not be held responsible.

After several days, I completed my report and turned in 22 pages documenting my findings, including copies of the signed statements from the soldiers I had interviewed. With a sly smile on his face, my CO skimmed through the document, signed his name, and forwarded the paperwork to the S-4 for final approval. A few days later, I was told to report to the S-4, a senior warrant officer. Bluntly, he said, "Why the fuck did you write a 22-page report?" I explained that I had read the regulations and tried to follow them explicitly. He informed me that the survey I did would have been fine if the loss had been a tank, but for $220 worth of equipment, a single paragraph would be more than sufficient. He tossed the paperwork back to me saying, "Give me one page, three paragraphs, and not a word more. Declare the SOB responsible for the loss of his equipment and we'll dock his pay. Get it back to me by tomorrow."

I headed back to the company office and to my typewriter. My CO had a great laugh. He knew that the S-4 would reject my report, but he had been so impressed with my research that he wanted the S-4 to see the effort I had exerted. I learned that in the army, it was always best to keep the effort in proportion to the scope of the job. That lesson helped me throughout the rest of my military experience and even into my civilian career.

~~~~~~

Letter: 2 July 1967, A Company, 1/325 Infantry, 82nd Airborne Division, Ft. Bragg, NC (Letter to college classmate)

You want to know about my reactions to my men. I haven't had too much contact with them, but for those I have been with, it has been quite an experience. Between 50–60% have not had a full high school education. They will do most anything you tell them. All are incredibly fit, but often you have to show them how to do a job and keep after them to insure it gets done. You must use a liberal sprinkling of shit, fuck, mother fuck, damn and hell. This is the language they use and understand. They will see through any snow job you try and hold it against you. They will not hold mistakes against you because they realize the lieutenant is a bit green, but if you try to cover up, you have had it. The best thing is to be truthful, and if you tell them you'll do something for them, you must do it. I know for a fact, even after this brief period of time, that if I told one of them to charge a machinegun nest, he would do it and not think twice. They will lay down their lives too although they keep their butts as low as possible. This scares me.

With the NCOs it's a different story. They have a lot of experience. This is very apparent. They are the ones who really run the men. You sort of sit back, keep quiet, and make timely suggestions. They are truly the backbone of the army. They respect your rank and are understanding of your newness. Most of them are fine people, but some do have problems: especially money, drinking and women.

~~~~~~

Finally, after six weeks, I received orders transferring me to Ft. Benning, Georgia, to attend the Airborne, Infantry Officer Basic, and Ranger School training courses. I loaded my car and headed south.

Weeks flew by at Ft. Benning. I made it through the four-week Paratrooper Jump School Course, as well as the six-week Infantry Officer Basic Training. I went through these courses with the graduating West Point class of 1967, all of whom had volunteered to be infantry officers. The West Pointers proudly wore their school rings and were a very close-knit group. They had spent the last four years going through most of the training and courses we were about to take. It was second nature to them. I learned that West Pointers made sure to "take care of their own" when it came to the assignment of leadership positions, and they insured their classmates always received top recognition during exercises. Those of us coming from ROTC tended not to be so buttoned up or gung-ho. We knew why we were training and where we would be heading within six to 12 months after graduation. The Vietnam War was escalating daily. TV and newspapers were filled with daily reports of battles and casualties—especially of lieutenant platoon leaders.

~~~~~~

Letter: 7 July 1967, A Company, 1/325 Infantry, 82nd Airborne Division, Ft. Bragg, NC (Letter to college classmate)

I went up in a C-130 yesterday to watch a parachute jump. This is the aircraft they make most military jumps from along with choppers. The plane has a big tail which opens to allow the extract of loads, or you can tail jump from it too. They can put one light tank in it, or three jeeps, or 84 fully equipped men, and drop them all.

It was quite an experience. I watched some of the men in my company go out the door. I even got to wear an Air Force parachute. I have never been so thrilled. 60 men cleared that plane in 20 seconds jumping out both sides of the plane. Honestly, Ken, to watch those men go out the door and see their chutes open was one of the most exhilarating things I have ever watched. It is beyond description (altitude was 1,300 feet.)

~~~~~~

After arriving at Ft. Benning and getting settled, I immediately started the four-week Airborne course. It was physically demanding. I started each morning in 90+ degree heat with a 2-mile run, gradually increasing to 5 miles in the final week. The run was followed by 20 pull-ups done in unison, a necessary requirement to pull on the risers (straps connected to your parachute harness and part of the parachute rigging). We had to be able to pull our body weight up and hold the risers to our chests to tip the chute and maneuver it. Men who couldn't complete the runs or do at least 20 pull-ups were quickly eliminated or recycled to the next program.

We ran in formation wearing white T-shirts, fatigue pants and highly polished combat boots. My legs were short which meant that I was always positioned at the front of the formation with taller men stepping on my boot heels. I quickly figured this was not a great position for me and when the request for a cadence caller was made, I volunteered. This allowed me to run to the side of the formation and call cadence to the rest of the soldiers. These sing-song cadences provided a diversion from the heat, sweat and exhaustion of the daily run. This cadence song earned me the moniker of "The Chaplain":

> I know the Lord will find a way for me
> I know the Lord will find a way for me
> If I live a holy life, shun the wrong and do the right
> I know the Lord will find a way for me
> I want to be an Airborne Ranger
> I want to live a life of danger
> Want to be
> Got to be
> Airborne
> Airborne
> Ranger
> Ranger

After the run, we were required to go through overhead spray showers in the push-up position, being careful not to get our boots wet. The heat was so intense there was a great danger of dehydration and heat stroke. Drinking plenty of water, taking daily salt tablets and hourly spray showers were the army's way of combating dehydration and heat stroke. This technique worked well.

In the first week we learned the basics of landing and rolling to absorb the shock. In the second week we practiced jumps from a 34-foot tower, riding a cable to the ground and landing. The third week found us dropping from a 250-foot tower. Our chutes were connected to a cable, but the landing was the same as if we had jumped from a plane. We were also taught how to release our harness when caught on the ground by a gust of wind.

Two things were memorable about Jump School: the increasing number of soldiers who showed up for church services on Sunday, and the parachute-malfunction orientation lecture at the beginning of the fourth week before our first live jump. The parachute-malfunction orientation lasted two hours and we hung on every word spoken by the instructor. We sat in the bleachers while a demonstrator hung from the ceiling in a parachute harness with a reserve chute attached. The instructing officer carefully discussed each step of the safety precautions. There was no sleeping in this class. We saw what to do if your risers got twisted (move your feet in a bicycle motion and twist); what to do if you landed on top of another man's parachute (run off the top of the chute and pull away from the other parachute). And most importantly, what to do if your parachute was a streamer (failed to open): pull the handle on the reserve chute, pull the silk out of the bag, and shake it to make sure it opens. If by some remote chance your chute got hung up on the tail of the airplane you were to put your hands on top of your helmet to show you were OK and do nothing else because the jump master would see you and cut you free. Once free, you were to pull your reserve chute.

The fourth week of Jump School was the easiest physically; there were no runs and no pull-ups. But it was the most stressful week of all as I made a parachute jump each day. After four jumps I was deemed Airborne-qualified and authorized to wear the paratrooper badge on my uniform and hat. Officers received an extra $110 jump pay per month (enlisted men earned $55). I was required to make a practice jump every six weeks to maintain my Airborne qualification and continue to receive the extra stipend.

I lived in a bachelor officers' quarters (BOQ) and shared a room with another officer. It was a spartan affair: one room with two desks, two chairs, two beds, a bathroom and two closets. I ate my meals in the air-conditioned Officers' Club. At the end of the day after a quick dinner usually of fast food and a drink or two, I returned to my room. I undressed in the hall, pulling off my filthy, sweat-soaked fatigues, T-shirt, underpants, and placing everything in a laundry bag that had my name on it. I took off my scuffed boots and left them outside my room as well. Then I would take a shower, and rub "Deep Heat" on my sore muscles. A heavily starched fatigue uniform was waiting for me in my closet along with my second pair of highly polished jump boots. I paid $50 a week for the laundry service, and it was worth every penny. The enlisted men going through training slept in a barracks and did not have access to this service. They would have to take their uniforms to a nearby laundry and spend hours each night cleaning and polishing their boots.

After Jump School, I enjoyed a weekend of relaxation before the start of the Infantry Officer Basic Course (IOBC). I spent the time moving into a new BOQ with a new officer roommate, getting my uniforms ready, sleeping, and relaxing. I remember going to the library and taking out several best-selling novels that I wanted to read (I had been a literature major in college). The books remained on my bedside table for the entire six weeks of training. I never cracked a cover.

The Infantry Officer Basic Course was uneventful. My classmates were the same infantry officers from West Point as well as graduating ROTC DMGs. We found the classroom training and field exercises much like a trip to Disneyland. It was repetitive of the training we had already had. The West Pointers remained incredibly gung-ho, skilled, fit, and hung together in cliques. The ROTC officers were forced to do the same, indicative of what would follow in Ranger School.

As I went through the six-week IOBC program, I realized this training would not prepare me to lead a platoon in combat. Ranger School, it was recognized, was the true preparation for becoming a skilled infantry officer and leading a platoon. Many of the classes were taught in classrooms by first lieutenants who had no prior combat experience. Field exercises were led by staff sergeants who had served at least one tour in Vietnam. Not surprisingly, there were only a handful of officers with any combat experience teaching any of the courses. They were all in Vietnam leading infantry units.

There was no physical training (PT) during the Basic Officer Course, so I focused every spare minute of my off-duty time on running and exercise. Each evening, I stripped down to a T-shirt and shorts, pulled on my jungle boots, and went out for an extended run with classmates. I typically finished doing as many pull-ups and push-ups as I could muster. I thought I was in good physical condition having made it through Jump School, but realized I needed to develop even more stamina—and I needed to do it fast.

Our schedule began each morning at 6 AM and ended at 5 PM. There was little time for anything beyond eating dinner, a nightly run, shower, quick study, and sleep. Despite the hectic schedule, one enterprising West Pointer, a jokester, who I later learned was the "Goat" of the class (he finished last in graduation standings), decided to sand the paint off his jalopy. He worked on it diligently each evening. His car was parked in the front row opposite the area where our company formed up each morning. Once all the paint was removed, he painted the car in camouflage colors. He finished the job three days before graduation. Everyone in the unit congratulated him on his perseverance and commitment to the military protocol and joked that his car had disappeared. His efforts were recognized during our graduation ceremonies with a round of applause and congratulations from all assembled.

On our last day of IOBC, we completed a field exercise that ended in a 10-mile forced march in the rain and mud with rifles and full combat gear, after which we loaded into trucks and returned to our billets, at about 6 PM. The training had run overtime. There was a reception for the commanding general that evening beginning at 7 PM. Covered in mud and grime, we were informed that we had to be in dress blue uniforms and at the Officers' Club within 45 minutes. Married officers' wives met the trucks bringing their husbands' clothes for them to change as there wasn't enough time to return to their billets.

I'm not sure how married officers survived this training. Every night we returned to our quarters totally exhausted, so the only time they would have with their wives was on weekends. In Ranger School, a married officer would not see his spouse for the entire nine-week program, except on one night in between each of the three phases of the training when we got a half day and evening off. Surprisingly, there were quite a few married officers in our unit.

I started Ranger School the day after graduating from IOBC—no breaks.

Letter: 4 September 1967, Infantry Officer Basic Training Course, Ft. Benning, GA
We had a full day's training on Saturday. We started at 6:30 in full combat gear. They showed us how a convoy operation is conducted and what to do in case of ambush. The demonstration was live, and the aggressors were dressed in black PJs. They used demolitions and blank ammunition to simulate very realistic tactics. The next segment was on cordon and search operations and how to clear a Vietnamese village.

They had an elaborate town set up right in front of our bleachers so we could view the entire operation.

After the formal "bleacher preacher," we were divided into our platoons and issued the operations order. Each of us had to prepare a platoon order and then one officer was selected to issue it. We critiqued him and worked out a revised plan. We then divided into squads and were issued blank ammo, automatic weapons, simulated grenades, grenade launchers and Claymore mines plus a lot of other equipment. We started out in convoy and met snipers, mines, and all kinds of obstacles.

We finally reached our dismount point (DP) and began to conduct our foot operation, establishing a blocking force around a VC training camp while another platoon attacked. Our route took us through a swamp! We walked, stumbled, and waded up to our chests in mucky goo and finally reached our positions. The attack came off on time and we heard bombs bursting, rifles shooting, machine guns and grenades—the works! We really blasted them.

It was 5:30 PM by the time we finished and returned by truck at 6:30 and were told we had 45 minutes to change from our muddy fatigues into Dress Blue Uniforms as this was the night of the commanding general's reception. One of the funniest sights I have ever seen was the married officers' wives beautifully coiffed and in formal gowns, meeting their tired, muddy, and dirty husbands, carrying their dress uniforms.

CHAPTER 3

Ranger School: Learning to Lead, Preparing to Kill

I was shocked to learn that West Pointers had rated me
poorly and I was in danger of failing the program.

The nine-week Ranger training program was spread out over three locations: Ft. Benning, Dahlonega, Georgia and Eglin, Florida. It was the most demanding experience of my life and far more strenuous both physically and mentally than anything I encountered in combat. The course conditions were designed to be as close to the combat experience in Vietnam as possible, with the exception that real bullets were not used. Ranger Cadre evaluated the leaders traveling in squad-size units of 10 to 12 men. Rangers who lacked the physical and mental stamina needed to lead men under these conditions were rapidly eliminated. The course in 1967 was composed of about 80 percent officers and 20 percent NCOs. It was the best combat training the army had to offer. It trained me to lead, command and tactically employ a small group under combat conditions, how to be self-sufficient, and how to overcome any adversity. It taught me how to plan and execute small-unit operations, to be aggressive, and kill. The object of the training was to take me beyond the point of physical and mental exhaustion and then, just as I was ready to succumb to that exhaustion, to be placed in a leadership role and tested to see how well I performed.

I knew from the outset how important this training would be. My class were all infantry officers and NCOs and knew we would receive orders transferring us to Vietnam within six to 12 months after completion of the course. Inwardly, I knew that the training was life essential. Lieutenant platoon leaders in Vietnam had one of the shortest life expectancies. Many were killed within the first 90 days in country. We all took this training seriously and did our best to master the skills of war and killing—regardless of any personal feelings or political perspective we might have on the war, or the current administration's direction of the conflict.

On the day after graduation from IOBC, I drove my car, again loaded with everything I owned in the world, including clothes, bedding, boxes of books and mementoes, to a secure area and parked. My first stop was the barber shop where all my hair was shaved off. We were told to save one uniform with insignia to be used for graduation ceremonies… assuming we made it through. Otherwise, everyone was to remove rank and uniform patches. I became "Ranger Bartlett." This allowed the Ranger School Cadre, many platoon sergeants with prior Vietnam experience, to give us orders, harass and try to wash us out. It was a voluntary course, so we could quit at any time. Ranger instructors would constantly ask if you wanted to quit, usually when we were exhausted, wet, cold, and demoralized. If someone responded "yes," or failed to pass one of the milestone confidence tests, he was immediately removed from the program and sent back to the rear.

We were also required to pass "buddy ratings" given by the other members of our squads. I started Ranger Class 8-67 with 210 officers and enlisted men; we finished with fewer than 80. Some men completed the course but failed to pass the final endurance test or received an unsatisfactory "buddy rating." Their records were marked showing they completed the training but were not permitted to wear the Ranger Tab on their shoulder. The thought of not being able to wear the Ranger insignia after enduring all the patrols, training, harassment, and physical demands was a major incentive for me to keep on going even when I was ready to collapse. I simply knew I could not return to the 82nd Airborne Division or to my college ROTC cadre, friends, and parents without having earned the Ranger Tab.

~~~~~~

Letter: 6 September 1967, Ranger School, Ft. Benning, Georgia

You asked about Ranger School and where I'll be living. I am not too sure of the conditions, but I do know a few facts. First, we wear no patches or rank insignia on our uniforms. We are all the same, officer and NCO alike. The first phase is conducted at Ft. Benning. I guess we will be living in old barracks. The Benning phase is all class work and PT with emphasis on the latter: 5-mile runs, obstacle course, hand-to-hand combat, bayonet training and confidence tests.

The second two phases are three weeks. They are usually four but have been shortened to prepare officers to go to Vietnam. These two phases are held in the mountains of Dahlonega, Georgia and in the Florida swamps near Eglin AFB. I think we will live in tents during base camp periods and "under the stars" for most of the time. The mountain phase is focused on mountain climbing, rappelling, and long-range recon, and combat patrols. In the swamps we'll learn more about guerrilla and counter-guerrilla operations and ambushes.

I am going to be extremely busy for the next two months or so and may not have much of a chance to write—if at all. I am OK so please do not worry if you don't hear from me for a while.

~~~~~~

Being lumped into the same class with the Infantry graduates from West Point, I was in for some major challenges starting on day one. My legs were short, and I was stocky. On the daily 5-mile runs and forced marches, I would always have to start at the front of the column, run or walk as fast and as hard as I could, but because of my short legs I would always fall behind. Then, I would run to catch up with the front of the column and start the process all over again. On one forced march, a burly 28-year-old SEAL team member (Sea, Air, and Land) named Church, who was going through Ranger training, noticed my plight. He told me to grab on to his pack frame and he literally pulled me up the hills, forcing me to keep pace with him. He saved me from dropping out. Church and his partner Sommers were in tremendous physical condition having endured SEAL training, uniformly recognized as the most demanding physical training given to any armed forces unit. Conversely, West Pointers showed no sympathy for ROTC grads. It became every man for himself against the West Pointers. ROTC grads and NCOs were on their own. I thanked God for the SEALs.

I went through the training with several enlisted soldiers from other branches including a few CIA guys who kept to themselves. It was hard to tell if the other Rangers in my platoon were officers or NCOs by looking at them, but after getting to know the two SEALs, it became clear that the physical part of Ranger School was a cakewalk for them. These two men taught me that SEAL training is many times more rigorous than anything Ranger School has to offer.

The SEALs' endurance was astonishing. The Ranger Cadre who made our lives miserable could not break them no matter how hard they tried. Every time my platoon passed a stream, pond, lake or even a large puddle of water on a run or forced march, the SEALs would make the sound of a seal: "ARC, ARC," and the rest of our platoon would take up the cry in support. We did this so often that the cadre got angry and made us jump into the water—even if it was a mud puddle. Every morning began at 4 AM with a 5-mile run, and it only took a few times of having to jump in the freezing water for us to soften our seal chants to a whisper.

Everyone in Ranger School was assigned a Ranger Buddy, and mine was Frisk, an ROTC grad just like me from Indiana University. He was on orders to join the 101st Airborne Division after completing the training. We never left each other's side. We slept side by side, ate meals together and partnered every step of the way. My Ranger Buddy was treated with equal disdain by the West Pointers.

The first phase of the program, based on physical development, took place at Ft. Benning, Georgia. If you could not run 5 miles daily carrying your M14 rifle, followed by negotiating the obstacle course, do 20 pull-ups in unison, holding on and waiting for each man to struggle to reach the bar, eat breakfast within 10 minutes and then be in formation by 6 AM and ready for the day's training, you became the target of the Ranger Cadre and received severe harassment. We ran everywhere, did push-ups and pull-ups by the dozens, and we were married to our M14 rifles. The weapon had a cord tied to it that slipped around your neck. It was never to be removed except when returning to the barracks. Given these conditions it would seem impossible for anyone to ever lose their rifle. Not so. One woebegone Ranger student removed his rifle's cord from his neck before sitting down during a rest stop while on patrol. He immediately fell asleep. When the patrol was instructed to move out, this Ranger woke abruptly and was so tired that he did not realize he had forgotten his rifle until he'd traveled several miles. At the end of the patrol, all members of his squad had to retrace their steps to retrieve the weapon, not an easy task in the dark. When that Ranger returned to base camp, he was trucked back to Ft. Benning.

The first phase ended after three weeks with a 20-mile forced march starting at 2 AM and ending at 6 AM. After a brief rest, we were required to negotiate the first of three arduous confidence tests. The Suspension Traverse Confidence Test required that I climb a 60-foot telephone pole and stand on a 6-foot square platform anchored to the top. There were two instructors roped to the railings. I was not. They attached a "snatch block" and I was told to grab onto it and hook it to a cable running overhead (a zip line). There was no harness, and the cable traversed a lake below.

I stood with my toes over the edge of the platform, facing an officer standing on a dock 600m away at the end of the zip line. I saluted with one hand and yelled at the top of my lungs: "Sir, Ranger Bartlett requests permission to negotiate the Suspension Traverse Confidence Test." I had to repeat these words until I got them exactly right. Mistakes meant extra push-ups at the end of the test. After I said the phrase correctly, the officer on the dock dropped his flag and I raised my feet, cleared the platform, and pulled myself into a pike position. I was required to scream "Ranger" all the way down the zip line. After I reached a speed of about 40 mph and was 100m from the officer on the dock, he dropped his flag a second time. I released the handles and landing on my butt in the water, went skipping across the lake much like a rock across a pond. After yelling "Ranger" all the way down the wire, I splashed into the water with no air in my lungs and had to fight my way to the top, grab a breath and then swim to the dock.

Being a good swimmer, I was able to complete this test with little difficulty. After the exercise each of us completed a "buddy rating" evaluating the other members of our squad. I was shocked to learn that the West Pointers had rated me poorly and I was in danger of failing the program. Again, it was clear they were sticking together and had no empathy for the ROTC graduates.

One of the most valuable skills I learned in the first phase of the Ranger program was point shooting where you pointed with the left index finger of your hand while holding the front of your rifle at a target rather than taking aim using the sights. We used BB guns to practice this technique. One man would stand next to the shooter and throw a 6-inch metal disk in the air while the man with the BB gun would attempt to hit the disk. I learned to point the forefinger of my left hand at the disk while holding the front stock of the rifle. After some practice, it became easy. Then we graduated to 3-inch disks. As a former skeet and trap shooter I was even able to hit quarters and pennies.

This skill saved my life on several occasions in Vietnam. All my enemy contacts in Vietnam were at close range (under 50m). I was faster on the draw than every enemy soldier I encountered, and I had great confidence as to exactly where my shots were going to hit. I pointed at my target and pulled the trigger. I didn't have to aim. (Of course, being able to fire the M16's full magazine of 18 rounds in two and one-half seconds also helped a great deal.) There was never a situation where I had an enemy soldier in view who escaped alive. Point shooting was our edge in close combat survival, thanks to Ranger School and the firepower of the M16 rifle.

The second phase of Ranger training, the mountain phase, took place in Dahlonega, Georgia. We learned to tie knots, rappel, mountain climb, hump a lot of hills and ridges, traverse long stretches of woods, and stay warm in the chilly October weather, especially at night. We placed our feet in plastic bags to keep them warm and wrapped ourselves in space blankets to conserve body heat. Each day brought new challenges and new leaders appointed to be tested on various parts of a mission. If you passed the patrol and reached the objective on time, C-Rations were provided. If you didn't, you went hungry.

I was appointed the leader for one mission and chose Randolph, one of the more friendly West Pointers, as my point man. I planned the mission to move through the woods toward our objective of meeting up with a friendly who was to provide us with enemy intel. But my point man moved out so quickly that I lost contact with him. He located the friendly and took over my mission responsibilities, completing the requirements of the exercise. Consequently, I received an unsatisfactory performance rating. In my mind I saw my Ranger Tab slowly slipping out of reach.

Fortunately, I came down with bronchial pneumonia. This meant I could not participate in night missions as my coughing would give away our position. After two days of hacking and sniffling, I was declared medically unfit to continue. I was returned to the rear to recuperate and be recycled to the next class going into the mountain phase in 10 days. This turned out to be the best thing that could have happened because even though I had to repeat a portion of the mountain phase, my previous scores were discarded. I re-entered the program with the Artillery branch graduates from West Point. These guys were not so cliquish as the infantry West Pointers. It turned out that my former Ranger buddy had also failed his buddy rating. He ended up passing the course but was not allowed to wear the Ranger Tab—the worst possible result.

Upon return to the mountain phase of the program, I had two weeks of experience under my belt. Even though the program changed from class to class, I knew something about what was coming and when to volunteer and when not.

My squad members looked to me for advice and intel. I sailed through three weeks of knot tying, rappelling, mountain climbing, and walking ridges covered with pine trees and shivering through cold November nights. This time I received excellent buddy ratings.

Rappelling off a 60-foot wooden tower was exciting and fun. I tied a rope around my waist and ran it between my legs forming a harness. Attaching a snap link (carabiner) I hooked myself to the rappelling rope. Wearing gloves, I applied the brake by forcing the rope against my hip. The action slowed or stopped me. We all got rather good at going down the 60-foot tower, bouncing out and dropping down the front of the tower in seconds.

Then it became time to rappel without the use of a carabiner. This is a much more challenging exercise. I had to run the rope between my legs and around my body, taking great care not to have the rope near my private parts. This technique used the friction of the rope wrapped around my body to brake and slow me down as I went down the 60-foot vertical drop sideways. Without a carabiner, the brake for this type of rappelling was to pull the rope into my chest rather than press it against my hip. On my first trip down the tower, I lost my grip with my left hand and failed to pull the brake into my chest. I panicked and simply grabbed the rope with both gloved hands and slid down about 40 feet. I landed hard and did a paratrooper roll. I was OK, but my hands were burned from the rope. I jumped up and said I was OK, but the trainers were furious that I had failed to brake properly and had come close to falling 40 feet down the tower. I was required to repeat the exercise, with the instructor screaming "Brake into your chest!" as I walked down the wall. I had to repeat this descent three times to prove my competence.

It was a cardinal rule in Ranger School never to walk on roads while on a patrol. Any leader who walked on a road even for a short distance would fail the exercise. You could cross a road, but never walk on or adjacent to one. We were taught to "bust trail" (walk through the bush and not follow trails) to avoid enemy booby traps and mines, today commonly called Improvised Explosive Devices (IEDs). One night, during the mountain phase, I was crossing a road just as a Jeep came around the bend. I knew that I had only seconds to get to the other side and not be observed. I dove for the edge of the road not realizing that there was a 4-foot drop on the other side. I landed on my chest and slid down a gravel slope. I was carrying the radio on my back, and it slammed on top of my head, knocking me out. I regained consciousness a short while later only to discover that I had landed on my right hip—right on top of an ammunition pouch filled with rifle magazines. I thought I had broken my pelvis. I was in agony.

I was evacuated by Jeep to a local civilian hospital where we woke up the physician on duty. At 2 AM, he x-rayed my hip to see if it was broken. Fortunately, nothing was, although I was in extreme pain. Subsequently transported to the medical clinic at the Ranger School base, I was given a warm bed and was able to grab several hours of sleep and a hot shower. Then, I was confronted by one of the cadre who informed me that I had a choice to make: I could be recycled again to the next incoming class, or I could suck it up and go back out to my patrol. I chose to go back to the field. I was given some Darvon to kill the pain. (A motto commonly used by the Rangers in my program was "take a Darvon and drive on.")

The next several days were agonizing as walking was excruciating. But I refused to be recycled again and forced myself through every exercise, taking the Darvon and ignoring the pain. It was cold in the mountains. When I stopped for a break, my hip would stiffen up and I would be in even greater agony when we started to move again. At night, we built fires to stay warm, but I could not lie on my right side. My front was always turned away from the fire. My back burned while my front froze. But finally, after a few days, I was able to keep pace with the rest of the patrol.

At the end of the second phase of training, I had to negotiate the "Rope Drop Confidence Test." This involved climbing a 40-foot telephone pole at the edge of a lake, walking across a 20-foot plank that was 8 inches wide and stretched to another telephone pole. There were three steps in the center of the plank that I had to step over. Then I grabbed a 20-foot rope and monkey-climbed to a height of 50 feet. At this point another transition was made to a horizontal rope pulling myself along for another 20 feet. I finally reached a large wooden Ranger Tab hanging at the center of the rope. After touching the wooden Ranger Tab, I hung by both hands and became motionless. When acknowledged by the officer on the dock, I let go with one hand, saluted the officer, and yelled: "Sir, Ranger Bartlett requests permission to negotiate the Rope Drop Confidence Test." The salute was returned, and the order given to "drop." I dropped 50 feet into the water yelling "Ranger" all the way down. Any error in carrying out this confidence test exactly as described would require that the exercise be repeated. I did it right the first time and passed my second confidence test.

I had not received a leadership assignment during the mountain phase; this was simply fine by me. I kept my mouth shut hoping they had overlooked me and did my best to volunteer only when the time was right and to keep up with the rest of the men. At the end of the mountain phase, I received a satisfactory buddy rating from my West Point Artillery colleagues and was approved to move on to the next training phase, which took place in the swamps of Florida.

During the third and final phase of Ranger training in Florida, I learned how to read and navigate using photographic maps. They were big, clumsy pieces of paper. It was hard to determine landmarks, especially at night under a poncho, using a flashlight with a red lens. The same rules applied as before: if you achieved your objective for the day, you were given a meal for the day. If you failed, you went hungry. There was great incentive to achieve the objective, but everyone looked haggard surviving on only one C-Ration meal a day. I felt my pants becoming loose around my waist.

Those of us who were airborne qualified enjoyed making several parachute jumps into our objectives during Ranger School. The most exciting jump of all was a night jump and it was my first one. The group of Rangers who were jump qualified strapped on parachutes at around 6 PM and were checked by the jump master. He pulled the back straps of my harness extra hard, and I felt the straps placing undue strain on my back. I endured the pain for as long as I could, but finally had to ask him to loosen the straps to relieve the pain in my back. He did and I returned to waiting along with the rest of our group. Then, finally, at around 8 PM, we loaded into a C-130 aircraft and took off. The flight and exit from the plane were uneventful. It was a very warm and humid night and that meant we would be floating down very slowly. After jumping, checking chute, and looking around to make sure I was not near any other jumpers, I looked down. All I could see were small strobe lights marking the corners of the drop zone. It seemed like it was taking forever to come down because of the humidity. Fortunately, there was no wind, and I was coming straight down. I took up the landing position and listened for the ground to come up. I started to stretch out one leg to feel for the ground and suddenly remembered that coming down on one leg was a guaranteed way to break it. The landing was one of the most comfortable I ever had. I landed so softly that I did not realize I was standing up and did not need to roll to absorb the shock.

I made a total of 32 static line parachute jumps before going to Vietnam, but this was my only night jump (except for the ones I made with my eyes closed!). I also made jumps out of helicopters, which was a hugely different execution because when you jumped you dropped straight down and needed to count to four to confirm that your chute was fully deployed. I also made jumps from Otters, C-130s and C-141s. When you jumped from a fixed-wing aircraft you were hit by a tremendous prop blast the moment you exited the door, and the count was to three before checking to see that your chute opened properly. It was an exciting time to be a paratrooper and we all took extraordinary pride in the special badges we were eligible to wear, as well as the extra jump pay.

The trick to navigating the Florida phase was to avoid the deep swamps. Traversing a swamp was no fun. Any leader that failed to learn the lesson of skirting a swamp rather than walking directly through it endured the wrath of the cadre as well as the rest of his unit. But sometimes our objectives were situated in the middle. Then, everyone was required to get wet in mucky water which could be as high as one's chest and filled with snakes and spiders.

Late one afternoon, while walking through knee-deep water, the word was passed back: "Ranger Bartlett to the front." I hustled forward to talk with the Ranger Cadre as we continued to move through the swamp toward our objective. He asked if I had ever heard of "Operation Red Dog." Being the smart-ass lieutenant that I was, I told him that I knew what a Red Dog was. The cadre officer asked me to tell him what it was. I said it was when the opposing football team rushed the passer. I was informed that I was full of shit and should shut up and listen.

We reached our objective and thankfully made it onto some dry land that had a C-Ration stash. I was told I had two hours to plan a night ambush and would brief my squad leaders at 8 PM. As I looked at the photographic maps, I was pleased to see that the terrain did not require any swamp navigation. My brain swung into high gear. Operations planning was an area of some expertise for me. I thought I would only have to create the plan and then pass the leadership responsibility on to another Ranger who would conduct the operation. That was the way leadership responsibility was typically managed: one man planned, one led the unit to the site, one executed the ambush, and one moved the patrol on to the next location. So, by the time the mission was complete, four or five Rangers had been tested.

The objective was to ambush the bad guys on the edge of a drop zone (DZ). I decided on using an L-shaped ambush formation which has a lot of killing power because you place two machine guns next to each other at the center of the L. However, I had to ensure the machine gunners knew their fields of fire and didn't shoot the friendlies located on the long or short legs of the L. That can be accomplished by placing stakes on either side of the machine guns so that the gunner knows exactly where to stop traversing when firing. I planned thoroughly and chose Church, my SEAL friend, to be my platoon sergeant. He would be judged on his execution of my plan, but fortunately did not have to write or present the plan as this was not his forte.

The 8 PM briefing of the squad leaders went smoothly. For the first time, I included the use of pyrotechnics. I had been carrying two star clusters (aerial rockets—similar to Roman candles) for many months, but no leader had thought to include them in their plans. Questions were asked and answered. I was feeling great with the plans I had laid out and had about 15 minutes after the briefing to rest before saddling up to begin the first leg of the move. Fully expecting to be relieved and for another Ranger to be appointed as the leader, I was told that: "No, you're still in charge... execute the mission." So, I saddled up and off we went.

Our night move through the sandy terrain went smoothly. We approached the drop zone, and I deployed my platoon sergeant, as originally planned, to scout the DZ and place the squads in position for the ambush. (This was the platoon sergeant's portion of the operational test.) He had difficulty returning to the unit after reconnoitering the objective, but eventually we linked up and put our men into position with five minutes to spare.

I was positioned at the apex of the L formation. I took out the aerial rockets and placed them in front of me. In about 30 minutes, a group of bad guys approached; everyone got ready to spring the ambush. The signal to shoot was the firing of a white rocket. (A red rocket meant to cease fire and for the hunter killer teams to move out to search the dead bodies.) It was time to spring the ambush, but I could not get the cap off the rocket. It had to be removed using a key, much like opening a can of sardines.

There was no time to fiddle with the rocket, so I did the next best thing and yelled "open fire" and shot off a magazine from my own rifle. Fortunately, everyone understood and began firing. They opened fire on the bad guys who dutifully died on the spot. (Obviously, we were using blank ammunition.) Having finally figured out how to open the flare canisters, I opened the red one, placed the cap on the bottom of the canister, pointed it straight up and slapped the bottom. A bright red flare shot 200 feet into the air above the DZ, providing illumination for the hunter killer teams to do their work. Unfortunately, there was a wind blowing against us and the flare drifted back and into the tree line. The remains of the flare landed in the woods and started a small fire which the Ranger Cadre rushed off to extinguish before it became a blaze. This gave me the time I needed to pull the men out of the ambush formation and move them about 100m to an assembly point, secure the area, count heads, and make sure everyone was accounted for.

Again, at this point, I fully expected to be relieved, and a new leader appointed, but had no such luck. I was still the leader and was told to redeploy my men back on the edge of the DZ because another group of bad guys was going to be parachuted in. They, too, needed to be ambushed. So, back we went to the DZ. The men were repositioned back into the L ambush formation.

I learned my lesson about the pyrotechnics the first time and passed the word that the ambush would be launched when the machine guns started firing. A whistle would signal the cease fire; a second whistle for the hunter killer teams to move out. Finally, a third whistle would signal the move to the assembly point. The second ambush came off smoothly although one of the machine gunners fell asleep and had to be awakened to begin firing. By this time, it was 1 AM. Everyone was beat from an exceptionally long day and even longer night.

At the assembly point I hoped and prayed that I would be relieved of leadership but was told to continue to execute the mission. So, we moved out. The patrol walked about 8km (klicks) through the sandy forest area taking breaks periodically as everyone was thoroughly exhausted. Finally, at first light, I came to an open area. My compass man and the soldier responsible for keeping count of the distance traversed indicated that we needed to proceed into the open terrain in front of us. I was told that our objective area was less than 500m ahead. Moving through open terrain was something that Rangers were forbidden to do, and I was extremely hesitant to modify our line formation. But I needed to trust my compass and the man responsible for calculating the distance, so I proceeded out into the open, changing our formation to staggered columns. After a couple of hundred meters, the Ranger Cadre stopped the formation and approached me. "You've done a decent job up until now," he said "but you are in danger of failing this patrol. Climb up on that mound and figure out exactly where you are." I realized that either the compass or the distance man was off on his count.

At the top of a 10-foot mound, I did a 360-sweep of the terrain and saw some smoke coming from a tree line to the right of our formation. The distance man was on target, but the compass man was off a few degrees. I moved the unit back into the tree line and, staying out of the open, rejoined the rest of the company. The Ranger officer gave me a grade of 85 for the exercise which counted as having led four patrols. There would be no more leadership tests for me. If I passed the final confidence test, I would be awarded the Ranger Tab.

I was ecstatic that I had passed all my patrols, but I was also hungry and exhausted. I grabbed a box of Cs and wolfed down the scrambled eggs and fruit. I laid out my poncho and was asleep instantly. A few minutes later, I was shaken awake to be informed there were several Rangers in our unit in danger of failing and they needed to lead make-up patrol assignments. I had to go on the mission. I complained bitterly that I had not slept in 48 hours and had nothing left in my tank, but it did no good. Thirty minutes later I was participating in another patrol… this time led by someone who had failed several previous attempts.

I walked back through the open area that had almost been the scene of my demise earlier that morning. The sun was up, and the temperature was in the high nineties. As I got halfway across the open field, the enemy opened on us, and we all hit the ground and returned fire. The leader called for "fire and maneuver." Everyone in the unit had been assigned a letter, either A or B. When A was called, the B Team was to lay down a base of fire and the A Team was to run forward. Then the A Team took up the fire and it was the B Team's turn to run.

The last thing that any of us wanted to do was run across an open field for 200m in the 98-degree heat. Most of us were already exhausted and the heat made things that much worse. Sweat dripped off my face, but the grass was cool and inviting. My letter was called, and I ran forward 10m and hit the ground. I was in high grass and could not see the enemy. Of course, they could not see me either. I fired a couple of blank rounds in the direction of the bad guys and waited for my letter to be called again. My eyes closed…

The next thing I knew, one of the Ranger Cadre was kicking my foot. I had fallen asleep while waiting for my letter to be called. I knew that I had to play this situation very cool, or I could be in big trouble. The Ranger Cadre asked me: "What are you doing, Ranger?"

By this time, I had my weapon up and pointed toward where I thought the enemy was located. I responded saying, "I'm waiting for them to call my letter, Sir, and then I will move forward." The Ranger Cadre asked me if I was still with my unit. I played the game to the hilt and poked my head up briefly and said: "Yes Sir, I'm an A. I'm waiting for them to call my letter."

I was then told to stand up and look around. Everyone had moved on to the objective while I had fallen asleep. Fortunately, the cadre officer knew that I had planned the previous night's exercise, was exhausted, and took pity on me.

(He thought it was funny that I had fallen asleep.) I was made to do 25 push-ups, pour a canteen of water over my head, and run the 200m to join my patrol. The unfortunate part was that the patrol leader had failed the exercise because he forgot to take a head count when the operation was over and discover I was missing.

Because I was short, I hated to carry the machine gun. Even though there was a strap on the gun that I could put over my shoulder, it was still too long, and the gun always hit me square on the thighs. I simply was not good at carrying it. I worked a deal with my Ranger Buddy: He would carry the machine gun when I got it, and I would carry the radio when he got it. Of course, what happened next was that I was assigned to carry the machine gun. I made the swap with the radio operator and put the PRC-25 (fondly called a "Prick 25") on my back. Somehow, I made it through the rest of that day and moved on to the final confidence test in the swamp phase of the program.

The third and last confidence test during the Florida phase of Ranger School was a 10-mile Ranger Buddy forced march to a final objective near the Ranger base camp. At 8 PM, we were all dropped off in pairs along a 10-mile line facing a large swamp with about 200m between pairs. I was told that we must cross through the swamp to the other side and make it to the finish line near the base camp by 6 AM. Any Ranger who failed to make it to the finish line by that time would pass the course, but would not be able to wear the Ranger Tab. Both Ranger Buddies had to cross the finish line together or both would fail to qualify for the Tab. Those who failed would immediately board trucks and be returned to Ft. Benning.

Everyone knew that taking a direct shot across the swamp meant suicide. The swamp was deep, full of roots and trees and impossible to navigate (never mind snakes and nasty water). There was no way we could get to the other side in time for the 6 AM deadline following a straight line. Ranger Cadre were posted every 500m along the route. If they found that we were trying to skirt the swamp, they would escort us back to the starting point. It became clear that the objective of this exercise was to avoid and bypass the Ranger Cadre and skirt the swamp. My Ranger Buddy and I decided on a plan of entering the swamp to a depth of about 100m, walk in knee-deep water past where the Ranger Cadre were positioned (they did not wish to get their feet wet) and then start skirting the swamp. The terrain was simply impassable, so my Ranger Buddy and I had to move out to dry land and play cat and mouse with the cadre. Fortunately, as this was the last exercise of the program the cadre were about as tired as we were; no one wanted to intentionally fail the Rangers trying to skirt the swamp. We spent a good deal of time that evening crawling around to avoid the pockets of Ranger Cadre. At 5:30 AM we emerged from the swamp with about 500m to go and easily ran to the finish line with time to spare.

Some Rangers were not as fortunate. Those that had tried to go through the swamp were delayed. Others had been caught and returned to the starting point. Some had fallen and were injured. Some were being helped and carried by their

Ranger Buddies. As 6 AM approached, we yelled and screamed encouragement to those who still had a chance to cross the finish line. Unfortunately, there were about five teams who did not make it. We watched as they boarded a truck and left the area. These men cried.

My first Ranger Buddy had failed the course because of poor buddy ratings from Infantry West Point graduates. I had been fortunate to be recycled and go through the program with a group of more sympathetic Artillery graduates. But there were still times of great frustration, exhaustion, and mental fatigue. I learned that it was possible to drive myself beyond the pain, beyond the exhaustion, and complete the mission. I learned to "gut it out." I "took a Darvon and drove on." Paramount in my mind was the fear of returning to my unit and college without the Ranger Tab on my shoulder. I had no choice but to succeed.

This accomplishment also helped me through my experience in Vietnam. There was never an instance where I was too exhausted or faced a physical or mental challenge that I felt I could not handle. I had been taught to execute operations viciously and to kill the enemy. Even if the tactical decision was wrong, we were taught that if the plan was executed viciously and aggressively, the outcome might still be successful. Killing enemy soldiers did not factor into the equation. What was important was surviving the ambush, attacking, and defeating the enemy force by any means possible. In Vietnam, I had to be careful not to unduly risk my men or expect the same level of aggressive commitment I knew I could demand of myself. Achieving a balance—between being appropriately aggressive and protecting the welfare of my men—was my goal.

Upon return to the base camp in Florida, we were instructed to take showers and put on our one clean uniform. As I put on my uniform with my rank and insignia, I discovered that my pants were a full 4 inches too large around the waist. I weighed myself after my shower and found I had lost almost 30 lbs while in Ranger School. I had to take 2-inch tucks on both sides of my pants and strap my belt around to hold them up. My weight had gone from 165 to 137 lbs.

One of the proudest moments of my life was when our Ranger Platoon sergeant, whose favorite saying was "move your boney legs," walked down the line to pin my Ranger Tab to my left shoulder. Tears streamed down my face. He saluted me and shook my hand saying: "Congratulations, Ranger Bartlett." I was so overcome I could barely utter a "Thank you, Sergeant." We graduated with a pass-in-review performed at double-time. We were exhilarated and yelled out "ARC, ARC" to show support for our SEAL comrades who graduated with us.

Graduation was followed by a marvelous barbecue dinner on the parade grounds with beer, soda, hamburgers, hot dogs, corn-on-the-cob, and fried chicken. I was so hungry that I stuffed myself. But I was exhausted too. I remember sitting on the grass eating my food and drinking a couple of beers. The next thing I remember was being shaken awake and told to go to my tent to sleep. We slept from about 5 PM that day until 8 AM the next morning and then boarded busses for the return trip to Ft. Benning. Ranger School was over; a new life was about to begin.

Ranger School turned out to be the best life insurance policy for any officer who was headed for Vietnam. The training was so valuable that the army shortened the course to eight weeks and made all infantry officers go through it. It was the most demanding and grueling training of my life. Not only was it the best preparation possible for Vietnam, but for the rest of my military and civilian life. It taught me how to overcome any adversity, no matter how physically or mentally challenging. At 21 years old, I now felt I had the practical experience and confidence I needed to lead men in combat, kill the enemy, and survive no matter how grave the danger or severe the situation. While often afraid, never once in Vietnam was I overwhelmed. Never once was I at a loss for what to do. I knew that no matter what enemy force I faced I was prepared mentally and physically to overcome all adversity, attack the enemy position, and kill them. And I did.

When Chief of Staff of the Army General Creighton Abrams ordered the formation of the Ranger Battalions in 1974, he directed that they would be the elite, setting the standards for the army.

They maintained a code of ethics, a Ranger philosophy to live by. Written by Command Sergeant Major Neal R. Gentry, the Ranger Creed would set forth this philosophy and be the hallmark of the spirit, discipline, and duty of all Rangers in peace and war. Gentry was selected to serve as the first command sergeant major for the 1st Ranger Battalion. Today, the Ranger Creed is a guide for Ranger conduct. It is the code that binds through loyalty the individual to his Ranger buddies and to his unit.

The Ranger Creed

Recognizing that I volunteered as a ranger, fully knowing the hazards of my chosen profession, I will always endeavor to uphold the prestige, honor, and high esprit de corps of my ranger regiment.

Acknowledging the fact that a ranger is a more elite soldier, who arrives at the cutting edge of battle by land, sea, or air, I accept the fact that as a ranger, my country expects me to move further, faster, and fight harder than any other soldier.

Never shall I fail my comrades. I will always keep myself mentally alert, physically strong, and morally straight, and I will shoulder more than my share of the task, whatever it may be, one hundred percent and then some.

Gallantly will I show the world that I am a specially selected and well trained soldier. My courtesy to superior officers, neatness of dress, and care of equipment shall set the example for others to follow.

Energetically will I meet the enemies of my country. I shall defeat them on the field of battle for I am better trained and will fight with all my might. Surrender is not a ranger word. I will never leave a fallen comrade to fall into the hands of the enemy and under no circumstances will I ever embarrass my country.

Readily will I display the intestinal fortitude required to fight on to the ranger objective and complete the mission, though I be the lone survivor.

RANGERS LEAD THE WAY!

CHAPTER 4

Back at the 82nd

I was on the phone, copying down the names of the soldiers who had just received orders to go to Vietnam when the sergeant read, "Lieutenant Robin Bartlett."

After Ranger School was over, I drove back to Ft. Bragg, North Carolina and returned to my unit, 1st Battalion, 325th Infantry at the 82nd Airborne Division. Now, Airborne and Ranger qualified, I was ready to meet my stateside troops. I was in the best physical condition ever—ready to be assigned as an infantry platoon leader within the division, a unit rich in heritage and one of the top fighting units in the US Army.

I linked up with three other second lieutenants who had gone through training with me, and we rented a house off post. After a couple of days to recuperate from the rigors of Ranger School, I reported to my battalion to be reintroduced to my company and finally meet the men in my platoon. Fate, however, intervened.

Arriving at battalion headquarters, I was introduced to the battalion commander, a lieutenant colonel, a man who had come up through the ranks and was proud of it. He was not Ranger qualified, but he was a veteran of one tour in Vietnam, a career officer with many years of military experience. Sitting outside his office waiting to report in, I noticed that there was a sergeant sitting at the desk normally occupied by the S-1, the adjutant or personnel officer. I asked the sergeant, who was typing away, where the S-1 normally sat and received the reply, "We don't have one, Sir. So many officers are in Nam." Then I asked what the requirements were for the S-1 job. The sergeant thought a moment and said, "Well, you really need to be able to write." Then he whispered to me, "If you are interested in doing this job, you should tell the CO when you go in. He really needs some help." At that point I remember saying to myself, "Well, as a comparative literature major in college, writing is certainly something I know how to do."

Shortly thereafter, I was ushered into the battalion commander's office; standing at attention, I saluted smartly and reported in. I had expected the officer to ask me to sit down, but he kept me standing in front of his desk as he asked a few perfunctory questions about my background and training. By now, I felt I had earned a measure of respect having completed Basic Officer, Airborne, and Ranger training, but I was still a second lieutenant, had never led men and was young and very green. The battalion commander knew it, even though I did not. The interview was about to end when the battalion commander said, "OK, I'm going to assign you back to your previous line company. Do you have any questions?" I said to myself, "Well, it's now or never." I told the commander that the sergeant had told me there was no officer in the S-1 slot. "Yes, why?" came the response. "Well, Sir, I'd like to have the job." He responded: "What do you know about being an S-1?" I replied, "I know how to write."

His response was immediate: "We'll see about that." Then he tossed a pad of paper and a pencil across his desk and said, "Write a response memo to the brigade commander. It needs to be short—three paragraphs, to the point, no bullshit, and short words." He passed the original correspondence to me and gave me some more rapid-fire instructions which I scribbled on the pad. He told me the sergeant would give me the proper format to be followed for the memo. I was to bring the memo back to him, typed, in 10 minutes.

Back outside his office, I got a copy of the memo format from the sergeant, spent a few minutes writing down the key things that needed to be said and then loaded a piece of paper into the typewriter. I worked feverishly for the next 9 minutes whereupon the battalion commander came out of his office and said: "Finished?" I stood up, pulled the paper from the typewriter, and handed it to him. The CO sat down at his desk as I again stood in front of him. He crossed out a few words and scribbled in the margin saying, "I told you no big words." He also circled a couple of typos that I had not had time to correct. After a few minutes, he said, "OK, clean this up and report for duty tomorrow morning." Flabbergasted, I said: "Here, Sir?" He looked at me strangely and said, "Of course here, this is where you will be working." Suddenly, I was the S-1, a second lieutenant filling a captain's slot.

I was elated with what had just happened. I had stuck my neck out and had qualified for a job that was normally held by an officer with much more experience. When my former company commander found out I was the new S-1, he was not so enthusiastic. He emphasized that what I really needed was to learn how to lead troops in combat and not write correspondence for the battalion commander. I considered this for a while and wondered if I had made a giant error. I had been looking forward to returning to my line company and to the challenge of leading my own platoon. But, in my gut, I knew my strengths. I believed it was a better use of my skills and knowledge as the S-1 than being a line platoon leader. While the job did not prepare me to become a combat infantry platoon leader in Vietnam, I still had Ranger training under my belt, and I was confident this job would prepare me for what I considered my future army career would be. In retrospect, there were times later in Vietnam when I wished I had had more troop leadership experience. But when in doubt, I naturally gravitated toward seeking and taking the advice of my subordinate leaders. This is what a good leader always does.

My life at the 82nd for the next six months was sweet. I lived in a nice little house off post. I had a 9–5 job handling all the administrative and personnel issues of the battalion. I made the obligatory parachute jump once per month to collect the extra $110 in jump pay. And when we went to the field, I accompanied the battalion commander, slept in a warm tent, ate hot food, rode in a jeep, and watched the troops slog through field exercises. My specialty, however, was planning parties. I planned the best parties our battalion had ever seen. I made sure that we had the best hors d'oeuvres possible, that every departing officer was recognized properly by the battalion commander and his name spelled correctly on the paratrooper statue awarded upon departure. And that's how I got to meet Miranda.

Every officer who joined our unit contributed $25 a month to a slush fund for our monthly officer parties. This money was used to buy hors d'oeuvres and fund an open bar, as well as gifts for departing officers. Attendance at battalion functions was mandatory unless you were at death's door. A farewell ceremony was held at each monthly cocktail party giving a sendoff to the officers who had received orders for Vietnam. The battalion commander would make a speech, say good things about each officer and then present him with a small airborne soldier statuette, inscribed with the unit crest, the officer's name, and dates of service. It was my job to order the statues, make sure that the name was spelled correctly, and write the CO's speech for each party. I also made sure that we had excellent food and drink for every party, as every officer certainly wanted to drink up his monthly $25 allotment.

Upon arrival at one of the first parties, I noticed that all the married officers and their wives stood over in one corner and the bachelor officers huddled in another. The bachelor officers hailed from many parts of the country and did not know any females in the local area. I decided I needed to change this picture.

One afternoon, I came home to find a mutual fund salesman talking with one of the other officers who lived in my house. Watching TV and eating a TV dinner, I listened as the salesman pitched my housemate. The officer said "No, I'm not interested," and the sales rep started packing up his briefcase. That was when an idea struck me.

I walked over to the salesman who immediately asked if I might like to hear the information about his mutual fund. I told him that I had been listening to the pitch and was mildly interested, but then asked: "Are you from around here?" His response was: "Yes, I was born in Fayetteville and went to school here." Then I asked, "Do you know any local girls?" He said that he knew a lot of them. Then I told him that I would buy his mutual fund on one condition. He was going to have to set me up with a date with one of his female friends. She had to be short, and good looking. And, if the date didn't work out, he needed to set me up again. His response was: "Sign here, Lieutenant."

About two weeks later, I received a call from the sales rep who passed on the name and phone number of a young lady living in Dunn, North Carolina, a 45-minute drive from Fayetteville. He said that this young lady was exactly my type. And so, a few days later I found myself driving to Dunn to have coffee with Miranda. It was about 8 PM when I arrived and walked up to the porch of a large Southern-style colonial home. It reminded me of a scene from *Gone with the Wind*, with large white columns on the porch. I was nervous. This was a blind date. The girl had been nice enough on the phone, but who knew what I was about to face. I rang the bell and waited.

The door opened and my mouth practically dropped to my chin because here, in front of me, was a beautiful, petite, blonde-haired, blue-eyed young woman (a true southern belle type). I could not believe my good fortune and told myself that buying that mutual fund was the best investment I had ever made (which, it turned out, was not the case.) Miranda and I spent the next two hours drinking coffee, exchanging stories, and getting to know each other. She was 19 and I was 21. We hit it off magically. At the end of the evening, I asked if she might like to see a movie or have dinner with me. She said she would. I drove back to Fayetteville elated at the prospect of having a drop-dead gorgeous date to take to the next battalion function.

And that is exactly what I did. I took Miranda to the next Officers' Club party and was the only bachelor to have a date. Upon entering the room, I could feel all the other officers' eyes looking at Miranda and me with great envy. I introduced Miranda to another junior officer friend of mine and went to get drinks for both of us. When I returned, I discovered that Miranda had been surrounded by about eight junior officers who crowded around her asking questions. I tried to muscle my way into the center and finally had to yell, "At ease troops, she's my date." Then I escorted her to the other side of the room to introduce her to my battalion commander, as well as protect her from the horde of bachelors. We enjoyed dinner, drank wine, danced, and had a wonderful time.

My dates with Miranda increased as time went by, and we would try to see each other every weekend unless I was participating in field exercises. On one Sunday, I was again visiting her home, drinking coffee, and exchanging stories when suddenly, a toddler came running through the room. On his second trip through, Miranda called the boy over and introduced him to me as Tommy, her son. Oh my, I thought, this situation just got a whole lot more complicated. Miranda was 19 and an unwed mother of a three-year-old.

She related the story of how she had become pregnant at 16 and had not wanted to marry the father who had subsequently moved away to college. She and her son lived at home with her parents while she worked part time and took some courses at the local community college. She was so open and honest about the situation that I told her it didn't make a difference to me, even though it really did. I was a 21-year-old second lieutenant with no ties to anything and would be heading to Vietnam within the next six to 12 months. The last thing I needed was to have an attachment to a ready-made family.

I invited Miranda and Tommy to come to my battalion's weekend parachute drop. The public could watch our drops; I told her where to meet me at the edge of the drop zone. The day turned out to be overcast, cold and windy, but the jump went off smoothly. I found myself at the end of the stick (a line of jumpers), pushing the other jumpers out the door. I hit the air, checked my risers and chute and everything seemed fine except for the smoke drifting across the drop zone. It was blowing much harder at low altitudes than above. As I approached the drop zone, I saw that the wind was pushing me across the field at an alarming speed. To counter the wind, I pulled in several armfuls of the parachute riser which tipped the chute in the opposite direction to the wind. This allowed me to come down straight, but it also increased my speed of descent. I was coming down fast. At the last second, I dropped the riser, and this allowed the chute to even out. I hoped I would not swing too much. I hit the ground hard landing in the following order: toes, buttocks, and head—all in quick succession.

I hit hard on my helmet and heard the cloth of the helmet liner tearing. I lay on the ground dazed, trying to figure out what had happened. I was shaken and knew that I had not landed well. I opened my eyes to blackness, and at first thought I had hit my head so hard that I had gone blind. When my helmet hit, I ripped all the webbing from inside the helmet liner. The helmet had slipped down over my face creating a total blackout. Thankfully, as I looked down, I could see daylight coming in from underneath.

Lying on my stomach and gradually pushing the helmet up toward the back of my head I looked out just in time to see my parachute fill with air and start to pull me across the drop zone. I was wearing a field jacket, so I stuck out my hands in the sandy soil trying to stop myself and regain my footing, but the wind was too strong. I was being pulled at an increasingly fast rate across the field. As I stuck out my hands, the sand shot up my sleeves, filling the inside of my field jacket. Realizing that the wind was not going to subside and that I could not get a solid footing, I flipped over on my back and tried to squeeze the quick releases on my chute. They were stiff but working with two hands I finally managed to pop one open and the chute deflated.

Slowly, ever so slowly, I picked my sore body up off the ground, took off my destroyed helmet and rolled up my chute. I shook the sand from inside my jacket and painfully walked to where the onlookers were assembled.

All this action had occurred right in front of the viewing stand. As I joined Miranda and Tommy, the little boy exclaimed: "Hey, Robin, did you have fun being dragged across the field?" Miranda gave me some aspirin for my pounding headache. We headed toward the Officers' Club for lunch and several stiff drinks. It had been the worst parachute drop of the 32 I made.

Each month, one of the duties of the S-1 was to receive a phone call from division headquarters providing a list of officers and NCOs who had received orders for Vietnam along with their future unit assignment. There was an attempt to send officers from the 82nd to other airborne units. This included a brigade of the 82nd, the 101st and the 173rd Airborne Brigade. So, one afternoon in April, I was on the phone, copying down the names of those soldiers who had just received orders to go to Vietnam when the sergeant read, "Lieutenant Robin Bartlett." I stopped copying for several seconds. Recovering from the shock, I asked the sergeant to return to the name after mine and resumed copying.

I was to report to the 101st Airborne Division, the "Screaming Eagles," in Vietnam within 30 days. Soon thereafter, at the next Officers' Club meeting, I received my Airborne statue for having served as the S-1 for six months. The battalion commander complimented me for stepping up to the plate without prior training and for performing efficiently. He hoped that the next S-1 would be as adept at throwing parties as I had been. My former company commander wished me well and told me to keep my head low and ass even lower. I assured him I would.

A few days later I said a tearful goodbye to Miranda and Tommy and promised to write. But at this point in time my future was uncertain, and my plans were focused almost exclusively on me. Furthermore, I knew that I was not excited about the prospect of taking on a ready-made family. Miranda and I corresponded for a time after departing for Vietnam, but both of us eventually moved on with our separate lives.

CHAPTER 5

First Days in Country

*On the bus from Tan Son Nhut Airbase to the "Repo Depo," in Bien Hoa, I noticed
a wire frame welded over each window of the bus. I asked one of the sergeants
returning for his second tour what was the purpose. His response was:
"To prevent Gooks from riding up on a scooter and dropping a grenade
through the open window." It hit me that I was truly in a combat zone.*

Before shipping out, I spent two weeks of vacation at my parents' home in Monterey,
California. Taking long morning and afternoon runs in my jungle boots and getting
as much exercise as possible, I tried not to think about what was coming my way
in a few short weeks. About five days prior to my scheduled departure, Dennis
Hastings, one of the lieutenants with whom I had shared the house in Fayetteville,
and who had received orders at the same time as me, unexpectedly gave me a call.
He had flown to San Diego and was driving up the coast in a huge white Caddy
convertible and wanted me to join him. This sounded good. We toured around
Carmel and Monterey before heading up to San Francisco, the top down, music
blaring on the radio.

My father, a retired Air Force colonel, pulled some strings to reserve a room for
us in a grand hotel, the Marine Memorial in downtown San Francisco. We split the
cost, $40 per night. The hotel sported a beautiful restaurant with gilded ceilings
and gold dinner service and charged "military prices." The two of us had some
cash to burn. We enjoyed grand dining on rich seafood and fine wines. We
rode the cable car, visited tourist attractions, and spent time going to clubs and
shows in the Haight-Ashbury district and trying to pick up girls. We ended up
drinking too much and crashing into bed at 2 AM and had severe hangovers
the next morning.

Before turning in the rental car and catching a bus for Travis Air Force Base
(AFB), I visited my grandparents' grave in the National Cemetery at the Presidio of
San Francisco. My grandfather, a former Cavalry colonel in World War I, had the
foresight to buy family plots inside the "Officers' Circle," a stunning location with an

incredible view overlooking the Golden Gate Bridge. The cemetery has thousands of white tombstones, some dating back to the Civil War, all perfectly aligned in rows, a mini version of Arlington National Cemetery. As I stood at the gravesite, I said a silent prayer that I would come back alive from this ordeal and that a place like this, while beautiful and serene, would NOT be my final resting place. I still had a lot of life to live and things to do. I didn't know what those things were yet, but I knew that I did not want to be buried in this cemetery—at least not now.

On the evening of my departure, I met my parents at the Officers' Club at Travis AFB. We were told that our flight would leave at 8 PM that evening. After dinner, I asked my parents not to stay but to say our goodbyes then. I knew my mother would become very emotional and I did not want her crying in front of the other officers in the club. Everyone, like me, was waiting for flights to Vietnam. So, we said our goodbyes and I hung around the Officers' Club when an announcement came that our flight had been delayed until 10 PM. Finally, we got on a bus, and made our way to the airport terminal. After another series of delays, we boarded a World Airlines jet for the first leg of our journey to Vietnam. It was 11 PM on May 9, 1968, a date that would become incredibly significant in my life.

~~~~~~

Postcard: 9 May 1968, En route to Vietnam, mailed from Hawaii
    Just stopped in Honolulu and now it's on to Okinawa. 18 hr. flight on a World Airlines jet—not bad! Was involved in the bomb scare at Travis AFB. Let me know if it hit the papers. Spent the whole time in the bar—oh, boy! Left on schedule, however. All is well except I am dirty and sleepy. Hope you enjoy the Mother's Day present.

~~~~~~

We stopped to refuel in Honolulu. It was 4 AM local time. We were allowed off the plane to stretch our legs and walk around the airport. Everything was closed except for a flower stand that opened at 6 AM. For $25 I could send a Hawaiian lei to some folks that would appreciate the gesture. I ordered three, one for my mother, one for Mitzi, my oldest friend and college classmate and one for the "girlfriend" I had recently met and with whom I'd formed a brief relationship.

Our plane was full of officers. The majority were second lieutenants from the 82nd Airborne Division. We were all infantry officers on orders to join the 101st Airborne Division. I wore a khaki uniform, highly polished jump boots and shiny brass insignia together with jump wings including the "flash backing" representing our respective units in the 82nd. Flight time passed very slowly as we all contemplated the next phase of our lives. There were a few captains and one or two field grade officers (majors and above) on the flight along with a few NCOs. Most of us chatted on the plane, except for the officers and NCOs returning for their second tours.

The Butter Bar Lieutenants were all FNGs to them and they kept to themselves knowing that many of us were in the largest "likely to be killed category."

* * *

As we touched down at Tan Son Nhut Airbase outside Saigon, everyone on the plane became quiet. The instant the door opened, the 105-degree heat, intense humidity, and acrid air filtered in. One of the stewardesses came on the intercom and asked us to pull down the window shades to keep the cabin cool for the returning soldiers. The plane would be taking off just as soon as it could be refueled and re-boarded with returning soldiers. As we walked down the roll-up ramp several hundred soldiers, the returning horde, dressed in jungle fatigues and a variety of uniforms filed past us, jeering, hooting, and making obscene comments. Mostly teenagers, these men had just spent a year in the Nam and were taking our seats for the return flight back to the World. My stomach churned as we trudged to an open-air hangar waiting for bus transportation to the Replacement Depot (Repo Depo) where we would receive further assignments.

The temperature and the smells were horrendous (something I would eventually take for granted). There were signs on the wall of the hangar telling us where the nearest bunkers were in case of a rocket attack on the airfield. It was common for the Viet Cong to drop a couple of mortar rounds on the airfield when a new flight arrived. I watched stoically as the plane that brought us in taxied to the end of the runway and took off. I grabbed my gear and loaded onto a military bus.

I had tried to carry the absolute minimum amount of clothing and personal items with me, but I still brought far too much. I had a duffel bag into which I packed underwear, toiletries, and spare uniforms plus some treasures from Ranger School—a 50-foot length of rope, a ball of twine, two carabiners, waterproof bags, extra socks, and foot powder. I also brought a set of two sheath knives with me. One blade was 9 inches long and it was piggybacked in the sheath by a smaller, 6-inch blade. The blades were super sharp, made of stainless steel, and were guaranteed never to go dull or rust. They came in very handy. Except for one uniform and my boots, nothing I brought returned home.

My father had given me a battery-operated, 3-inch reel-to-reel tape recorder that fit in a custom-made briefcase with Styrofoam cutouts so that the recorder, extra tapes, and extra batteries fit snugly. It weighed in at about 8 lbs. There were times that I cursed carrying it, but I recorded six tapes in my first three months before it mysteriously disappeared from my company headquarters. He also gave me a Kodak Instamatic camera with six rolls of pre-packaged film cartridges. This was one of the first autofocus cameras to hit the market; it took excellent pictures even in low light. I was able to snap a lot of photos and mailed the cartridges home for my parents to develop. Realizing that my folks would see the photos first, I was careful to keep them to shots of my men that were positive and general in nature. I always loved photography and thought this would be a terrific way to capture some memories. I carried the camera in a waterproof bag in an ammo pouch on my pack frame. Unfortunately, I forgot to remove the camera from the pouch one day when I crossed a stream and that was the end of the camera. While the tape recorder and camera represented excess baggage, I could not leave my father's thoughtful gifts behind.

Everyone saddled up with their gear to board the busses. We were all quiet. speaking only in hushed tones, sweating profusely, and longing to get into fatigues. On the bus from Tan Son Nhut Airbase to the "Repo Depo" in Bien Hoa, I noticed a wire frame welded over each bus window. I asked one of the sergeants returning for his second tour what was the purpose. His response was: "To prevent Gooks from riding up on a scooter and dropping a grenade through the open window." It hit me then that I was truly in a combat zone.

I arrived at the Repo Depo to be told I would be spending three to five days there. There was an air-conditioned Officers' Club where I could go to get cold drinks and food, but I was advised to stay out of it and begin the acclimatization process that would take at least three weeks. Due to the recent Tet Offensive and the extensive officer losses throughout units in Vietnam, we were informed all previous orders had been canceled. I was to be reassigned to a new unit depending on the greatest need. It was important to stay near our bunks as we might be called to move to the airfield at any time. The airborne officers were disappointed not to be going to the 101st, thus losing out on the extra jump pay. In retrospect, this turned out to be a positive experience for me.

God, it was hot. I was miserable. I lived in a large tent with sandbag walls. Even though we rolled up the flaps, there was no air. For several days, my routine was the same: Wake up. Shuffle to the mess hall. Eat some food and return to my bunk. Strip down to my shorts. Read, write letters. And then, every four to six hours, take a shower. Showers were my salvation. It felt so good to cool off and wash the sweat away. I dried off and walked back to my tent and then started the process all over again. A wet towel, hung outside, was dry in five minutes. Finally, at about 4 PM I made a trip to the post exchange to buy a magazine or paperback and browse useless items. I purchased a cheap wristwatch which lasted about two months before it stopped. Ultimately, because of the sweat, most officers pinned their watches to their uniforms in the way many nurses wear a watch. I tried to wear my college ring, but it too ended up with my other personal effects stored in a waterproof bag back at our company headquarters.

Occasionally, when I couldn't stand the heat any longer, I made a trip to the Officers' Club or O Club to watch a movie or drink a beer. It was always standing room only, but the temperature was 20 degrees cooler than outside. If you got lucky, you found a seat, grabbed a hamburger, and relaxed for a half hour before being ushered out by other officers waiting their turn to come in.

The most uncomfortable thing about the Repo Depo was that no one knew one another. We were all army officers and separated from the enlisted men—and treated a bit better. While waiting for orders to our new units we were herded together like cattle. I saw Dennis Hastings, my housemate from the 82nd and San Francisco Road warrior, briefly one afternoon. He understood he was still headed for the 101st the next morning as originally scheduled. I wished him well and that was the last I ever saw of him. I learned Dennis' fate sometime later. An officer from the 101st told me that on his fourth day in the field, while leading his platoon in combat, Dennis was directing an incoming chopper to land. He made the fatal error of standing on a mound to do so. He was decapitated by the rotor blades and died instantly. I could not believe it, but subsequently observed firsthand how these kinds of careless, non-thinking accidents can happen and could cost a life.

Sleep was impossible. I slept in my underwear and sweated into the mattress. Finally, at some time between 2 and 4 AM the temperature dropped a few degrees. Only then was I able to drift off to a light sleep. I dragged through the day acting and feeling like a zombie. Those first few days in country were awful. I did not know my next assignment. I had no friends. I felt miserable because of the heat. I was alone in a mass of other officers all feeling and reacting in the same way.

That was the routine I followed for four days after arriving in Vietnam: I took 6–8 showers a day trying to "stay alive." I read a half-dozen paperbacks, and I wrote "cheerful" letters back home telling everyone that I was fine… ridiculously hot, but fine.

~~~~~~

Letter: 12 May 1968, Bien Hoa, 90th Replacement Depot, Long Binh, III Corps, Vietnam

The temperature yesterday was 95 degrees and that was only average. We are in a large compound which is clear of everything from the edge of the perimeter as far as one can see. It is a fine place. There is an Officers' Club with air conditioning, a field ration mess, PX, and the standard, platoon size, double bunkbeds BOQ, plus cold showers. It is said to be a very secure base.

I should be here for 24–48 hours while someone determines if I should go to the 101st or if I am needed somewhere else. So, we sit, relax, and take cold showers. Every five minutes they call someone's name over the loudspeaker; he goes to the processing room, gets his assignment, packs up and leaves. This is what will happen to me sometime in the near future.

I hit the sack early last night only to be awakened at 11 PM by five rocket rounds crashing into the compound! I was out of the sack and into a bunker as fast as

I could go. All I had on was a T shirt, shorts, and boots. We spent one and a half hot sweaty hours in that bunker until they decided it was all clear. Two enlisted men (EM) were killed and several wounded. The choppers went out and there was a great deal of Arty booming. This is all I know for now.

Then, on the fourth day, I was awakened at 4 AM by a soldier and told to be ready to leave in one hour. I was shipping out to the 1st Air Cav Division. The division's rear was in An Khe, located in II Corps, and I would be catching a flight at 6 AM that morning. This was actually good news. My brother, an artillery officer, had been in that division a year earlier. Although he had been gravely wounded in a mortar attack, he had fine things to say about the unit. As those of us with assignments prepared to leave, the stories started to circulate. The Cav was a great unit to be in because they were airmobile and had more helicopters in the division than in all of Vietnam. The line units had extensive helicopter gunship and air support. Soldiers didn't have to carry as much equipment on their backs as other infantry units and thus could carry more ammo and water. If I got into trouble, helicopter support was only a call away. But because the unit was airmobile, it also meant that we could be picked up at a moment's notice and combat assaulted into the thick of a suspected enemy action. This was a unit famed for finding, trapping, assaulting, and killing the enemy no matter the terrain.

I humped my duffel bag, which I was now beginning to curse, and my fancy reel-to-reel tape recorder in its fancy case into a C-130 airplane for the 45-minute flight to An Khe. Upon arrival, I was ushered into a tent and continued to follow the same routine as I had at Bien Hoa: take frequent showers, read books, write letters, visit the Officers' Club and, oh yes… sweat.

Two days later, I went to the S-4 and drew equipment. I received a pair of jungle boots, six new jungle fatigue uniforms, six pairs of socks, a steel helmet, a camouflage cover and band, flak vest, pack, pack frame, load-bearing equipment, two one-quart canteens, a two-quart bladder canteen, four ammo pouches, mosquito repellent, first-aid pouch, 22 magazines and an M16 rifle (but no ammo). The rest of the day was spent sorting through the equipment, packing it together along with my personal possessions. Officers were told that they were required to have black patches with name, rank, and insignia and the 1st Air patch sewn onto their uniforms, so I dutifully took my six uniform shirts to the tailor, paying about $15 for the job. Some savvy officers had patches sewn on one uniform only.

Letter: 14 May 1968, 1st Air Cav Division Rear, An Khe, II Corps, Vietnam
I have joined the 1st Air Cav Division. The base camp here at An Khe is much larger than at Long Binh and it has all the facilities: PX, Officers' Club, showers.

We will draw our weapons and equipment today. It will be so nice to get into some jungle fatigues. These others are so hot. Tomorrow or the next day we will fly up north. They have moved the entire division into I Corps, to Camp Evans, about 10km south of Hue. I shall be going through a five-day training period before joining my battalion (or troop as they call them in the Cav.) I'm told we'll get our assignments today or tomorrow.

Right now, I just sit and wait for something to happen. I guess I will be stomping through the boonies very soon. Can't think of anything else I need except an air conditioner or a tub of ice. You might send another set of penlight batteries as I gave some to a friend for his shaver. That certainly won't be of much use in the field.

Two more days passed as I packed and repacked my gear, trying to reduce my load which had now grown with the equipment I had been issued. I was told to keep only one khaki uniform, my jump boots, and a change of civilian clothes for when I took rest and relaxation (assuming I made it to R&R). I spent several hours at the rifle range sighting in my rifle and practicing with a .45 pistol. I was issued only enough ammo for zeroing the sights. I was still an FNG, not to be trusted with a loaded gun.

The division rear was nestled in a valley with trees and plenty of overhead cover. It featured an Officers' Club where I could buy a steak dinner and a beer, watch movies, and eat popcorn. I slept in a comfortable bunk. There were showers and hot food every day. There was even a stream running through the camp where we could go skinny dipping to cool off. On my eighth day in Nam, I boarded a Chinook helicopter together with about 30 replacements and was shuttled to Camp Evans, in I Corps. The new camp, still under construction, was in the middle of a blazing desert. There was no overhead cover, no shade and sand blew everywhere and got into everything. The heat was intolerable. Many of the fortifications were still being prepared. Sandbags surrounded the tent in which I slept, but protective bunkers were still under construction.

The daily acclimatization process continued; I was not required to do anything except adjust to the heat. The army had learned that it took most soldiers three to four weeks to adjust to the average daily temperatures of between 100F and 115F. Soldiers could not be called upon to be effective fighters until their bodies adjusted to these temperatures. It was so hot that I had little or no appetite. I must have lost 20 lbs in the first three weeks and my pants kept getting looser and looser. I would try to eat some food in the morning and drink water and juice, but hot food was unappealing. We ate C-Rations for lunch (mostly the fruit) and had a simple meal for dinner. Drinking water and lots of it was a requirement, as was taking daily salt and malaria pills. Slowly, I noticed that my body was adjusting to the temperatures.

Upon arrival at Camp Evans, I was instructed to remove all patches from my uniforms. "Cut those fucking things off," one crusty training sergeant told me: "The snipers love to see those nice black patches. They are perfect aiming points. As officers and NCOs, you don't want anyone to know you are a leader because you will become an instant target. You've got to be careful about things such as checking maps out in the open, talking on the radio or giving directions to your troops. Keep your hand and arm movements to a minimum. The Cong are always looking for you. That's why your life expectancy is less than 90 days. Hide the fact that you are a leader and if you do, you'll have a better chance of making it through the next 365 days in one piece… but not much."

~~~~~~

Letter: 16 May 1968, Camp Evans, 1st Air Cav Division, I Corps, Vietnam

I got my assignment today: 1st Battalion, 5th Cav Regiment. After training, we will move out from Camp Evans where we are now to another base camp where the 1/5 is located. I was told the unit is presently engaged up around the DMZ.

It was hot this morning and my arms got sunburned as we sat and listened to lectures all morning. The afternoon cooled off a bit when clouds moved in, and it rained for a few minutes. The classes were repetitive except for one on airmobile assault from the CO of the training center. We also had a "fun" exercise in the gas chamber. I got a healthy lung full of CS gas and proceeded to vomit all over. I got the point of the exercise but am OK now. Tomorrow we will have more classes and spend the night on the perimeter.

I can send you a tape but will have to wait for more news to add. I know I won't have a chance to use it when we go to the field. I know now that I really brought too much stuff and may even send some back if I get a chance. I'll try to send my pictures home too to be developed as there are no facilities here to do it.

~~~~~~

I spent the next five days continuing the acclimatization process and participating in modest training exercises. I went to the rifle range and sighted in my M16 again. I watched a demonstration on the use of the jungle penetrator (a device at the end of a long cable with a pull-out seat or hook to lift a person or stretcher into a helicopter). I took refresher courses on calling in artillery, mortars and most important, how to direct ARA or helicopter gunships. I received a refresher course on basic first aid, treating traumatic wounds and administering morphine as well as protection from malaria and water-borne diseases. I was given a demonstration of how to direct the Cobra helicopter gunship and how important it was to clearly mark your position before directing them to fire on an enemy position. The firepower of this versatile helicopter was truly devastating and not something to be taken lightly. The nose gun was equipped with a minigun which fires at a rate of 3,000 rounds a minute. It also carried a rocket pod on each wing of the aircraft. If you were in close contact with the enemy, it was comforting to know that you had such a powerful and versatile weapon at your disposal, one you could call on to support you in a moment's notice when you got into the shit.

I also took refresher classes on small-unit tactics, fire, and maneuver, conducting an ambush, use of the Claymore mine, throwing hand grenades, the M60 machine gun and firing the M79 grenade launcher, as well as the diverse types of rounds that were available for the weapon, from flechettes (1-inch steel darts) to high explosive. I knew that I would not be called upon to fire any of these weapons, but I did need to know how to best deploy the men who did. I received refresher training on conducting combat assaults by helicopter and was informed that the platoon leader would always ride on the first bird accompanied by his radio operator, machine gunner, M79 grenade launcher, squad leader and riflemen. I discovered that, in the event a landing zone was under fire by the enemy (hot LZ), only the first bird would be permitted to land. The men on the first helicopter would have to fight it out on their own before any other helicopters with troops would be placed at risk. I paid close attention to the combat assault (Charlie Alpha) procedure, as I knew that I would be making plenty of them in the months to come. I personally made more than 60 helicopter combat assaults during my time as a combat platoon leader, sometimes making two assaults on the same day.

Finally, the five days of training culminated in an all-day exercise where our group left the base camp, walked 5km around the outer perimeter and directed helicopter gunships to fire on a suspected enemy target. One hundred and twenty-five men started the exercise, but only 80 completed the walk. The rest fell out due to heat exhaustion. Several had to be medevaced.

Letter: 20 May 1968, Camp Evans, 1st Air Cav Division, I Corps, Vietnam,

I have a nice suntan on my arms, neck, and face, but the rest of me is all white. I am slowly, very slowly beginning to acclimatize. At least now I can sit under a tent without my shirt and not sweat—too much.

We finished the training course yesterday. The pilots have already moved out and I should be going to the 1/5 very soon. Our last classes yesterday were extremely interesting. I learned that more than likely I will only be a platoon leader for six to seven months, then transition to a less hazardous staff job. We had a class from the Civil Affairs and Psyops officer [Psy Ops]. I spoke with him after the class and asked how difficult it would be to work in this area after 6 months as a platoon leader. He told me he would be glad to have me. I am going to think about this seriously.

Sure wish you could send me a cold drink, of anything. I figure that my weight loss has been between five and ten pounds… so far

---

Camp Evans was a sprawling base camp about 2 miles in diameter. The location had not been well chosen as there were large hills to the south and west. I was told there had been many enemy probes to the perimeter and that on two occasions sapper teams (enemy soldiers carrying satchel charges) tried to get through the wire and into the camp to throw explosives into command bunkers (the ones with lots of radio antennae sticking out of the top). The enemy was observing the camp every day. It was only a matter of time before Charlie would try something. I was not surprised when the "shit hit the fan" on the night after our big field exercise. It was my 19th day in Vietnam and the beginning of the "Mini Tet" offensive of 1968.

It started with a mortar and rocket barrage at 2 AM. I was in my bunk and instinctively rolled out of bed, keeping low, and crawled into a corner of our tent platform where I could be protected by two walls of sandbags. The nearest bunker was still under construction. It consisted of a hole dug in the ground with a large semicircular piece of aluminum placed on top and then covered with sandbags. But the top of this bunker still had not been covered with bags. The bright aluminum was an ideal target and stood out in the dark like a beacon. No one wanted to go near it during a mortar or rocket attack.

There was little I could do except slip into my flak vest and stay low while mortars and rockets pounded the camp. I had no ammunition so could not defend myself or others in the event of a sapper attack. There was always the danger of being shot by friendlies as a suspected sapper if I had been seen running around in my shorts. I decided, "What the hell," and reached for my tape recorder and started to record a message for back home with the loud booms resounding in the background. As I reached the end of the tape, I said that I would turn the reel over to the other side. I thought I had threaded the tape properly, but it was pitch black and I could not see what I was doing. Thinking I had threaded the tape properly, I kept recording and discussing what was going on, speaking very softly. Then, suddenly, the VC attackers hit what they were aiming for… the fuel depot. Fuel was stored in large rubber bladders which lay on the ground surrounded by sandbags. Only a direct hit would cause the bladder to explode, but that's exactly what happened. Although it was a mile away, the heat from the exploding gasoline singed the hair on my arms. Night turned into day. I thought I had captured the entire event on the tape but failed to replay it before sending it home to my parents. I learned later that my parents had listened intently to the sounds of the battle on the front of the tape but when they flipped it over they were met with total silence—a cause of great concern.

By now it was about 4 AM. After the gasoline dump exploded, someone informed us that we must move to the unfinished bunker near our tent. We complained that the bunker offered less protection than the sandbags around the tent, but we were ordered to move. I stayed in that bunker—eaten alive by mosquitoes—for another hour. Finally, the all clear was sounded and we returned to our tents.

A day later we packed up and moved out to join our units. I had been in country for three weeks, adjusting to the heat and "getting organized." I honestly felt out of control and was at a loss as to what to do with all my stuff that I laboriously packed and repacked each day. That problem would be solved the next day when I joined my company with the 1st Battalion of the 5th Cav Regiment.

On my 21st day in country, five other officers and I were loaded onto a Huey helicopter with all our gear and choppered out to a field position near Quang Tri. We spent the entire day waiting to see the battalion commander. While waiting, we were given the news that all of us had just been promoted to first lieutenant as we had been in the army for one year. I was no longer a "Butter Bar." (By comparison, it took my father eight years to advance to the rank of first lieutenant and it took my brother four. I made it in one. Such was the need for platoon leaders during the Vietnam War.) Finally, at 8 PM that night, five first lieutenants were ushered into the battalion commander's bunker. We went in alphabetical order; I led the group.

We stood at attention and saluted. The battalion commander was dead on his feet. He could have put his head down on his desk and gone to sleep immediately. He spoke with a slow southern drawl, as if he had to think about every word that he wanted to say. I was so nervous that I didn't remember much of what he spoke about during the two or three minutes we stood there. He clearly wanted to get us the hell out of his bunker and go to sleep. He muttered something about having had five platoon leaders killed in the last month and we were the replacements. With that, he asked the S-1 where replacements were needed, and we were told that B Company needed two platoon leaders; the rest needed one. The battalion commander said, "Well, it really doesn't matter where I assign you." So, he pointed at me as the first in line and counted us off, "You will go to A, the next two to B, the next to C, and the last to E. You're dismissed." We saluted and walked out of his bunker.

Of that group of five officers entering the battalion commander's bunker that night, I was the only one to survive the tour. It was the sheer luck of the order in which we entered the battalion commander's bunker that determined who lived and who died. The four other officers who reported to the battalion commander that night were subsequently killed in various firefights.

A runner was called from A Company to get me. This soldier helped me carry my duffel bag and equipment to Company A's command post. I entered another tent at 10 PM on my 21st day in Vietnam to be introduced to the first sergeant. He was "the Hulk" personified. He weighed in at about 350 lbs, shirtless, sweating, and chain smoking and drinking beer by the case, a stash he kept in a cooler adjacent to his desk. A cold beer was the first thing he offered me. I thanked him but said no. By now I had a headache and was beginning to feel the strain of the heat, stress, and exhaustion of the day. He gave me a couple of aspirin and a Coke instead.

Then he told me to unpack everything I owned and lay it out in front of him. He relieved me of all my spare uniforms and put them into the company uniform supply. The first sergeant informed me I would be issued clean uniforms periodically, depending on where I was and if clothing could be flown out to me. "All you need now are the clothes on your back," he said. He had me write my name on a waterproof bag and I placed my personal possessions in it: my one khaki uniform, my dress boots, civilian clothes, and a few personal items along with my tape recorder in its case. The first sergeant eyed the case suspiciously and wanted to see the contents before allowing me to put it into the waterproof bag. He placed our bags in the pile along with all the others from the company, one for each man. He also relieved me of my flak vest, informing me, "These fucking things are too heavy to carry in the boonies. Besides, they wouldn't stop a bullet, so they're basically worthless."

I was left with three pairs of socks, my rope, carabiners, a couple of waterproof bags, toothbrush, toothpaste, soap and razor, map case and what I had in my pockets plus the rest of my military equipment. I had learned in Ranger School about the value of having extra socks and waterproof bags, and I was not about to give them up. I also hung on to my non-regulation sheath knives which were attached to my belt and hidden under my shirt. I thought they might be confiscated and was glad they were not. These knives turned out to be valuable possessions.

Again, a runner was dispatched to take me to meet with my company commander at his command post which was nearby. It was now past midnight. I was truly exhausted from the ordeal of the day. I met with the captain, an easy-going guy, who asked for a quick assessment of my leadership experience. When he discovered I had been the battalion S-1 and not a platoon leader at the 82nd Airborne Division, he decided to assign me as the mortar platoon leader for a while. In this way I could "take some time to become more acclimated to the weather and the routine of the company's operations." I was relieved with this decision. At this point, I was tired, confused, and frustrated with the heat, my excessive equipment and the fear that kept creeping into my mind whenever I had a chance to think. My CO was smart about not assigning an FNG first lieutenant who had just been promoted that day to command a platoon of experienced troops. I did not object to this decision. In fact, I was truly relieved to have an assignment that would be less responsibility starting my 22nd day in country.

~~~~~~

Letter: 31 May 1968, A Company, 1/5 Cav, 1st Air Cav Division, LZ Hardcore, I Corps, Vietnam

I have, at long last, joined my company. We have a comparatively new CO, but he knows his stuff. He has assigned me as the weapons platoon leader. This is a most fortunate stroke of good luck.

Presently, we are in a company perimeter and are linked up with our direct support battery as well as a mechanized company with tanks and armored personnel carriers (APCs). Our responsibility is to secure two bridges which are about 200m apart. I am still in the same general area as before, near Utah Beach, also called Wonder Beach.

Two of the battalion's five companies are operating in the area of operation (AO) conducting search and clear, search and destroy and cordon and search operations. We are in a very secure position at present, and everyone has been resting and taking it easy. There is a lake nearby and I took a long swim today.

My mortar platoon has only 13 men. We carry one tube and as much ammo as each man can. It is a fortunate job for me because our primary responsibility is CP security. Therefore, I do not have to take a point position, lead a line platoon, go out on ambush or be on the perimeter. I am as safe, if not safer than the CO himself. I think it will be a most valuable learning experience.

Finally, at 1 AM, I met my mortar platoon sergeant. The man turned out to be a hell of a nice guy. Our company was camped in an old stone building; the mortar had been positioned outside in the center of a courtyard. While only 20 years old, Staff Sergeant John Deerling was clearly experienced, knowledgeable, and competent. I trusted him immediately. He surveyed all my equipment and said: "Sir, why don't you let me help you get organized? You have a lot of stuff here, and there are better ways for you to carry it. Tomorrow, we will load your 22 magazines with ammunition, and give you several hand grenades, four smoke grenades, three star clusters and maps. You must be able to carry all this stuff easily and efficiently. Let me set you up so that you can carry your equipment on your back, drop your pack quickly if you hit the shit, and still have the most important things you need with you: water, ammo, map, compass, smoke, and grenades."

I thanked him and turned over all my equipment. Then, I sat down and watched him create an expedient field pack. He removed the pack from the pack frame and attached my web belt around the bottom. Then he attached two ammo pouches and a canteen to the belt. My camera, wrapped in a waterproof bag, went into one ammo pouch; extra grenades and two white phosphorus (WP) grenades went into the other. A plastic one-quart canteen of water and metal cup were inserted into the canteen pouch. Two smoke grenades were also attached to the frame. My rope and carabiners were lashed to the side. My personal items (toothbrush, toothpaste, razor) went into a waterproof bag and were wrapped inside my poncho and poncho liner. A second waterproof bag held extra socks and foot powder and was also wrapped inside the poncho/poncho liner. Select C-Rations (mostly fruit) were dropped into a sock and strapped to the top of the pack frame. Three star clusters (much like roman candles in a tube) were also strapped on. I carried a two-quart bladder of water with the strap slipped over my shoulder. Two bandoliers of 18 magazines of ammunition (with four magazines containing tracer rounds) were tied around my middle and two hand grenades inserted into ammo pouches in the bandoliers. Two additional smoke grenades and hand grenades were attached to the rings on the straps of my pack frame.

Overall, the pack weighed about 45 lbs. This compared very favorably to officers in other units who carried packs as heavy as 70 to 100 lbs. It was a very efficient field pack system thanks to Sergeant Deerling. The bandoliers of ammunition protected my mid-section. A first aid kit was attached to a clip on the pack frame. Mosquito repellent was placed under the helmet band. Two items that I always wanted close at hand were water—that went into my left thigh pocket—and my map, which went into the right.

I wore no insignia. The only way anyone would know that I was an officer, and the leader, was to read my name written in pen on the ¼-inch helmet liner band: "LT BARTLETT." My call sign was "Foggy Day 4-6 (meaning the platoon leader of the fourth platoon, the mortar platoon). I was 22 years old, the second oldest man in my unit. It was my 22nd day in country. In the morning, I would meet the other men in my mortar platoon, but for now all I could do or think about was sleep.

Letter: 3 June 1968, A Company, 1/5 Cav, 1st Air Cav Division, LZ Jane, I Corps, Vietnam

Our company does not return to "a base camp" per se except to pull security missions. All I have is what I carry on my back. My personal clothing, towels, underwear, all items of personal equipment I decided I could not carry were given away. I only have one towel that I wear around my neck, the clothes on my back and a very few miscellaneous items. It is too hot to wear underwear, although I do wear an OD T shirt (only have one of those). This is the way we live, and everyone is in the same boat. You get used to it and it really isn't so bad once you get used to the smell.

I have not mentioned many names in my stories. This is because while I spent a lot of time with my CO and with my men, we never got close to one another. I always had to recognize that I might be giving an order to one of my men (or my CO to me) that would end up getting the soldier wounded or killed. With few exceptions we called each other by our numbers and nicknames and not actual names. It was a very impersonal existence. An officer only had to endure six to seven months in the field, so the countdown clock started ticking the moment you stepped foot in country. Consequently, I never got close to my CO or my men. There were exceptions of course, but that was the way I managed my year in "the Nam" and why I refer to the officers and soldiers in my stories most frequently by nickname or number and not by name.

1. QUANG TRI, Quang Tri
2. THUA THIEN, Hue
3. QUANG NAM, Hoi An
4. QUANG TIN, Tam Ky
5. QUANG NGAI, Quang Ngai
6. KONTUM, Kontum
7. BINH DINH, Bong Son, Qui Nhon
8. PLEIKU, Pleiku
9. PHU BON, Hau Bon
10. PHU YEN, Song Cau, Tuy Hoa
11. DARLAC, Ban Me Thuot
12. KHAN HOA, Nha Trang
13. QUANG DUC, Gia Nghia
14. TUYEN DUC, Dalat
15. NINH THUAN, Phan Rang
16. LAM DONG, Bao Loc, Di Linh
17. BINH THUAN, Phan Thiet
18. PHUOC LONG, Phuoc Binh
19. LONG KHANH, Xuan Loc
20. BINH TUY, Ham Tan
21. BINH LONG, An Loc
22. BINH DUONG, Phu Cuong
23. BINH HOA, Bien Hoa
24. PHUOC TUY, Ba Ria
25. TAY NINH, Tay Ninh
26. HAU NGHIA, Khien Cuong
27. GIA DINH, Gia Dinh, Saigon
28. LONG AN, Tan An
29. KIEN TUONG, Moc Hoa
30. DINH TUONG, My Tho
31. GO CONG, Go Cong
32. KIEN PHONG, Cao Lanh
33. VINH LONG, Vinh Long
34. KIEN HOA, Truc Giang
35. CHAU DOC, Chau Doc
36. AN GIANG, Long Xuyen
37. SA DEC, Sa Dec
38. BINH BINH, Phu Vinh
39. KIEN GIANG, Ha Tien
40. PHONG DINH, Can Tho
41. BA XUYEN, Khanh Hung
42. CHUONG THIEN, Vi Thanh
43. BAC LIEU, Bac Lieu
44. AN XUYEN, Quang Long
45. SPECIAL CAPITAL ZONE, Saigon

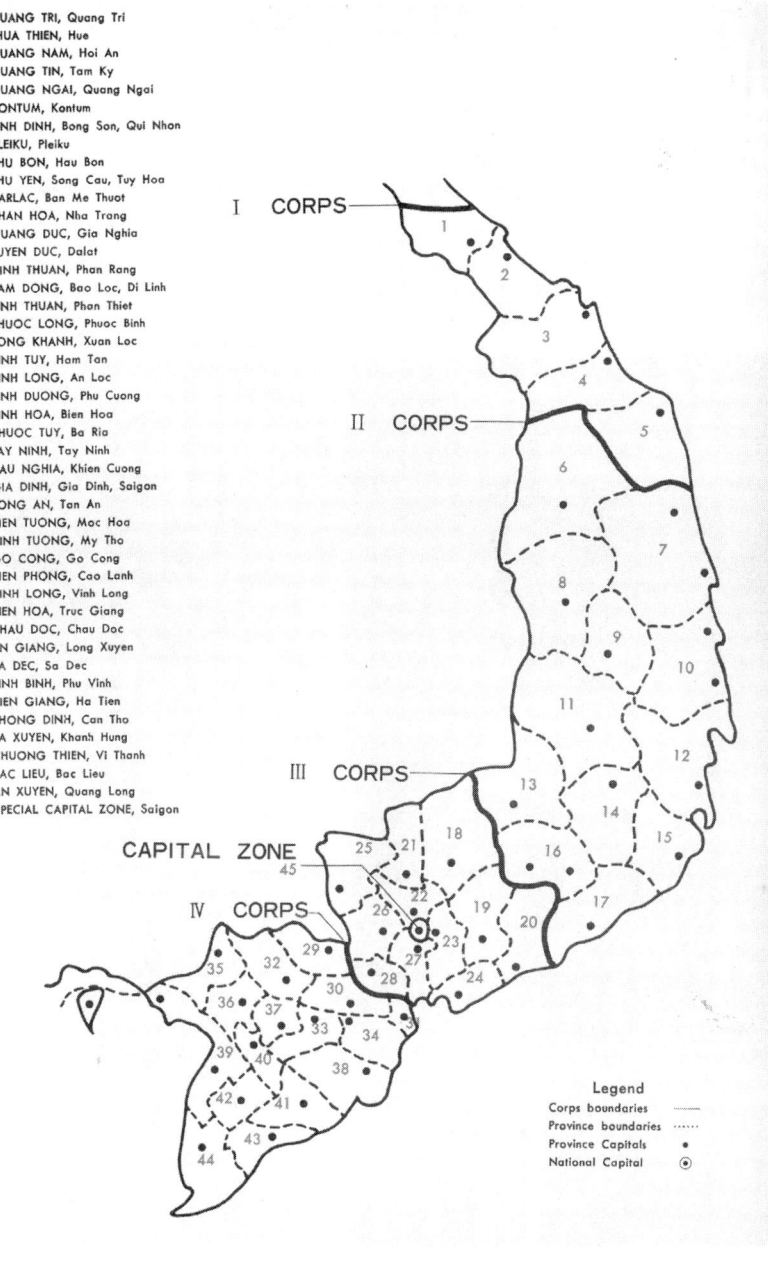

Four Corps areas of South Vietnam, circa 1969. (Public domain)

Major Unit Locations

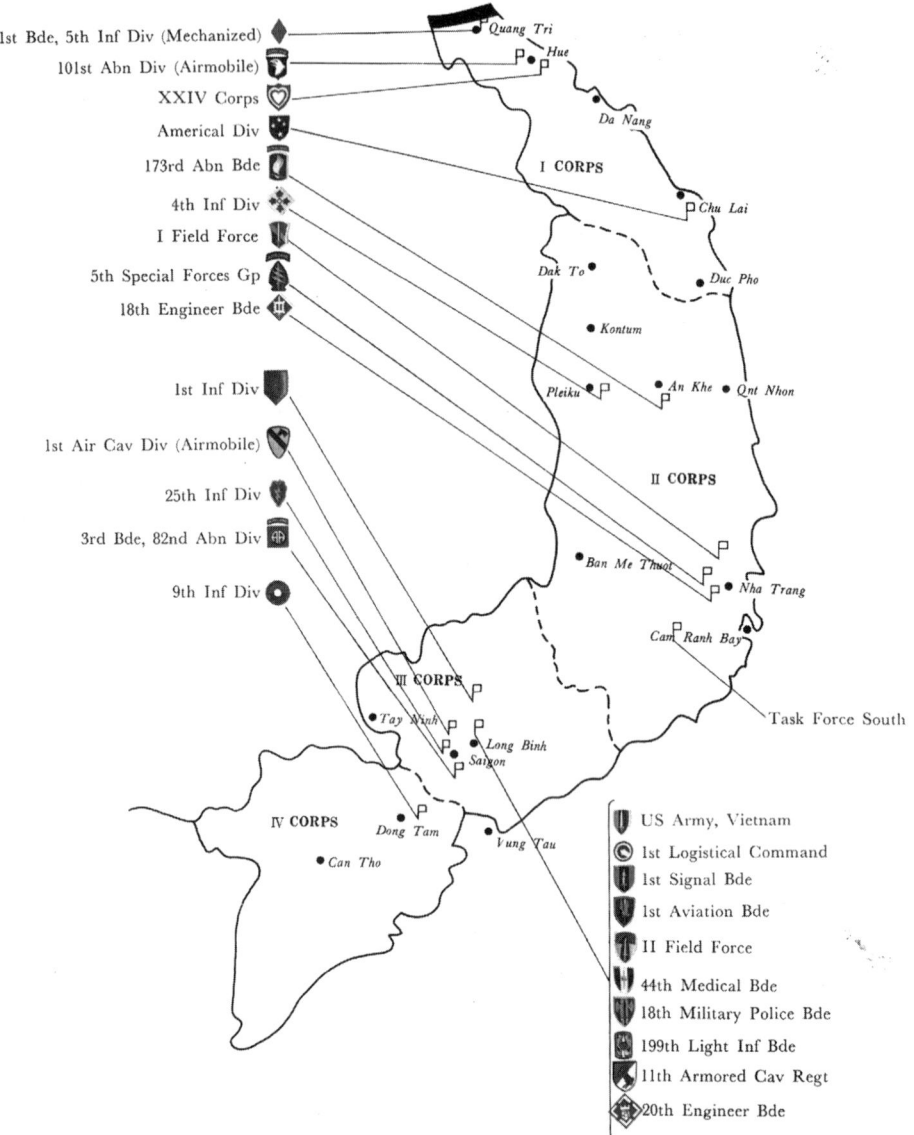

1st Bde, 5th Inf Div (Mechanized)
101st Abn Div (Airmobile)
XXIV Corps
Americal Div
173rd Abn Bde
4th Inf Div
I Field Force
5th Special Forces Gp
18th Engineer Bde

1st Inf Div

1st Air Cav Div (Airmobile)

25th Inf Div

3rd Bde, 82nd Abn Div

9th Inf Div

Quang Tri
Hue
Da Nang
I CORPS
Chu Lai
Dak To
Duc Pho
Kontum
Pleiku
An Khe
Qnt Nhon
II CORPS
Ban Me Thuot
Nha Trang
Cam Ranh Bay
Task Force South
III CORPS
Tay Ninh
Long Binh
Saigon
IV CORPS
Dong Tam
Vung Tau
Can Tho

US Army, Vietnam
1st Logistical Command
1st Signal Bde
1st Aviation Bde
II Field Force
44th Medical Bde
18th Military Police Bde
199th Light Inf Bde
11th Armored Cav Regt
20th Engineer Bde

American unit locations, circa 1969 (Public domain)

CHAPTER 6

Ambushing Gazelles

The bad news was it was always slow going carrying that equipment through whatever terrain we were walking through. The good news was we did not go out on ambushes at night.

The 1st Battalion, 5th Cavalry Regiment has a long and impressive history. The first commander was Lieutenant Colonel Robert E. Lee, who resigned to lead the Armies of the South during the Civil War. The unit served with distinction during the Indian Wars of the 1870s, fought in Puerto Rico against the Spanish in 1898, and saw action against Pancho Villa in Juarez, Mexico in 1919. The unit became part of the 1st Cavalry Division headquartered in Fort Bliss, Texas, on December 18, 1922. It earned Presidential Unit Citations for actions in the Philippines and the Republic of Korea. In Vietnam, it earned Presidential Unit Citations for the Pleiku Campaign. Company A of the 1st Battalion, 5th Cav, was distinguished by earning three oak leaf clusters to its Presidential Unit Citation for engagements in 1967. (An oak leaf cluster represents a subsequent earning of an award. A Presidential Unit Citation is the highest distinction a unit can earn and is only given as recognition for exceptional success in major battles against enemy forces.)

When I joined the battalion, the division had moved its forward base of operations to I Corps. The mission of the division was to conduct search and destroy missions along the Demilitarized Zone (DMZ) from the Gulf of Tonkin in the east to the Laotian border in the west. It was felt that the airmobile assets of the division and its quick reaction capability would help to curb and prevent enemy infiltration across the zone as well as from the Ho Chi Minh Trail in Laos. Consequently, units of the division operated in a variety of terrains—from the sandy soil along the Gulf of Tonkin with blazing hot sun and no overhead cover to three-canopy, mountainous jungles along the Laotian border. The tactics employed had to change for each type of terrain which, along with the 105-degree daily temperatures, made for some challenging daily humps. It was a pleasure to be picked up by choppers conducting combat assaults (Charlie Alphas) as it was the only time when one could cool off, if only for a 20- to 30-minute flight.

The mortar platoon was a squad-size unit consisting of one E-6, seven men, me, and one mortar. (Normally, a mortar platoon would consist of three mortars and many more men, but the tube and ammo were so heavy that one tube was all that could be carried.) While 13 men were officially assigned to the unit we rarely had that many in the field. The assignment allowed me to become more familiar with leading men and with the company's daily action plan, and to gain confidence before taking over a line unit.

The mortar platoon would walk with the company commander, carrying its one 81mm tube, base and 10 rounds of ammo. Five soldiers carried two rounds each in addition to their regular gear, each round weighing about 45 lbs. The bad news was it was always slow going carrying that equipment through whatever terrain we were walking through. The good news was we did not go out on ambushes at night. Additional mortar rounds would be flown in each evening and taken out the next morning. And unless we were moving our company CP, our little band had an easier time of it than the line platoons. The mortar, when set up, was ready to provide close-in fire support to the patrols that would be sweeping the area surrounding the CP. While waiting for a fire mission, we would set up our poncho liners overhead to provide shade, read paperbacks, sleep, and generally take it easy.

On one occasion, my company commander noticed that we were enjoying our "preferred status" just a little too much. He decided to have some fun with us by calling in a fire mission. Poncho liners came ripping down and men jumped into firing positions. I manned the radio and replied, "Fire mission, Roger, what is your mission?" Not receiving a reply and by now sweating profusely, I again called to ask about the fire mission. At this point, I heard ecstatic laughter coming from the other side of the company CP and realized the joke that had been played on us.

My CO was a smart guy. He realized that I was green and nervous, but he also recognized my leadership skills. He felt that I only needed some adjustment time to gain confidence and be prepared for the more demanding assignment of a platoon leader. Those leadership skills kicked in at about three weeks into the job. I was beginning to feel a little bored and started to look for more responsibility.

I was asked to test and then report on a new product designed to alert troops who were on guard at night of an approaching enemy force. The product consisted of four stakes with wires protruding from them, a small battery radio and headphones. Each stake was numbered: 4, 3, 2, and 1 and the idea was to place the stakes along the probable enemy approach route coming into the CP or an ambush. Stake #4 was to be placed 500m out and would beep four times if anyone walked within 20 feet. Stake #3 was to be placed at 400m and would beep three times, stake #2 at 300m beeping twice and stake #1 at 200m beeping once. The idea was for the man on guard to listen on the earphones and to wake everyone if he heard the stakes start to chirp.

The concept was a good one, but the execution was problematic. The stakes were extremely sensitive and would chirp if an enemy walked nearby, but they would also chirp if a rabbit or other ground animal ran past. They would also chirp if artillery rounds landed hundreds of meters away. We tried using the product several nights in a row, but always received false readings. First the number #4 stake would chirp, then the number #2 stake, then the number #4 again. There was no consistency in the chirps, and the men were getting tired of being alerted in the middle of the night. Furthermore, it was sometimes difficult to locate and retrieve the stakes the next morning. One stake is still out there somewhere in South Vietnam. We just couldn't find it. I wrote my report to say positive things about the product's overall concept, but realistically it was a bust and totally unreliable.

Letter: 13 June 1968, A Company, 1/5 Cav, 1st Air Cav Division, near LZ Jane, I Corps, Vietnam

My mortar platoon is a good one. They work well together and no gripes. We carry more weight than any of the others and hump the boonies just as fast. We also pull all the "ash & trash" details to relieve the line platoons. When you have to do this type of work it's hard to keep morale up (and the heat doesn't help), but my boys come through like champs. They are really tough. My platoon sergeant is a 20-year-old E-6, a draftee, but bright and cautious. We had a harassment and interdiction (H&I) fire mission last night. I was the FO and we put the rounds on target on the third adjustment. I just can't praise these men enough.

Tonight, we are going to employ a new anti-intrusion device. We call it the beeper. There are four transmitters and one receiver all run off transistor radio batteries. Each transmitter has a stake that is stuck in the round at 100m intervals. If anyone walks within 20 meters of the device it emits a radio signal (a beep) which is picked up by the receiver, about one-half km away. The uses seem to be unlimited: mortar ambush, regular ambush, and perimeter security. We'll try it out and see how it works.

After about three weeks with the mortar platoon, I decided that I wanted to do something that would demonstrate my leadership skills. From our field CP position, we could clearly observe a saddle between two hills about 3km in front of our position. The saddle created a natural area through which enemy soldiers would have to travel if they were approaching our position. I convinced my CO to allow my platoon to walk out to the saddle, call in a fire mission on the area and string trip flares. We planned to watch the area all night and if the trip flares went off, we would drop mortar rounds onto the spot.

We walked out to the location late in the morning (3km out and 3km back), and I stood on the top of one hill and called in a fire mission on the center of the saddle.

The first round landed a little too close to where we were standing. I adjusted the rounds and pulled back several hundred meters—just to be safe. The second round landed right on target. I told the mortar gunner to lock in the location. Then we proceeded to set up our trip flares and prepare for our mortar ambush.

We ordered extra mortar rounds that night and made doubly sure that rounds were pulled from their containers and laid out, so they could be dropped down the tube at a moment's notice if a flare went off. An 81mm mortar round has two safeties on it that must be removed for it to fire. The first safety is a bore safety that prevents the mortar round from accidentally sliding down the barrel unless the safety is removed. The second safety is at the tail of the mortar round and prevents the mortar round from exploding upon impact. Both safeties must be removed to have the mortar fire and explode successfully.

Our night began without incident. The men took turns sitting at the perimeter of the CP and watched through binoculars for the flares to pop. Suddenly, at about 2 AM one of the flares exploded. Just as suddenly, a second flare popped. Our guard immediately alerted the gun crew, and we sprang into action. We fired six rounds in quick succession and waited for them to land and explode. All six rounds fired out of the tube properly, but there was no explosion in the kill zone. In the excitement, the gunner had forgotten to pull the tail safeties.

We quickly realized our error and we dropped five more rounds into the tube making sure that the safeties were pulled. Our spotter, looking through binoculars, said that he thought he had seen some movement in the area, but could not be sure.

The next morning saw our group going back out to the target to inspect the area. There was blood everywhere we walked. We were starting to feel proud of ourselves for killing several enemy soldiers; however, one member of our platoon walked a bit further into the saddle between the hills to discover several dead gazelles lying on the ground. Our mortar ambush was further complicated by the fact that we now had six unexploded mortar rounds with fins sticking out of the ground. They had to be destroyed because if we left them in the ground the VC would steal them and use them as booby traps.

So, the Explosive Ordinance Disposal Team (EOD) was called in to destroy the rounds—a job that did not please them as live rounds are always handled with great caution. You never knew what might happen.

Our mortar ambush proved to be a bust, but my CO was impressed with my initiative and felt confident that I was ready to lead a line platoon. As it turned out, the first platoon leader was wounded in a firefight and the next week the CO assigned me to command the first platoon of the company. The platoon sergeant is usually the most experienced man in the unit. Mine was a good man, dedicated and smart and able to keep the troops in line, but was only 19 years old. He had gone through a 90-day NCO training course irreverently called "Shake and Bake School" designed to promote him to platoon sergeant upon successful completion.

My squad leaders were 19 and 20 years old, and I realized that I was the second oldest man in my platoon at 22 with one man at 25. It looked like I was in for the greatest ride of my life. And I was.

Letter: 2 June 1968, A Company, 1/5 Cav, 1st Air Cav Division, LZ Jane, I Corps, Vietnam (Letter to college classmate)

We have just returned from an eight-day operation—search and clear. We got a body count of ten gooks which isn't too bad for this area, with only one friendly KIA.

I think I told you I have been assigned as the weapons platoon leader. We hump one tube and about 20 rounds of ammo and can provide quick fire support to one of the line platoons if they need it.

I came up with an innovative idea: a mortar ambush. We sent out a patrol about 3km within view of our forward operations base (FOB). I found a likely ambush spot and registered the tube onto the area. We then set up trip flares and returned to the FOB. That night at 2 AM, one of the flares popped. We slammed 20 rounds down the tube. It really must have fucked with Charlie's mind to have popped a flare and have no one shoot at him. Then, 20 seconds later, have the world come crashing in on top of him. The next morning, we found pieces of bodies, bloody clothes, and blood trails, so I guess it must have been a successful endeavor. We will try it again with a few minor variations (i.e., having a quick reaction force nearby).

CHAPTER 7

The Jungle Penetrator

In the midst of this melee, three yellow and white butterflies flew past my face.

Smoking pot was common among troops in Vietnam. The local children sold it openly, along with cold black-market Cokes, in the streets, villages and at watering holes. We were near civilian villages whenever my company pulled battalion perimeter security. The troops would gather at a local swimming hole, buy pot, and take trips into the bushes with prostitutes. Children flocked around the pond to sell their wares. Pot smoking was often tolerated or ignored by line officers, except when conducting field operations.

Some hard-core officers never allowed it and would court martial any soldier found smoking pot. Officers who were prone to deliver court martials for pot smoking or minor infractions made themselves possible targets of "fragging." Fragging, where a hand grenade was rolled by a disgruntled soldier into a sleeping officer's hooch, tent, or bunker, was something that every platoon leader became aware of. Most often, as a warning, a grenade would be rolled in at night without the pin being pulled. The message was clear, "Change your aggressive attitude and unnecessary risk-taking or the next time it will be a live grenade." No one in my battalion was ever fragged, but it was commonly discussed by officers and soldiers alike.

Like many officers, my attitude was to ignore pot smoking while in base camp as long as it didn't interfere with operational security. I had to be vigilant at night to make sure the men were alert when they pulled guard. The situation became more serious if they smoked pot in the field when hunting Charlie. This placed everyone in jeopardy, but it still happened occasionally. My unit was out in the boonies for four to six weeks at a clip with no friendly contact and no access to pot, so it was not a problem. In my unit, on a few occasions when a soldier was found smoking pot in the field, he would immediately be relieved of duty and returned to the rear facing disciplinary action. Our lives depended on one another. While pot smoking might not have severely impaired one's mental capabilities any more than drinking a couple of beers, running the risk of enemy activity while under the influence, especially at night, was too dangerous.

I had too many more critical issues to deal with than pot smoking. I needed every soldier in my platoon armed and ready. I averaged 24 to 28 men in the field at any one time. That gave me three squads of eight or nine men each. I never had a full-strength platoon (40 men), so sending a man to the rear for pot smoking reduced my fire-fighting capabilities. I also didn't want to deal with the paperwork involved to initiate an Article 15 punishment (administrative justice) or court-martial proceedings that would lock up a healthy soldier for six or more months, the typical sentence for smoking pot.

I made it clear to my troops that I would employ every combat asset at my command to reduce the risk of ambush or close contact with an enemy force. My men knew that their safety and security always came first in my mind, and I proved this on more than one occasion. I accomplished this goal by firing lots of artillery on suspected enemy targets before we moved through an area. This technique was referred to as "reconnaissance by fire." My men also knew that in the event one of them was wounded, my priority was to get him medevaced and taken to a medical facility as quickly and safely as possible. Officers with the reputation as gung-ho leaders looking to win medals and make a reputation for themselves tended to have abbreviated tenures. These officers might suddenly find themselves out in front of an engagement with no support from behind. They rapidly learned to temper aggressive combat enthusiasm with greater concern for their troops' welfare, especially in the late 1960s. Mission accomplishment and enemy engagement were not avoided but became secondary to keeping my troops safe from unnecessary danger.

We humped the boonies for several weeks at a time, conducting search and destroy operations in an area where the Laotian border met the DMZ. The terrain was mountainous, three-canopy jungle (three layers of growth overhead). We slogged our way through. Often we had to slice a trail through thick, thorn-infested animal trails using a machete and replacing the lead man doing the cutting every 10 to 15 minutes. We couldn't afford to allow a man to cut trail for longer periods for fear of heat stroke. The cover man who kept watch for booby traps and signs of enemy ambush was also changed frequently. Because of the sound of the machete chopping trail, it was extremely difficult to be alert to enemy noises. Our 90-man company would be strung out in a single line about a mile long. It ebbed and flowed accordion-style trying to stay as quiet as possible but knowing that the enemy would hear us, nonetheless. We traversed up hills and skidded down slippery slopes teeming with "wait-a-minute vines" (thorny vines that tripped and cut you). Under ideal conditions, I could see 15–20m to the front, but usually it was less than five. As the days warmed, sweat poured off our bodies. We had to be cautious and conserve water because there was often no resupply until the evening when we could create a perimeter to receive a helicopter. It was stop and go, stop and go, with the sound of the machete filtering back through the otherwise quiet jungle.

Letter: 7 June 1968, A Company, 1/5 Cav, 1st Air Cav Division, in the boonies, I Corps, Vietnam

I made my first Charlie Alpha day before yesterday. It starts with a five-minute artillery (arty) prep, then ARA gunships, then the birds land the troops. It's an exciting affair and I took several pictures. We do it so frequently however that it is old hat after the first few times.

We are operating with only three officers and the FO. It is rough terrain, changing from bushy hills to two and three canopy jungle in the mountains. The company is holding up well, but movement is often restricted to 150–200m per hour. The point man has to cut trail through thick vines, bamboo, and stickers with a machete. My arms look as if a cat has attacked me: a mass of scratches. The heat doesn't bother me so much under two or three canopies and water consumption is also reduced. It's usually cooler and you frequently run across creeks. These are great and you can wet down completely.

The leeches are a problem however and you have to stop frequently to burn them off with a cigarette. I have had several on me already. You must be careful in removing them. Got to get the whole head out or it will become infected. As they fall off, the leech injects an anti-coagulant into the wound, so it bleeds a lot. Spraying with insect repellent seems to help.

We'd walk for 45 minutes, then take a break, sending out security to the front, back and sides. Everyone collapsed. I sympathized with my radio telephone operator (RTO) who carried a 35-pound radio plus two extra batteries each weighing 4 pounds in addition to his regular gear. This added another 43 pounds to his load. I allowed my RTOs to reduce the amount of ammo they carried to one bandolier and at least two smoke grenades, as compared to the usual four. In truth they usually humped the full load because they knew how vulnerable they were with a 3-foot radio antenna sticking up over their head.

My RTOs were a special breed, typically short, stocky, and tough. They would complain bitterly about the weight of their radios but were always right behind or in front of me within arm's reach of that lifesaving tool. (The radio was the lifeline to calling in artillery, helicopter gunships, medevacs, and support from other platoons.) I once got tired of listening to my RTO, Kennedy, complain about humping his heavy load. I said that I frequently carried the radio in Ranger School and never had a problem. At the base of a steep mountain, I traded packs with him and carried his to the top. The climb nearly killed me. We switched our packs back at the summit. From that point on I never said another word about his bitching.

Humping the boonies, chopping trail, slogging our way along animal trails—that's how our days went. We weren't too concerned about enemy contact in deep jungle. If there was no trail network, the likelihood of encountering enemy troops was slim. In more open terrain, our greatest fear was an ambush. The point man and cover man are extremely vulnerable, as are the first six or seven men in line—including myself, the RTO and the men carrying the M79 grenade launcher and M60 machine gun. A well-entrenched enemy squad might wait until the first five to seven men were exposed, then spring the ambush, killing as many as they could and then taking off through pre-planned escape routes while the rest of our unit fell on their faces to avoid fire. My posture was always tense because of the near-constant threat. I could only relax after we pulled base camp security where there were bunkers for the men, concertina wire, and immediate artillery and mortar support.

After several days of this up-and-down humping, the company formed a perimeter in a fairly open area on the top of a mountain where we could bring in helicopters. Using machetes, we cut down trees in a wide circle and cleared a space for a chopper to land to bring in rations, ammo, water, and supplies. It was always dangerous to land a chopper in dense jungle. If the clearing wasn't large enough, the bird's rotor blades could clip a large tree, resulting in damage to the helicopter and even the possibility of a crash.

When it was impossible to clear a large enough space, the chopper would hover at 10 to 30 feet above the hole that had been cut in the canopy and kick out supplies. But only if the chopper landed could we get the lukewarm beer and soda we loved, or even hot meals if cooks were available (much to their concern about the possibility of being placed in harm's way). If hot meals could be flown out, we might have meat and potatoes for breakfast or pancakes for supper. We luxuriated in hot food whenever it came.

We remained on this mountaintop for several days while waiting for a new company commander to join us. Under the temporary command of a lieutenant who was only days senior to me, we sent out daily patrols and set up night ambushes. Then, it was my turn to take a reinforced squad down to the base of the mountain and sweep the area. We were to follow the creek bed for a couple of klicks (kilometers) and then work our way back up to the top of the hill. As a standard procedure, we plotted several artillery positions along the route on key terrain features in case we came into contact. I put dots on my map next to each plot so I could quickly recognize them and call for artillery support if needed. This strategy was a great idea in theory, but useless if you couldn't identify exactly where you were on the ground. And when we were walking through three-canopy jungle, losing our bearings and misidentifying landmarks was an easy thing to do.

Letter: 22 June 1968, A Company, 1/5 Cav, 1st Air Cav Division, LZ Jane, I Corps, Vietnam

Our 1-6 was wounded the other day, so I have taken his place as the 1st platoon leader. Now I must start learning names all over again! I am going to be a bit busier than before. It seems to be an exceptionally good group of troops although they are all young, young. I am the second oldest in the platoon.

We had a cordon & search mission yesterday and the CO liked the way I handled my part. It is a more hazardous job than being 4-6, but I do what I am told and make the best of it. Don't worry though as I keep my "gown down." We have another mission today, so must wind this up. We'll be in the field until the 23d, I think. Will write again soon.

Before leaving the company perimeter, I checked my reinforced squad of 12 men to make sure they had the required equipment. Each carried at least two bandoliers of ammunition and a magazine in his gun, two smoke grenades, two white phosphorus grenades (for marking targets for helicopter gunships), four hand grenades and at least four quarts of water. Every man wore a steel helmet and carried an M16. I also included the grenadier and machine gunner on this patrol. The grenadier carried 70 rounds of high-explosive ammo plus buckshot, white phosphorus, a couple of flares and several flechette rounds secured in a slotted vest that hung down below his knees. The machine gunner carried a belt of ammo wrapped around his shoulders and his assistant carried two canisters of ammunition, about 2,000 rounds. This equipment was the minimum carry, although each man could carry more if he wished. I had each soldier jump up and down to ensure his equipment wasn't rattling or clanking and everything was secure. We each carried a C-Ration meal for lunch, but no packs. This was a lighter load from what we normally humped each day.

We left the company perimeter to slowly work our way down the mountain. The terrain was steep and treacherous, made even more difficult by a slick slope whose undergrowth was wet from overnight dew. After a half hour of cautiously snaking down we reached a shallow creek at the bottom and, walking in the water, we began to circle the base of the mountain. The creek's uneven bed of rocks and boulders made walking difficult. It required that we keep our eyes on the ground to avoid tripping. This placed my point man in a precarious position making his forward progress slow.

The heat was oppressive, and we felt as if we were being baked in an oven. I wore a T-shirt with a towel draped around my neck. Covered with sweat, I had to wipe my face periodically to keep the sting of sweat out of my eyes. It was super humid at the bottom of the mountain. Heat stroke could be a real factor, and I moved the unit slowly so as not to push too fast or too hard. The only redeeming feature was that we could dip our towels, bandanas or sweat rags in the creek to cool off for a few minutes of relief.

After an hour of stumbling and tripping in the creek bed, I called a halt to cool off and eat. I sent out security to prevent being surprised; we sipped water and ate the fruit from our C-Rats. It was too hot to eat anything more substantial. C-Rations came in a 6x4x6-inch cardboard box. Each box consisted of a can of pre-cooked meat, a can of fruit, a can of crackers, an accessory packet with coffee, cocoa and toilet paper, and cigarettes. Most men ate the fruit and chucked the meat and crackers, unappetizing to eat when it was so hot. We all stayed in the shade, smoked cigarettes, and splashed water from the creek on our heads and faces. I reminded the men to stay alert and keep the noise down. We hadn't seen signs of any enemy activity, but the jungle was exceedingly quiet and that made everyone edgy. Normally, we would hear birds chirping or an occasional monkey scream out... but on this day we heard nothing.

After 30 minutes, I gave the word to saddle up and get ready to move out. I was surprised when my squad leader, Sergeant Thomas, approached me to say he was going to take over the point. He had been bringing up the rear of the unit. I thought Thomas was acting kind of goofy. He had a funny smile on his face and was laughing to himself, but if he wanted to walk point no one was going to argue with him. I was preoccupied with getting the patrol moving and didn't think more of it. Thomas moved out to take the lead.

We continued walking through the creek, sweating, moving cautiously in the eerie silence surrounding us. After five minutes, Thomas dropped to one knee and whispered for me to come up to his position. He pointed to a wet footprint on a rock. I brought up two more men, but the creek bed was too narrow for any formation other than single file. We continued to walk, slowly, cautiously, crouched, weapons ready, listening and watching for any movement. After another five minutes of walking, a single shot rang out and then, suddenly, all hell broke loose, with two or three of my men firing on full automatic. Everyone hit the ground and I gave orders for the men around me to low crawl forward and provide support to the men on point. Lying on my belly, half submerged in the stream, I could only see about 5m in front of my face. But I crawled forward trying to reach the point men with my RTO in tow behind. The shooting continued and was fierce, but all the shots were coming from our guns and not the enemy. The single AK-47 shot must have come from a sniper. Our M16s have a distinctive sound when fired, quite different from the AK-47s.

Then I heard a muffled cry from one of my men. Thomas had been hit.

Danny Small, our medic, immediately rushed forward. Still not able to see anything to the front, I directed two men to branch out to the left and two to the right to protect us from being caught off guard should the enemy attempt a flanking movement. These men struggled to penetrate the morass of jungle; almost immediately they were out of sight of one another. The rest of the unit continued our low crawl forward, not knowing what we were getting into.

Then Danny yelled: "It's Thomas; he's got a sucking chest wound. Call for a medevac and ask for a doctor on board." My heart was in my throat. I knew how critical immediate medical attention was to survive a sucking chest wound. (The hole created by a bullet pierces the chest and allows air directly into the lungs and prevents the wounded man from being able to breathe normally.) Regulations required that requesting a doctor be on board a medevac could only be done if the soldier was in imminent danger of death, and a sucking chest wound, or amputation, would be the only type of wounds warranting this type of request.

I could feel the eyes of my men on me. What were my priorities? Would I pursue the enemy contact first or would I try to save Thomas? The answer was easy. I reached for the radio to call the company commander requesting an immediate medevac, jungle penetrator with doctor on board.

"What are your coordinates?" came the reply. I knew that I did not want to give my location in the clear over the radio, but there was no time to grab my code book and convert my coordinates to code. I had a general idea of my location and relayed the position providing distances and direction from the closest artillery plot we'd drawn up before leaving the CP. I told the CO I was 300m south (Sierra) of Red 3.

This caused some initial confusion—our forward observer called me and asked me if I wanted to call in artillery. "No, no, I'm not calling for arty!" I radioed back. "I'm providing my location for the medevac." The FO suggested he would fire a smoke round to confirm my position. I agreed. Within seconds I heard an artillery round fly overhead and land. The sound was much closer than 300m. That scared the hell out of me. I could not positively verify the distance or direction to the smoke round lying on the ground or try to estimate where it had landed. The FO then wanted to fire a high-explosive round (HE) to help me confirm my positioning. I told him to fire on Red 4 instead as it was much further away. He did this and I heard the round land, a full kilometer to the north of my position. I now had enough confidence to confirm my location.

While still trying to direct the artillery, I told the men immediately at my front to spread out and lay down a base of fire. I also yelled at the men on both flanks to concentrate their fire on the suspected enemy position and not advance further. Still unable to see through the jungle growth, we could only estimate where the enemy position was and fire in that general direction. They fired single shots to conserve ammunition. Meanwhile my medic and I grabbed hold of Thomas by his shoulder web gear and dragged him back to a small clearing behind a large boulder. That was where the rest of my squad waited. By this time, Thomas's chest was covered in blood. He was conscious, but bleeding profusely and unable to speak.

My mind spun. I tried to think of all I needed to do to keep control of the situation and ensure my men's safety while attempting to get Thomas medevaced. Everything and everyone seemed to be moving in slow motion. I realized that I was experiencing tunnel vision, so I stopped, took some deep breaths, and gulped water from my canteen. I directed men to our rear to provide security and began planning my next move.

Danny was working on Thomas. He abruptly announced that Thomas did not have a sucking chest wound. He'd been shot through the throat and had blood pouring down his chest. Unable to speak, Thomas could only make gurgling noises that confused the medic into thinking he had a more serious, life-threatening wound.

"Well, what the fuck," I said. "Let's get him out of here as fast as we can. He's losing blood like a stuck pig." I was worried about losing him, as there was no way to tie off the wound and stem the blood flow. We couldn't put a tourniquet around his neck. There's not a lot to be done for a man who has been shot through the throat.

We wiped the blood from Thomas's mouth and pressed a bandage on the wound, but all this did was to force blood into his mouth, causing him to choke. Soon we were all covered in blood.

Word came over the radio that the medevac was 10 minutes out. I left Thomas in Danny's capable hands and began to prepare for its arrival. It was then that I realized that my location was going to be extremely difficult to identify from the air. Given the density of the jungle with my men in position and laying down suppression fire toward the suspected enemy, I realized that if I popped smoke to signal the chopper it would go unseen because the dense overhead cover would hold the smoke in.

I grabbed Johnson, our machine gunner, and the strongest man in the unit. I had him start hacking down trees that were 6–10 inches in diameter with a machete. I rotated other men in to help as he became exhausted. They felled a dozen trees, despite a dull blade and slippery hands. Their efforts opened a 15-foot hole in the canopy—just large enough to see daylight. Through it all, we kept low to avoid the possibility of enemy fire.

I crawled to the radio and made a call to the medevac to determine if the helicopter was in my area. The pilot replied that he was circling over my coordinates. I told him I was going to fire a star cluster through the canopy so he could locate our position. (A star cluster is a rocket that shoots 200 feet into the air and bursts at the top.) Grabbing one of the three star clusters tied to my RTO's pack I crawled out to the center of the clearing, took the top off the tube, placed it on the bottom of the can, and while holding it vertically, smacked it, sending the rocket off. It was stopped by tree limbs before reaching the hole. I crawled back to my RTO and spoke with the pilot for a second time, telling him I would fire another. The second one shot straight, but the pilot missed seeing it. Finally, just as I was getting ready to fire the third and last star cluster, I said a quick prayer. This was Thomas's last chance to be seen and evacuated. In the midst of this melee, three yellow and white butterflies flew past my face. It was so incongruous that, for a second, I was removed from this horrendous situation. Thoughts of my dear childhood friend, Mitzi, "the Butterfly Lady," flashed through my mind. (We were eight years old the summer we first met while I was visiting my grandfather in Sacramento. We caught butterflies together and stayed in touch all our lives. See Chapter 32.) I fired the rocket, and it went through the hole trailing smoke and exploded 200 feet overhead. "I've got you," came the pilot's voice over the radio and I said a quick silent prayer of thanks.

For good measure, we tied a smoke grenade to the end of a 25-foot tree branch, popped it and held it overhead. Much of the smoke was still trapped by the canopy, but enough got through so the pilot could clearly confirm our location. Told that we weren't taking any incoming fire, the pilot wanted to know the direction of the enemy contact so he could position the chopper's tail toward it (his least vulnerable position). I gave him a compass reading from the hole in the canopy to the contact area, and he asked us to lay down heavy suppression fire on the enemy position as he dropped the stretcher for Thomas.

I yelled to my men to lay down a base of fire as we grabbed the stretcher and tied Thomas onto it. I had only seen the use of a jungle penetrator demonstrated in training and not in three-canopy jungle. But even strapped in, Thomas was too weak to manage sitting on the seat. I had requested the stretcher, but it wasn't clear to me if I should hook him up to be hauled up vertically or horizontally. I called the pilot to ask. Sensing my lack of experience and frustration, he said he'd send his crew chief down to make sure Thomas was secure.

The pilot then announced he could see white smoke coming from the enemy contact area. I informed him this was one of the hooches that had been set on fire from tracer rounds. He wanted assurance before he came in again to hover, drop his crew chief, and possibly place his helicopter in peril. He needed to know that the area was secure. I told him that we were no longer taking enemy fire, and he directed me once more to lay down covering fire when he started his hover. We did and it sounded like the Fourth of July, with six guns blasting and M79 rounds going off.

The chopper swooped in and lowered the crew chief on the jungle penetrator. He wore a Mickey Mouse helmet and carried a .45 pistol in his hand. This hilarious scene should have lightened the mood, but the chopper was extremely vulnerable and all we wanted to do was to get Thomas out as quickly as possible.

"What's the fucking problem?" the crew chief yelled above the rotor noise.

"There is no fucking problem," I yelled back. "I just didn't know if the man should go up vertically or horizontally." He grabbed one end of the stretcher, and we hauled Thomas to the center of the clearing. The top of the stretcher was clipped to the end of the cable and Thomas was hauled up vertically. The chopper flew off and returned minutes later to pick up the crew chief. The wire was lowered and mounting the seat, he disappeared as quickly as he'd arrived. The entire process took no more than a few minutes but seemed like an hour.

With Thomas on his way to the battalion aid station. I returned my attention to the enemy.

The adrenalin had started to wear off. Cautiously, I regrouped my squad and redistributed ammunition, making sure that those who had been laying down fire support were replenished. Then, ever so slowly, we moved forward, safeties off and ready to shoot at first sign of movement.

After about 100m, we came to a small clearing with three large hooches made from cut timber, an unusual find in dense jungle. Two of the hooches would have slept four men each, but the largest could have housed at least ten. We tossed grenades through their doors to be on the safe side, then looked inside. There was little of interest in the two smaller hooches, but the large one had medical supplies and food. We had discovered an enemy aid station!

I called in a situation report (sitrep) to my CO who told me to inventory all the items and call back with the list. We spent the next hour counting and sorting through medical supplies and other items we'd found. There were numerous bandages and some drugs, and the most interesting of all, a bag of American-brand rice in a gunny sack. It must have been donated rice that had made its way through the black market into enemy hands.

There was also a small wooden box, 6 inches wide by 6 inches high and 12 inches long. I slid the top back slowly to reveal three small, light-blue bras. I couldn't believe what we had found and made great fun of showing the bras to all the men. Those bras immediately became prized souvenirs of the day. When I called in the inventory report I left the bras as the last item, having to spell "Bravo, Romeo, Alpha, Sierra." The RTO copying my message couldn't believe what I was telling him. Laughing, my CO said to make sure to bring him one. Those bras suddenly disappeared into various packs and were never seen again.

I was ordered to pull back from the area and set up an ambush, in hopes that the enemy would return after we left. By this time, I was exhausted and could barely hold my head up. I told my troops that I had to sleep. We formed a wagon wheel ambush formation with me in the center. I fell asleep instantly and slept soundly until I was shaken awake—my snoring was so loud my men were afraid I'd alert the enemy.

With no sign of the enemy returning, we obeyed the command to torch the hooches, saddle up and move back uphill to our base camp.

~~~~~~

Letter: 13 July 1968, A Company, 1/5 Cav, 1st Air Cav Division, still in the boonies, I Corps, Vietnam

I was in a firefight yesterday. I led a sweep into a streambed near our FOB. We found three hooches and some bunkers, NVA type. I had security out and the place looked deserted. We started finding things: medicine, cooking equipment, 300 lbs of rice, etc. We were just about to leave when a sniper shot one of my squad leaders in the neck. He was in pretty bad shape, bleeding heavily and had trouble breathing.

We couldn't get the sniper either. It looked as if we would be unable to medevac the man. The canopy was so thick that it was impossible to bring in a bird. We had one machete and used it to cut down several large trees. A medevac finally came in and dropped a stretcher. We tied the man to it and the chopper dropped a jungle penetrator and hauled him 75 feet into the air and safety. He is still in serious condition, but we saved his life.

I was never so scared in my life as I was yesterday, but after a good night's sleep I'm back in the pink again and ready to go.

As we progressed up the winding slope, following an animal trail, my point man alerted and called for me to come forward. We were about halfway up the mountain. The point man had walked up on an unexploded bomb. This was an exceptionally large, 500-pound bomb, probably dropped by a B-52. There were ropes attached to the handles; the enemy had been trying to haul it down the hill. We marked the location, called in a sitrep, and continued up the slope to the company CP.

A day later, my platoon sergeant escorted a group of combat engineers back to the bomb. They strapped it with C4 explosive, attached blasting caps and lit a 15-minute fuse. You never saw a squad clear the area faster and hustle back up the hill. They made it to the top of the mountain just as the bomb exploded with an earth-shaking bang.

I recommended Danny Small for a Bronze Star for his work in saving Thomas and wrote up the paperwork. He crawled through enemy fire to pull Thomas back to safety; he treated his wound and controlled the bleeding as much as he could. I too felt I should be written up for the Bronze Star, but there was no love lost between Lieutenant Ross, my hard-core temporary CO, and me, and he nixed both awards. He said the medic was just doing his job and I shouldn't have called for a doctor to be on board the chopper because Thomas didn't have a sucking chest wound. While true, it was unavoidable at the time.

Letter: 28 June 1968, A Company, 1/5 Cav, 1st Air Cav Division, LZ Jane, I Corps, Vietnam

We are still operating out of LZ Jane, and I expect we will remain here until 1 July before going back to the boonies. Our company commander left yesterday. I was sorry to see him go. He was a fine officer and leader. He inspired confidence in me and the other leaders. When I was in the field, I had a great feeling of security just knowing he had my back and ready to give me any type of support needed. The XO, also a 1 LT, is now in charge and will remain so until we get a new captain. He is a good man, but I'll be happy when we get a more experienced CO.

My new role is progressing well. I have not had any problems, yet, and the men are doing an excellent job for me. I now have 32 "boys" to work with. My platoon sergeant is one of the "Instant NCOs." He is an E-6 and is only 19 years old (birthday a month ago!). He is a good boy though but requires close supervision. I wish I had one of those hardnosed Regular Army (RA), tough platoon sergeants who would boss me around a bit. As it is I am the leader and must make all the mistakes by myself.

~~~~~~

A couple of weeks later, one of my squad leaders received a letter from Thomas. He had been evacuated to Japan for surgery and was recuperating from wounds that would keep him from returning to Vietnam. He asked that a bag of pot be removed from his personal effects he'd left behind. The man had been high when he offered to walk point. I had not realized this when he volunteered to walk point, and no one was going to argue. I got Thomas out alive and saved his life with no fire directed toward the helicopter. To my mind that was enough.

CHAPTER 8

FNGs in the Field and Base Camp

FNGs were a liability. We watched them carefully for 30 days. By then
they were wounded, dead, removed to the rear as liabilities or
had become trusted members of the platoon.

An infantry company in the 1st Cav typically humped the boonies for four to six weeks before coming into base camp to pull perimeter security for five days. In the field, you had to be self-sufficient, carrying all the things you needed to survive. C-Rations were delivered every day by helicopter and each man grabbed one or two meals from the carton. The ones with fruit were the most highly valued because they gave you some liquid and nourishment without having to drink your water. We also kept the crackers, coffee, hot chocolate, cigarettes, cigars, and toilet paper, throwing most of the rest away. Each man had his favorite meal. Mine was spaghetti and meat balls, but they always gave me indigestion and my parents constantly sent me rolls of antacid tablets which I shared with other troops. Every man carried about a gallon of water at the start of each day. I carried two one-quart canteens and a two-quart bladder. Some men like the radio operator, grenadier, or machine gunner, who carried heavy loads, often carried two two-quart bladders plus two one-quart canteens. In the 105-degree heat, it was not unusual to run out of water by midday.

The daily routine was to assemble and then have each platoon move out following a different prearranged route assigned by the CO. The CO and FO would also follow a separate route together with the mortar platoon. The mortar platoon could provide rapid support to an infantry platoon that got into trouble but carrying only six rounds limited their capability without immediate resupply by helicopter. The platoons would start humping at 7–8 AM and arrive at a company command post (CP) usually by 3–4 PM. Walking 8–15 klicks by the end of the day, depending on the terrain and the heat, was common. We would hole up from 12 to 1, eat a noon meal, rest and drink water and stay out of the sun during the hottest period of the day. If there was no overhead cover, we would pull out poncho liners and create little tents over our heads to keep the sun off.

Because the Cav had so many helicopters available, I had more immediate support for our operations than most other units in Vietnam. This meant that I could get tactical and logistical support overhead usually within 10–15 minutes of a call and even faster if I was in contact. We received resupply each evening and sometimes that included waterproof bags filled with a little bit of ice and containing one lukewarm beer and one soda per man per day. (Each man contributed money from his monthly pay for these drinks and they were a welcome relief from the chlorinated water we drank every day.)

Clean clothes came out about every three to four weeks and when they arrived you stripped down, took off the very ripe ones you'd been wearing and put on clean ones. After leaving base camp and humping for a couple of days, the body odor was horrendous but in time you got used to it and ignored the smell.

There was usually enough water to drink, and I used a small amount each evening to brush my teeth, but water could not be spared to shave or wash. During the monsoon season, it was common for men to strip down, soap up and wash allowing the rain to rinse them off. Similarly, if we were near a stream, and time permitted, we posted security and allowed the men to go down to wash. We were forbidden to drink stream water even though it appeared to be fresh and clean. The army said "no," and it was one of the restrictions we faced each day. Water had to be flown out to us each evening in five-gallon Jerry cans, and the men topped off their canteens for the next day. I wore an olive drab (OD) T-shirt with an OD towel wrapped around my neck with the ends slipped under my pack straps. We wore no underpants. It was too hot. My jungle fatigue shirt was wrapped in my pack and brought out at night to protect against the mosquitoes. When we came to a stream, I usually dipped my towel into the water, wiped my face and wore the wet cloth around my neck. It typically dried within an hour in the intense heat. We had no body armor, only flak vests. We only wore the vests when we were required to pull night security at base camp, and even then, the troops usually sat on them or used them as pillows.

Each day our medic distributed a daily malaria pill, and each Monday he distributed a large weekly pill that was a prophylactic against the disease. All men were required to demonstrate they had taken their pills to the medic and the medic had to certify that the pills had been administered. We were also given several large salt tablets. Most men broke up the pills and put them into their canteens along with packets of Kool-Aid to help kill the taste of the salt and chlorinated water. Even so, it was common to lose a man to heat exhaustion if it was extremely hot or if the day's march was long.

Pulling base camp security was easy duty. I would send out a patrol each day to accompany the mine sweep team that checked the road leading into the base camp. After the sweep, the patrol would end up at a stream or pond near the base camp where local civilians would come to sell pot, cold beer, and soda along with prostitutes. All items were purchased with military payment certificates (MPCs) called scrip.

FNGs received light duty for several weeks. They were jumpy and anxious and could not be relied upon until fully acclimatized and field tested. We assigned an experienced soldier to be the FNG's buddy and work with him to get his equipment organized, overcome the jitters of being in combat and teach him to the point where he could be trusted by the other men in his squad. I was in constant need of replacements. My three squads should have been four. Each squad averaged eight men and should have been ten. Several weeks were needed to get an FNG up and running and reliable in the unit. After a month, if the man proved to be too nervous and too unreliable, we often tried to find him a "straphanger" job (a relatively safe position) at base camp or at the division rear. After the transition period, if a man could not be relied on during a firefight, it was better to transfer him to the rear rather than try to continue to get him adjusted to combat.

Without exception, we watched each FNG carefully for 30 days. By then they were wounded, dead, removed to the rear as liabilities, or became trusted members of the platoon. In the field, we carried our weapons loaded, but without a round in the chamber unless we were on patrol. The fire selector switch was always set to safe except for the point man and cover man. When we came into base camp, the first thing that we did was to pull the magazines from our weapons and clear them of ammo. This was standard operating procedure (SOP) and a cardinal rule of being in base camp.

I had one FNG who failed to do this and was standing in line waiting to get a haircut. He had the tip of the rifle resting on his foot. Another experienced soldier noticed he had a magazine in the weapon. The man scolded the FNG saying weapons were not to be loaded in base camp. The experienced soldier reached over, pulled the magazine out of the weapon, moved the selector switch to fire and pulled the trigger. Unfortunately, this FNG had also failed to remove the live round from the chamber after his last patrol and the bullet severed two of his toes. He was evacuated to Japan, and this ended his military experience.

Base camp meant light duty for everyone. You could get a haircut, eat hot chow, and take a cold shower each day. We all took advantage of these facilities. The men slept on top of the bunkers surrounding the perimeter and built poncho tents overhead to keep the sun off. The four-man bunker team pulled security each night and rotated on hour-long shifts. It was common to sleep until 10–11 AM the next day if you did not have to go out on patrol. Afternoons were spent reading paperbacks, writing letters, and receiving letters and care packages from the World, and playing blackjack and poker.

The engineers built shower stalls in each base camp. The showers consisted of concrete platforms with shower heads connected to pipes running overhead. Tents were erected over the structure and water was stored in several 55-gallon drums; a pump powered the water to the showers. Water was always at a premium, so to take a shower, you fired up the generator and turned on the pump. You quickly wet yourself, turned the water off, soaped up and then rinsed using the least amount of water possible. The water truck would come by each day to fill the drums. Within an hour or two the water would be warm or even hot by the end of the day. If there was enough water, it was great to take a hot shower late in the day or early in the evening. This was a real treat, but usually all the water had been consumed by that time of day. Cold showers, therefore, were most common.

The engineers also built two-man latrines. These structures were small buildings enclosed by screens to keep the flies away. They were elevated and allowed for a 55-gallon drum that had been cut in half to be inserted underneath each of the toilet seats. Each day it was the job of an FNG to go to the latrine, pull out the cans, put in fresh cans and burn the shit. This process eliminated the need to dig holes and then fill them in and relocate the latrines once they had become full.

One FNG in my platoon was designated to perform this duty, so my platoon sergeant carefully explained the procedure, step-by-step. The FNG was to go to the artillery battery and pick up a 105mm howitzer shell casing. The casing, made of brass, held a quart of liquid. Then the FNG was to go to the diesel fuel bladder and fill the canister. He would proceed to the latrine, pull out the cans full of shit and insert clean cans under each seat. He would then pour half of the diesel fuel into one can and half into the other. The last step was to light a match, throw it into the dirty cans, ignite the diesel fuel and burn the shit. My platoon sergeant asked if he understood what he was to do.

The FNG said that he understood and set off to the artillery battery up the hill to get a howitzer shell casing. We watched him fill the canister from a huge bladder and then walk over to the latrine. He pulled the half drums from underneath the latrine and inserted fresh cans that were standing nearby. We noticed that the dirty cans seemed very heavy, so the FNG only pulled them about 10 feet away. We guessed this would be a safe enough distance from the wooden structure as diesel fuel does not flare up when ignited. What we didn't realize was that the gasoline bladder was located right next to the diesel fuel bladder, and the FNG had filled his canister with gasoline instead of diesel fuel.

The FNG proceeded to step back and throw a lit pack of matches into the first can. Well, of course, the can exploded sending burning shit in a 50-foot radius of the can. The burning refuse landed on the latrine and set it on fire. Men came scrambling out the doors grabbing their pants as they ran. The latrine burned to the ground. Meanwhile, the FNG and everyone near him were covered in excrement.

While this was a serious event, it was also one of the most hilarious things I had ever seen. Those of us who were watching laughed so hard we had tears streaming down our faces. Some men laughed so hard that they could not stand up.

The poor FNG spent the rest of the day cleaning up the shit and had to help the engineers build a replacement latrine. He was also on latrine duty for the rest of the time we were in base camp. He was happy to eventually go to the field with the rest of us and end his shitty experience.

CHAPTER 9

Face-to-Face

I violated the cardinal rule of combat—never *be caught without your weapon.*

I came face-to-face with enemy soldiers on four occasions. The first time it happened my platoon had been following a trail through dense jungle forest for the entire day. It was one of those wet, rainy, monsoon days when you ended up being soaked through with fingers starting to wrinkle from being wet for so long.

Monsoons were both a blessing and a curse. The benefit was that it was not so bloody hot. The curse was that there was no way to stay dry or warm. Everything got wet: your clothes, your boots, your socks, your feet, and everything in your pack that was not wrapped in a waterproof bag or poncho. It took forever to dry things out and you ended up just sucking it up and learning to live a cold, wet miserable existence for a couple of hours each day. If we were holed up at a CP, some men would try to strip down and take a monsoon shower, but often there wasn't enough water to wash all the soap off. A trick I learned in Ranger School when wet and miserable was to sit on the ground covered by your poncho and make a cup of coffee or cocoa between your legs. A heat tab placed in a C-Ration can would help to warm you for a while and you had something hot to drink after the tab burned out. But usually, we simply endured the wet and cold, shivering and wrapping ourselves in wet ponchos and poncho liners. Being wet and cold was demoralizing and my troops complained bitterly. It was dangerous to be on patrol or ambush during a rainstorm because you could not hear anything with the rain beating down on your helmet and poncho. You hoped that Charlie was as miserable as you were and had decided to hole up until the rain stopped.

We spent the day slipping and sliding through wet, dense jungle terrain along the I Corps corridor near the Laotian border. The Ho Chi Minh Trail was about 25 klicks to our west and the DMZ was about 25 klicks to our north. The terrain was rugged, mountainous, and almost impenetrable. Often, we had to chop our way or follow animal trails. When we came to a real footpath, we took extra caution because of the possibility of encountering an enemy patrol walking in the opposite direction or an ambush. When a footpath was discovered, the point man always went on extreme alert. I had to rotate him every hour so that he would not become too nervous or get tired and lose alertness.

It was about 4 PM and my men were tired. We had slogged through the wet, dense underbrush for the entire day, walking for 50 minutes and taking 10-minute breaks. We were strung out single file along a 100m line following a rabbit trail moving from point A on the map to point B. Intelligence told us we were on a Viet Cong supply route, but if this was the case there was no evidence of anything more than individual troops walking down the trail—usually at night to avoid US patrols. We had seen no evidence of any enemy activity for the entire day.

The three platoons in our company had taken alternate routes through the jungle, searching for signs of enemy paths, encampments, patrols or hooches. The Viet Cong had a habit of creating small encampments hidden deep in the dense jungle. You would only discover them by mistakenly walking into them. We were on alert for footprints, broken tree limbs, camouflaged trails, chopped brush—anything that might look out of place.

But by the end of the day all that my men wanted to do was to join up with the rest of the company, drop their loads, dig holes for the night, grab some food and sleep. We were close to our objective, only about a klick more to go. But when men are tired, caution often starts to drop and carelessness creeps in. I was alert to this, so even though we only had a short distance to go, I called a halt to the march and had the men rest for 10 minutes. It was not a comfortable rest as everyone was feeling cold and miserable. Some men pulled out their ponchos and draped them over their heads to keep the big drips from falling on them from the trees above.

I called my platoon sergeant and told him to put out security to the rear and then walked forward to speak with our point man. There was no need to put out flank security because the jungle was so dense that you couldn't see 15 feet into the bush. It was critical that the point man and cover man be on alert. They were the first line of defense in the event enemy soldiers should come walking down the trail.

Usually, the cover man would join up with the point man and take up firing positions that were about 50m in front of the platoon. My platoon's policy was that the point man always carried his weapon set to full automatic while everyone else kept their weapons on safe with a round in the chamber. We always carried our weapons at the ready and never over our shoulders, with thumbs ready to flip the selector switch from safe to single or full automatic fire. However, it was the point man who was always the most vulnerable. Our rules of engagement stated that there were no friendlies in our AO. If we contacted anyone, they were considered to be the enemy and the point man was authorized to kill first or be killed. The common wisdom was "he who shoots first—lives" and my point man's life often hung in the balance of this rule.

It was always scary to be in the point man's shoes or even the covering man. Carrying your weapon with the selector switch set to full automatic with your finger just off the trigger was dangerous. On occasion I had a point man trip and pull the trigger by mistake, spraying bullets into the brush and sending everyone into a panic. He had to be cautious, survey the ground in front looking for booby traps and be alert to any noise, even something as faint as the click of a safety switch. I was often called to the front to help evaluate a noise, clearing, or anything that looked suspicious. This placed me in a highly vulnerable position. But always being prepared to spray bullets to the front was the best protection the point could have against ambushes or enemy encounter. Being the first to fire saved lives and while always a harrowing experience, it was the edge that we trusted to give us the advantage in a firefight.

The M16 rifle can fire a magazine of 18 rounds in full automatic in about 2½ seconds. As you fire, the weapon tends to creep from lower left to upper right. So, if the point carried his weapon pointing to the lower left and fired on full automatic, the bullets would spray up and to the right across his front and hopefully hit the target. In the dense jungle this was the best plan to follow.

Called to the front, I could see that something had spooked the point. He and the cover man were in a crouched stance looking and listening intently down a well-worn footpath. I immediately alerted the men behind me by placing my fist in front of my face, the hand signal for enemy. With this signal I heard a dozen safeties clicking to automatic fire, including my own.

Crouching low, I waddled forward to where the point man and cover man were now taking cover to the left and right of the path behind some trees. I realized that I was totally exposed in the center of the trail. If an enemy soldier was coming, I would be the first person they would see. But there was no cover in sight except for 15m in front of me where the point man and cover man were now lying behind tree stumps. This was where I also planned to move to seek cover. I continued to move forward slowly in my crouched position, weapon at the ready and switched to full automatic.

At that exact moment, at about 20m to my front, a Viet Cong soldier came walking around a bend in the path. He was a teenager dressed in black pajamas and carrying an AK-47 slung over his shoulder. He looked straight at me and I at him, both being incredibly surprised. The shock of seeing my first enemy soldier face to face lasted about one second. I saw him stop, open his mouth, and begin to unsling his rifle. At this point my reflexes and training came into play. I pointed my M16 in his general direction, being careful not to aim near either of my two soldiers lying on the ground to my front, and pulled the trigger. The weapon performed exactly as it was designed. The first few rounds landed in the dirt a few feet in front of the Viet Cong soldier, but the next four rounds found their mark in his leg and across his body. The soldier fell back 4 or 5 feet as if punched by a prize fighter. The enemy soldier was dead before my point man or cover man could bring their weapons up to take aim.

I immediately dove for cover expecting additional enemy soldiers to be coming up the path. After a few seconds, I gave the command to fire down the trail to kill any enemy following the now dead Viet Cong. Two M16s opened in full automatic and made a tremendous thunder. With ears ringing, the point man and cover man dropped their magazines and reloaded, and I did the same.

We lay on the wet ground for five minutes, allowing our breathing and heart rates to return to some semblance of normal and the adrenalin to purge from our bodies. There was no further enemy activity. My platoon sergeant and radio operator cautiously joined our little group. I also brought up my M60 machine gunner and M79 grenadier to have plenty of firepower immediately available. Cautiously, we advanced on the dead soldier. We searched his bloody body, finding only a bag of rice and some personal papers which we confiscated along with his weapon and bandolier. We moved down the trail, found a suitable ambush site, and set up waiting for an hour to see if any additional troops would show up. None did. We decided we had simply encountered a lone soldier en route to who knows where, or if there had been other enemy soldiers they had run in the opposite direction.

The death of an enemy soldier or soldiers was not something we celebrated. The bodies were always badly torn up having been hit with numerous bullets at incredible velocity, tearing big holes through their bodies. There was blood everywhere and any papers or documents were always covered in it. The man or men who had done the firing had to be moved to the rear of the column because they became too hyped on adrenalin to continue at point. It took them hours to come down, myself included.

My second face-to-face direct encounter occurred in the same area of operations, to the east of the Laotian border and south of the DMZ. Our company had chopped a company CP out of the jungle and had dug in for the night. Morning came, and we busied ourselves with eating some C-Rats, making coffee or hot chocolate, and trying to wake up after the very few hours of sleep from the night before. I ate some fruit and drank a cup of coffee, but the sun was up, and the heat and humidity had started to rise. I didn't feel much like eating. Plus, I had to take a crap.

When a soldier takes a crap in the field the protocol is to leave the company perimeter, telling those on the line that you are going to walk a short distance away and "dig a hole." This is exactly what I did. Our CP was on a hill, and we had cleared fields of fire in front of each foxhole to a depth of 50m. The area in front of each foxhole was totally exposed. I proceeded down the slope and moved into the underbrush for 5m for some privacy. As it turned out that was a big mistake.

I dug a small hole with the heel of my shoe, then proceeded to relieve myself. I used some C-Ration toilet paper, dumped it into the hole and covered the hole with dirt. As I fastened my pants, I looked up to see an enemy soldier standing not more than 10m in front of me. He was smiling and did not appear to be armed. As we looked at each other he waved at me. Immediately, I reached for my rifle only to realize that I had left it behind at the CP. I had been so intent on the task at hand that I violated the cardinal rule of combat—*never* be without your weapon.

I turned and ran back up the slope and yelled at the men in the foxhole that I had seen an enemy soldier. After conferring with the CO, I pulled a patrol together and we searched the area, but the enemy soldier was long gone.

I was one incredibly lucky person on that day. Had the enemy soldier been armed I might well have been killed. I never made the mistake of being outside of arm's reach of my weapon again.

My third face-to-face encounter occurred in the lowlands near the Gulf of Tonkin. We continued our mission of "search and destroy," looking for pockets of the enemy, blocking them and doing our best to annihilate them. We were moving in company formation across a large rice paddy with my platoon at the front of the column.

As we approached a wooded area, my point man alerted and let loose with a volley of automatic fire. He had uncovered an enemy soldier who was hiding in some deep brush. The soldier had been shot in the stomach, was quickly bleeding out, but was still alive.

We had a Kit Carson Scout (usually former VC soldiers who switched sides) with our company. These soldiers underwent special training and were taught some rudimentary English. They were used in more populated areas to question villagers and help determine if a captured person was a VC soldier. The Kit Carson Scouts were vicious soldiers who did not hesitate to beat the crap out of someone being interrogated.

Our scout approached the wounded soldier to try to extract some intelligence. He refused to allow the medic to treat the soldier until he talked. In truth, the man was so gravely wounded that he only had minutes to live, but the Scout did his best to gather information before the soldier died.

Many of the Kit Carson Scouts were captured VC or NVA soldiers or who surrendered in response to "Choi Hoi" leaflets dropped by American Psyops units from airplanes and helicopters throughout South Vietnam. There were many varieties of these leaflets encouraging soldiers to surrender and join with soldiers of the Army of South Vietnam (ARVN) or US Army units. Some leaflets offered money for turning in enemy weapons. Others pictured dead soldiers and indicated this is what would happen to them unless they surrendered. Some NVA units prepared similar leaflets of their own, printed in English and specifically exhorting US soldiers and even soldiers of the 1st Cav Division to abandon the unjust war created by Johnson and Nixon.

CÙNG ĐỒNG-BÀO   N THÂN-MẾN.

Chúng tôi kêu-gọi sự giúp-đỡ c   đồng-bào để bảo-vệ

cho đồng-bào và những người dân lương-thiện. Chánh-Phủ

Việt-Nam Cộng-Hòa sẽ có giải-thưởng về những tin-tức vũ-

khí và hầm chôn-giấu đạn dược của bọn Việt-Cộng.

Qui đồng-bào sẽ nhận được phần-thưởng xứng-đáng ngay

khi đồng-bào hướng-dẫn cho chính-quyền, Quân-Đội Việt-Nam

Cộng-Hòa hoặc Đồng-Minh đến nơi có vũ-khí đang được chôn-

giấu chở khỏi phải mang các vũ-khí đó đến chúng tôi.

Nếu có tin-tức, xin cầm tờ truyền-đơn nầy đến gặp bất

cứ một quân-nhân thuộc quân-đội Việt-Nam Cộng-Hòa hoặc

Đồng-Minh nào gần nhứt. Trong tờ truyền-đơn nầy đã nói

rõ-ràng đồng-bào sẽ được thưởng ngay nếu có những tin-tức

nêu trên. Tên họ đồng-bào sẽ   ữ kín.

NOTICE TO MEMBERS OF U S FORCES

The person showing you this leaflet has information concern

Weapons turn-in leaflet (front), picked up in I Corps jungle near Laotian border, June 1968. (Author's collection)

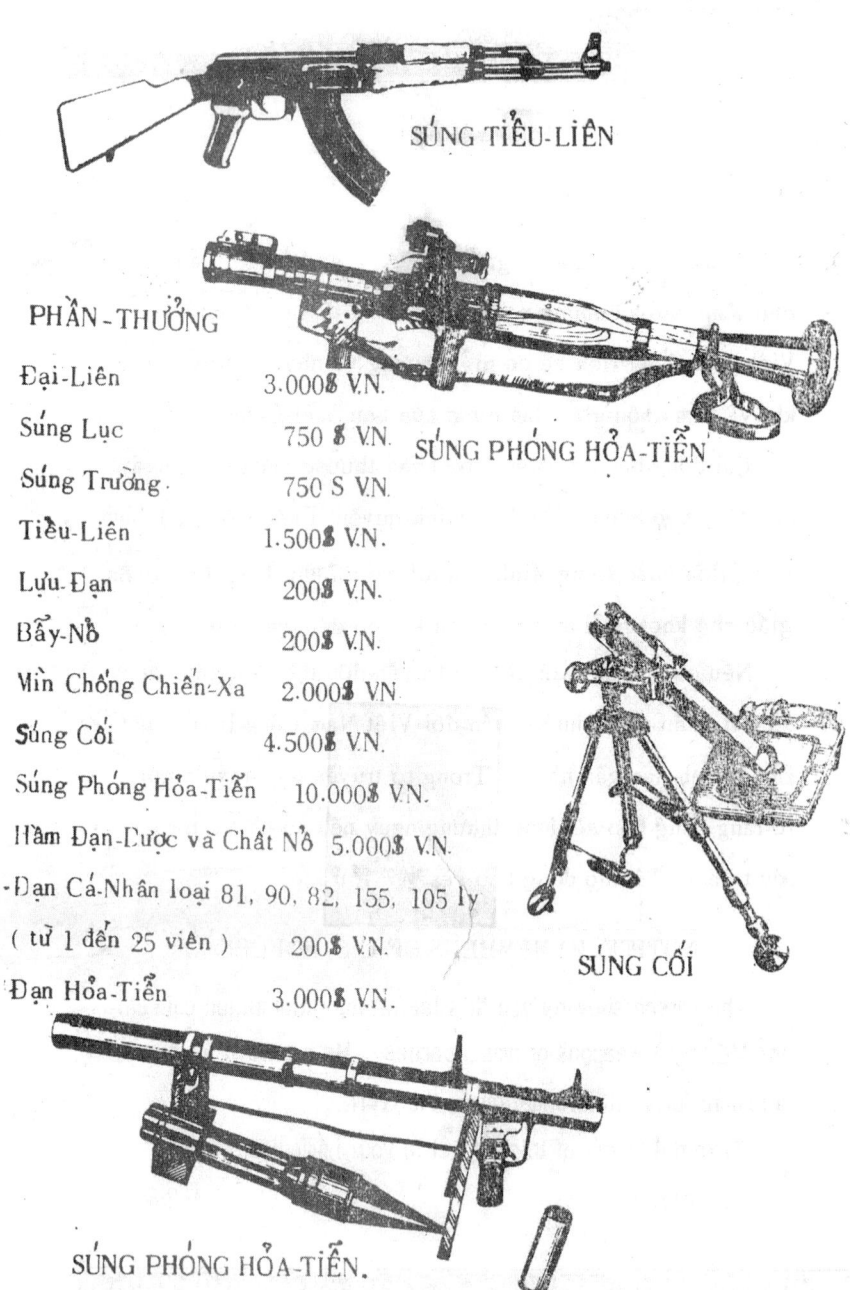

SÚNG TIỂU-LIÊN

PHẦN - THƯỞNG

Đại-Liên	3.000$ V.N.
Súng Lục	750 $ V.N.
Súng Trường	750 S V.N.
Tiểu-Liên	1.500$ V.N.
Lựu-Đạn	200$ V.N.
Bẫy-Nổ	200$ V.N.
Mìn Chống Chiến-Xa	2.000$ VN
Súng Cối	4.500$ V.N.
Súng Phóng Hỏa-Tiễn	10.000$ V.N.
Hầm Đạn-Dược và Chất Nổ	5.000$ V.N.
-Đạn Cá-Nhân loại 81, 90, 82, 155, 105 ly	
(từ 1 đến 25 viên)	200$ V.N.
Đạn Hỏa-Tiễn	3.000$ V.N.

SÚNG PHÓNG HỎA-TIỄN

SÚNG CỐI

SÚNG PHÓNG HỎA-TIỄN.

Weapons turn-in leaflet (back), picked up in I Corps jungle near Laotian border, June 1968. (Author's collection)

LỜI KÊU GỌI
CỦA ỦY BAN HÒA BÌNH MIỀN NAM V.N
gởi binh sĩ trong quân đội viễn chinh Mỹ

HỠI BINH SĨ MỸ !

CHÍNH quyền Giôn-xơn đã phải chấm dứt ném bom và bắn phá trên toàn bộ nước Việt-nam Dân chủ Cộng hòa.

Rõ ràng đây là một thất bại to lớn trong chánh sách leo thang chiến tranh của bọn diều hâu trong tòa nhà trắng và lầu 5 góc, đồng thời cũng là báo hiệu sự thất bại hoàn toàn của đế quốc Mỹ trong âm mưu xâm lược miền Nam Việt-nam.

Rõ ràng đây là thắng lợi vẻ vang của nhân dân Việt-nam ở hai miền Nam Bắc đang chiến đấu để bảo vệ nền độc lập, tự do của xứ sở mình.

Đây là thắng lợi rất có ý nghĩa của những người yêu chuộng hòa bình, công lý trên thế giới và ở nước Mỹ đã đấu tranh không mệt mỏi, không khoan nhượng đòi chấm dứt cuộc chiến tranh phi đạo lý mà bọn cầm quyền Giôn-xơn, Đin Rát-xcơ gây ra ở Việt-nam.

Và rõ ràng đây cũng là thắng lợi bước đầu của những binh sĩ Mỹ khôn ngoan và có lương tâm đang kiên quyết từ chối không chịu ra trận chết vô ích để thu thêm tiền lời cho bọn lái súng và bọn ngụy quyền thúi nát Thiệu, Kỳ, Hương.

Nhưng bọn diều hâu ở Phố U-ôn, những kẻ có nhiều đơn đặt hàng chiến tranh vẫn ngoan cố với mưu toan dùng binh sĩ Mỹ để duy trì lửa đạn ở miền Nam Việt-nam.

Chúng không thể nào thực hiện được ý đồ đen tối của chúng.

Nhân dân Việt-nam anh hùng và kiên cường nhứt định sẽ chặn bàn tay xâm lược đẫm máu của bọn hiếu chiến Mỹ.

Hàng triệu nhân dân Mỹ và nhân dân thế giới đang thừa thắng đấu tranh mạnh mẽ hơn nữa đòi bọn cầm quyền Mỹ phải chấm dứt ngay chiến tranh văn hồi hòa bình ở miền Nam Việt-nam.

CÁC BẠN BINH SĨ MỸ !

Là những người trực tiếp phải chịu đựng mọi hiểm nguy gian khổ trong cuộc chiến tranh ngày càng gay go, ác liệt, hẳn các bạn không ai muốn tiếp tục bị đẩy ra chiến trường. Hình ảnh ước mơ của các bạn hẳn là con tàu cập bến quê hương và khung cảnh đầm ấm của gia đình đoàn tụ.

Muốn hòa bình chống được lập lại ở miền Nam Việt-nam, muốn sớm được trở về đất nước, các bạn phải đứng lên hành động !

— Cương quyết không ra trận, không đi tiếp viện, không đi phản kích lùng sục !

— Không chống lại Quân giải phóng; khi lâm trận nhanh chóng hạ vũ khí để được đối xử khoan hồng.

Các bạn hãy cùng nhân dân Việt-nam, nhân dân Mỹ và nhân dân thế giới đấu tranh đòi chánh quyền Mỹ :

— Chấm dứt chiến tranh, văn hồi hòa bình ở miền Nam Việt-nam.

— Rút quân Mỹ và chư hầu về nước.

— Công việc của người Việt-nam do người Việt-nam tự giải quyết.

ỦY BAN HÒA BÌNH MIỀN NAM VIỆT-NAM

Choi Hoi surrender leaflet in Vietnamese, found in I Corps, near DMZ, June 1968. (Author's collection)

APPEAL
OF SOUTH VIETNAM PEACE COMMITTEE TO G.I'S IN THE US EXPEDITIONARY CORPS

AMERICAN G.I's!

Johnson Administration had to end the bombing and strafing throughout the Democratic Republic of Vietnam.

This fact is a clear proof of big failure of the War escalation policy pursued by the White House and Pentagon Hawks, at the same time it tolls the complete failure of U.S Imperialism in its evil scheme of aggression against South Vietnam.

This is a clear proof of glorious victory won by the Vietnamese people, both in South and North, fighting for the defence of Independence and Freedom of their country.

This is a significant victory of the peace-and-justicel loving people of the World and of America, tirelessly and uncompromisingly struggling for an end to the immoral War being waged by the Johnson—Rusk Administration in Vietnam.

And this is also a clear proof of victory firstly won by wise and conscientious G.I's determinedly refusing to go out to the field to uselessly die for more berefite for the arm-dealers and the corrupt puppet administration of Thieu—Ky—Huong.

But the Wall Street Hawks who receive orders of war materials and equipments still obstinately cling to their scheme of continuing fire and bloodshed in South Vietnam with lives of G.I's.

They will be unable to realize their dark designs.

The heroic and indomitable Vietnamese people will successfully check the bloody hands of aggression of the American war-mongers.

In the impetus of victory, millions of American people and people the world over will push up their struggle forcing the U.S Administration to end he war and restore peace in South Vietnam.

G.I's!

Directly bearing the brunt of hardship and danger in this ever harde and more dangerous War day by day, surely no one of you wish to be driven out to the field. Your dream must be the image of your ship landing home harbor, and the warm happy atmosphere of your family reunion.

For the early restoration of peace in South Vietnam, for an early home return, you should stand up for action by:

—Determinedly refusing to go out to the field, refusing to reinforce, refusing to take part in counter-Offensive and sweep operations!

—Not resisting the Liberation Armed forces; in contact, quickly lay down your weapons for lenient treatment.

You should join the people of Vietnam, of America and of the World in the struggle forcing the U.S Administration to:

—End the war, Restore Peace in S.V.N.

—Bring American and Satellite Troops home!

—Let the Vietnamese affairs be settled by the Vietnamese people themselves.

SOUTH VIETNAM PEACE COMMITTEE

NVA surrender leaflet in English for all GIs, found in I Corps near DMZ, July 1968. (Author's collection)

G.I's IN THE 1st CAVALRY DIVISON!

Johnson has had to stop the bombardment on the whohe territory of North Vietnam.

Both Johnson and Nixon have aknowledged that the « desamericanization » of the U.S aggressive War in South Vietnam must be done to avoid shameful failure.

Yet, why have you been in this hot battlefield of South Vietnam to suffer untold hardships and dangers and finally to die a senseless death?

You should:

— Demand an end to the war!

— Demand to be repatriated at once!

— Resolutely refuse to go out on operation!

— By all means, cross over to the National Front for Liberation, you will receive fair treatment and have good occasion for your return home.

THIS LEAFLET CAN BE USED AS A SAFE CONDUCT PASS

Rare NVA surrender leaflet in English directed at 1st Cav soldiers, found in I Corps near Laotian border, July 1968. (Author's collection)

Choi Hoi surrender leaflet with photo (front), I Corps, found near LZ Jane, July 1968. (Author's collection)

SINH BẮC   TỬ NAM

Hàng vạn gia đình ở miền Bắc không còn được tin tức gì của con cái họ trong bộ đội. NHỮNG NGƯỜI CON THÂN YÊU CỦA HỌ ĐÃ CHẾT. Đó là số phận của những người xâm nhập miền Nam. Trước lực lượng hùng hậu của Quân Đội Việt Nam Cộng - Hòa và Đồng - Minh, bộ đội Cộng - sản xâm nhập miền Nam không thể nào tránh khỏi sự THẤT BẠI HOÀN TOÀN. CHỈ NHỮNG NGƯỜI BIẾT KỊP THỜI RỜI BỎ HÀNG NGŨ CỘNG-SẢN MỚI SỐNG SÓT DỄ CÓ NGÀY TRỞ VỀ SUM HỌP VỚI GIA ĐÌNH Ở MIỀN BẮC.   49

Choi Hoi surrender leaflet (back), I Corps, found near LZ Jane, July 1968. (Author's collection)

* * *

I was involved in many firefights and ambushes during my tour. I saw plenty of enemy killed by Claymore mines, rifle fire, artillery, or ARA fired by Cobra helicopter gunships. I have searched enemy bodies for documents, but these soldiers were all dead by the time I got to them. As with the death of one of my own men, I was dispassionate about enemy kills. Killing a soldier was not something I thought about or allowed to affect my emotions. I blocked the experience and got busy with the search of the body and making sure my unit was secure.

There was a fourth instance when I faced the enemy at close range, but that story bears telling in its own chapter, called "Saturation Ambushing."

CHAPTER 10

Pay Officer

After humping the boonies and sleeping on the ground for weeks at a time, being pay officer was a real joy.

American soldiers in Vietnam were paid in cash every month. When you came into country you met with a personnel specialist. This specialist made sure your beneficiaries were properly designated and arranged for your pay to be deposited in a stateside bank. You were asked how much money you would like to receive each month. As there was no place to spend money when you were at base camp or in the field, $50 was more than sufficient. Some soldiers who were heavy gamblers would take $100 or more in hopes of success at blackjack or poker. Soldiers and officers alike were paid in scrip each month and one officer from each company was designated as the "pay officer."

Scrip, also known as Military Payment Certificates (MPC), was used by soldiers to buy things from Vietnamese locals who would "hang out" near the base camp. When my company pulled base camp security, I would send a squad out with the engineers to check the road for booby traps each day. In the afternoon that patrol was allowed to go down to the river so they could swim and wash. Soldiers would buy cold sodas, pot, and more and pay with scrip. Security was always present during these mini afternoon R&Rs, and the troops were usually well behaved. It was always a pleasure to take a dip in the stream and cool off from the heat. But about every six months, without warning, the army would change the color of the scrip. There would be a lockdown on the base camp, and soldiers had one day to exchange their scrip for the new color. When this happened, you could see the Vietnamese civilians lined up at the gate begging soldiers to buy their scrip for pennies on the dollar. Any soldier who tried to help these civilians risked serious punishment. Civilian fortunes in scrip were won and lost in the space of a day and depending on the color and design of the notes.

As the senior lieutenant in my company, I was assigned the duty of being pay officer on several occasions. Being the pay officer was a special pleasure. It meant that I first spoke with all the soldiers in my company to determine if they were experiencing any personnel or pay problems. I made note of the problems and then traveled by helicopter to the division rear in An Khe. This travel took a day. Solving the personnel problems and drawing cash to pay the men in the company took another day or two if things worked out right. The return trip to the field took another day. After I paid the troops and did the necessary accounting paperwork, the remaining cash had to be turned in at the battalion base camp and that accounted for yet another day. So, with any luck, as pay officer, you could enjoy at least two nights sleeping on a cot, one or two steak dinners at the Officers' Club, a movie, and drinks. After humping the boonies and sleeping on the ground for weeks this duty was a real joy.

It is important to note that when an officer drew cash to pay the troops, he became personally responsible for the money. I would draw about $8–10,000 in scrip and place it in a small briefcase that was provided. The briefcase, which resembled a Samsonite case, was made of plastic. There were locks on the case, but the keys had long been lost so there was no way to lock it. If I came up short in returning the leftover cash, the difference was deducted from my own pay. Thus, I took this responsibility very seriously.

Letter: 20 June 1968, A Company, 1/5 Cav, 1st Air Cav Division, LZ Jane, I Corps, Vietnam (letter to college classmate)

I have just returned from a five-day spree to An Khe. I was the pay officer for the company this month. I drew a payroll of $10,520 in scrip and was held personally responsible for it. After paying the troops in the field, I went to Camp Evans to try to settle pay and personnel complaints. Evans couldn't help me, so I had to go to An Khe. I stretched my trip to two days in the division rear visiting the finance department by day and the Officers' Club by night. It sure was great to have something cold to drink, and I had plenty too! I also saw two movies, but don't remember what they were and ate a steak dinner.

I returned to the company today in the field. The company has seen considerable contact since I last wrote. This time we didn't do too well. The VC enjoy employing snipers in a booby-trapped area. They shoot at you and then run for it (DiDi Mau). You haul ass after them and get zapped by a booby trap. We lost four men this way last week (one KIA, three WIAs, with one man losing a leg.)

We sprung several ambushes on Charlie and have gotten one or two. We don't take too many prisoners or WIAs. They either surrender without a scratch, or we blow them to hell. We got one sniper the other day. Upon further examination we found it was a VC nurse, about eighteen years old. She had a medical bag, three grenades and an AK-47. Most of her head was missing.

There were three or four lieutenants who were appointed as pay officers, one from each company. We would all join up, board the same helicopter to An Khe, hang together, drink and tell stories in the O Club.

On one occasion, several in our merry band were very hung over from partying at the club the night before. At the airstrip we waited for a plane to take us to the battalion CP. One officer from E Company was wasted, having overindulged in both food and drink. He was having severe intestinal problems, retreating to the woods every 10 minutes or so.

Our plane finally landed and the four of us boarded for the 45-minute flight to the division forward. We landed and had to prop up the sick lieutenant who by this point had become dehydrated. We asked if he wanted to go to the aid station to recover, but he declined, stating that the cool air of a helicopter ride out to his company was all he needed to recuperate.

We walked over to the helicopter landing pad to be informed that the S-4 runs (nightly supply run) out to the company CPs would be leaving shortly. We were welcome to ride along to our respective companies.

A few minutes later, we found ourselves jumping onto a chopper loaded down with ammunition, C-Rations, water canisters, mortar rounds, hand grenades and flares. Each officer held his plastic case close to his chest as we balanced ourselves in the chopper and found room to sit.

As we lifted off, the one poor officer who was experiencing intense pain and intestinal problems could hold back no longer. He dived for the edge of the open door to the chopper, vomiting all the booze he had enjoyed the night before and splashing the helicopter door gunner who sat at the side of the helicopter. After vomiting, the poor guy lay on the chopper floor while the surprised door gunner attempted to wipe his boots and pants legs clean. After 15 minutes of dry heaves, the officer picked himself up and wobbled to his seat. As he did, he dropped his plastic case which bounced against the chopper floor and out the door. As if in slow motion, we all watched the case pop open and more than $5,000 in scrip scatter to the wind. A collective scream of "Oh, noooooo!" was heard. Unfortunately, there was little that we could do as we were 1,500 feet in the air over dense jungle.

I heard through the grapevine that after a hearing, the officer was to be held accountable for the funds, but luckily for him there was a scrip exchange. It ended up that the lost scrip had become worthless. I never saw that officer on pay duty again.

CHAPTER 11

Blown Ambush

I mashed the handle on the Claymore, bracing for a massive explosion…

The Claymore mine was one of the most formidable antipersonnel weapons used in Vietnam. It consisted of a convex plastic case, 8½ inches wide by 5 inches high and 3 inches thick. It had two scissor-like legs on the bottom and an open sight on the top. Inside were 700 tiny steel balls, one-eighth inch in diameter, embedded in the case and backed by C4 explosive. It weighed three and one-half pounds. If placed and aimed correctly, it had an effective kill zone of from twelve inches off the ground to 6½ feet high in a 50m arc and an effective range of 100m. This is the same as firing 700 .22 rounds in an arc 50m wide. It is a devastating weapon.

The mine is placed 75 feet in front of your defensive or ambush position at dusk. To set it up you simply pull down the legs, press the mine into the ground, lie down and look through the sight to make sure the weapon is pointed in the right direction with the bottom situated a few inches off the ground. Then you slide in the blasting cap into the mine. The cap is connected to a long wire that is then carefully uncoiled back to your ambush position. The last step is to connect the wire to a trigger that looks like an oversize staple gun. There is a safety wire that prevents the firing handle from being mashed until you push the wire out of the way when ready to fire. Firing the mine propels the 700 steel balls in a cone from one to five feet high with a kill radius of 50m. Nothing, absolutely nothing, lives in front of a Claymore after it is blown.

Every morning in the bush, just before dawn, troops would fire up their C-Ration stoves to make coffee or hot chocolate. The stove is made by punching holes with a beer can punch in the crackers can that comes with the C-Ration pack. Soldiers are issued "heat tabs" (individually wrapped hexamine tablets that burn smokeless and with high intensity) to place in the stoves. One tab will heat a canteen cup of water. If the stove is positioned at the bottom of the foxhole, no light can be seen while the water is heated. Thus, at first light in the cool mountain air, as you looked at the foxholes to your left and right, you could see shafts of steam rising out of each of the holes. You could spot troops holding canteen cups to their lips taking sips of the warm liquid with minds coming awake and alert. This was often the time when Charlie would throw a grenade at you or fire a rocket-propelled grenade (RPG). My company often practiced a "Mad Minute" at first light with everyone firing off a clip of ammo to the front, just to make sure that any attempt by the enemy to slip one in would be foiled.

But if you spent five or six weeks in the field with only occasional resupply when choppers could land, you lived off Cs. Heat tabs were often in short supply. A perfect alternative, however, was to pry open a Claymore mine, extract a small amount of the C4 explosive and burn it in the C-Ration stove. (Too much C4 will burn so intensely it will melt the stove and the fumes were toxic, but soldiers had to have their morning coffee.) So, after many weeks in the field, a few Claymores had become completely useless with all the C4 having been taken out to make hot drinks. After the explosive was removed, the Claymore was snapped back together waiting for an opportunity to dispose of the weapon so that it could not fall into the hands of the VC. Of course, it was forbidden to open and remove the C4 from the mines. The men usually kept close watch on those Claymores that had been dismantled, placing a mark on the weapon to indicate that the C4 had been removed. Therein lay the danger and unfortunately, sometimes in haste or in the dark an inactive Claymore might be pulled for a night ambush.

As usual, the platoons followed different routes to each day's objectives and were dispersed to prevent the entire company from being ambushed, but if one platoon got into trouble the other two would not be too far away and could rapidly come to the rescue. As the platoons neared the end of day's objective, they would begin to recon several ambush sites. We knew that Charlie was always watching us, so it was important to identify several possible sites. While watching us, he would not know which one we chose for that night's setup. An ideal ambush site would occupy the high ground and be located along a trail or be positioned at a trail intersection. The men would be located 50–75 feet back from the trail, ideally with some cover and in a place where they could get comfortable for the night.

I remember identifying a prime spot for an ambush with clear fields of fire adjacent to a well-used trail. There was a slight depression where we would place our ambush team and thus would be shooting slightly uphill, which was not ideal. We planned to install our Claymores 10–15 feet back from the edge of the trail and aimed to cover the approaches from both the left and right as well as the center. Of course, we stopped and made a big fuss over several other sites, but I already knew which one was the best choice for that night's ambush.

The three platoons would rendezvous at the company CP at around 3 PM, and each platoon was assigned a sector of the perimeter. My platoon sergeant placed two-man foxholes within our sector making allowances for the 10 men who would go out on ambush that night. Each platoon would send out a 9- or 10-man heavily armed ambush team. My platoon sergeant and I alternated taking ambushes out each night. It was my turn to pull ambush duty. The only real benefit to pulling ambush duty was that you didn't have to dig a foxhole, so you could rest while the rest of the platoon dug in.

At 45 minutes before dusk, the ambush teams were assembled, and each man was checked to see that he had the necessary equipment and nothing rattled. Our packs were left at the CP, so we could carry the minimum gear, water, and extra ammunition. I checked to ensure the men had all their gear. The ambush team also carried three Claymores. We marked our faces with camouflage sticks, put on floppy hats, buttoned our shirts at the collar and sleeves and slathered on mosquito repellent. We wanted to make the minimum amount of noise as we moved into position. The radio speaker was turned off, and the volume set to the lowest setting. Common radio procedure to respond to a request for a sitrep was by breaking squelch with the handset (pressing the "push to talk" button sent a "click" to other radios). This communicated a silent response rather than spoken words: one click for yes and two for no.

Before departing, I checked with our FO and learned where he had pre-plotted three artillery positions near my ambush. If we got into trouble, it was easy to call for artillery support and adjust without having to pull out a compass and try to shoot an azimuth (point on a compass) in the dark.

Our team moved out quickly as the light started to fade. We had to cover several klicks before reaching the ambush site. We broke brush, not following any trails, to avoid being ambushed ourselves. Traveling at near dark was always extremely stressful. We walked single file, just close enough to the man in front so as not to lose contact. This was a dangerous formation. If we were ambushed, many men would be killed or wounded, but this formation was essential so as not to lose sight of the man in front of you.

It was still extremely warm. We sweated as we moved single file through the dense brush, sweat and camouflage paint dripping into our eyes. Finally, at about 8 PM and just before moon rise, we arrived at our site. The squad leader and point man moved forward to scout the location, leaving the rest of us behind. The squad leader would leave the point man at the ambush site and return to bring the rest of us into position. This was the most dangerous part of the mission because the two men could easily become disoriented, unable to return to the rest of the team or be mistaken for the enemy. But we had practiced this tactic repeatedly and the men on the team were familiar with the need for caution.

After 10 minutes, the squad leader returned and led the rest of the team to the site. The men were placed 3 feet apart in a line formation. Each soldier spread out his poncho liner and took up a prone position, weapon pointing toward the trail. Three men would always remain awake, rotating responsibility every hour to three other men. Each man pulled two shifts each night, alternating every two hours.

The last thing, before starting the shifts, was to place the Claymore mines. Three men crawled forward at the same time, to the left, center and right. At 75 feet away they stuck their mines in the ground, aimed, and inserted the blasting caps. As they crawled back, they uncoiled the wire back to their ambush positions. They then connected the firing triggers to wires and made sure the safeties were in place.

The signal to blow the Claymores would be given only by me, located at the center of the line. The idea was to wait until the enemy force entered the kill zone, blow the center Claymore, and then blow the mines on either end after a few seconds' delay. In this way, any enemy trying to escape to the left or right and not killed by the initial blast would be killed by the mines located on the ends of the formation. The Claymore explosions were also the signal to the rest of the ambush team to open up with their weapons. Every other man would fire on full automatic. This would allow the men to reload while the other half of the team continued to fire single shots and maintain continuous fire. The machine gunner would fire a full belt in three-round bursts and the M79 grenadier would fire flechette rounds consisting of 50 steel darts with a range of 500 feet. The noise of an ambush was deafening, and our ears would be ringing for hours following the action.

The firepower released within the first minute of an ambush was devastating: Claymore mines exploding, machine guns firing, flechette darts blasting and M16s firing full and semi-automatic. It was rare that any enemy force escaped a properly executed ambush. That was unless the enemy soldiers were strung out along an extended line.

By 9 PM, my ambush team had our mines in place and the shifts began. We lay on our stomachs, which made it easier to grab our weapons and start shooting. It also reduced the possibility that one of the men would fall asleep and start to snore. I had the third shift of the night and knew I would be awakened promptly at midnight. I pulled down my hat and shifted my body until I was able to get comfortable and get rid of the aches and pains of the day.

True to form, my RTO started kicking my foot promptly at midnight. I took a slug of water and splashed some water on my face. My RTO was sound asleep by the time I was fully awake. I looked to my left and right to make sure there were men on either side of me awake and alert. Our lives depended on each other. It was a violation of this trust if you fell asleep during guard duty. There were numerous tricks to staying awake. The one that worked best for me was putting water in my eyes. I would first take a slug from my canteen, wet my mouth, and then spit some into the palm of my hand. Then, I would rub my face and eyes with the water. In this way, I not only got a drink of water, but it served to keep me awake for about 15 minutes, and then repeat the process.

At 12:45, I thought I heard a noise coming down the trail. I couldn't be sure; and I looked to the man to my left who was looking at me. I gave him the enemy sign, a closed fist in front of your face and shrugged my shoulders. He nodded vigorously.

He had heard the same noise. The adrenalin kicked in and I immediately touched the feet of the men lying to my left and right with my foot. I whispered in their ears, "Charlie's coming—wake up!" The men came awake instantly and rifles were put to shoulders, safeties quietly clicking to semi and full automatic. (Everyone had rounds in the chambers with weapons cocked so we only needed to flick the safety indicators to fire.) I picked up the Claymore firing handle and moved the safety wire to the firing position. Out of the corner of my eye I saw the man to my left, the direction from which the noise was coming, also pick up his Claymore firing handle.

Our ambush team peered to the front, squinting our eyes, and looking above the target area. (It is easier to see an object in the dark if you look above it, rather than directly at it.) I wished I had remembered to bring the platoon's starlight scope, but it was in my rucksack back at the FOB.

The noise of people walking on the trail was clearly audible now and it was obvious that an enemy force was coming into our kill zone. The adrenalin was pumping through my body. My heart was beating so loudly I thought the enemy could hear it. Then, as if in slow motion, the shadows of men walking down the trail came into murky view. The night was very dark with only a sliver of moon. It was difficult to determine how many men were in the force, how fast they were walking or how heavily armed they were. I could feel and smell the tension among the men on my ambush team. Fingers were all resting on triggers just waiting for the signal to fire.

* * *

To the best of my recollection and from what I could make out in the dark, there was an enemy force of about four or five men. They were well spaced with about 3m between each man. What I couldn't tell for sure was how many more men might still be coming down the trail behind the first group. I remember wishing that I had told the men setting the Claymores to point them up and down the trail rather than at it. "Well, perhaps they did," I said to myself… but I couldn't be sure. I just had to hope that there wasn't a larger force following behind this squad that was in my kill zone. My radio operator was kicking my foot at this point telling me that it was time to blow the Claymore. His tension and anxiety were understandable. He wanted to be able to call the CO immediately once the ambush was initiated to let him know what was happening. I delayed a few seconds more to make sure that we had the entire enemy force in the kill zone. I wanted the Claymore to do its work and ensure that no enemy troops escaped.

I mashed the handle on the Claymore—bracing for a massive explosion—only to hear a very loud "pop" as the blasting cap exploded, and the plastic case blew apart. But there was no blast. The ambush team was so surprised by this noise that they too hesitated several long seconds before someone yelled, "Shoot the mother fuckers." And then, all hell broke loose. But those few seconds of delay were all that was needed to give the edge to the enemy soldiers. They dropped to the ground and unleashed a stream of AK rounds in our direction. Fortunately, we were in a slight defilade position (a depression in the earth) and the enemy rounds zipped over our heads. By now our weapons had opened up and two loud explosions occurred on the left and right as the other Claymores were set off and blown. The problem was that these mines were indeed pointed up and down the trail, but all the enemy soldiers were positioned in the center of the kill zone where the dead Claymore had been. The enemy were now flat on their bellies and our rounds also flew over their heads. The firing went on for many minutes more with men dropping magazines and reloading with fresh ones. My machine gunner reloaded a second belt. He continued to spray the area in six-round bursts. The M79 grenadier switched from flechette rounds to high-explosive and launched rounds up and down the trail as well as straight ahead. He was thinking that the enemy force would naturally want to run in the opposite direction of the contact.

I got on the horn and called in fire missions on Red 3 and Red 2 hoping that I might catch some of the fleeing troops. But it was the middle of the night, and it took Artillery several minutes to wake up to shoot a couple of smoke rounds—testing to make sure that we were safely away from high-explosive rounds when they hit. I adjusted the rounds and shifted them to the left as this was the direction I thought the enemy was likely to try to escape. But it was too little, too late. The enemy had escaped. There was nothing I could do to recapture the element of surprise or put them back into the kill zone. We waited until first light before going out to the kill zone to look for blood trails. There were none. Our ambush had been a failure. The ambush had been blown.

My CO was furious over the Claymore and did an immediate inspection of all the remaining mines in the company. Five more empty Claymores were discovered, but of course no one would own up to removing the C4.

Interestingly, there was a big bag of heat tabs and replacement Claymores on the next supply chopper.

CHAPTER 12

Saturation Ambushing

The CO's words came over the radio: "Take him out... silently."

It was so damn hot. Unbearably hot. You woke up sweating and kept sweating all day long. You were beyond stinking. Smelling other soldiers' body odor ended after about the third day in the field. Your clothes were stiff from sweat and drying. You were dirty all the time. Your hands were dirty. Your face was dirty. You just got used to it and lived with it. The only thing you washed was your teeth if you could spare the water. The humidity was equally fierce. There was no end to it. I drank gallons of water just trying to avoid heat stroke, but if the terrain was steep, if we had to cut trail or if we were out in the open, some men would pass out. No one was immune; even those who had been in country for months could be susceptible to heat stroke or heat exhaustion no matter how much water they drank and how many salt pills they took. You could be walking along and suddenly someone would keel over. The soldiers carrying the heaviest loads were the most vulnerable, like Kennedy, my RTO, Cowboy, my machine gunner, or Johnson, my M79 grenadier. Even at night when the temperature dropped a few degrees, it remained hot, sticky, and uncomfortable. We were required to wear our long-sleeved shirts at night with buttoned cuffs and collars to keep the malaria-carrying mosquitoes from biting.

During one challenging period with daily temps rising as high as 115 degrees, we had to medevac so many men because of heat stroke and heat exhaustion that the battalion commander called a halt to our typical search and ambush routine. We were ordered to use the tactic called "saturation ambushing." The plan was to create a series of ambushes along a trail network, separated by 500m. Each platoon deployed two ambushes for a total of six ambushes for the company along a 5km trail. The concept was simple: if an enemy force came walking down the trail, we would allow the lead group to pass the first and second ambushes and spring the trap with the third ambush. Then, if any survivors tried to escape running either up or back down the trail, they would be taken out by the fourth or second ambushes in line. This tactic was ideal for extremely hot weather because the troops could set up in ambush formation, conserve water and not have to hump the jungle. Long Range Reconnaissance Patrol (LRRP) rations were issued which were a welcome alternative to the C-Rats we normally ate daily. LRRP rations required no heating but did require sufficient water to reconstitute the dried food. Fortunately, we had extra water flown in to go with the rations.

~~~~~~

Letter: 24 July 1968, A Company, 1/5 Cav, 1st Air Cav Division, LZ Jane, I Corps, Vietnam

Today we got hit by a typhoon! It was quite a blast with winds up to eighty mph. Of course, we are now all wet and the storm has settled to a steady drizzle. The power went out and several tents went down, but there was no major damage. There is a lot of cleaning up to do and we will be eating Cs for a few days as the mess tent is in shambles. Boy, what a climate, from 115 degrees to freezing rain!

This storm will cancel our forthcoming mission for a few days. It's a new mission called "saturation ambushing." The object is to break down into reinforced squad size units and "saturate" a small area with ambushes. You hump heavy (carry heavy packs) and are not resupplied for several days. You wear camouflage and run recon patrols during the day in addition to the ambushes. It's a Ranger type mission and not too dangerous unless you run into a large force. If so, the troops have to be quiet and try to avoid contact.

~~~~~~

The success of the tactic was dependent on keeping the troops quiet throughout the day and night. This was difficult because the soldiers would become bored with sleeping or reading paperbacks and want to play blackjack. Inevitably, there was an outburst of noise when one soldier won a big hand. Even with these challenges, saturation ambushing provided a great respite and we did not lose troops from heat stroke.

American troops, in general, had a tough time keeping quiet. Some VC reported that American troops coming through the jungle sounded like a herd of rogue elephants. American soldiers were also big smokers, and the cigarette smoke could be smelled tens of meters away, but I chose not to be too strict with the noise makers and smokers, except at night which was the ideal time for ambushes to take place.

My unit's ambush was the third in line. We set up along a ridge with steep drops-offs on either side. We were designated as the ambush to spring the trap on any enemy soldiers coming down the trail. The trail itself was a well-used Viet Cong travel route; in fact, we had killed two enemy soldiers on the first day using this tactic. We hoped that other enemy soldiers would come looking for the bodies, so we left them where they lay in the ambush zone. After the better part of a day, the bodies began to bloat and stink. The smell became intolerable, and we dragged the two dead men down the hill away from our ambush position. There are lots of stories about American troops desecrating enemy bodies, cutting off ears and stealing valuables. My troops did search the bodies for documents and maps but left the bodies alone except for frequently placing a 1st Cav patch in the mouth of the dead enemy soldier. I never permitted the cutting of ears.

A night ambush is always a hairy experience. It's dark and quiet and there are the unknown noises of the jungle. But it is essential to maintain absolute silence during an ambush. The men are always restless, nervous, trying to sleep, and often must be jostled to prevent snoring. At about 10 PM on the second night of our saturation ambush tactic, the first ambush position placed a hushed radio call to the company commander, who was located at the fifth ambush position. An enemy soldier had just passed their location. The first ambush could not verify if there was an enemy force following this soldier or if he was alone. The CO told the second ambush to allow the enemy soldier to walk past their location and for the first ambush to report if there were additional troops following him. Ambush #2 gave two clicks on the radio advising that they understood. A short while later, ambush #1 advised that no additional soldiers had come down the trail. They thought they heard noises heading their way but couldn't be sure.

Upon hearing this information, the CO gave the order over the radio to me to "take him out ... silently." This meant that the soldier had to be killed with a knife. I quickly asked if any of the men wanted to volunteer to take the soldier out. No one did, so the job fell to me. I told my men not to fire under any circumstances and told my radio operator to draw his .45 pistol, make sure there was a round in the chamber and follow me. We crawled from our ambush to a large tree adjacent to the trail. I whispered to my RTO that if I got into trouble with the kill, he was to put the gun to the head of the enemy soldier and pull the trigger—just be careful not to shoot me in the process. My RTO was just as nervous as I was, but I wanted to make sure I had backup in the event something happened that I could not control.

We both lay in the brush alongside the tree, trying to get control of our breathing and staying as quiet as possible as the adrenalin kicked in. After what seemed like an hour, but was only a few minutes, I heard the soldier coming toward us. It was pitch black. I couldn't see more than a few feet in front of me. I welcomed the dark as it meant that the soldier couldn't see us either lying next to the trail. As soon as I heard the noise of the man coming, I rose and crouched next to the tree. Pulling out my 9-inch hunting knife from its sheath on my belt, I pressed my body against the tree with knees bent. It seemed like I stayed in this position for a long time, although it could only have been a few minutes as the soldier got closer and closer. With the tree in front of me, I could only hear his footsteps; I had no idea of his height or size. A flood of thoughts flashed through my mind: What if he hears me before I grab him? What if he's bigger or stronger than me? What if I miss him with the first blow of my knife? What if he screams?

I didn't have time to think these thoughts through as the enemy soldier walked past the tree. My training and experience kicked in. I jumped on his back, put my left hand over his mouth, pulled his head back towards my shoulder and simultaneously thrust my knife into his chest just below the rib cage and then upward toward his heart. There was a popping sound as the knife pierced the skin. I immediately felt hot blood spilling over my hand. The man struggled, but the knife had found its mark and the wound was mortal. He fell back and collapsed into me almost causing me to fall backward. I continued to shove the knife into his body as deeply as I could. He made a gurgling sound as he hit the ground. I saw his eyes were wide open. His rifle had been slung over his shoulder and it clattered to the ground. I immediately pounced on top of him, straddling his chest, pressing my left hand over his mouth so that no sound would escape while I continued to shove the knife deep into his chest. Blood was now pouring out of the open wound and all over my hands. The man struggled and brought his hands up to grab my hand, but his grip was weak and there was little he could do with me sitting on his chest. Gradually, his hand fell back as I continued the pressure on his mouth and the knife in his chest.

Suddenly, my RTO was hovering next to me, his pistol drawn and placed at the man's temple. I hissed at him to put the gun away as this guy was finished, and we wanted no noise to alert any possible followers. My RTO and I grabbed the body and pulled it off the trail toward our ambush position. We grabbed his AK and ammo belt. I whispered to my RTO that we would search the body tomorrow as I wanted to get back to our ambush position as quickly as possible in case any enemy troops were following. We low crawled back to our position and whispered to the men on ambush that we were coming in.

I grabbed my canteen and drank about half of it, then poured the rest over my hands and arms which were drenched in blood. I lay down on my poncho liner. After a minute, I started to shake uncontrollably. I instructed my RTO to call in a sitrep as I was in no condition to talk. After shivering for about five minutes, my body gradually started to come down off the adrenalin high and relax. My breathing slowly returned to normal, and a deep fatigue overtook me. I fell asleep, waking only when one of my men kicked me in the foot, telling me to turn over because I had started to snore. No further enemy soldiers came down the trail that night.

We searched the body the next day. He was a skinny VC, in his late teens. He carried a rice ball in a pouch and had a wallet with a few papers and some photos in it. This got passed on to the battalion headquarters. The big prize was the AK-47. It had been unloaded along with a bandolier of ammo. This, too, was passed back to HQ.

Thinking back, what I remember most was the smell of the soldier's sweat and the feel of his blood on my hands as it poured out of his body. There was a warm gush of blood on my right hand as if someone were pouring a bucket of fluid on my hand and arm. I remember the feel of his stubbly beard on my left hand as I clamped it across his mouth and the sweat on his face. I remember the grip of his hand on mine and how it weakened as I drove the knife deep into his chest. And I remember the little gurgling sounds he made as his life slipped away and his body stopped struggling.

To this day I can recall the actions, emotions, and sensations I felt that night, as clearly as when they happened. Twenty years later, I started to have daydreams and relive this experience as well as others on a frequent basis. I was worried that I was losing control.

I sought the advice of a psychiatrist friend to help me deal with the unwelcome thoughts. I made an appointment with her and ended up talking with her for more than three hours, reliving this and other killing experiences. I confessed that none of this had bothered me for many years and I was extremely concerned that now, after 20 years, these horrific experiences were starting to re-visit me. She listened to my stories and finally offered a simple exercise for me to practice. She told me to see the enemy soldier that I killed and allow myself to relive the trauma in as much detail as I could remember. "Visualize the soldier and speak to him," she said. "Tell him that you are sorry you killed him, but you were doing your job as an American soldier and platoon leader. Tell him that you are sorry he died and ask him to forgive you."

"Really?" I said. "It's really that simple? That's all I have to do? Are you telling me that this is going to make those images disappear?"

"Yes," she replied. "Just give it a try."

Amazingly and fortunately, after a few practice sessions of my psychiatrist's advice, the images stopped, and I was no longer tortured by these memories. For a very long time, I had locked this and other horrific experiences away in the back of my mind. I kept thinking I had a titanium trunk there and I could bury these memories and thoughts and lock them away forever. But gradually, some of the experiences seeped back into my consciousness. To this day, I can sharply recall and intensely feel many of the emotions from more than 50 years ago, but I have always adopted a stoic mindset and a resolve to never allow the experiences to affect me. I rarely talk about them, and they remain locked in my magic trunk... but I know they are always there.

CHAPTER 13

Recon by Fire—Enemy Base Camp

"You've been assigned a budget of twenty-five rounds—max."

I always tried to make full use of artillery support and used it generously and carefully. It was an amazing tool, and I formed a great relationship with our FO. I was always careful to coordinate with him before going out on an ambush or on patrol, making sure that he knew my route of travel and identified key landmarks for preplanned fire. Artillery could be extremely precise. The Cav batteries that supported us could put a smoke round or White Phosperous (WP) on target usually within one or two minutes and even faster for preplanned targets. This expertise was always appreciated when I had my face pressed to the ground with bullets flying overhead and could not see more than a few feet in front of me. Furthermore, once rounds had been adjusted, the "fire for effect" using all three guns was overwhelming destruction. Artillery was the first fire support measure I always applied when entering a suspicious area or in a firefight.

My CO received daily intelligence briefings via radio with coordinates encrypted using a code book that changed hourly. These intel estimates came from Division Headquarters and wound their way down through battalion and out to the companies in the field. By the time the information reached the company level, it had been watered down to simple instructions to explore and recon an AO from coordinates X to coordinates Y. The actual routes and tactics to be employed were left up to the CO and the individual platoon leaders.

This daily plan could easily become mundane. But because we had access to tremendous helicopter resources we could be called on at a moment's notice to combat assault into a suspected enemy location. Assuming a clear LZ was available we might be asked to make major terrain relocations at any time of the day. It was common to be "out by the beach" walking through sand, low brush, and tumbleweed, and with little notice be picked up and Charlie Alpha-ed (the letters CA for combat assault) into a one-bird clearing in a densely wooded area or mountainous jungle. The terrain we were in dictated the formation we used and the tactics we employed.

It was not unusual to receive a call to immediately find a landing zone and prepare for pickup within 30 minutes. I would receive the coordinates from the CO where the combat assault was to take place along with a sentence or two of intelligence information about the area, if any. When it was my platoon's turn to lead the assault, I always rode in the first helicopter. It was my responsibility to advise the trailing helicopters if the LZ was "green" or "hot." If it was a hot LZ, the following birds would not be placed at risk, but would circle the area providing covering fire, leaving it up to the men on the first chopper to fight it out with the enemy force on the ground.

Being on that first helicopter was dangerous and nerve-racking. I encountered several hot LZs where we were met by sniper fire or sporadic ground fire aimed at our landing helicopter. The two door gunners on either side of the helicopter would provide intense supporting fire with their machine guns as the birds came in for a landing. I was also on several missions where other platoons encountered hot LZs. When that happened the rest of the company was sometimes diverted to land nearby and move rapidly to support the first bird under fire. When we reached the unit, they often had suffered heavy casualties and the first helicopter was destroyed on the ground.

But the greatest danger of the daily routine was to become complacent. This was easy to do. With the intense heat, soldiers became tired, irritable, and nervous. They had not slept well and became inattentive, weary of carrying their packs, ammunition, water, and weapons. They lost focus and the late afternoons were always the most dangerous time when ambushes could occur.

While my troops acknowledged me as the leader, their trust did not come without reservations. It had to be earned. As their platoon leader, I had to re-earn that trust every day. It meant being as fair as possible about assigning the point team, switching walk positions with my radio operator, being extremely cautious about not pushing the men too hard during high heat and, most important, being cautious about walking through an area that looked or felt suspicious. Employing simple leadership skills—and not taking unnecessary risks—was the way that I won the trust of my platoon sergeant, squad leaders, my immediate support team, and men. Trust was further established because I always rode in the first bird and walked at the front of the line, placing me at continuous risk. These leadership skills were taught as a part of the Infantry Officer Basic and Ranger School training programs, but trust was earned or lost by example in the field.

Another way that I gained the trust and respect of my men was to exercise a strategy of "recon by fire." This meant that I would preplan several artillery plots along my route of march with our FO. These were marked on my map in grease pencil and were easily recognized terrain features such as hill tops, trail intersections or bends in streams. They were given simple names like Red 1, Red 2, and Red 3 and were spaced at 3–5km intervals along the route I was scheduled to follow. This planning was done with the FO before the start of each day's mission.

The FO made sure that his pre-plots were marked on the platoon leader's and platoon sergeant's maps. The advantage was that in the event we got into contact with an enemy force, it became faster and easier to call in the preplanned concentration and then adjust it rather than start from scratch and try to provide one's coordinates, give a compass azimuth to the target, and range. Furthermore, if you were lying on your stomach in a firefight or in deep jungle, it was impossible to know your exact position and try to adjust artillery fire. In deep jungle, adjustment was by dead reckoning. The first round fired was always a smoke round, and adjustment was accomplished by listening to where the round landed, and then estimating its position and distance from your location. Dead reckoning was not a very accurate method, but if you had bullets flying overhead it was often the only choice. The greatest fear I had was making a mistake and calling in fire that was too close to my own position and injuring my men.

But often when I needed to move through areas that had no preplanned artillery concentrations I would exercise "reconnaissance by fire." On one mission, my platoon came over a rise in the terrain that overlooked a thickly wooded area. I had trained my point teams to be alert to any open area where we might see signs of an enemy encampment or where we might be observed by the enemy. We looked for smoke coming from cooking fires or listened for noises coming from enemy soldiers who were not aware we were in the area. My point teams were also trained to trust their gut instincts. If they were suspicious, had uneasy feelings about an area they were approaching or if things didn't seem just right, such as no jungle noises, no birds chirping, no monkeys howling, they were to stop, alert, and call me to the front.

The ideal location for recon by fire was where you could observe a large area, see potential enemy signs, and watch the artillery rounds land and adjust them. So, I made it a habit to call in artillery quite frequently. In fact, I reconned by fire so often that the artillery battery that supported us came to know my call sign by heart. My standard tactic was to provide my grid location in code, compass azimuth, and distance to the center of the target and request "one-gun fire for adjustment." This meant only one artillery piece would fire while I adjusted the landing rounds, but once on target all three artillery pieces in the battery would plot the same corrections as the lead gun and be prepared to fire. If the command "fire for effect" was given, three guns would fire multiple rounds at the target. When this happened, it was a formidable sight.

As my platoon walked through the dense forest my point man alerted. I went forward to see the lead men lying on their bellies at the edge of a ridge and observing the area below. I asked the point man what was happening. He told me he had an uneasy feeling about the area we were scheduled to walk through. Observing the area, I saw what appeared to be a dense and more forested area than what we had just walked through.

I got on the horn to the FO and called in a fire mission using one of the pre-plots he had set up. I gave the standard "recon by fire" as the reason for the fire mission.

There was a longer delay than was usual in responding to my request. Because I shot so much artillery for this purpose, the battery commander had become familiar with my cautionary tactic. When I finally received the call back from the FO, he advised me "You've been assigned a budget of twenty-five rounds—max," I understood that the battery was exercising a measure of cost control. This budget did not include the smoke rounds needed to adjust before firing HE rounds.

I acknowledged the 25-round budget and fired five or six smoke rounds, making 100- and 200m adjustments until I saw the rounds land where I wanted them. I then called for fire for effect adding 100m adjustments in between each set of three volleys. This allowed me to adjust the fire wide and long throughout the area where we were scheduled to walk.

After the 25 rounds had been fired, I told the point man to walk directly through the center of the area that had received the fire. I cautioned him to look for blood trails and body parts. As the platoon moved into the area, we discovered several blood trails which made us move even more cautiously. Again, the point man alerted, and I came to the front. He had stepped into a latrine and the smell of shit permeated the area. We cautiously approached a clearing and entered a sizeable enemy base camp extremely well concealed in the heavily forested area. The camp was complete with a dozen bunkers made from cut timbers with lots of overhead cover for camouflage. We did not encounter any enemy soldiers, and this relieved my troops' anxiety. We had given the enemy plenty of time to leave the area and take their wounded with them. After a sweep of the area, we performed an inventory and reported our find to the CO. This report filtered its way up the chain of command. Cut timbers in a large concealed enemy base camp were a surprise and a real find. The enemy would typically use poles cut from trees to create their camps. Cut timber indicated a more substantial camp.

My platoon was ordered to secure the area and we were eventually joined by the entire company. Later that day we were advised that General William Westmoreland, commanding general (CG) of Vietnam, had decided to pay us a visit at noon the next day to view the bunker complex in person. Wow! That raised the pucker factor tenfold. A visit to the field from the commanding general of Vietnam was most unusual and necessitated cautious planning and security preparation. I made sure all my men were briefed and highly vigilant. We cleaned weapons that night and dug our foxholes a little bit deeper.

The next day, we took great care and precaution to make sure that our company perimeter was dug in, tied in and secure. The last thing anyone wanted was to have General Westmoreland land and have an enemy force attack his helicopter. We sent out security patrols early in the morning to make sure there were no enemy forces in the area. By noon, we were prepared for the CG's visit. Since my platoon had found the enemy base camp, I was told that I would host the general and escort him into the complex. I immediately made a point of cleaning my boots and straightening my uniform. I tried to look as presentable as possible. I even poured a canteen cup of water and lathered my face with soap to wash and shave off several weeks of growth on my face. There was nothing I could do about how I smelled; the CG was just going to have to keep his distance.

As the CG's chopper landed, my greatest concern was whether to salute or not. Because of the danger of snipers, it was forbidden to salute officers or to use their rank when referring to them. But this was the highest-ranking officer in Vietnam, and I was not about to fail to salute him. The chopper landed and it was the Deputy Commanding General, Creighton Abrams, who stepped off. We were notified only moments before that Westmoreland sent his second in command to view the enemy encampment. General Abrams was a two-star general at the time, but I was not disappointed in the least as I met him just off the landing zone. "Lieutenant Bartlett reporting, Sir," I said to the general and proceeded to deliver as snappy a salute as I could muster with my M16 slung over my shoulder. The general did not return my salute, but instead stuck out his hand and shook mine, saying: "I understand it was your platoon that discovered this base camp. How did you find it?" "We smelled the latrine, sir, and that led us into the center of the camp." "Shit does smell, doesn't it, Lieutenant?" "Yes sir, it sure does," I responded. "It's a dead give-away."

I took a minute to brief the general on the positions of my platoon and the company around the perimeter and reassure him that he was in a safe and secure area. We then proceeded down the hill from the LZ into the enemy camp. As we approached the first bunker, the general walked through the doorway without hesitation. It was pitch-black inside and the first thing he said was: "Do you have a flashlight?" Having thoroughly explored all the bunkers, I had the foresight to hand him the only flashlight we had in our platoon. We sat down on the rough benches inside the large bunker and carried on a brief conversation about the location of the enemy camp, its size, and the number of men likely to have occupied the area. We were joined by my company commander. I was happy to have another officer there to comment and answer the general's questions about how well camouflaged and hidden the camp had been. It had been dumb luck to have walked into it. The general wanted to know if we had encountered any NVA troops and we told him, "Not recently, our firefights have all been with VC."

After about 20 minutes, the general's aide stepped into the bunker. He said that the chopper was in-bound to pick him up. We promptly stood within the tight confines of the bunker, saluted, and watched as the general left, climbed up the hill and back into his chopper as it landed to pick him up.

The entire visit lasted a total of 30 minutes. I was amazed that a two-star general would fly out to look at an empty bunker complex where the most outstanding feature was cut timbers. But I assume it was significant because of its size, location, and degree of camouflage. The top brass and planners wanted to "see for themselves" what we had stumbled upon.

Our company hung out for another day as another chopper landed bearing demolition specialists who rigged explosives throughout the camp. Then, our company packed up and moved out, taking three different routes to our next night defensive perimeter (NDP). After about 45 minutes of walking, we heard the explosions of the bunkers being blown. The whole event was treated as just another day in country, although for me, the meeting was a never-to-be-forgotten experience.

CHAPTER 14

Beyond Artillery Cover

"Turn around. Come back. You're out of artillery range."

The 1st Air Cav Division prided itself on aerial troop support. This not only included fire support in the form of Huey and Cobra helicopter gunships, and jets, but also close-in artillery support from 105mm, 155mm and 8-inch howitzers. As a combat infantry platoon leader, I had experience using and directing all these assets. The gunships and the ARA were sometimes easier to direct because the pilots could often see your position and I could talk with them to give instructions. When calling in ARA, it was critical to mark my forward position with smoke and have the pilot confirm the color and the direction of the path of attack to avoid hitting friendlies. While the attacks were fearsome and deadly, being able to talk with the pilot in a firefight was always reassuring. The pilots I encountered were super-cautious about wanting to know exactly where my troops were and refused to fire unless positions were clearly marked. They also made doubly sure of the enemy intelligence I was giving them: location of the enemy position and how close to my lines before they fired rockets and minigun bursts.

The Cobra helicopter, armed with rockets on the wing pods and a front nose minigun firing bursts of thousands of rounds, was always a welcome sight when my unit was pinned down by enemy fire in a firefight in open terrain. However, these incredible resources were not as effective in mountainous jungle where smoke would be caught in three-canopy growth overhead. On several occasions, I resorted to chopping down trees to open a hole in the canopy and tying a smoke grenade to the end of a long branch, raising it high overhead to allow the smoke to penetrate the hole and confirm my position.

I was always leery of having that first artillery round land too close. Short rounds (rounds that land short of the target) and the danger of being hit by friendly fire were always something I was extremely concerned about. Consequently, I always asked for the first shot to be a smoke round. This was a safe technique only if you could actually see or hear the round land. It was also extremely important that

I knew exactly where I was on the map. A miscalculation by a few hundred meters with any of these measurements could spell disaster. My habit when requesting a fire mission was to state, "danger close," and when finished with adjustments and ready to give the command "fire for effect," I frequently requested only "one-gun fire and one-gun fire for effect" (rather than three). This controlled the volume of high-explosive (HE) rounds landing on the target.

But the use of artillery support was a godsend. Even smoke rounds landing anywhere near an enemy position was usually enough to rout them and cause them to break off a firefight. When HE rounds are fired, they carry a tremendous punch and will typically wipe out anything within a 50–75m radius, not to mention causing soldiers (both friend and foe) to lose their bowels on the spot. They were less effective in dense jungle because of trees and undergrowth that absorbed the shrapnel, but when the call came and 6–10 rounds were dropped on top of a suspected enemy position, the impact was overwhelming. I often wondered how anyone, or anything, could survive such a deadly barrage.

On one hot, sweltering day (hotter than usual at around 110 degrees), we were operating in hilly terrain. I was leading the platoon on a search and destroy mission, taking a semi-circular walk of 5–6km out from the company CP. My landmark was a dirt road (actually more of a foot trail) that would lead us back to the company CP. Our FO had plotted the usual artillery concentrations along the way, placing them on recognizable terrain features.

The trip out was uneventful. I had my point man and cover man far out front because we were in semi-open terrain. I could see for several hundred meters for a change. It was difficult to navigate, however, because everything was relatively flat, and the available landmarks were inconsequential. There were no streams, no trail networks, and no distinguishing features showing on the map other than a lonely hill with only slight elevation. Consequently, my point man ended up walking farther than expected. After about an hour's march, I called a halt, and we took 10 minutes to rest and drink water. I put out security to the front, rear and both sides. We had not seen any sign of Charlie all morning, but I did not want to take the chance of having a sniper sneak up on us and put a bullet into someone or me.

I examined my map and called in our coordinates using the current security codes issued to us. A new code book was issued weekly with a new page of codes for each day. Numbers and letters had to be looked up and substituted for map coordinates. The codes changed every hour. Within five minutes of calling in my position, I received a call from the FO asking me to confirm the coordinates I had just given. I double checked my map and the code book to make sure I had provided the right numbers and transferred the codes correctly. I was positive I was within 100m of where I was positioning myself on the map. I called the FO back and confirmed my location. The FO came back on the radio asking what code book and time I was using, and I again confirmed the code book for that day and time.

Then he called back and told me: "Turn around. Come back. You're out of artillery range." We had walked too far and had exceeded the maximum range of the 105mm battery that was providing cover support for our mission. So, we packed up and headed back the way we came.

After 500m, we branched off and continued our original line of march moving in a semicircle—this time under the safe canopy of artillery cover. While the terrain was easy to move through, it was exceedingly hot. My men were sweating, tired and running low on water. I called another halt and had the men take cover wherever they could find it. About this time, I got a call from the company commander informing me that a resupply bird was on its way to the CP, and it was bringing ice cream. He encouraged me to make our way back to the CP as quickly as possible—before it melted. Ice cream was a real treat. We rarely had it and unless we hurried back all that would be left would be warm cream.

So, I got the men saddled up and started our movement back to the CP at a rapid clip. We were strung out in a long line that began to experience the accordion effect. If the point man walked slowly, the men following him would bunch up and lose proper interval. If the front of the line walked too fast, the men at the rear would have to run to catch up. And that was what was happening to my platoon. In my desire to have the men enjoy some cold ice cream, I had pushed forward too quickly and the men at the rear of the column had to run to catch up. After about 10 minutes of forced march, I got a call from my platoon sergeant at the end of the column telling me that if I kept up the pace, several men would pass out from heat exhaustion.

I decided that ice cream was not worth having men pass out and called for another 10-minute break. My platoon sergeant came forward to bitterly complain about the rapid pace I had set. I explained about the ice cream, but with sweat pouring off him he told me that making men run to catch up in 110-degree heat was not a very smart thing to do. He was right.

That day resulted in two important lessons I never forgot: first, always stay under the canopy of artillery cover and second, never make your men run unless you are in a firefight and lives are at stake… no matter how great the ice cream might have tasted.

CHAPTER 15

LZ is Green

*I told my RTO: "After you hit the ground, count to 15 slowly and
if you don't hear any fire and if you are still alive, call the battalion
commander and say: 'LZ is green, I repeat, LZ is green.'"*

I made at least 60 "Charlie Alphas" (helicopter combat assaults) during my time in
the field and was awarded the Air Medal with oak leaf cluster. You earned one Air
Medal for the first 30 combat assaults and an oak leaf cluster for the second 30.

Each day, one platoon was designated as the quick reaction force (QRF). The
position was alternated through each regiment and battalion so that a fresh platoon
was assigned the responsibility. The designated platoon was to be on full alert for the
entire day. The men were stationed at the helipad, armed, loaded, and ready to go as
quickly as the pilots could fire up the engines on the Hueys that were also stationed
on the helipad. If the division intelligence (G-2) received information about enemy
movement, they could have a combat platoon of 30 men in the air and assaulting a
position within 10–15 minutes of the alert. The rest of the company—and even an
entire battalion—could be in the air within two hours should the contact escalate.

Being the QRF platoon was not a pleasant duty assignment because you never
knew if you were going to be called on to make an assault, or if you would spend
the day sitting in the shade. The latter meant waiting at the edge of the helipad,
smoking cigarettes, drinking water, eating C-Rats, and hoping for 5 PM to arrive,
bringing an end to your assignment and another platoon to replace you.

If a platoon was to be combat assaulted, the platoon leader received a briefing
from the battalion S-2 prior to launch advising him of the nature of the potential
engagement. Sometimes, however, there wasn't time for the S-2 to come to the
airfield. Then the briefing was delivered over the radio. Often, there was only a brief
radio communication with the pilots who were also receiving a briefing on weather,
wind direction, and landing conditions if known.

One day in late July my platoon was designated as the QRF platoon. We hung
around all day trying to avoid the heat, reading anything that was available, catching

up on sleep, and letter writing. At around 2 PM, a call came over the radio from my company commander instructing me to get my platoon ready to make an immediate assault. He told me that a reinforced enemy company had been spotted and the entire battalion had been put on alert with my platoon leading the engagement. Only eight helicopters were available for the mission, and of these, two were reserved for the battalion commander. This meant that the six choppers carrying my platoon would be dropping us into a potentially "hot LZ," then returning to pick up the rest of the company and assaulting one platoon at a time until all three platoons were on the ground. This was a hairy situation because my platoon would be on the ground fighting it out while the helicopters were making the return trip to pick up more troops.

I roused my men and told my platoon sergeant to double check their gear and make sure there was plenty of ammo and water. I ran to the edge of the airfield where I was met by the S-2 who was a captain. He showed me where the LZ was located; I marked the location on my map with a grease pencil. His briefing lasted about three minutes and went something like this:

> We have intel of a suspected reinforced enemy company moving through this area from north to south within the last two hours. We suspect they are still in the area. The LZ is within three hundred meters of their last known location. It will be prepped with arty for 10 minutes and then lifted to allow two Cobras to work the perimeter. Your mission is to secure the LZ so the rest of the company can be inserted. The LZ is small and will only allow one bird to land at a time. As there are only six choppers available, you will hold the perimeter for 20 minutes while the choppers make the return trip to pick up the next platoon and return. Cobras will be on station for close air support if you get into trouble. The battalion commander will be overhead directing the operation.
>
> You are to notify the battalion CO within 15 seconds of landing if the LZ is red (hot) or green (safe). If hot, you will fight with what you've got on the first bird. We won't risk additional men or choppers if you hit the shit. You will have to fight it out on your own. So, make sure you have a heavy machine gun and grenade launchers with you. We will not send in additional support until you can verify that you have a secure perimeter. Understand?

Those were my instructions. I asked how firm the intel was and was told "about 60 percent." What he did not know was if the enemy force was still in the area or if they had moved on. The S-2 also advised me that from experience, he knew that the enemy *may* have identified the LZ, and *may* have dug in, waiting to fire on the first helicopter to land. They would take out the first one as it came in for a landing thereby preventing additional choppers from coming in. If this should happen, there was another LZ about three klicks away where the rest of the company could go in. If the LZ was hot, I was to call in ARA and arty and hold my position. I was not to engage any enemy positions directly, just return fire. The final instructions were: "Secure the LZ, and make sure there are no enemy in the immediate area that could attack landing helicopters. Other birds will not land until you report the LZ is green."

I returned to my platoon to brief my platoon sergeant on what I had been told. I asked if he thought I should tell the squad leaders. We talked about it for a few minutes. There was always a danger in giving the troops too much unsubstantiated intel because it just made them nervous and more trigger-happy than usual. In this case, because only one bird would be landing at a time, we decided to tell the men everything. If we were going to get into trouble, it would be after the first several birds had landed. Then the enemy had a clear opportunity to take out one or more of the landing helicopters making it impossible for subsequent birds to land. We decided to downplay the intelligence, telling the troops that it was strongly believed the enemy force had moved on.

Riding in the first bird, I brought extra firepower with me consisting of two machine gunners, two ammo bearers with M16s, and two grenadiers. This left positions for myself, my radio operator, and the squad leader, all armed with M16s. Nine men would be on the first flight. One machine gunner and ammo bearer would be on each side of the bird and the rest of us on the floor and seat of the chopper. After landing, the men would immediately move to either side of the perimeter and set up firing positions. My radio operator and I would exit on the right side and tie in with the soldiers on that side. I showed each man where we were going to land and the locations of the preplanned artillery fire that surrounded the LZ. In the event anyone was hit, each man would be able to call in both artillery and ARA fire support.

I double checked each man making sure he carried an extra bandolier of ammo and several smoke grenades. I told them if the LZ was hot, the plan would be to move to the opposite end of the LZ from where the enemy fire was coming. We would set up a secure firing position, return fire and call for fire support.

Every man, myself included, was extremely nervous at being on the first chopper going into that LZ. I reassured the men that the LZ would be thoroughly peppered with artillery for 10 minutes. Nothing could survive a barrage like that. Furthermore, ARA assets would be flying overhead. I assured them we would be well supported.

As I finished my briefing, I could hear the first chopper winding up. I directed the platoon to split in half. Each squad would load half its men from the right side of the helicopter and half from the left. We moved into position and waited for the crew chief to signal he was ready for us to board. After receiving his signal, we ran, holding on to our helmets, bending low, and squinting to avoid the dust from the rotor wash. There was room on the bench seat for four men. I sat in the middle with my RTO and squad leader next to me. The rest of the men sat on the floor. I noticed no one slung his feet outside the door as the men usually did when the ride was routine.

The lead bird lifted off. I pulled out my map to try to get some idea of where we were, but it was impossible to navigate as the chopper was flying too fast. So, I put the map back in my thigh pocket and took a big swig of water. I knew the flight time to the LZ was about 10 minutes. After about 5 minutes, I crawled forward, and put on the spare headset and told the pilot that I wanted my men to chamber their guns and test fire a few rounds out the door. The pilot said OK and that he would tell me when we were five minutes out. He added that the artillery would end its prep with white phosphorus (WP) rounds to signal they were finished. If his helicopter started taking fire as he came in for a landing, he was not going to risk the chopper. He would pull up and get out of the area. I told him that was fine with me.

Five minutes passed and I got the signal from the crew chief. I told each man to put a clip in their guns and fire three rounds out the door. We took turns moving to the door and firing quick bursts. Then off in the distance, through the front of the helicopter, we could see artillery rounds landing. We were close enough to hear and feel the shock waves as we got within a couple of miles of the LZ. The pilot had told me that as soon as the arty was lifted the two Cobras escorting our flight would work the area. They would use their miniguns and save their rockets in case the LZ was hot. I acknowledged this about the time that the WP rounds landed signaling the end of the artillery barrage.

At that point, the two Cobras flying parallel to us lowered their noses and flew at high speed ahead of my lead bird. We watched as they flew in tight circles around the LZ and saw streams of tracers coming out of their miniguns. This reassured me somewhat that we would have a safe landing. We knew the Cobras would provide close air support upon landing if we got into trouble. If there was an enemy unit in the area they would be spotted and eliminated.

The crew chief yelled above the noise that we were "three minutes out." I held out two smoke canisters: one green and one red. I would pop the correct color depending on what happened after we landed.

I leaned over to my RTO and told him: "After you hit the ground, count to 15 slowly and if you don't hear any fire and if you are still alive, call the battalion commander and say: 'LZ is green, I repeat, LZ is green.' Don't wait for a reply, just say 'LZ is green.' If we are taking fire, tell him 'LZ is hot, I repeat, LZ is hot—we are taking fire'—and give him the direction where the fire is coming from." I then made the RTO repeat these instructions back to me. He got it right the second time. It was clear he was nervous about the landing and making the call. I was too.

Then the crew chief screamed "Get ready!" and the door gunners on the chopper opened fire toward the edges of the perimeter as we slowed. The tail of the chopper dipped as we started to land. The door gunners fired for 20–30 seconds and ceased the moment we touched down. We waited for the crew chief to give us the signal to dismount. By this time, my machine gunners were both standing on the skids on either side of the chopper, holding on as we came to within 15 feet. This was a dangerous move, but they had done it many times before. They wanted to dismount and start running for cover just as soon as possible. The chopper hovered for a few seconds and then we felt the skids touch the ground. The crew chief yelled "Go,

Go, Go!" and we were out the door, bending low, running for the right edge of the perimeter.

Or at least I thought we had all dismounted. My radio operator was still in his seat, trying to unbuckle the seat belt he had fastened around his waist. He couldn't figure out how to release the buckle. The crew chief came over, unfastened the belt, and helped him out the door. The PRC-25 radio on his back weighed about 35 lbs. It was positioned high at the top of his pack frame and back, just below his helmet. The cord to the handset ran under his arm and clipped into the loop on his load-bearing equipment (LBE). A plastic bag covered the handset protecting it from sweat. As my RTO finally jumped down from the chopper, he bent too far forward. The momentum of the jump with the radio high on his back caused him to do a forward roll. This shook the poor man up even more; I turned around and ran back to try to help him to his feet. He had landed hard, and he had lost his helmet and the handset had come loose. The fall knocked the wind out of him and bloodied his knee. So, I lay down beside him, and told him to relax and catch his breath. I pulled the handset cord to us as we lay in the center of the LZ. Meanwhile, the chopper rose and left us, blowing dust and dirt everywhere. Suddenly, all the noise of the helicopter and rotor wash was gone. An eerie silence came over the area. I yelled at my men on either side of the LZ asking if they were OK and if everything was secure. I got an OK back from both groups.

By this time, my RTO had regained his composure and said he had lost the count. I told him to go ahead and call the battalion CO and say the LZ was green while I got ready to pop the green smoke grenade. He did this perfectly, saying: "LZ is green, I repeat LZ is green." The battalion CO acknowledged the transmission personally, saying "Roger, LZ is green," and then added, "Who are those men lying at the center of the LZ? Get them out of there. They're supposed to be securing the perimeter." I told the RTO to acknowledge with a "Roger that," and to pick himself up and follow me to the edge of the perimeter. I threw the green smoke grenade into the center of the LZ and grabbed the radio handset saying, "Smoke popped." I got a response from the next helicopter pilot saying, "Roger, I have green smoke." I acknowledged the use of green smoke. (The practice of popping smoke and having a pilot confirm the color was standard procedure and avoided the possibility that an enemy force might pop a smoke grenade and try to lure a chopper into a different location.)

The birds carrying the rest of my platoon landed, each bringing an additional eight men. As they offloaded, they fanned out in an ever-widening circle taking up firing positions around the perimeter. At the same time, the Cobra pilots circling overhead called and asked if I wanted them to fire on any suspected areas. I responded saying that I could not direct their fire because the jungle was too thick to see any terrain features.

The Cobra pilots said they could see our smoke and they would stay on station in case support was needed while the transporting choppers returned to base to pick up the next platoon. They would concentrate their fire well away from our position after the last chopper had departed. The two Cobras continued to patrol around the LZ in ever-widening circles in search of any enemy. My men gradually relaxed having not encountered any enemy fire.

The second platoon soon landed. They moved into their sector of the perimeter and sent out a patrol toward the last known enemy location given to us in the briefing. The third platoon and the company commander followed suit. Each platoon moved off in a different direction in search of a non-existent enemy force—fortunately—this time.

My medic bandaged my RTO's knee. The man walked with a limp for several days afterwards. The assault turned out to be a non-event. If enemy had been present they left as soon as the bombardment began.

CHAPTER 16

Autorotate

*Suddenly, there was no noise. No noise at all. The engine had
simply stopped, and I knew we were all going to die.*

I did a lot of flying in Vietnam: Caribous, C-130s, and even an Otter, and, of
course, helicopters—both Chinooks (commonly called "Shit Hooks") and Hueys
(UH-1Ds). I even had a short ride in a Light Observation Helicopter (LOH). We
went everywhere by chopper. I made a lot of flights, often every day and sometimes
twice a day.

In the afternoon, in dense jungle, we would chop down trees with machetes to
clear a hole so that supplies (water, ammo, C-Rats) could be kicked out to us. If a
helicopter could land, water was delivered in 5-gallon "Jerry cans." We had to be
careful cutting a hole large enough for a chopper to land. There was no worse sound
than hearing helicopter blades chop through branches if you failed to cut the hole
wide enough. And if this happened, pilots would refuse to hover until you chopped
down more trees and eliminated the danger.

If opening a large enough hole in the canopy was impossible, water was placed
in washed out 8-inch artillery powder containers and kicked out of the door by
the crew chief along with C-Rats and ammo. A common delivery method in dense
jungle, this was often the only way to get fresh water, but it always had a metallic
taste even if the canisters had been thoroughly washed. When this happened, we
were faced with the problem of what to do with the containers the next day after
everyone had filled their canteens and bladders. The danger was that the canisters
could be turned into excellent IEDs by the enemy. The only solution was to place
them in a foxhole and throw a thermite grenade on top which would burn a hole
through the metal. Using thermite grenades was always a dangerous proposition.
But in dense jungle with no way for a bird to land to retrieve the canisters and
no way to carry the containers, thermite grenades were the only answer. Access to
fresh water was essential as the army did not want troops drinking from streams
or trying to purify the water. Resupply of ammo in a firefight was also a common
practice. The helicopter would fly over and drop a bag filled with bandoliers of

ammo from 50–60 feet overhead. This was a very welcome sight—as long as you weren't directly underneath.

Getting on and off choppers became commonplace in the Cav. The doors were always wide open and within a few seconds of lifting off everything became cool. The sweat and dirt dried on your skin. Flying was a welcome relief from the intense heat.

Many of my men were comfortable sitting in the door with feet dangling out. As the bird approached an LZ, they would step out onto the skids and jump to the ground just as the skids were touching down. The crew chief and pilots hated this because these soldiers became prime targets for snipers on final approach. Not only that, if incoming fire was received as the bird started to land, the pilot would want to "pull pitch," accelerate, and fly out of the area, possibly leaving behind a soldier who had already jumped to the ground.

The Bell UH-1 Iroquois Helicopters (Hueys) we flew had a canvas bench seat along the back wall between the door gunners where four men could sit. The rest of the men sat on the floor or in the door. It was not a comfortable seat but being cool for any length of flight time was always welcome.

We were trained and constantly reminded to be alert to the main and tail rotor blades when exiting the aircraft. You learned to bend low and never stand up straight until you were well clear of the aircraft. Blowing dust and dirt made helicopter landings or takeoffs dangerous. When directing a bird to land, you never stood on high ground for fear of decapitation.

There was a strict procedure for calling in helicopters to land or hover. We would receive a radio call from the pilot that the bird was inbound. Everyone was told to move to the edge of the perimeter and secure their gear, as the rotor wash would blow up anything that was not tied down. Upon final approach, the pilot would radio to "pop smoke." A smoke canister would then be thrown into the center of the LZ, and the pilot was told that smoke had been popped. The pilot would confirm the color of the smoke, followed by a reply from the ground that the color was correct. This insured a friendly landing zone. The smoke also helped the pilot determine the wind direction and speed. (The NVA and VC also had smoke canisters—usually ones we had left behind.)

You were surrounded by a cloud of dust and grit as you tried to direct a helicopter to land. The pilot would lower the tail of the helicopter just before landing to reduce forward motion and transition to a hover. At this point, he was dependent on the man in front on the ground to provide hand and arm landing signals. This man directed the pilot when to hover (holding arms horizontal) and when to lower the craft to the ground (pumping arms up and down) as well as move left or right. The door gunners and crew chief were always alert to flying debris that might be blown into the engine. Loose gear could be a major problem. Troops were notorious for not lashing down ponchos and poncho liners. If one of these came loose and was sucked into the engine the helicopter could be wiped out.

Sometimes my platoon sergeant would volunteer to take the lead bird into a CA. This was a responsibility I took very seriously and did not share. But when returning to base camp, I would usually let my platoon sergeant (1-5) take the lead.

A minister came out to our company on one occasion to deliver Sunday services. Our company was suddenly called to prepare for a Charlie Alpha and my platoon was designated as the lead. The minister asked if he could ride in the lead bird with me. I respectfully declined, but the minister wanted to see what it was like to be in the lead helicopter, watch the artillery preparation and see the Cobras work the perimeter before the first troops landed. He appealed to the company commander who informed him that the decision was mine. I had to tell the minister no. If he was in the lead helicopter and we got into a firefight, it would reduce my firepower by one man. Should the LZ be hot I needed every gun I could get. (The minister ended up riding in the second bird, much to his regret.)

Helicopters are noisy. If you're not wearing a headset, it is impossible to hear what's being said unless you're shouting right into the ear of the person next to you. Because of the noise and the inability to communicate during flight, travel time was usually spent sitting quietly. This was a chance to reflect on whatever was in your mind at the time. Thoughts of home would often come to mind: girlfriends, parties, good times shared and, occasionally, what thoughts and plans you had for the future—assuming you made it through the shit. And everyone... everyone wanted to make it through.

As we got close to the LZ, I tried to pinpoint our location often speaking with the co-pilot to have him point it out on my map. I'd then give the command to my soldiers to load and check their weapons and fire a few rounds out the door. We waited for the helicopter to hover with men sometimes standing on the skids ready to jump off. If we landed or hovered a few feet above the ground the crew chief would give the command to go, go, go!

Landing and taking off were always the most vulnerable times for a helicopter, crew, and the men on board. Helicopter pilots were busy making sure that they could put the bird down safely. The door gunners were usually blasting away at the surrounding perimeter so that if there were any enemy present, they would be ducking down, not able to draw a bead on the chopper, pilots, or men. And the troops all wanted to get off and away from the landing helicopter and take cover at the edge of the perimeter as quickly as possible. The dirt and grit thrown up by the rotor wash always complicated landings. Everyone worried about being shot at during this most vulnerable moment. The pilots were supposed to wear heavy bulletproof vests with thick ceramic breast plates slipped into them. These vests and plates weighed in at more than 30 lbs and were hot and restrictive. It was rare to see the pilots wear them. Rather, they would sit on the bulletproof plate to give themselves a slight measure of protection from below. The most vulnerable parts of a helicopter are the front windows and the transmission. A bullet through the front window was bound to cause injury to the pilot or co-pilot; and a round in the transmission could cause the engine to fail. Bullets in the tail rotor could also cause the helicopter to rotate wildly and go into a crash landing. That is why door gunners opened up in bursts as the first bird came in for a landing. The men, of course, were always cautious of the door gunner's fire. The door gunners were supposed to stop firing as the troops disembarked, but sometimes continued to fire over their heads. This was a scary situation. The whole landing process usually took less than 20 seconds, but often seemed like an eternity.

Letter: 28 August 1968, A Company, 1/5 Cav, 1st Air Cav Division, 33 days in field, I Corps, Vietnam (letter to college classmate)

Made a Charlie Alpha yesterday together with three other companies and a group of "baby carriages" [APCs—Armored Personnel Carriers] to cordon a large village where an NVA battalion was suspected to be hiding. We were positioned in a rice paddy with warm, leech-infested muddy water up to our knees about 500m from the village. They prepped the village with four batteries: three 105s, and an 8-inch. I have never seen such destruction. The first three minutes was all Variably Timed artillery shells (VT), designed to explode in the air. It blew the village apart. We killed 67 NVA and captured another 30, beaucoup weapons and equipment. Now I am back in the hills performing our screening mission. The fire power of the Cav never ceases to amaze me.

My knowledge of helicopter mechanics was limited to getting into and out of them, flying from point A to B, speaking briefly to the pilots and following the instructions of the crew chief. My greatest concern was for the safety of my men, getting them on and off. I wanted them off the bird with no sprained ankles or spills and then quickly moving to secure the perimeter for the next bird to land. I had never heard of the term "autorotate." I did not know that a pilot could do a controlled crash landing in the event of main engine failure. I had heard about helicopter crashes in other battalions but had been fortunate never to witness a crash.

On one occasion my platoon had been called on to secure the perimeter for a downed helicopter that had crashed after taking enemy fire. We landed near the crashed bird, secured the site, and watched as a giant Sikorsky crane helicopter came in and hovered overhead. A sling was connected to the crashed bird. The Sikorsky simply picked up the damaged bird and flew it away either to be repaired or used for parts. Our division went through a lot of helicopters. There were always plenty of stories circulating about choppers that had been fired on or shot down. But I ignored most of these stories because there was little I could do to change the equation. I was the leader; I was to fly in the lead bird and what would be, would be. We simply prayed for cold LZs.

In August, my company had been called upon to be a blocking force surrounding a village that was being searched by the Army of South Vietnam (ARVN) soldiers. The company was picked up at first light and dropped about 3 klicks from the village. The idea was to set up a perimeter around the village. If any Viet Cong troops were trapped in the village, they would be found by the ARVNs conducting the village search. It was always preferable to have South Vietnamese troops conducting searches because of language issues. My troops were nervous and trigger-happy because we were used to operating in areas where there were no friendlies. If we encountered someone in the boonies, the rules of engagement for our AO allowed us to shoot to kill. No friendlies were to be found in the area.

But the blocking force mission was an exception. It was one of the very few times when I was even close to a "friendly" village. It was early dawn as we moved through low, brushy terrain into our blocking positions. My point man suddenly alerted; I was called to the front. He had discovered an American hand grenade with the pin pulled, stuffed in a C-Ration can with a tripwire across the trail. If he had taken another step along the path, his boot would have caught the tripwire and pulled the hand grenade out of the can. This was one of the most common types of booby traps used against us. The VC used our own hand grenades and C-Ration cans to create these booby traps.

We cut the tripwire and marked the area where the grenade was located with toilet paper, so an EOD team could be called in to disarm it. We did not deal with such situations ourselves as it was possible that the grenade might have been hooked to another booby trap. Nobody wanted to touch a live grenade.

The day proved uneventful. We set up our blocking perimeter and tied into the platoons on our left and right. Two men were stationed every hundred meters or so. The men pulled out their poncho liners to keep the sun off while one man stood guard and one man slept, read, or ate. The men took turns watching the village for any signs of escaping enemy soldiers. We saw the ARVNs land and move into the village. They would methodically go through every hooch in the village looking for weapons, tunnels, and interrogating villagers, but our blocking force was far enough away that we did not directly observe this activity. If ammo caches or weapons had been found, the people living in that hooch would have been taken into custody. Then the hooch would have been burned. But throughout the day, we heard no shooting and no hooches were set on fire.

At around 4 PM, I received a call from my company commander directing me to return to the booby trap and help the EOD team locate the hand grenade. (The toilet paper we used to mark the spot had been blown away.) I took my radio operator and two men. We met the EOD team and showed them where the grenade was on the trail. They blew it in place, and we returned to our perimeter. After that, my CO called and told me to assemble my platoon in the same area where we had landed in the morning. Birds would be in-bound to pick us up in 30 minutes. I moved the platoon and we quickly humped back to the LZ, secured it, and got ready for the call from the inbound helicopters.

It wasn't a long wait. I separated my three squads so that the four helicopters could land in the field with plenty of space between them. Four men were placed on the left side of where the chopper was to land; three on the right with the fourth man responsible for popping smoke and directing the chopper where to land. Again, I would be riding in the lead helicopter.

Things went smoothly. Smoke was popped, the birds identified the smoke and there was plenty of room for them to land in the field. As soon as the birds touched down, the men ran to the doors from the left and the right. I was the last man to board the first chopper. The only space available was sitting in the door with my feet dangling out, a position I was not fond of. As we lifted off the ground, we heard three pops coming from the field between our location and the village. We were taking fire. The pilot pulled pitch, turned, and accelerated at a tremendous rate of speed. I grabbed onto the door frame as we launched into the air away from the enemy fire. The door gunner on the right side opened up with a blast aimed at a puff of white smoke where the enemy fire had originated.

Within seconds, we were away from the LZ and climbing to about 1,200 to 1,300 feet above the ground. The helicopter had been hit by the three rounds, but everything seemed fine. We were on our way back to base camp. Then, suddenly, there was no noise. No noise at all. The engine had simply stopped, and I knew we were all going to die. Flashing lights appeared on the helicopter dashboard. Loud chirping noises came from the instrument panel. The three enemy shots had hit the transmission and that was enough to cause it to stop working. The blades were still turning, but there was no engine. We were at some 1,200 feet in the air and the engine had just stopped. The nose tipped down and we started to descend at an alarming rate. I was frozen, hanging on to the door frame and seat leg. I started to pray as I knew these were going to be my last moments alive. We were going to crash and die in a burning mess. I heard several men start to pray as well as a few who screamed "Ohhhhhhh, shit!" The pilot kept yelling "It's OK, it's OK, I'm gonna autorotate."

"What the fuck is autorotate?" I thought while mentally preparing myself for the crash. We were going down, the nose pointing toward the ground. I briefly thought: "This must be the way people in a falling elevator must feel moments before it crashes at the bottom." I held on to the door frame and seat leg with all my might.

Looking through the front window of the aircraft, I saw the pilot was aiming for a small clearing. The ground was coming up fast and everything remained quiet except for the chirping instrument panel. My men were all saying prayers and holding on to anything they could grab. The pilots were busy with hand movements and instrument panel switches which were beyond my comprehension. As we got within about 100 feet of the ground, the pilot suddenly pulled hard on the control stick and the tail of the helicopter dipped down dramatically. The helicopter flared, nose rising high in the air. Then, the rotor blades suddenly engaged. I didn't know it then, but this maneuver is like placing a car's engine in first gear when going downhill. The helicopter's descent slowed, and we coasted forward just enough to come down in the open area. We hit hard but did not crash with full force. I bounced about 3 feet in the air when it landed. I would have fallen out of the chopper if I had not had a death grip on the bench seat. We hit so hard it spread the skids—as I later learned, this is a feature helicopters are designed with. Acting like shock absorbers, they cushion the body of the helicopter and thereby allow it to survive a controlled crash.

The crew chief and pilots were all yelling: "Get out, get out, get out!" The danger at this point was not only the possibility of enemy in the area, but for the engine to catch fire. I saw the crew chief had grabbed a fire extinguisher and I needed no further encouragement to get out. I yelled at my men to get out, run and take up firing positions, but they were already out the door. Fortunately, there was no fire. My legs were rubbery as I jumped out and ran with my RTO, keeping my head low and away from the still swirling main rotor blades. We quickly set up a perimeter on the left and right sides of the bird. We had my eight men, plus the crew chief, two door gunners and two pilots who were armed with .45 pistols. Pistols don't provide much firepower and it was hard to create a complete circle around the downed helicopter with so few men. We did the best we could, finding cover and taking up firing positions.

Two other helicopters had followed us down and began to circle our makeshift perimeter, but they were fully loaded and could not pick anyone up. Thanks to our pilot's skill, no one was injured—although we were all thoroughly shaken. The pilot spoke on my radio with the two helicopters overhead and were told they would stay on station for as long as they could. Unfortunately, their fuel was running low, and they could circle for only a few minutes. A mayday call had been put through; Cobra helicopters would be overhead in 10–15 minutes and two replacement choppers were also en route with another platoon coming in to reinforce and provide security to my downed squad.

It seemed like hours as we lay in wet grass waiting for the replacement choppers and reinforcements. We were fortunate there were no enemy in the area as we were in an extremely vulnerable position. If Charlie had been in the area he could have easily attacked and killed all of us. Finally, the replacement birds arrived and were able to land near the damaged chopper. We loaded up and completed the ride back to base camp leaving the additional platoon behind to secure the downed chopper.

I thanked our pilot profusely for saving our lives. He told me that they had had plenty of training on how to autorotate in the event a situation like this might occur. I told him that was certainly a good thing to know, but it would have even been better if someone had explained what autorotation was to me before this had happened. The pilot told me that they don't do that intentionally because sometimes autorotation doesn't work.

Getting off the return flight back to base camp was one of the happiest moments I spent in Vietnam. I got down on my hands and knees and kissed the ground. But, after a few minutes of thanking God for still being alive, it was time to move on, get my men into the chow line and assigned to their bunkers. The daily routine continued, and we moved on. After a lot of talk about what each of us thought and did during those tense moments, we put the incident behind us and took it for granted.

CHAPTER 17

Stream Crossing

Then, after a minute, we felt two strong tugs on the rope.
We pulled hard to bring the man to the surface.

One of the most valuable lessons I learned in Ranger School was the importance of having a coil of strong rope and a couple of snap links (carabiners). So before leaving for Vietnam, I visited an outdoor sports shop and bought 100 feet of half-inch rope and two strong snap links. I carried this coil of rope and the snap links looped around my pack frame for my entire field tour, but only used them twice.

The first time I used the rope was in a training exercise that I ran with my platoon one morning when we were in base camp. In Ranger School we were taught how to use a rope to belay when mountain climbing (one man on the upper slope ties into the rock and protects the climber, tied to the other end, from falling). I didn't want to get into that type of training, but one of the other techniques we learned was how to descend a steep slope rapidly by using a rope that was tied to a fixed object at the top. Wearing gloves, you held onto the rope and pointed your lead hand down the slope. Your other hand grasped the rope behind you. Then you ran down the slope, pointing the rope in front of you as you went. To slow or brake, you pulled your lead hand into your chest and the friction would slow you down.

I had each of the men in the platoon make a run down the slope, practicing this technique. We only had one pair of gloves, so each man had to hike back up the hill after his turn and pass the gloves to the next. It was a simple exercise as long as the soldier did not run too fast and trip and knew how to properly apply the brake.

The training proceeded very well until one soldier, who was a bit uncoordinated, took off down the slope at high speed. I yelled at him to slow down and brake, but the soldier had forgotten how to do it. He tried to stop by squeezing the rope with both hands. This effort succeeded in causing him to trip, fall, and roll down the slope, ending up with severe lacerations to his arms and legs. This injury also ended the training exercise. Later, my CO pulled me aside to discover how this man had been injured. I explained the technique and received the comment: "We have enough injuries just humping the boonies; don't complicate matters with a training exercise." This made a lot of sense. There was no need to place my men at unnecessary risk.

The second time I used my rope was to cross a swift, deep stream. During a search and destroy mission, my company was directed to send three platoons on parallel tracks through what was suspected to be enemy territory. It was a 10km trek with 3–4km in between platoons. Spacing was needed to avoid any possibility of firing on friendly troops if one of the units got off course. If any platoon encountered an enemy force the other two platoons could quickly be called on for support. It was not a particularly effective method for searching an area since the terrain was thick jungle and each platoon was forced to walk single file. An enemy force might well have hidden itself in the undergrowth between the platoons' parallel lines of march.

My platoon had the middle route of the three. It was especially difficult because we had to chop trail as well as go over two large mountains to remain parallel to the other two platoons. The other platoons, with easier routes to follow, arrived at "the blue line" (a stream) much earlier in the day than mine. I listened on the radio as each of the platoons talked about the difficulty they encountered crossing a fast-moving and deep stream. We crossed a couple of creeks (knee high), so I thought that we too had encountered "the blue line" and were staying even with the other two units. In reality we were several kilometers behind.

Finally, my point man alerted, and word was passed back to me that there was a stream ahead. I came up to the front and surveyed the situation. It was in fact a fast-moving stream and the depth was well over a man's head. We walked up and down the bank looking for a suitable place to cross. We found a narrow gap in the stream, but it was deep, and the current was swift. There were two sturdy trees on either side of the bank. I decided to use a stream-crossing technique I learned in Ranger School to get my men across. The idea was to send one man across the stream without his gear and fasten the rope to the tree on the other side. Once attached, the rope was stretched very tight using a snap link as a pulley. Then, one man at a time would go across pulling himself hand over hand.

All proceeded smoothly and my men, one by one, loaded down with their packs, ammo, water, and equipment, were able to make the traverse without too much difficulty. That is until it came to the machine-gun ammo bearer. This man carried two heavy canisters of machine-gun ammunition along with his usual gear, an M16 and bandoliers of ammo. As the man got about halfway across the stream, his feet slipped, and he lost both canisters of machine-gun ammo as well as his M16. Fortunately, the soldier hung on to the rope and was able to pull himself to safety. He was shaken and cold, but alive.

Losing two canisters of machine-gun ammo was not too serious, and they could easily be replaced. As they had sunk to the bottom of the stream, I was not concerned that the enemy might find and recover them. But the loss of an M16 was far more serious. Losing one's rifle was simply not something that was allowed, even if a soldier had been wounded or killed. If a man was killed, it was mandated that both the body and the man's weapon should never fall into enemy hands—under any circumstances. Loss of a weapon created grave consequences for the platoon leader. And now, my machine-gun ammo bearer had lost both ammo and weapon. This was not good… not good at all.

Fortunately, my machine gunner was a courageous soldier. It was his ammo bearer who had lost the equipment and he realized the severity of the situation. After all the men had crossed, the machine gunner stripped off his clothes and prepared to jump into the stream. We tied the free end of the rope around his waist, and he dove down into the water. Several of us held on to the other end ready to pull him out if it looked as if he was in trouble. The water was moving so fast that it was impossible to see the man as he dove underwater to try to recover the lost equipment. Suddenly, I felt a sharp tug on the rope and several of us pulled the soldier out of the stream. He came out gasping and holding the two canisters of M60 ammo attached to the gunner's load bearing equipment (LBE). I asked if he had spotted the M16. He told me that the stream was so swift that it was impossible to see anything underwater. After resting for a few minutes, the soldier jumped back into the stream and again dove down to the bottom.

It seemed like ages that he was under water, and I was just getting ready to pull him up when we felt another tug on the rope. The soldier came up empty-handed and my heart sank. I could see myself trying to explain to my CO how one of my men had lost his rifle crossing the stream. We started to pull the sergeant out of the water, but he said no, he wanted to try one more time. He said he may have seen the weapon down-stream from where he was diving.

He dove underwater again, and we paid the rope out as he searched the bottom of the stream bed. Then, after a minute, we felt two strong tugs on the rope and pulled hard to bring the man to the surface. This time the sergeant came up holding the sling of the M16 and we pulled him ashore. Shivering, he quickly pulled on his clothes as I coiled up the rope, attached the snap links and put it back on my pack frame. What had cost $15 before leaving the States had been a lifesaver in more ways than one. Without the rope, my men would have had great difficulty crossing the stream and my machine gunner might have drowned trying to recover the lost equipment.

My machine gunner's only concern was that I not report his ammo bearer for losing his gear. Of course, I agreed, as the man had done such a marvelous job. I wanted to acknowledge his bravery but could not, due to the circumstances of the loss.

My platoon proceeded on to the rendezvous coordinates, arriving at dusk an hour after the other platoons, in time to dig foxholes and take our posts along the perimeter. I remember being exceptionally tired that evening. I ate some fruit from my C-Rations and fell asleep almost immediately. It had been a harrowing time, but my rope and snap links had saved the day. I was happy to have kept the equipment with me even though I was urged to discard them several times during my field tour.

Unfortunately, the next morning I discovered my Kodak Instamatic camera (that I kept in a waterproof bag) had become thoroughly soaked and would no longer function. No more photos would be sent back home! Another casualty of the war was my reel-to-reel tape recorder, which was mysteriously stolen from the company rear. I can only hope the person who stole it recorded some tapes and sent them home—just as I had done before the machine disappeared.

Letter: 20 September 1968, A Company, 1/5 Cav, 1st Air Cav Division, out in the sticks, I Corps, Vietnam

I sent you a roll of film yesterday and I'm afraid it is probably ruined. We crossed a deep river and everything I had in my pack got wet. My camera too is ruined, all corroded and rusted inside. I shall take it with me on R&R, but think it is a casualty. Please do not send me a replacement or any more film.

There is no way to protect your things from the elements or weather. I had the camera wrapped in two plastic bags and inside an ammo pouch and it still got ruined. How my tape recorder has held up for this long I'll never know. It is in the rear in a waterproof bag, but still is exposed. You just can't attach any feelings to personal possessions here, there is no way to keep them secure or protected from the elements. If they make it through that's great, but don't count on it.

When I finally left the field after seven months, I gave the rope and snap links to my platoon sergeant. He probably ditched them as no one wanted to carry any additional weight, but the rope had certainly saved our butts the day we crossed that stream.

CHAPTER 18

Letting It All Hang Out

"It looks like you need a new pair of pants, son."

On one mission, after four weeks in the bush, we all began to anticipate being rotated into base camp to pull perimeter security. It meant access to showers, getting clean clothes, hot food, taking easy patrols outside the perimeter and ending at the local watering hole to swim. Each man would receive a semi-cold Coke and a beer each afternoon and relax by sleeping, reading, writing letters, and playing cards during the day. It also meant being away from the stress of searching for and running into the enemy. Unfortunately, during this mission, one of the other companies in our battalion had been ambushed by an NVA force and had suffered heavy casualties including their CO. Consequently, that company had to be pulled offline and returned to the division rear to receive replacements, acclimatize, train, and get prepared to return to the battalion. As a result, the other companies in the field were forced to pick up the slack and could not be rotated into base camp on the usual schedule. This translated into a much longer stay in the field than usual.

In compensation, clean clothes and water in 5-gallon "Jerry" cans were flown to our position. There was enough water for the men to wash, shave and change into clean fatigues. I was leading a patrol during the time these supplies were delivered to our company CP and my unit did not return until well after the clean clothes had been distributed. Upon return to the company CP, I reported to the CO, informing him of the results of my patrol. When I finished and searched for clean clothes to wear there was only one uniform left, and the pants were a size small. I wore a medium.

Arriving in Vietnam I weighed 165 lbs; after six weeks in the field, I was down to around 150, a weight I maintained throughout the rest of my tour. It was too hot to wear underpants in Vietnam and they were not available even if you wanted to wear them. But even at 150 lbs, a size small was a tight fit around my waist and crotch. The pants I had on were so dirty they could have stood up by themselves, so I put on the small pants. I held on to my fatigue shirt which was a medium and was not too dirty as I only wore it at night.

We continued that mission for another two weeks for a total of six weeks in the boonies without a break. The only relief from the heat was the frequent helicopter combat assaults where you relished the cool air for 15–30 minutes before being dropped back into the soup. Our daily patrols continued, and we moved through dense jungle, trying whenever possible to follow animal trails or stream beds. While these routes made movement easier, they were inherently more dangerous because of the ambush possibility by VC or NVA forces.

On the third day after receiving clean clothes, I stepped over a large log on the trail and heard the crotch of my small pants rip at the seam. At that moment, I was "hanging all out." It was an uncomfortable feeling to say the least. I asked my medic if he had any safety pins, and he gave me two: one large and one small. I did my best to pin the crotch of my pants which now had a split of about 6 inches right in the front.

Of course, the pins held for only a short while as I continued to lead my platoon on patrols and night ambushes. After several days, the small pin was lost, and my pants were held together by one pin holding torn and ratty fabric across my groin. This was my uniform for two weeks. Then one morning my CO called me to his CP. He informed me that my platoon was to be picked up and taken to secure the perimeter of an artillery battery firebase. Furthermore, I was informed that I was to report to our battalion commander, a lieutenant colonel, who was at the firebase once I had my platoon moved into the bunkers surrounding the hilltop.

An artillery battery firebase was typically located on the top of a high mountain. It needed to be the highest peak in the area and wide enough to secure the three 105mm howitzers in the battery, plus ammunition and the men who manned them. The position was always super-fortified with perimeter bunkers made from cut timber and hardened with tons of sandbags. A platoon would normally secure the firebase with three to four men in each bunker surrounding the perimeter.

My men were overjoyed when I gave them the news. This meant we would only need to send out patrols during the day to sweep the base of the mountain. And even though that usually meant a 3–5km walk down the hill and then back up, it was still easier to pull this duty than to hump the jungle as we had been doing for six weeks. At night we would keep watch, alternating the men on 1- to 2-hour shifts. It was comparatively easy duty.

So, at around 4 PM that afternoon, choppers arrived at our company CP, picked up my platoon and flew us 20 minutes to the artillery battery's firebase perched on one of two adjoining mountain tops. Upon arrival, we discovered there was a saddle in between the two hill tops about 150m apart. The terrain configuration necessitated the placement of two men in a listening post (LP) on top of the second hilltop, outside the perimeter at night. Equipped with a radio, these men were to protect us if an enemy force tried to infiltrate from the adjacent mountain top. No one liked to pull LP duty, as these men were extremely vulnerable to both enemy and friendly fire, positioned in an unfortified foxhole. It also required longer shifts of being awake throughout the night. Every little noise created fear, anxiety, and concern that an enemy force was sneaking up on the LP. It was always a "short straw draw" as to who would man the LP. Furthermore, there was danger that if the LP did encounter an enemy force and tried to return to the perimeter they might be shot by our own men. But in this case an LP was a necessity to protect the main base camp.

After walking the perimeter, my platoon sergeant and I positioned the men into bunkers making sure that each one had three or four men. Then, I found my way to the battalion commander's bunker near the center of the base camp. This bunker also housed the artillery battery's command center with extensive radio communications with the FOs. FOs from an artillery battery were assigned to every infantry company. They would constantly plot and shoot harassment and interdiction (H&I) fire throughout the night to protect the company from enemy infiltration as well as support daytime patrols.

Reporting to the battalion commander in his bunker I noticed he had a cot with an air mattress, jungle blanket, desk, a gas lamp, and radio. I did my best to look as presentable as I could, blousing my pants and putting on my fatigue shirt. There was nothing I could do about the split crotch in my pants. It was now being loosely held together with one large safety pin that did little to prevent me from completely hanging out. I tried to compensate by holding my legs close together hoping that some of the remaining fabric would hide my genitals. This was a lost cause.

I stood in front of the battalion commander and saluted and said, "Lieutenant Bartlett reporting, Sir. I have all my men in position around the perimeter with three or four men in each bunker. I will have two men manning the LP tonight."

The battalion commander returned my salute and with an amused smile questioned, "How long have you been in the boonies, Lieutenant? It looks as if you could use a new pair of pants, son."

I responded, "Six weeks, Sir. I was late coming to the clean clothes pile and a small pair of pants was all that was left. I lost the crotch after three days… sorry. I sure would appreciate a medium if you have one, Sir."

The battalion commander went over to a shelf built into the wall of his bunker where several pairs of pressed clean pants were stacked. He pulled out a brand-new pair of fatigue pants and asked if I needed a shirt too. I told him that the pants would be fine, but a T-shirt would also be great—if he had one.

I walked out of the bunker with a new pair of medium pants, a new shirt, and a new T-shirt courtesy of my battalion commander. Quickly, I changed my pants and T-shirt, throwing the old ones in the trash heap.

My platoon pulled security duty at that firebase for five days while the rest of my company continued to hump the boonies. I sent out daily patrols to skirt the mountain top, but these patrols were easy duty. My men benefitted from the one hot meal flown in daily and the ability to sleep and relax during the day.

〜〜

Letter: 19 August 1968, A Company, 1/5 Cav, 1st Air Cav Division, somewhere in the boonies, I Corps, Vietnam

Just a short note for now. We are still out in the field and rain after more than three weeks. The men are really beat, and I am not too far off. It seems that the NVA are massing outside several of our LZs, and the higher ups do not wish to disturb the integrity of the base defense companies. So, we stay in the field and suffer.

I am really quite a sight: beard, skin peeling off my hands from the wet weather, infected cuts and scratches on my arms and a most pungent odor! Oh well, someday I'll get to take a shower.

(Later), OK, that now makes four weeks in the field straight. I am a real beauty and there is no word as to when we will go in. The NVA are still reported to be in the area. I guess it is true too as we took six mortar rounds the other night. We suffered three WIAs (all slight) and brought artillery (Red Leg) and our own mortar tube to bear on the enemy position. Our patrols and sweeps have been uneventful.

The wind comes up every now and then and the weather is at least bearable. Often there is no canopy and the sun shines on your head all day. I don't know which is worse, the brushy hills or the jungle. They are both pretty bad.

I received a care package from you today. It was the one with the peanuts and blue baby bottles filled with bourbon. I shared with my men. We all got one swallow. It sure was good.

〜〜

After this, my longest field mission, I was informed that the second platoon was being rotated in to replace us. We would use the same helicopters to return to the field and rejoin our company. At this point, my platoon sergeant informed me that one of my men was refusing to return to the field stating that he had a toothache. I called the man to my CP and spoke with him. This soldier was one of my machine gunners and thus an important member of my platoon. I could not be in the field without him. I told him so. But the man was adamant about having a toothache and said that army regulations permitted him to refuse to go into the field under the circumstances.

I was aware that if a soldier's teeth were broken or if he could not chew his food for some reason, there were regulations prohibiting him from field duty. But I did not know about a toothache. I also had some suspicion about the man's story. He had not reported any problems previously while we were on the firebase. He hadn't asked my medic for aspirin or a painkiller. I was in a quandary as to what to do or what the regulations were.

I called my company commander to explain the situation emphasizing I needed to have the machine gunner on patrol with my platoon. He told me to put the man on the radio and he spoke with him. Then my CO told me to stand by. About 15 minutes later I was told to take the man to the battalion commander's bunker. I escorted the soldier to the battalion commander where they met for about 15 minutes. The man stuck to his story and indicated that he was not trying to avoid duty, but he was suffering a severe toothache. It prohibited him from eating and he was in constant pain.

The battalion commander came out of the bunker with the man and told me to return to my platoon. The man was to collect his gear and would be medevaced to the rear later in the day for dental care. He could not return to the field if he was unable to eat and in pain. I would have to survive without my machine gunner.

At 2 PM that day, the second platoon arrived, dropping off a squad and picking up one of mine to return to the company position. I briefed the second platoon leader on placement of his men, the need to have daily patrols and place men in the LP at night. The birds continued to come in dropping off members of the second platoon and picking up my men. I caught the last bird out and returned to my company.

My company spent another week humping the boonies for a total of eight weeks in the field before finally being pulled into the battalion base camp for security detail. It was my longest single mission in Vietnam. I certainly appreciated the warm shower, shave, hot food, and sleep that finally awaited me at base camp. But what I appreciated even more was the new pair of medium-sized pants, T-shirt and even a new fatigue shirt given to me by my battalion commander that afternoon in his bunker... after letting it all hang out.

CHAPTER 19

Tracer Rounds

"I don't see 'em, Sir."
I yelled back: "Watch my tracers."

The terrain along the DMZ where we patrolled was always different. One day we would be walking through flat terrain with sandy soil, tumbleweed, and no overhead cover. The next we might be in thick forest sometimes peppered with Agent Orange (AO). And as we moved farther west, we entered the mountainous jungles along the border with Laos and the Ho Chi Minh Trail. Each terrain necessitated different unit formations and tactics, but most often single file in deep jungle and forested areas. But Charlie knew we had superior firepower. He knew we could call for helicopter gunships that could be overhead in minutes, so he always holed up by day and moved by night. We knew this too.

Walking fourth or fifth in line positioned me behind either my machine gunner or my M79 grenadier. The M79 grenade launcher was used for the first time in Vietnam. The weapon looked like a large bore, break-action sawed-off shotgun weighing in at 6.5 lbs loaded. The weapon is single-shot firing a 40mm high-explosive round. It was a devastating weapon because of its versatility and became one of my favorite support pieces. It provided a close-in artillery-like firing option. The grenadier's vest held HE and flechette rounds, as well as smoke, illumination, and buckshot. An experienced grenadier could lob an HE round accurately from 75m out to 375m. The explosion carried the same impact as a hand grenade with a 5m killing radius. The grenadier's vest carried 25–30 rounds in what looked like an overcoat without sleeves with pockets on the inside for ammo. An HE round needed to travel at least 30m to be armed, so lobbing a round into the air was always the best practice. Really good grenadiers could drop rounds on top of a 5-foot square simply by evaluating the distance between themselves and the target and adjusting the angle. For close-in support (less than 50m) in deep jungle, the weapon rarely fired HE rounds because the distance required to arm the shell was too great. In these cases, the grenadier would use buckshot or flechette rounds. The weapon could be used to attack enemy soldiers spotted up to 300m away without revealing our position or requiring a fire and maneuver assault (i.e., soldiers advancing directly against an enemy position). It was also a superb weapon to be used in ambush situations. The only drawbacks were that it fired only one round at a time and could not be used in dense jungle or when surrounded by trees.

* * *

One late afternoon, with temps hovering between 105 and 110 degrees, we had been walking single file through a forested area that had been sprayed with Agent Orange. The orange/red dust was all over our pants and boots. Most of the trees and vegetation in the area were dead or dying. The leaves on the ground made it look like a late autumn scene in New England—dry leaves and dead brush everywhere. We had already called in a medevac for one victim of heat exhaustion.

I was fortunate not to have walked through very many Agent Orange-sprayed areas. Most of the defoliated areas were closer to the Ho Chi Minh Trail, designed to reveal enemy pinch points and storage areas as bombing targets. Talk of the concern about Agent Orange had begun to circulate among the troops. There was no way to walk through an area that had been sprayed without becoming covered in the dust. Some of it had to have been ingested. We knew it was not a healthy situation regardless of what we were being told from the top brass and we avoided these areas wherever possible.

My point man alerted as he broke through from the dead forest area into an open field. He called me to the front to say that he had seen two enemy soldiers running about 150m to the front, through the middle of a field of chest-high dry grass. I called several riflemen to the front, and we formed a line in case I needed immediate firepower. I also called for my grenadier to come forward. I radioed the CO to let him know that we had two suspected VC hiding in tall grass about 150m to our front. He gave the OK to attack. At about the same time, I also saw the two VC stand up, run about 10m and drop back down. We fired several rounds at the VC in the general vicinity where we saw them drop. We had no idea what their cover was like, but it could not have been much in the tall, dry grass.

When the grenadier arrived, I told him to drop several rounds out at 150m near where the two enemy soldiers had been seen. He told me, "I don't see 'em, Sir." I yelled back, "Watch my tracers."

I carried several magazines of red tracer rounds at the front of my bandolier. Tracers were extremely valuable to mark a target, so others could concentrate their fire. But they also revealed my position, so troops typically would not carry them, only the leaders.

I quickly unloaded my M16 and inserted a mag of tracer rounds. I took careful aim at the area where I thought the two VC had taken cover and fired several rounds. My grenadier saw where the tracers landed and proceeded to drop three rounds on the spot in quick succession. Then I had him drop one round to the right and one to the left of where his first rounds landed.

We hadn't anticipated the grass fire that started from either my tracer rounds or the impact of the M79 HE rounds. At first, we only saw a small plume of smoke coming from the area, but the wind was blowing—and in our direction. The wind fanned the flames, and the dry grass caught fire very quickly. Suddenly, we were faced with a huge wall of flame advancing on us. Fanned by the wind, the smoke and flames were coming at us at an alarming rate; my platoon was bunched up and in great danger.

I quickly got on the radio to tell my platoon sergeant, at the end of the column, that we had started a fire, and it was quickly advancing on us. He needed to turn the line around and have the platoon run back in the direction we had come. This was the equally dangerous dry wooded area through which we had just walked. It too would quickly catch fire as the flames grew. We were facing a fast-advancing ground fire and in great danger. And, as we were in a single line formation it was taking too long to reverse course and get away from the flames.

Meanwhile, seeing the smoke and flames, my CO was yelling at me over the radio to get the platoon the hell out of there. I realized that there was not enough time for my entire platoon to turn around and reverse course. My only option was to move parallel to the wall of flame at a full run to reach an area that was not so dry. I radioed the platoon sergeant that I was splitting the platoon in half and would lead my group toward a safe area to the north. He was to lead his group in the direction he was now taking and also break off to the north. Once he was back into the forest and had avoided the fire, he was to move to rejoin us.

There is nothing worse than to have men run at full speed in 110-degree heat with a fire at their backs and little or no water left to drink. The danger of being burned by the fire was real. Our only hope of avoiding severe injury was to outrun the fire by moving to the far edge of the field. That is exactly what we did. Feeling the heat of the fire on our backs, we ran as if our lives depended on it, and they did.

Fortunately, the plan worked, and my half of the platoon was able to find clear ground. The fire passed behind us. When we saw the edge of the forest go up in flames, I radioed my platoon sergeant to tell him to move north as the fire was sweeping in behind him. His response was garbled because he and the radio operator were running at full speed, but I knew he had heard my warning.

My group was able to return to walking, but none of us had any water left. We were suffering from dehydration and potential heat exhaustion. My mouth felt like it was full of cotton. I couldn't even make spit. I swallowed the last drops from my two-quart bladder and radioed the CO that we were in immediate need of water resupply. I requested that a chopper come out with as many Jerry cans as it could carry.

My group of soldiers arrived at the company CP at about the same time as the supply chopper landed. Several men were on the verge of collapse and supported by other soldiers. We grabbed the Jerry cans off the chopper and began filling canteens.

Some men were in such bad shape that we whipped off their steel helmets, filled them with water and splashed it on them.

My CO realized my full platoon was not present and screamed at me: "Where the hell is the rest of your platoon?" I was so involved in helping get water to my men that he had to come over to me and grab me by the hair to get my attention. I informed him that we had to split the platoon into two groups to avoid the fire. I did a quick count to confirm that I had all the men in my group. I got on the radio and called my platoon sergeant to ask for a sitrep. He called back saying that he needed help. He was about a kilometer away but had four men who had collapsed from heat exhaustion. I grabbed five men and had them fill their two-quart bladders. We immediately moved in the direction of the rest of my platoon carrying as many bladders as we could.

We found the rest of the platoon and were able to pass the water around to the men who needed it most. Dousing the men who had collapsed, I called in a medevac to evacuate two of the men who were suffering the most. After the dust-off (medevac) left, I led the rest of the platoon back to the company CP. Everyone again filled their canteens and took long drinks to rehydrate.

Fortunately, no one was seriously hurt. The men who had been evacuated with heat exhaustion returned to duty after a day's rest and IV fluids at the battalion aid station. It was a critical lesson learned: don't fire HE rounds and tracers into dry grass even if you see the enemy—unless the wind is blowing in the opposite direction.

Letter: 31 May 1968, A Company, 1/5 Cav, 1st Air Cav Division, LZ Jane, I Corps, Vietnam

My recent operation was a real experience, and I learned a great deal. It was exciting too because we did have several contacts. We also had an unfortunate experience three days ago. We were moving from one FOB to another and spotted two "gooks" running to our front and opened fire on them. They went into a hole, and we proceeded to call in M79 rounds on top of them.

The M79 fire itself was very close about 150–200m from our position. When ARA came in the gunners must have been a little jumpy: two rounds fell short, slightly wounding a man in the platoon. Furthermore, a fire was started, and the wind was blowing it right into our position. We had to DiDi the area pronto (short for DiDi Mao—Vietnamese for go quickly). In so doing we lost some equipment and suffered several heat casualties. The temp was at least 115 degrees. We were finally able to reach the top of a hill, set up, and medevac our casualties. Needless to say, it was a very unhappy time, all caused by two gooks.

The following days of the operations were a bit better. We set out several ambushes and scored three times with a total body count of ten. We did not suffer any additional WIA.

CHAPTER 20

Surviving Leg Cramps

"But I did take my salt pill."

The most common reasons for calling a medevac were heat exhaustion and heat stroke. As hard as I would try to encourage the men to stay hydrated, it was not unusual for them to exhaust their water supply, become lightheaded, cold, and clammy and literally fall over and pass out because their body temperature spiked. Every man carried at least a gallon of water, but sometimes even that was not enough. If the temperatures were more than 110 degrees and we were chopping our way through three-canopy jungle, a soldier could easily go through a gallon by midday.

A soldier suffering from heat exhaustion or heat stroke had to be placed in the shade with any available water poured over him to cool him off. But no one wanted to give up their drinking water; so sometimes cooling the soldier became a life-threatening issue. (It's been said that "urinating on a soldier would cool him off," but I never encountered an instance where this was necessary.) When a man was in danger of heat exhaustion or heat stroke, everything stopped and a call for an immediate medevac was made. An LZ had to be located and the area needed to be secured. If the unit was in dense, three-canopy jungle, the solution was to chop out a hole with a machete and evacuate the man via jungle penetrator. Evacuation became the top priority. This type of medevac happened to me and to our company on a regular basis as there was rarely enough water to stay hydrated. We did everything we could to ensure men did not become casualties. We put salt tablets into our canteens mixed with Kool-Aid to kill the taste. Every time a man took a drink, he swallowed some salt water. Each night we typically received a helicopter resupply of ammunition, mortar rounds, C-Rats and Jerry cans heavily laced with chlorinated water.

Water resupply was always a major issue. When a unit was in contact with the enemy, resupply of ammunition and water became the highest priorities. Men in contact would consume every drop from their canteens in a matter of minutes. Resupply of these essentials became as critical as air support, artillery, and reinforcements. For this reason, extra canteens in waterproof bags and Jerry cans full of water were stored on the helicopter landing pad at base camp and could be loaded onto helicopters at a moment's notice to support a unit in contact.

On one extremely hot morning, my company was walking through dense jungle terrain as we had for several days. We had been resupplied with C-Rats and water placed in 8-inch howitzer powder canisters the night before, but the canisters had not been thoroughly washed, so the water tasted awful and could not be consumed. We tried to conserve every drop available, but most men were down to a quart or less—myself included.

Our route found us heading out of the mountains and into open terrain, but for the first part of the journey we had to bust trail. The temperature on this day had soared to well over 110 degrees. By mid-morning, everyone was out of water with blazing sun overhead. Fortunately, we had reached some level ground and had only about 8km to go to our CP rendezvous point for the night. At around noon, my platoon found some shade and took a 45-minute rest. The men opened cans of fruit from their C-Rations. They drank the juice and ate the fruit. The fruit in the C-Rations was the most valuable part of each meal and became a trading commodity. I was fortunate to have a can of peaches and consumed it as we settled in and tried to cool off. I was out of water but feeling OK. I felt I could easily make it another 8km. My medic came around with more salt pills for everyone, but I told him I was out of water and could not take it. He gave me a sip from his canteen, and I swallowed the giant pill.

At about 2 PM, we saddled up to continue to move toward our objective. The men were clearly dragging and suffering from the intense heat. Normally, we would have covered the 8km in an hour's walk, but due to the heat, we were forced to stop every 30 minutes to rest and find shade. This was the only solution available to protect against heat exhaustion.

Finally, at about 4:30 PM, my platoon pulled into the company CP and took up positions in our assigned sector of the perimeter. A logistics helicopter had been called and plenty of water was on its way along with the night's provisions. We were told that one beer and one soda per man had been placed on the chopper in waterproof bags with ice and were also on the way. This cheered us all and we couldn't wait for the bird to arrive.

I suddenly started to feel lightheaded. I told my radio operator that I wasn't feeling well and sat down in a shady spot. I tried to relax but continued to sweat profusely. Then the leg cramps started. I got cramps in my toes, in my calves and in my thighs. I got them in both legs at the same time. At first, I was able to stretch out my legs to relieve the cramps, but as soon as I sat back down the cramps came back. The pain was excruciating. I was in agony. It was difficult to stifle my screams. My medic came over to give me a drink, but by this time it was too late. Both legs continued to spasm uncontrollably. I had two men massaging my legs, trying

ROTC Graduating Class 1967, Claremont McKenna College. Author is in the first row, fifth from the left. (Author's collection)

Author after earning paratrooper wings. (Author's collection)

Ranger School Training. (Public domain)

I survived my first worst day in Vietnam, I Corps, jungle. (Author's collection)

Walking the trail, Quan Tri Province. (Public domain)

Soldiers engaged in firefight in Hue during Tet 1968. (Public domain)

Our forward observer. (Author's collection)

Cav Cobra. (Public domain)

Helicopters fly over jungle. (© Ratpack2/Dreamstime.com)

Huey Nose. (Public domain)

Flying Cobra. (© Ivan Cholakov/Dreamstime.com)

Cobra Nose, 1/9 Cav. (Author collection. Used with permission: Vietnam Center and Sam Johnson Vietnam Archive, Texas Tech University)

Chinook landing. (Public domain)

First days in country, Long Binh Repo Depot. (Author's collection)

Transfer to Camp Evans, I Corps from Long Binh. (Author's collection)

Mortar platoon setting up, A 1/5 Cav. (Doc Cleary collection)

Mortar platoon takes action, A 1/5 Cav. (Doc Cleary collection)

1st platoon, A 1/5 Cav in jungle. (Author's collection)

Payday in the field, A 1/5 Cav. (Doc Cleary collection)

Command group, 1st platoon, A 1/5 Cav. (Doc Cleary collection)

Deep jungle patrol. (Author's collection)

Medevac of wounded soldier using jungle penetrator. (Robert Lafoon Collection. Used with permission: Vietnam Center and Sam Johnson Vietnam Archive, Texas Tech University)

Author switching packs with RTO. (Author's collection)

Vietnamese boys posing near watering hole. (Doc Cleary collection)

Burning shit. (See disclaimer)

1st platoon, A 1/5 Cav 1969. (Doc Cleary collection)

Religious service, LZ Jane. (Public domain)

Author using tape recorder at LZ Jane. (Author's collection)

Kit Carson Scout, A 1/5 Cav. (Public domain)

Set up for saturation ambushing. (Author's collection)

Taking a break from the heat. (Author's collection)

Combat assault, platoon leader view. (Courtesy of Wayne Guffy, http:www.118ahc.org/PhotoAlbum5.htm)

Combat assault, door gunner view #2. (Public domain)

Combat assault, door gunner view. (Photographer unknown, Courtesy of Edward Vigil, 1st Cav. See disclaimer)

Combat assault en route to Cambodia. (See disclaimer)

Combat assault, helicopter is getting ready to land, A 1/5 Cav. (Doc Cleary collection)

Jumping off. (Public domain)

Jumping off and falling down. (Courtesy of Askanod.com, Photographer unknown)

On the horn calling in a fire mission. (Public domain)

105mm howitzer. (Author's collection)

Troops waiting to be picked up. (Public domain)

Soldier landing a helicopter, A 1/5 Cav. (Author's collection)

Village blocking force uses Armored Personnel Carriers (APCs). (Public domain)

Soldier with APC blocking force. (Public domain)

Village search. (Public domain)

Huey after controlled crash using autorotation. (Used with permission: Bill Hirtle, Thunderbird 10 next to Blue 6 following engine failure. Http:www.118ahc.org/PhotoAlbum5.htm. Original photo Joe Lemieux)

Author crossing a stream, which appeared in the Cav newspaper. (Public domain)

Washing off. (Public domain)

Machine gunner, A 1/5 Cav. (Doc Cleary collection)

Author takes cover from heat under a poncho. (Author's collection)

Soldier tries to stay cool. (Doc Cleary collection)

Lieutenant Richey and friend. (Richey collection)

Medic and RTO, A 1/5 Cav. (Doc Cleary collection)

Medevac. Battle casualty of 1/4 Marines. (Photo by Jim Falk. 222362762 © US Navy Medicine|Dreamstime.com)

Firefight Leader. (Public domain)

Firefight. (Public domain)

Spider hole. (Public domain)

Booby trap. (Public domain)

Author walking point. (Author's collection)

Camp Evans, where the author was based as part of the 14th Military History Detachment. Photo taken September 1968. (Public domain)

Author enjoying R&R in Tokyo. (Author's collection)

Author, 14th Military History Detachment, Phuoc Vinh, III Corps. (Author's collection)

14th Military History Detachment. (Author's collection)

Santa delivers toys at a Christmas party for orphans. (Author's collection)

Author handing out gifts at Christmas party for orphans. (Public domain)

Ann-Margret and General Creighton Abrams. (Public domain)

Bob Hope Show, Long Binh, 1968. (Public domain)

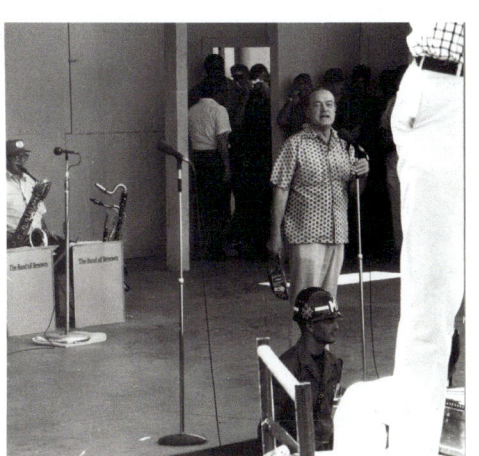

Bob Hope Show, Long Binh, 1968. (Public domain)

Combat scout team, 1st Cav. (Public domain)

Combat tracker team patrols in the field. (Public domain)

Rocket attack damage, Phuoc Vinh, III Corps. (Public domain)

122mm rocket remains, Phuoc Vinh, III Corps. (Public domain)

Reinforcing protection on the bunker building, Phuoc Vinh. (Author's collection)

Perimeter bunker, Phuoc Vinh. (Public domain)

Tower lookout on perimeter, Phuoc Vinh. (Public domain)

Short-timer: sky trooper of 1st Cav Division (Airmobile) keeps track of time left. (111-SC-647323, courtesy of the National Archives)

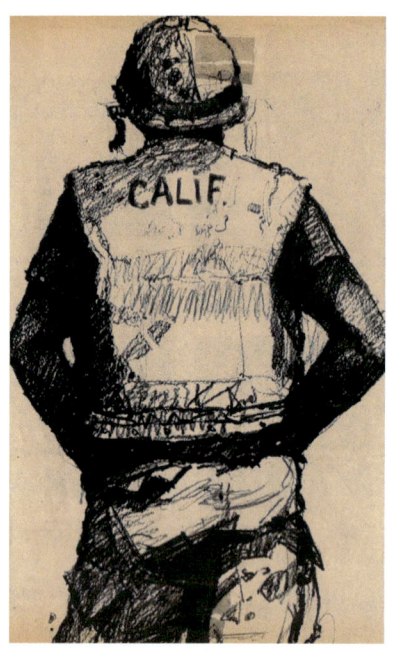

Combat Art: landing a chopper. (Public domain)

Combat Art: California dreaming. All the
artwork created by combat artists assigned
to the 1st Air Cav Division. (Public domain)

Combat Art: the face of combat. (Public domain)   Combat Art: Madonna and child. (Public domain)

Combat Art: preparing for ambush. (Public domain)

Combat Art: RTO. (Public domain)

Combat Art: planting. (Public domain)

Combat Art: fatigue. (Public domain)

Combat Art: the face of death. (Public domain)

Combat Art: a tight landing. (Public domain)

Combat Art: child washing. (Public
domain)

Combat Art: the general's face. (Public
domain)

Author's Disclaimer: Every effort was made to locate copyright holders and obtain permission for material used. After exhaustive research, author was unable to find the owner of this photograph.

to stretch the muscles out and relieve the cramps but to no avail. A cramp would subside for a few seconds and then return.

My screaming brought my CO over to investigate. He asked if I was going to be able to recover. I asked him to give me a few more minutes to see if the cramps would subside as the two men continued to massage my legs. He told me that the logistics helicopter was on its way, and it could take me back to base camp if the cramps continued. I acknowledged this in between bouts of pain and screams.

The CO spoke with the logistics helicopter. He informed the pilot that he needed to take me to the battalion aid station. The pilot informed him that he was not authorized to evacuate a soldier, and he needed to call for a medevac. By this time, I was screaming from the unceasing pain. I knew I needed to be taken to the rear.

About 10 minutes later, a medevac landed. I was placed on a stretcher and taken to the helicopter along with my equipment. Within minutes, we were flying, with doors open and a temperature drop of at least 20 degrees or more. Suddenly, the leg cramps disappeared. The sweat dried and although I was exhausted from the ordeal, I was thankful not to be experiencing the severe pain.

~~~~~~

Letter: 1 June 1968, A Company, 1/5 Cav, 1st Air Cav Division, LZ Jane, I Corps, Vietnam

Our 6 decided to move our FOB that morning. It was a long hump with many hills. It turned out to be the hottest day I have ever experienced in VN. I had to medevac several men along the way for heat stroke and cramps. With only a few hours of sleep, I too was not quite in the pink. I did make it to the new FOB, and then my body went berserk. I had cramps in my legs, my back, fingers, and arms. It was very bad, and I don't remember too much except I was in continual pain and screaming.

I woke up in the hospital back at Jane with a bottle of salt fluid running into my arm. Three bottles did the trick, and I am A-OK now, but still tired. I shall take it very easy today and go back to the field tomorrow. It was quite an ordeal, but happens to men all the time, so please don't be alarmed. I was amazed at how fast they got me back to the rear and treated. The medevac took a total of about 10 minutes.

~~~~~~

When we landed, I attempted to get up and climb out of the helicopter, but two orderlies grabbed my stretcher and ran with me to the battalion aid station. The stretcher was placed on two sawhorses. Another orderly shoved what looked like a giant stick up one of my pants legs. In an instant he cut the material from the bottom to top. Then he did the same to the other side. Another man did the same thing to my shirt. Within 10 seconds, I was lying on the stretcher completely nude.

A surgeon arrived, looked at me and asked where I was injured. I told him that I had been suffering tremendous cramps in both legs and could not walk or get rid of them. His response, "Well, you should have been taking your salt pills." I responded: "But, I did take my pills. We ran out of water." The surgeon seemed annoyed that my case was not more serious and ordered an IV drip for the next 12 hours. The two orderlies who had pulled me off the medevac picked up the stretcher and transported me into the battalion aid station tent where I was transferred—still nude—to a cot. After being placed on the cot, one of the men came over with a bottle of fluid, applied a tourniquet, found a vein, and started the drip. My arm was strapped down so that I could not move or adjust my position on the cot for the next 12 hours.

The drip worked. After an hour, I began to feel much better. I was lying nude on the cot with my arm locked in position. Finally, an orderly came by, and I asked if he could get me a jungle blanket to cover me. He came back with one a short while later. The blanket helped, but I alternated between being too cold and too hot under it. I asked if I could have a drink and was finally brought a small cup to wash my mouth out. After four hours of lying on the cot, I became extremely uncomfortable. I told the orderly that I had to have my arm released from the restraints as I needed to shift my position on the cot. He told me that his orders were to keep the arm restrained. I told him that I promised to keep my arm extended, but that I had to shift onto my side.

Aside from feeling extremely uncomfortable at being nude I was annoyed at the way the orderlies were treating me. Perhaps it was because I was an officer or perhaps because I was not severely wounded, but they had no empathy for what had befallen me or for my discomfort. I thought about complaining but decided these soldiers could make my life even more miserable if they wanted to, so I kept my mouth shut. In a way it was a good lesson to learn. The battalion aid station was there to stabilize wounded men and transfer them to a field hospital or to a hospital ship as quickly as possible. My case did not merit any special treatment and no sympathy was given.

At about 8 PM, I asked if I could get a pair of pants or shorts to wear. I was told that they didn't have any. I asked if they could call my company CP and ask the first sergeant to send over some shorts or pants. About an hour later, one of the men in my company showed up with a pair of shorts and a pillow. I was finally able to cover up and get comfortable. After two full bottles of fluid, the drip came out of my arm. At 6 AM I was told to lie there for another hour and would then be released.

I had to walk back to my CP barefoot and wearing only a pair of shorts and wrapped in a jungle blanket. Fortunately, the first sergeant took pity on me and gave me a beer to drink. Then he let me use his personal shower consisting of a bucket with a shower head on a rope with a pulley. I filled the bucket with water, wet down, soaped up and rinsed off. It was like taking a spit bath, but it was a welcome relief and made me feel 100 percent better. I was given new boots, socks, pants, shirt, and T-shirt. I located my M16 and equipment. I went to the mess hall, ate a hot meal, and came back to the tent to rest. Then I slept soundly for the next six hours.

I returned to my company that evening on the logistics helicopter and resumed my duties as platoon leader.

~~~~~~

Letter: 3 July 1968, A Company, 1/5 Cav, 1st Air Cav Division, in the boonies, I Corps, Vietnam

I have had no problems with the heat since my last bout. I guess I have adjusted pretty well although I do sweat a lot. I am surprised how well I have been feeling. I have begun to physically surpass my men and have had no problems with my feet or jungle rot. It's surprising too because my hands and arms are covered with scratches. I guess I just have a tough hide.

Things are working smoothly. The men are working as a team and getting the work done with less direction and pushing from me. My platoon sergeant still needs a lot of direction. He is so young, inexperienced, and immature. He is a boy, really, only 19 years old and is being called on to do the job of a 30-year-old man. My squad leaders, too, are just boys, but they have been here for quite some time and know their stuff. They give me a lot of help and advice. I still have that problem of talking first and thinking second. I must try to use my brain a bit more.

~~~~~~

CHAPTER 21

Ambush in the Rain

"Mash the plunger."
"No, wait," he replied, "I think the Claymore's been turned around."

When setting up an ambush I always planted two or three Claymores in front of my ambush positions; firing the Claymore triggered the start of the ambush. When fired, an enemy soldier might be hit with many steel balls and killed instantly depending on where he was struck. And, if the Claymore blast didn't kill him, the ensuing fire from our machine gun, M79 grenade launcher and M16s certainly would. It was rare that enemy soldiers escaped from a Claymore blast and one of our ambushes. We killed a lot of monkeys and several large animals as well.

The enemy knew our tactics and knew that we used trip flares in front of our Claymore ambushes. Sometimes they would try to crawl in, disarm the trip flare, locate the Claymore, and turn it around so that it would fire back on the ambush force. Then they would withdraw and make noise so that the ambush Claymore would be fired, thus killing, or injuring the American troops. This happened in our battalion on two occasions. The soldiers on ambush duty were cautioned to stay awake and alert but throughout the night, even in one-hour shifts, this was hard to do. The men were tired from a long day's hump and were lying on the ground in relatively comfortable positions. One or two men stayed awake while the rest of the ambush team slept, but try as we might, heads would droop, and eyelids would close.

Ambushing in the rain was a worst-case scenario. When it rained, you pulled out your poncho and wrapped up, placing the hood over your head. You could not wear your steel pot, as the noise created by the rain hitting the helmet was deafening. Jungle hats, if you had one, also became wet, soggy, and miserable to wear. When the rain hit the plastic hood of your poncho, especially a heavy rain, it became impossible to hear anything. And when conducting an ambush, especially when there is no moonlight, hearing enemy movement is critical. Furthermore, in a heavy rain everything becomes wet. Your feet are wet, your pants are wet, your rifle is wet and puddles form underneath where you are lying. The skin on your hands shrivels up. It does not take long to become uncomfortable and miserable. You want to sit up to avoid the wet ground, but you must remain lying prone in the ambush. And, because it is raining, an enemy soldier has the potential advantage of sneaking up on your position, disarming your trip flares and turning your Claymore around.

Letter: 2 August 1968, A Company, 1/5 Cav, 1st Air Cav Division, still in the boonies, I Corps, Vietnam (letter to college classmate)

This operation is going well. We have had several contacts and got two NVA. There have been no friendly WIA or KIA. We also got a new CO today. It is his second tour, and he looks pretty good. It will be a while however, before we get him squared away. This is the case with every new man.

I do not like our present mission just too scary. It's called "saturation ambushing." We are in small ambush groups and must be quiet all the time. It is especially bad at night and even worse in the rain. You wake up with every slight noise. It begins to wear on your nerves after a while. I hope we'll be going back to the old patrolling and FOB type mission soon.

The monsoon rains started like clockwork at 4 PM but on one particular day, instead of ending about an hour later as they usually did, the rain continued unabated. It didn't take long, even wearing our ponchos, for everything to become soaked. The rain was cold. We did our best to remain quiet and out of the puddles that seemed to form everywhere. Our feet were soaked and that made everyone miserable. And, to make matters worse, the rain intensified. We were in the midst of a tropical storm.

I instructed that Claymores and trip flares be placed to our front, left and right sides of the ambush because we had no idea what direction the enemy might come from. The only direction we were confident in was to our rear where there was a 50-foot embankment. Anyone coming up that slope would have an extremely tough time and make a lot of noise doing it. I split our ambush into three groups, each one focused on a different direction of enemy approach: front, left and right. This meant four men pointed in each direction and as night came, the watch was alternated in one-hour shifts.

The rain abated for a time and some of the men were able to sleep—myself included. But then at 2 PM it started up again—ferociously. I covered my head with the hood of my poncho, pulled my feet up under it and tried to doze. Suddenly, the man on watch crawled over to me and whispered in my ear that he thought he heard movement on the left flank. We woke everyone and took up firing positions. I moved up adjacent to the machine gunner and pulled the hood off my head in hopes of hearing something. But all I could hear was the rain beating down on my poncho and the leaves on the trees. Nothing was visible.

Suddenly, I thought I saw a shape moving about 100 feet to the front. I couldn't be sure, but my intuition told me I had seen something that should not have been there. I whispered to the machine gunner to "mash the plunger." "No, wait," he replied, "I think the Claymore's been turned around." I thought to myself, "How the hell could an enemy soldier have disarmed our trip flare and reached the Claymore in front of our position to turn it around?" The answer became clear: The soldier on watch had been sleeping or nodding off. But now was not a time to dwell on what had happened or to take a chance on the Claymore being reversed. I instructed the machine gunner to fire several short bursts to the side of our position and traverse the landscape. The machine gunner fired, and this was accompanied by the other men who also fired their M16s. As soon as he had finished, I made the machine gunner relocate the weapon as it was dangerous to have revealed the machine gun's position.

The firing necessitated a quick call with the CO who wanted to know what had happened. I told him that we had movement to our front. He wanted to know why we had revealed our position and had not blown our Claymores. I told him I was afraid that the enemy had snuck into our position and turned them around. Of course, this upset the CO, but to his credit, he did not pursue the conversation at that time. I was in for a lengthy explanation the next day. He asked if there was anything he could do. I requested that flares be fired overhead so we could evaluate the situation. Seconds later, a series of flares fired by a 105mm howitzer appeared overhead and we scanned the area. By this time, if there had been any enemy in the area, they had certainly left, so I called for a discontinuation of the flares.

The next morning, we checked our Claymores and trip flares. We discovered the trip flare had been disconnected, despite the "butterfly switch" that was supposed to prevent this from happening. It was clear an enemy soldier had penetrated our outer perimeter but had not had a chance to turn the Claymore around before his movement was detected. If the machine gunner had not detected the movement when he did, the outcome might have been costly. A potentially disastrous situation had been averted. At the same time, the importance of staying awake and alert throughout the night had been reinforced.

My CO was upset we had not blown the Claymores and had revealed our machine-gun position but understood the difficulty of conducting an ambush in the rain. We saddled up and continued humping the boonies.

An important lesson learned.

~~~~~~

Letter: 7 August 1968, A Company, 1/5 Cav, 1st Air Cav Division, LZ Barbara, I Corps, Vietnam

I wanted to fill you in about ambushing. The saturation ambushing type mission is for the birds. It really gets on your nerves to sit on ambush night after night with no breaks. We were in several contacts too which didn't help with the anxiety and stress. Fortunately, we took no casualties and did kill three NVA.

I was in my first night firefight. It was very scary, much more so than during the day. Every little noise turns into an enemy, and you can't see what you are shooting at. Needless to say, you don't get too much sleep. The ambushing force always has the advantage just as long as they are quiet and do not try to tackle anything big. The NVA have been moving in small groups so there is really no worry about that. It is still very scary especially at night. The men get very irritable, and you really have to push hard to get the job accomplished.

CHAPTER 22

Escort to Laos

Eight men had gone out but only four retuned.

The term "Tiger Force" was made famous by Colonel David Hackworth of the 101st Airborne Division, who in 1965 established a platoon of paratroopers who would "out-guerrilla the guerrillas." This unit was a predecessor of the first long range reconnaissance patrol (LRRP) teams that were established in every American infantry unit. LRRP teams of five to seven men were often inserted in a clandestine manner behind enemy lines. They provided intelligence on enemy movements such as infiltration routes, the location of large NVA units, location of caches of supplies and other similar missions. Such operations were sometimes considered secret black ops missions because of where they were placed. Commanding generals at the division level depended on this intelligence to formulate search and destroy or blocking strategies. The teams hid themselves during the day in the densest jungle they could find. They would observe trail and road intersections and move silently only at night. The men who participated in this activity were volunteers, willing to undertake great personal risks. On a mission they could not talk or smoke and knew how to move silently at night. Their security depended on total camouflage and concealment. The work was extremely dangerous because the men were always outgunned and, if discovered, would be immediately killed or captured. Inserting and extracting LRRP teams were also extremely dangerous operations for the helicopter pilots who flew them in and for the soldiers themselves. Some of the Special Ops teams gained adverse notoriety because they committed assassinations. But LRRP teams provided extremely valuable intelligence that could not be obtained any other way.

When I served in Vietnam, American units were forbidden to cross the borders into North Vietnam, Laos or Cambodia when conducting patrols or operations. Our maps were not entirely clear as to where the exact border line was, and it was impossible to determine in dense jungle. On several occasions, I know I walked very close to the Laotian border and may have even crossed over unintentionally. It was on one such mission that I was informed by my CO that our company was to be joined by a "Tiger Team" the next day. I was to take a reinforced squad and escort the team to the Laotian border. Four days later I was to meet the unit at the same location and escort them back to the company CP. The mission was to be considered secret and I was not to ask any questions and to have minimal communication with the American team leader.

The next morning two choppers landed in our company's LZ, and eight men dressed in tiger fatigues jumped off. Two of the men were Americans and the rest were either ARVN or Kit Carson Scouts. The men carried extremely heavy packs, enemy AK-47s, and did not speak with us. They carried many bandoliers of ammunition and grenades. They also carried multiple Claymores and I watched as one soldier unpacked and repacked blocks of C4, detonation cord (det cord) and blasting caps. I surmised that the unit's mission was to go into Laos, blow something up and return. I did not ask any questions as originally ordered. The men wore no American uniforms, insignia, or helmets. They didn't even wear American jungle boots. The team did not carry a radio but may have had hand-held radios in their packs.

I spoke with the unit leader, a man of about 25 or 26, and went over the route that he wanted to follow. He briefed me on what he wanted to accomplish; he said that he should move out at 2 PM that afternoon as it would take about two hours to get to the Laotian border. I casually asked the man if he was with the 1st Cav and he responded, "No, the Agency." I asked no further questions. From his response I assumed he was CIA.

I assembled my reinforced squad, and we moved out in line formation promptly at 2 PM. The Tiger Team occupied the center of the group. I was ordered to have my radio turned "off speaker," and not to have any communication while the unit was being escorted. The going was extremely difficult as the route we were following was up a steep mountain slope and through dense jungle. After two hours of slogging through the jungle, the men rotating on point were exhausted from having to cut trail with machetes. I called for a break. The American leader of the Tiger Team came forward and asked why we were stopping. I informed him that my men were exhausted from cutting trail. He told me that his team would take over the point and I gladly agreed.

The Tiger Team chopped their way through the dense terrain at an amazing clip. These men were in exceptional shape despite the heavy loads they were carrying. We picked up the pace dramatically as the Tiger Team led the way.

Finally, at about 3 PM, we reached a small clearing. I put out security and looked at the map with the Tiger Team leader. We discovered we had crossed the border by a half-kilometer or so and were already in Laos. This made me extremely nervous because it meant that we were no longer covered by artillery. We had also violated military rules that stated American troops would not cross the border. The Tiger Team leader didn't seem to mind, however, and told me that we would meet at this clearing at 2 PM in four days. I was to wait for his unit until 4 PM. If he did not show, we were to repeat the trip the next day. We established a challenge and password that would be used. He cautioned me several times to brief my men and make doubly sure they would not fire on his men upon return. With that, the American "Agency Man" and his seven team members formed up and continued to move west. During the entire time we were together there had been no other communication. I formed up my squad and headed back in the same direction from which we had come, arriving at the company CP at around 5 PM. I briefed my CO on the operation but did not mention that my unit had crossed the border into Laos.

My company continued to stay at the CP we had established for the next four days. This was unusual because we normally changed our CP every day. My CO wanted to have a good helicopter LZ available to extract the Tiger Team upon their return. So, we continued to send out patrols and ambushes in the surrounding area each day to make sure that there was no enemy activity in the area.

Four days later, I assembled the same reinforced squad to go back out, find the Tiger Team and escort them back to our LZ. I chose the same men for the trip because we were the only ones who knew the route that had been chopped through the jungle. I left the CP early as I wanted to arrive at the clearing with security set up before the Tiger Team returned. I made sure that my men understood not to fire on any noises they might hear coming in our direction and to use the challenge and password that had been established with the Tiger Team leader.

Promptly at 4 PM the remains of the Tiger Team returned. Eight men had gone out, but only four returned. One man was limping badly. My medic ministered to him, saying he thought it was either a broken ankle or severely sprained. He wrapped the ankle. I assigned one man to help the soldier hobble along as there was nothing else we could do for him. I asked the leader where the other four men were; he simply said, "This is it—no one else is coming." I asked if they had been killed and he replied, "This is it." I did notice the four remaining men all had smaller packs than when they had gone out. They had no Claymores left and only a few grenades.

We packed up and made our way back to the CP. Shortly after our return, a chopper landed, picked up the four men and whisked them off. I never found out what the Tiger Team had done in Laos or what happened to the four missing Tiger Team members. I had strong suspicions that they had gone in to blow up something big and had encountered enemy forces coming out and lost four of their members. So much for American soldiers never being in Laos!

~~~~~~

Letter: 20 September 1968, A Company, 1/5 Cav, 1st Air Cav Division, Out in the sticks, I Corps, Vietnam

We are on the second leg of our mission and still in very thick terrain. It seems that we have intruded into one of Charlie's hiding places and found a Regimental Headquarters with bunkers, weapons, ammunition, and we have had some contact.

I lost a man just the other day. He was trying to throw a grenade into a bunker. He was a sergeant and a very fine man. He was married too. I felt bad about it, but you have to keep pushing and not let these things bother you.

Well, not surprisingly, my R&R has been changed. Now I am going to Tokyo! I am due to get out of the field on 7 October and the R&R will run from the 11th to the 16th. I am not disappointed. This means I'll return to the company in late October. I may have to spend a few more weeks in the field, but more than likely the Colonel will want me to work with the old S-1 and S-3 before they leave Vietnam. Both men are scheduled to depart in November so I may not have to go back out to the field at all or if I do it won't be for too long.

It is probably just as well that I take my R&R soon. The ground pounding is beginning to get to me. It is very hard to withstand the constant humping, heat, rain, and strain as well as the firefights and loss of life. I need a good rest.

CHAPTER 23

Tear Gas Attack

I thought I would be able to simply take a deep breath, hold it, remove
my mask, pull out the lenses and then put the mask back on.

I am nearsighted. Prior to leaving the World, I had a pair of eyeglasses made for me at the military base in Ft. Ord, California, near where I stayed with my parents. At the same time, the optometrist told me about an eyeglass insert for the regulation Army gas mask. Gas masks were issued to all soldiers coming into country and having them in the field was a requirement. I thought this was a clever idea, and had the inserts made along with the traditional pair of eyeglasses. The gas mask inserts were small, funny-looking granny glasses that were held in place within each eyepiece of the mask by a simple expanding wire spring. They were among the personal possessions I brought with me to Vietnam.

I tried to bring only what I thought were the minimum personal effects. After a few days of lugging around a duffel bag of personal gear plus the briefcase that held my reel-to-reel tape recorder, it became abundantly obvious that that I had brought too much crap. I saw officers returning for their second tours carrying only a small overnight bag and wondered why someone hadn't clued me in as to what to bring. But I was reluctant to give up any of my personal possessions because I had no idea about what I would use and need. It wasn't until I finally joined my company at the battalion base camp and my personal possessions were placed in waterproof bags that I was relieved of all the equipment burden.

It was just too damn hot to wear eyeglasses; I kept them with me but after a few weeks I discovered they had been broken. I went without eyeglasses for the entire time I was in Vietnam. This didn't help my eyesight, but I rarely needed to see long distances anyway; operating in dense jungle, I never needed to see more than 50m. I did remember to insert my granny glasses into my gas mask where they stayed for the entire time I was in the field.

The gas mask was placed in an awkward, half-moon shaped bag like an airline flight pillow with straps that wrapped around your waist and leg. There was a zipper in the front of the bag that let you rapidly remove the mask in the event of a gas attack. CS gas or tear gas with a vomiting agent added was rarely used in Vietnam. However, when dropped from the air, it spread uncontrollably, and the concern was that American troops would need gas masks with them at all times in case gas was used. The NVA certainly never had access to gas, but we put up with the masks as it was a requirement to carry them, and they most often became our pillows.

All American soldiers were required to go through a tear gas familiarization and training exercise. Wearing his mask, the soldier enters a tent where gas has been exploded. He then must remove the mask and state name, rank, and serial number. The exercise is long enough so that you have to inhale the gas. It is an experience that you never forget. As soon as you remove your mask and try to take in a breath, you find your throat constricted, you cannot see, and the gas burns your eyes and throat. You become totally incapacitated and are forced to run from the tent to find clean air.

* * *

My battalion had been chasing an NVA regiment in dense jungle bordering Laos for several weeks. We conducted several combat assaults into various LZs surrounding the area where the regiment was suspected to be holed up. My company was chop-pered into a blocking position in hopes of preventing the enemy from escaping across the Laotian border. Other companies were designated to pursue the enemy, locate the force, and destroy it. A cat-and-mouse game ensued as the NVA were familiar with our tactics, and masters at breaking into small units to escape our attack. But our battalion commander wanted to mix it up with this regiment in the worst way.

We were successful at ambushing several smaller groups of the enemy force at night. After capturing some NVA soldiers and accompanied by some strong inducement, the intel staff was able to determine the approximate location of the main body of the regiment. When it came to extracting information from enemy soldiers, our intelligence people, accompanied by Kit Carson Scouts, were often successful. However, one never knew how accurate the information was. Even if we had a fix on where the enemy unit had been the day before, they frequently changed their position throughout the night. The enemy was impossible to spot from the air given the three-canopy jungle. An enemy force would have to pass directly in front of our ambush or a patrol for us to be completely sure of their location.

My company had set up a perimeter on the top of a hill as usual. We cleared brush in front of our positions, dug in and sent out patrols during the day and ambushes during the night. This was SOP. We had been in place for two days due to having difficulty chopping out an LZ where one bird could hover. Being stationary for two days was a pleasure for those soldiers who were not required to go on patrol or pull ambush duty at night.

It was my platoon sergeant's turn to take out the day patrol and I would be taking out the night ambush. The weather was very warm, so most of the troops were staying in the shade, sleeping, writing letters, or eating, with one man on duty in each foxhole. Abruptly, I was called to the company CP for a briefing by my company commander. I learned that one of the other companies had spotted a large enemy force in the area and was pushing it in our direction. I was told to contact my platoon sergeant who was on patrol and order him to return to the CP immediately. We were to prepare for potential immediate enemy contact. Furthermore, F4 Phantom jets were being dispatched to be overhead within 15 minutes. They were going to drop canisters of CS gas within 500m of our company CP. As soon as the gas was dropped, we were to open up for a "mad minute" of sustained fire to hopefully catch the enemy force unaware of our position. The order came down to make sure our gas masks were functioning properly.

My platoon sergeant responded to my call to return immediately, saying that his patrol was more than 30 minutes away. He was right in the path of the gas drop. Furthermore, the patrol members were carrying only light loads of water and ammo and no masks. I relayed this information to my CO, and he barked: "Tell them to run. I don't know if I can delay the jets."

Running through three-canopy jungle and up a mountain to the company CP was challenging. It would be equally dangerous if the patrol was caught without masks in the area where the gas was dropped. My platoon sergeant said he would rush the patrol back to the CP as fast as was humanly possible. He did not think he could get back within 15 minutes. He was especially nervous about having his men caught in the gas drop without access to masks.

All the men at the CP began pulling out dusty and dirty gas masks and cleaning off the lenses. They put them on and checked to make sure that the seal was secure and filters in place. I did the same and discovered that my mask was equally dirty and dusty even though I had never opened the case. Wiping the mask down with a wet cloth helped. I put on the mask and checked to make sure that there was a tight fit around my face. For the first time, I discovered the granny glasses I had installed many months before. I pulled out the glasses and wiped them but had a devil of a time trying to put them back into the eyepieces. I checked my mask again by placing my palms over the intake vents and sucking in. When no air came into the mask I was assured of a tight fit and no gas would enter the mask from around the edges. My mask worked fine. I was even able to look through the glasses and see distances clearly for the first time in several months. After checks had been made, we stored our masks back in their cases. We waited for the official word to put them on in preparation for the drop of gas by the jets.

New filters were also passed out; all the men were instructed to change the filters. At about the same time, one of my squad leaders informed me that a couple of the men did not have gas masks. When I asked why, I was told that they had not been issued. I knew this was not true but suspected these men had thrown their masks away or left them in the rear not wanting to carry them.

Fortunately for these men, there were several others in the company who also did not have masks. An immediate resupply was requested, to be delivered by helicopter. This really angered my CO as well as the battalion commander, as the jets would have to be delayed.

Meanwhile, my platoon sergeant was pushing his patrol to climb uphill to our company CP. The men were simply not able to make the climb on time in the intense heat. The sergeant called for a short stop to give the men a chance to rest and catch their breath. Given the fact that some men did not have masks and more filters were needed, the gas drop was postponed for 30 minutes, then an hour and then for a second hour. The patrol finally made it back to the CP, checked their masks and hurried into their foxholes.

Two hours after the first alert, we were instructed to pop purple smoke from all perimeter positions surrounding our CP. This would mark our position for the jets and insure they did not drop the canisters too close to our position. The word was given to put on our masks as the planes were inbound. Everyone dutifully pulled out their masks and put them on. Two jets came screaming over our position and dropped their canisters to within 500m of our perimeter. Our FO was talking to the pilots asking them to do a second run placing the second round of gas in closer. On their second pass, after the jets released the gas at about 200m off the ground, they were so close that we could see the pilots in their cockpits. The gas billowed up and surrounded us. Men who did not have a tight fit on their masks started to choke and cough.

It was so hot inside my mask that the granny glasses fogged up. It was impossible to see what was happening and to check if my troops were wearing their masks properly. Everyone was getting ready to fire the mad minute in hopes of catching enemy soldiers near our position and trapped by the gas. I thought I would be able to simply take a deep breath, hold it, remove my mask, pull out the lenses and then put the mask back on again. However, I did not anticipate how long it would take to remove the lenses. I tried to keep my eyes closed and remove the lenses by feel but couldn't do it. Eventually, I opened my eyes ever so slightly to pull out the lenses. That's all it took. My eyes immediately started to tear and burn from the gas. Now I could not see to pull out the lenses and I was running out of breath. I handed my mask to my RTO and told him to pull out the lenses. In doing so, I ran out of air and sucked in some gas. Things were not going well for me. I was experiencing exactly the distress I had wanted my troops to avoid.

Finally, my RTO was able to extract the lenses. He handed my mask back to me. By now, I was in agony from the gas and unable to check on my men or direct the mad-minute firing. As I pulled on my mask, I inhaled another lungful of CS gas which caused me to continue to choke and squirm. I made sure the mask fit tightly and took deep breaths. It took several minutes to regain my composure and start breathing normally.

This was the only time I encountered the use of CS gas in Vietnam. I suspect that someone in the G-2 intelligence shop had the bright idea to try to gas the NVA. The problem was the suspected enemy force never materialized. The entire exercise was a major waste of time, material, and planning. Unfortunately, this was not an unusual situation and indicative of how American taxpayer dollars were wasted during the war.

CHAPTER 24

Night Firefight

I turned over, groaned, and heard someone say: "Hey, it's One-Six—he's not dead."

When we worked the lowlands area near the Gulf of Tonkin, even though the heat was oppressive, the terrain made it so much easier to navigate and maneuver. Our company would typically get started with a daily move as early as possible before the sun became too oppressive. We would hump from 7 AM until around 11, stop to eat C-Rats, drink water and "hole up" during the hottest hours of the day. Men stripped down to T-shirts with towels wrapped around their heads and shoulders, wiping the sweat away. We sweated—a lot. There was no end to it when we were humping.

As soon as we stopped for lunch, we grabbed sticks and put poncho liners up over our heads to get out from under the sun's intense rays. The lowlands were a grueling experience. We all looked forward to being picked up by helicopters and flown to a new location. We were grateful for the cool air in the open helicopter cockpits—if even for a short flight.

In the lowlands, we assumed that Charlie was watching us all the time. The VC were masters of hiding. They would dig spider holes, camouflage them superbly well, and hide—watching the American movements and evaluating our activities. It was rare that we would spot them. Their spider holes were so well camouflaged that sometimes the point man would crash into one. The enemy seemed to be aware of our every move, knew our routines, loved going through the trash we left behind and planned carefully to ambush us when they felt very sure of having the advantage. But because of the firepower we could rapidly bring to bear in any firefight, the VC picked their battles very carefully. They used booby traps and snipers to harass and pick at us rather than direct confrontation. But the monitoring of our movements and anticipation of our activities was reported back through their chain of command. Occasionally, NVA troops would mass to conduct a larger attack given this detailed information.

We countered these VC activities with a variety of deceptive moves. When the company started to move, usually in the early afternoon, each platoon needed to scout for night ambush sites. As the platoons traveled our respective routes, we stopped at several possible ambush locations. We would stop, evaluate the terrain, use lots of hand gestures, and make it appear as if we were planning to use that spot for the night's ambush. We therefore believed it was very difficult for Charlie to know which spot we ultimately decided to use. This deception worked—most of the time.

The day I was wounded started out just like every other. It was super-hot, the men were tired, and we were in the low country with the prospect of 105-degree heat facing us. The CO gave each platoon leader a route to follow. We saddled up and moved out at around 7:30 AM through low, scratchy brush. As usual, I cautioned the men to stay alert even though they were tired and hot. We knew Charlie was in the area and did not want to take the chance of being ambushed.

We reached our noon stopping point, set up a perimeter, ate some fruit from our C-Rations, rested and drank water. We tried to keep the chatter down, but even so the men smoked, joked, and talked. With security posted, some men played cards, some read, and some wrote letters home. You could try to snooze, but the heat made it extremely difficult.

Finally, at around 2 PM we saddled up again, continued our move toward that night's CP and started to scout ambush sites. It was my turn to lead the ambush. We stopped at three different locations that looked promising and made a big fuss over each one. Arriving at the company CP around 5 PM, we sighed with relief when a slight breeze came up and cooled things off slightly. The men perked up, enjoying the drop in temperature. The men who were not going out on ambush that night dug foxholes just as we did every night. In the lowlands, the digging was much easier compared to the forest, mountains, and jungle. The soil was sandy and there were no roots to cut through. It was easy to dig the two-man holes four to five feet in depth, piling the sand and dirt in front of the hole.

The squad that was going on ambush with me rested, ate, and prepared their equipment. The reinforced squad consisted of 12 men, including a machine gunner and ammo bearer, the M79 grenadier, my squad leader, RTO, six riflemen and me. Each man carried at least two bandoliers of ammunition, four hand grenades, a smoke grenade, and a white phosphorus grenade. We brought four Claymore mines and two flashlights with red filters. My radio operator switched his PRC-25 radio to silent mode and attached three smokes and three star clusters to his rig. I carried two smokes and two star clusters, my compass, and a small penlight flashlight, in addition to the same ammo and water load as the others. We cleaned our weapons, left our packs and steel helmets behind, put on floppy bush hats, darkened our faces with camouflage paint and carried our poncho liners to lie on when we reached the ambush position.

As was the usual standard operating procedure (SOP) my FO gave me pre-planned artillery concentrations adjacent to our chosen ambush location, marked and labeled on my map with a grease pencil. Squad leaders were briefed, and we got ready to move out. My L-shaped ambush location had been randomly chosen on the other side of a muddy rice paddy with our machine gun placed at the corner of the L. We would catch any enemy troops that were moving across the area. After inspection we moved out and soon arrived at the edge of a low brush line adjacent to the rice paddy.

I thought I did everything by the book, and perhaps that was what caused us to be ambushed that night as we started to cross the rice paddy. The proper way to cross an open space, like a rice paddy, was to send two men across and have them check the other side. Then, they would signal using their flashlights covered by a red filter. It was getting dark as I sent my point man and cover man across the 150m open space. After a short while, I saw two short red flashes from the other side of the paddy. This was the all-clear signal to send the rest of the squad to cross the paddy. We walked along a dike. It was about 12 inches high and as hard as concrete. The squad moved out with 5m between men. When our unit was fully exposed, an enemy machine gun opened up on us.

All hell broke loose. Two men at the head of the column were instantly killed by the initial burst. Another was hit in both legs and started screaming, fully exposing our position. The rest of the men hit the ground behind the rice paddy dike as rounds thumped into it. My men returned fire which brought immediate return fire from the machine gun. We were pinned down. I heard the thump, thump, thump of a mortar being fired. I grabbed the radio handset from my RTO and yelled the FO's call sign, saying that I was under attack by an enemy machine gun and mortar. I requested he fire the Red 1 pre-plot and only one-gun fire for adjustment and one-gun fire when the target was confirmed, as the target was "danger close," within 100m of our position. The FO acknowledged my call. Within a minute I heard the FO come back on the radio and say "Shot, over," meaning that the first round was on its way.

My men buried themselves behind the paddy dike wall. While it was only about 12 inches high it seemed to be stopping the machine-gun bullets from hitting us—but we were clearly pinned down and in dire straits and I had a man screaming in pain. My squad leader crawled over to attend to his wounds. There was nothing that could be done for the two dead soldiers. I called my company commander, quickly explained the situation, told him I had KIAs and a WIA and needed reinforcements immediately. He wanted more information, but the FO broke in saying that rounds were on the way, and he wanted adjustment. At that moment enemy mortar rounds began to land behind us. The enemy unit had their mortar fire zeroed in on the dike and I knew that the next rounds would bracket us. I needed to get my men out of harm's way and away from the open area. I yelled at the men to my left to keep firing but to start crawling back to the area we had come from using the rice paddy dike for cover. I had no idea what had happened to the two men who had already crossed the rice paddy to the other side. Every time one of my men fired his muzzle flash gave away his position and the enemy machine gun would zero in on it, placing the shooter in grave danger.

Our first artillery rounds landed; I put my left arm on top of the rice paddy dike and lifted my head up to see where the rounds were landing. I had my compass out and was preparing to adjust the fire when an enemy mortar round landed on the opposite side of the dike. A piece of shrapnel tore into my exposed arm knocking me backwards. It felt as if I had been hit by an NFL linebacker and I rolled over several times, lost my rifle, my helmet, and the radio handset. I was stunned and in shock at what had just occurred. I was also bleeding badly from my left arm, and it hurt like hell.

Slowly, I pushed myself up to a kneeling position and opened my eyes. I was groggy and light-headed, feeling sick to my stomach. I could feel the blood dripping down my left arm and onto the front of my shirt, but I was able to move it—though painfully. I recalled thinking "Thank God it's not severed." I looked up and noticed that green tracer rounds were flying over my head, but they were going away from me. I was confused. Why were tracer rounds going away from me? Then I realized that I was kneeling with my back to the enemy contact.

Another mortar round landed in front of me and fortunately it sank into the deep muck of the rice paddy before it exploded. Water, mud, and shrapnel flew all around me, slapping me hard in the face and chest. Why I was not immediately killed was pure luck. Landing in the soft mud had curtailed the explosion of the mortar round. I was incredibly fortunate that I caught only one piece of shrapnel in the groin. Again, I was thrown backwards. The back of my head hit the rice paddy dike and it was lights out for me. I was knocked out cold.

When I came to, I was somehow back in the brush where we had started. It was totally black, and I couldn't see anything. I sensed bodies lying near me; heard men yelling commands and firing their weapons. There were occasional rifle shots and bursts from our machine gun returning fire and bullets whizzing overhead from the enemy. I was disoriented, and I had the worst headache of my life. I remember thinking, "How did I get here?" And there was blood dripping from my left arm and across my hip. I felt the area; I was wet with blood, and I was continuing to bleed. I was groggy, lightheaded, and dizzy. I tried to sit up and as I did, I promptly fainted due to blood loss. After a few minutes, I regained consciousness. I turned over, groaned, and heard someone say: "Hey, it's One-Six—he's not dead."

My squad leader crawled over, cut open my shirt and applied a pressure bandage to my arm where I had taken the shrapnel hit. Then he opened my pants and placed another bandage on my hip. It hurt like hell when he moved me to tie the bandage. He spoke quietly to say I was going to be OK, and he was going to get me out as soon as he could. He told me I had lost some blood, but all I had to do was hang on as medevacs would be arriving soon. I felt so woozy that my conversation with him was incoherent. I came to understand that the two other bodies lying next to me were our KIAs. We had two others wounded, one suffering from severe leg wounds. I instantly regretted my decision not to have my medic come with us on this mission. But my squad leader had brought a medical bag. He stopped the bleeding and had given shots of morphine to the men who were in extreme pain. He asked if I wanted a shot. I told him no, that I was in shock and very cold. In fact, I was shivering from loss of blood. He then crawled away, but soon returned with a poncho liner which he wrapped around me and tucked under me to try to maintain body heat.

There was nothing I could do. I couldn't sit up. Every time I tried, my head would spin, and I would faint. My squad leader told me to lie still and not disturb my bandages. My wounds were not severe, but if I wasn't careful, I might bleed out. He had done all that he could until the medevacs arrived.

So, I lay there—trying hard not to move a muscle; listening to the sporadic fire and return fire. Suddenly, there was a yell from one of my men. I heard my squad leader yell "Left flank, left flank—they're on our left flank. Move that gun over here." There was a brief pause, and our machine gun opened up firing a full belt load of ammo. Return fire was sporadic. I could hear bullets hitting the bushes overhead. I heard my squad leader yell again "Move that gun back—reposition yourself or they're going to have you sighted in." There was a short lull in the fight and then our machine gun picked up again, firing in sporadic bursts.

I heard my RTO quietly giving instructions to our FO. Artillery was in play. The RTO was shifting the fire from the original plotted point to where he thought the enemy was located. He moved the fire gradually, shifting in 50m intervals, walking the shells toward the direction from where the enemy was shooting. He screamed "Fire for effect." In a few seconds 20 or 30 artillery rounds landed within 300m of our position. The ground shook and the noise was deafening as the rounds landed. After that, there was an eerie silence.

We heard noise coming from behind our position as many soldiers came running into our position. At first, I thought we were being overrun, but realized it was our company commander and two platoons of men brought in to reinforce us. Commands were given, men yelled, and a cordon was formed around our meager position. I felt great relief that we weren't being overrun. My CO came over and shined a flashlight in my face. He spoke to me, but I was too disoriented from blood loss and the blow to the back of my head. I do recall him saying to hang on—choppers would be coming in at first light. "First light?" I said, "Holy shit—that's hours away."

What time was it now? We had started out at about 7:30 PM, so it must be after 9 or 10 by now. It was actually after 2 AM and I had been lying on the ground unconscious for several hours. The company medic came over to check my bandages.

He applied a new bandage to my hip as the one previously applied was soaked with blood. This time he tied it very tight to apply pressure to the wound. It hurt like hell. I screamed in pain, but he kept on pulling the bandage tighter and tighter. He said bluntly that if he didn't stop the bleeding, I was going to die before they could medevac me.

So, I lay there. I lay there from 2 AM to 6 AM. I thought about what was happening to me. I thought that I might be close to death. All kinds of thoughts flashed through my mind. What would my parents think if I died? What would my friends and relatives back in California think? What would they say? Who would come to my funeral? But mostly I thought about the life I had lived so far. If I were to die, would my life have had any meaning? Would my death have made a difference? If I died right then, would it have been worth it? What had I accomplished so far in my life? What had been the value of my existence?

I had more questions than answers. But I did know one answer was, "No, I have not accomplished anything in my life. If I died right then, it would not have served a purpose." I had more to do and more to give. I needed to stay alive to do those things—whatever they might be. And for the first time I realized that my time in Vietnam had been meaningless. I took some solace in the fact that I had done my best to lead my men fairly and securely and not to endanger their lives or mine unnecessarily. I had worked to fulfill the orders and accomplish the mission I had been given, but I did so with caution. I never intentionally gave orders to my men that I knew would get them killed. Some had died, but I never asked a man to blindly charge an enemy position or risk his life unnecessarily. I don't know if I was thinking these thoughts or saying them out loud, but I know that these were the things that were going through my head at the time. I did not want to die. It was basic, simple stuff, but that's what you think about if your life is slipping away.

I kept passing out, losing consciousness, but our medic would slap my face to keep me awake. That pissed me off and I told him to stop it. He said that he would if I kept my eyes open and kept talking to him. Finally, after what seemed like many hours, I heard choppers coming in. Four men grabbed on to the edges of the poncho liner that I was lying on that was now soaked in my blood. They scooped me up and half carried, half dragged me over some rough terrain to an open area where a medevac chopper was coming in. Purple smoke and dust blew in all directions; I was hoisted into the chopper and placed on a stretcher. I grabbed on to the poncho liner so that it would not blow away. I was freezing and I wanted it wrapped around me.

The chopper stayed on the ground while the other wounded men were loaded in. Two were walking wounded and two, including me, were on poncho liners. Four of us had been wounded; two seriously. Two had been killed. The dead would be placed on the next bird along with all their rifles and equipment. It seemed as if our chopper was on the ground forever, but it was only a few minutes. The crew chief came over to me to ask how I was doing. I smiled and told him OK now that I was on his bird. He gave me a thumbs up and moved to the other man lying on a stretcher at the back of the chopper. We lifted off. The cool fresh air blew over me. As we flew back to base, the anxiety of the engagement lifted. My fear of dying evaporated with the cool air. I took a deep breath and shut my eyes. There were tears in them because I knew I was not going to die. I knew that I was going to be patched up and live—and God had answered my prayer. There was more for me to do. There were other contributions I was yet to make with my life.

I learned much later that at first light, the two men who had crossed the rice paddy came out of the woods and rejoined our unit. There had been so much shooting going on they were afraid to come back during the night for fear of being shot by our own men. They had taken cover on the far side of the rice paddy and did not want to reveal their position to the enemy. They were also in no position to attack the enemy with a force of only two.

After a blood transfusion at the battalion aid station and some taping of my wounds, I was transported to a hospital ship off the Gulf of Tonkin. The shrapnel was removed, and the wounds in my arm and groin were sewed up. Three days in the hold of that ship were more than enough. I requested permission to be flown back to my battalion where I could recuperate at the battalion fire base. I was walking around slowly and able to take care of myself. My battalion commander wanted me back as he wanted me to write an account of the contact as well as write awards for the soldiers involved. So, on the third day, I flew back to my battalion base camp and was on light duty for the next 10 days until my stitches were removed. I wrote awards for the Bronze Star for Valor for each man involved in the fight. My platoon had been returned to the base camp and I had the chance to interview the men who had been in the fight, especially my squad leader and RTO who played critical roles in directing the squad after I was taken out of action.

All the men thought that I had been killed. They saw the two mortar blasts and my body being thrown backward to the dike. There was so much blood on my shirt and pants, and I was so unresponsive that they dragged me back and put me in the dead pile. No one thought to check for a pulse, understandably as they were so busy trying to handle the situation that decisions were made in a split second.

I learned from my RTO that it had been my squad leader who had saved the day. Almost single-handedly, he and another soldier had pulled the wounded men out of the rice paddy and back into the safety of the brush line—one at a time, making repeated trips out under fire to retrieve the wounded and dead. My squad leader set up a defensive perimeter and got all the men who were not wounded into position. He was also responsible for repositioning the machine gunner and riflemen and told them to conserve ammo and gave them firing directions. After securing our position, he and another soldier crawled out several more times to drag the KIAs back to the perimeter including me.

I spent a week seated at a typewriter writing a sitrep for the battalion commander, letters to the parents of my men who had been killed and writing award recommendations for all the men in the contact. After finishing, I was sitting in our company CP when the battalion commander entered our tent. I immediately started to rise, but he ordered me to sit. He had just finished reading my sitrep, letters and award recommendations. He complimented me on the write ups and wanted to know more about my background. He planned to recommend me for a Bronze Star with V device. I told him I had been a comparative literature major in college and had done a lot of writing as an adjutant with the 82nd Airborne Division. Being a battalion adjutant or S-1 was my secondary military occupational specialty (MOS). The battalion commander told me that my report, letters, and award recommendations were the best he had ever read. He wanted me to be his adjutant as soon as my field tour was up. I gratefully accepted his offer.

He then told me that he was upgrading my recommendations for my squad leader and RTO from the Bronze Star with V device to the Silver Star as these men had shown exceptional courage, bravery, and leadership under fire. My squad leader was responsible for saving my life and the lives of the other men caught in the ambush.

While these events did not change the thoughts, feelings, and decisions I had made lying on the ground that night, I was grateful to the two men who saved me and the rest of the squad that repulsed the enemy attack. I might not be alive today had it not been for their bravery, leadership, and courage under fire. I was proud to be among these men, and even more pleased to get my stitches removed and return to my platoon after 10 days of light duty.

~~~~~~

Letter: 7 September 1968, A Company, 1/5 Cav, 1st Air Cav Division, LZ Jane, I Corps, Vietnam

It has rained for the last four days without stop. Everyone and everything is wet. It's better to be here on the LZ though than in the field. At least you have a chance to dry out and eat some hot chow. I guess the higher ups realize this, so we are going back out to the field again tomorrow! I am not real happy about it, but what are you going to do?

LZ Jane is really soaked. We had several bunkers collapse. In fact, a man was killed when one fell in on him. My bunker is still dry with only a few leaks. The front part, the fighting position did collapse. This required us to work in the rain to repair it. I have some funny pictures of our attempts at rebuilding in the rain and mud.

My spirits are down a bit. They seem to get this way every time we are due to go out. Then we go out and I perk up a bit. As the days and weeks wear on, I am down again. We come in and I'm up. It's a constant change of ups and downs…c'est la vie.

Please do not worry if you do not hear from me for 20 days or so should that happen again. The mails are slow in the monsoon season and there are a thousand reasons why my letters don't get mailed. Do not worry. I am OK and plan to take excellent care of myself.

In case I'm wounded, notification is very prompt (2–3 days), and exact extent of wounds is usually included. But you won't be receiving anything like that. I am usually too low to the ground. So please don't be concerned. I'll keep the letters as regular as possible.

CHAPTER 25

Hard Luck Simons

Sometimes the greatest challenge is to believe the things that are hardest to believe.

I arrived in Vietnam at the age of 22 and had my 23rd birthday in the field. I was the second oldest man in my platoon. The oldest man was Peter Simons. He was the old man at age 25.

About once every six weeks, we manned the perimeter bunkers, providing security at our battalion base camp, LZ Jane, located near the DMZ in I Corps. The greatest pleasure was sleeping during the early morning hours before it got too hot. We would put up poncho liners on top of our bunkers, strip down to shorts and sack out. Even though it was extremely hot, it gave us a chance to recharge and come down from the daily grind and extreme stress of walking through the jungle and looking for and setting ambushes each day for Charlie. After a good morning's rest, time was typically spent writing letters, reading circulated paperbacks, and going down to the nearby pond for a swim as well as "shooting the shit." At some point in the afternoon, blackjack games would start up, usually a dollar a hand, and would continue until dark. Then it was time to return to the bunkers and begin nightly security, rotating one man awake for an hour at each bunker and three sleeping.

Although we were paid $50–$75 monthly in scrip, there was simply nothing to spend money on except betting on poker. Scrip was worthless outside the country and was exchanged frequently to kill the black market trade. Some poker games were legendary and would last for many hours and sometimes for days. There was little else to do and because no one had very much money, no one lost too much. The first time that I had an in-depth conversation with Private Simons was at the end of one such marathon dollar blackjack game that had taken place at my platoon command post. It was 7:30 PM, the game was over, and the participants had begun moving off to their bunkers. I was getting ready to make my rounds of the bunkers in my sector of the perimeter, ensuring that a relief schedule was in place and the men were alert and ready. I also made sure that each bunker had plenty of ammo, flares and Claymore mines set and armed, M16s, machine guns and M79 grenade launchers clean, operational, and strategically placed.

At 8 PM I was approached by my medic who informed me that Private Simons wanted to speak with me in confidence. I had an "open door policy" but it was unusual for a platoon member to request a private meeting unless the matter was of some urgency. I told the medic to have Simons come into my bunker. The medic turned to get Simons, but added on the way out, "By the way, the man is drunk."

Simons had been in Vietnam for about four weeks, had finished processing, training, and acclimatization. He had just joined my platoon but had not spent any time in the field. He was scheduled to go out on his first mission with us the next morning. Simons came into my bunker and saluted sloppily. The minute he opened his mouth, I knew this conversation was not going to go smoothly. I could smell the alcohol on his breath and his speech was slurred. He wavered forward and back as he stood in front of me. I told Simons that he should not be speaking to me when he was drunk. He told me that he knew that, but that he had received a letter from his wife that day with some very disturbing news. He was so depressed that he wanted to get drunk. I told him to go ahead and tell me his story, but that I did not want him pulling security duty tonight because he was so intoxicated. He said he understood.

In most units, being drunk on duty could result in an Article 15 (administrative judicial punishment with the potential for loss in rank and pay). But ours was not the typical military environment. An officer could exercise discretion over how troops should be disciplined. I needed every soldier in the field. The last thing I wanted to do was to lose a soldier in the field because he had a personal problem, or to fine him or reduce his rank because he was upset and drunk.

With slurred speech Simons told me his story in bits and pieces. Before being drafted, Simons had married a woman whose father was a multimillionaire and disapproved of the marriage. Against her father's wishes, the couple got married and proceeded to overextend themselves by buying home furnishings for their first apartment. Simons had been drafted even though he was married, and his wife was pregnant. At that time, the government's policy was not to draft married men whose wives were pregnant. So, if Simons' story was true, he should not have been drafted. Simons had contested the draft board's decision but to no avail and into the army he went. After basic combat training (BCT) and advanced infantry training (AIT), Simons received immediate orders sending him to Vietnam. His wife remained in their apartment. On this day, he had received a letter from his wife telling him that the furniture they had purchased together had not been paid for. The store was going to foreclose on the items if an immediate payment of $1,000 was not sent. The letter went on to say that her affluent father would not give her any money nor help in any way. She was upset over her pregnancy, his being away, the financial burden she had to bear alone and felt that under the circumstances it would be best if she divorced him. Simons topped off his story by saying, "Furthermore, because I was illegally drafted, I should not be in Vietnam at all."

At this point in the conversation, Simons was so drunk that he started crying, swaying back and forth, and having trouble standing on his feet. It was apparent to me that intelligent conversation was going to be useless from this point on, so I told Simons that I would do what I could to help him in the morning after he had sobered up, but that there was nothing I could do for him right now. I further informed him that I knew that American law states that it is unlawful for a wife to divorce a serviceman who is serving in combat, and that a company could also not repossess goods sold to a soldier who was on active combat duty. Both issues would have to wait until the soldier returned from combat duty.

I then called my platoon sergeant to inform him of Simons' condition and to insure he would not be pulling security duty that night. I dismissed Simons and told him to go back to his bunker and sober up. Simons gave me another sloppy salute and left my bunker. It was dark outside, and I heard a muffled thump as he left my bunker but didn't think much of it.

Suddenly, my medic screamed out: "Simons has fallen, and he's hit his mouth. His mouth is all bloody and he's not breathing." The medic started mouth-to-mouth resuscitation only to further scream: "Call for a medevac; he's broken his teeth and there's blood everywhere."

I immediately got on the radio and called the company commander. I informed him that I had a man who had tripped and fallen on a tent rope outside my bunker. He had broken his front teeth, was bleeding profusely, and had passed out. We needed medical assistance immediately. The CO said he would drive his jeep over to my bunker right away and bring men and a stretcher.

The CO arrived a few minutes later. By this time Simons had started to breathe on his own but had proceeded to puke all the alcohol he had consumed over himself and our medic. The medic was covered with vomit and blood, but he had saved Simons' life by clearing his broken teeth and giving him mouth-to-mouth resuscitation. As my CO arrived, he slipped and fell down a steep gravel hill en route to my bunker, gashing a 6-inch-long cut in his calf. The CO became another casualty for my medic to treat. Then we had to carry two people back up the hill: Simons, on the stretcher, still puking his guts out, and the CO, who by this time had discovered that Simons was drunk. He cursed and said he was going to give him an Article 15. Both men went to the aid station. Simons ended up having his stomach pumped and taking a day to recover from his drunken ordeal. My CO received 10 stitches for his efforts to rescue an inebriated soldier.

The army has many requirements for all soldiers who are directly involved in combat. Soldiers must be able to walk, carrying packs on their backs; they must be able to shoot their rifles; and they must be free from illness or physical impairment. And their teeth must be in satisfactory condition for them to eat and participate in combat activities. We discovered that Simons had, in fact, broken his front teeth, but those teeth were dentures. Dentures are still teeth and as the army's rule stipulates: "No teeth, no field duty." Simons would have to go back to the rear to have new dentures made before he could return to the field.

My CO was angry at himself for having fallen and gashed his leg trying to rescue the soldier. I was able to talk him out of the Article 15 punishment, by telling him part of Simons' story. I assured him that I had prohibited Simons from pulling guard duty that night, and the accident had occurred because he tripped on the tent rope when leaving my bunker. We were scheduled to return to the field later that day so fortunately the CO got busy with other important matters and did not pursue the punishment.

About an hour before we were scheduled to be at the helipad for the afternoon flight back to our jungle AO, I stopped by the battalion chaplain's tent. I asked him to visit Simons who was still recuperating at the battalion aid station from his drunken ordeal. I gave him a quick overview of Simons' story but told him that I did not have much faith in what he had told me. The chaplain said he would talk with him but if he had been illegally drafted, Simons might have a case to be dismissed from active duty. At 4 PM, I was on the lead chopper that flew my platoon and company back to the jungle. For the next five weeks we humped the boonies while Simons recuperated and visited the dentist at the division rear in An Khe. He spent a week while dentists crafted and fitted him with a set of new dentures. It then took the better part of another week for Simons to find transportation back to the division forward at Camp Evans, then to the battalion base camp at Camp Jane and finally on a flight out to rejoin our company. Simons' time in country was now at two months and time in the field: zero days.

The company had been walking through dense mountainous terrain near the Laotian border for the better part of two weeks. It was slow going. We were searching for trail networks and supply routes that fed into South Vietnam from the Ho Chi Minh Trail. The trail ran through Laos, just a few miles over the border from South Vietnam. Fighting in the country of South Vietnam was akin to fighting in an area larger than the states of California, Oregon and Washington combined. Military regulations at that time prohibited American troops from crossing the border into Laos or Cambodia to pursue the enemy or to find and destroy caches of enemy equipment and supplies. Conversely, the NVA and VC could come across the border into the South, all along the border, and did so with impunity.

Finally, after slogging and cutting our way through dense, three-canopy jungle, our company came down off a mountain top and into a large valley. Late in the day, we set up a perimeter on a small hill. For the first time in several weeks, we did not have to cut down trees to establish an LZ for helicopter resupply. The logistics helicopter brought ammunition, water, C-Rations, 81mm mortar rounds, mail, and the ration of one soda and one beer per man.

Because of our accessible location, we were told that the chopper would bring us hot food the next morning. It would be the first hot food we had had in three weeks, and we were all looking forward to it. The food was finally flown in at around 11 AM and cooks offloaded field stoves and prepared pancakes, eggs, and bacon for us. I remember that meal as one of the best I enjoyed in Vietnam, as everyone was sick of eating C-Rations. When the chopper came in to collect the cooks and their equipment, Simons was on the flight returning to our unit.

This would be his first day in the field. The other men in my platoon started to give him a hard time about his being a "straphanger" (one who works in the rear and hangs up equipment by its straps) as well as shirking his duties as an infantryman. Simons didn't like what was being said to him, came to me, and requested to walk point when the platoon started to move out. I was a bit skeptical about letting him walk point because of his lack of experience and time in the field, but we had not had contact with any enemy for several days and I saw that he was trying to reestablish his reputation within the platoon. Reluctantly, I agreed to let him do it.

The afternoon monsoon rains started right on schedule at 2 PM. We saddled up and moved off the hilltop and down a steep incline following the route we were to patrol. The rain made the ground slick and slippery. We switched back and forth down a steep grade; men were hanging onto trees, roots, and anything that would keep them from falling. As we snaked down the mountain side, the ground was torn up and the trail got muddy. Rocks were dislodged and started to tumble down the steep slope. When this happens, the man who dislodges a rock yells "Rock!" and everyone is supposed to turn their backs uphill. If you got hit, you were hit in the back which hopefully would not be as painful or debilitating as being hit in the front.

Someone from above yelled "Rock!" and everyone dutifully turned their backs, except Simons who by this time had reached the bottom of the slope as the point man. Simons looked up, just in time to see a large rock come crashing down and land on his right ankle. When our medic reached him, the man was in severe pain and the ankle was swollen to twice its normal size. Doc examined Simons and declared the ankle was broken. He would have to be medevaced. A squad was selected to take Simons back up the hill to the LZ we previously used to bring in the cooks. We all took turns carrying Simons and his equipment, piggyback style, to the top of the hill with me in the lead.

It was a real struggle to carry the man back up the hill. It continued to rain as we tried to work our way up the slippery slope. It had taken us only 20 minutes to get to the bottom of the hill, but 45 to work our way back. We swore and cursed Simons with every step. When we finally got back to the LZ, everyone took a breather and had a smoke while we waited for the medevac chopper to arrive. The helicopter called us, and we popped smoke, so the pilot could identify our position and see which way the wind was blowing.

As the chopper landed, men rushed out to put Simons' equipment on board. Simons was sitting on a big boulder resting his broken ankle. I told him to climb on my back, so I could piggyback him out to the waiting chopper. Simons climbed on my back and as I started to move toward the helicopter, he started to slip. I stopped and boosted him higher on my back. As I did my head came back and my steel helmet shifted backwards and crashed into Simons' mouth, busting his new dentures. So now Simons had a broken ankle and broken dentures. We threw him on the chopper, collected our own gear and headed back down the hilltop to join the rest of the platoon. Simons was taken back to the field hospital where his ankle was set in a walking cast and arrangements made to send him back to the division rear in An Khe to have new dentures made. After two weeks, Simons returned to the company with new dentures, but still in a cast. He was assigned to light duty while his ankle healed.

At about the same time, I was designated to be the pay officer for the company and was choppered out of the field late one afternoon to our battalion base camp. I would be heading to An Khe early the next morning to draw funds to pay the company in the field. I was exhausted, and it was a real pleasure to grab a hot meal and sleep on a cot in the company tent. I was sound asleep by 9 PM. At around 11 PM, the battalion executive officer, a major, came into the tent, shook me, and woke me up. I was groggy and half asleep. He wanted to know if I had a man who was on light duty who could guard the battalion's truckload of soda and beer which was being driven up from An Khe in III Corps to the battalion base camp in I Corps. I thought for a moment and asked if a man who had a cast on his foot would qualify. The XO said that would be perfect.

I found Simons sleeping in an adjacent tent. He had just returned from An Khe that same day, but still had another two to three more weeks of light duty before the cast on his foot could be removed. I told him he was to fly down to An Khe the next day at first light to guard the battalion's load of soda and beer. Simons readily agreed as it would give him more to do than hang around the company CP and take crap from the first sergeant.

I struggled back to my tent, fell on my cot and was asleep in minutes. I was awakened by the duty NCO at 5:30 the next morning and headed for the airfield. My only mistake was that I completely forgot to tell my company commander and the first sergeant that I had assigned Simons to this guard duty. Furthermore, our first sergeant had not been informed that Simons had returned from An Khe. Consequently, several days later when Simons had not returned to the company, the first sergeant reported him as absent without leave (AWOL).

I continued my way to An Khe, spent a day in the Officers' Club, picked up the pay for my company, handled some administrative matters requested by the soldiers and made my way back to LZ Jane and then on back to the field and my company. Simons and the guard duty to which I had assigned him were completely forgotten.

Simons guarded the truck full of beer and soda. However, the truck broke down halfway to the battalion base camp. This happened in a secure area, but repair parts had to be ordered and it took two weeks for the parts to work their way to the truck's location and for it to be repaired. Dutifully, Simons stayed with and guarded the truck. It took him another week before he and the truck finally returned to battalion headquarters.

By this time, my company was back pulling base camp security again. After Simons reported back, the first sergeant wanted to have him arrested for being AWOL. Simons blurted out the story of how I had assigned him to guard the truck, how the truck broke down and how he had stayed guarding it until repairs were made. Finally, the battalion XO was consulted and Simons' story was verified.

Our time at base camp came to an end the next day, and we choppered back out to the boonies to continue our daily mission. Simons stayed behind to have the cast removed from his foot and spend a week on light duty as he exercised it back into shape. One week later he was flown out to join our company. Simons' time in country: four months; time in the field: zero.

Simons again came out to join the company on a noon "hot food flight." We were balancing paper plates heaped high with roast beef, mashed potatoes, vegetables, and gravy along with lukewarm Kool-Aid. We looked for places to sit and eat our food. My troops again started to give Simons a hard time. He had been in Vietnam for more than four months and had yet to spend one full day in the field. Simons again asked me for permission to walk point, but this time I declined and told him to just shut up, eat his food and keep a low profile. He could prove himself to the others just by doing his job.

Like the rest of us, Simons had a paper plate full of food. He finally found a place to sit, away from the troops who were harassing him, on what looked like a grassy spot… except that it wasn't a grassy spot at all. It was a thistle bush. As he sat down, Simons thrust a 3-inch thistle deep into his ass cheek causing him to scream in pain and drop his food.

The medic was called, but the thistle was in too deep and could not be extracted. Simons again found himself being flown back to the battalion aid station along with the returning cooks and food containers. At the battalion aid station, it was learned that the thistle that Simons had sat on was poisonous and he developed a severe infection once the thistle was removed from his butt. He ran a high fever which lasted several days. Antibiotics were administered, but the wound became infected. Simons was laid up for another two weeks of recovery.

After seven months of leading my platoon in the field I was rotated to a staff job. By comparison, the average soldier spent 11 to 12 months in the field. (Short timers, those with less than one month left to serve, were often pulled out of the field as they became "squirrely" when they had less than 30 days left in country. They were given straphanger duties in a rear area.) Officers were assigned staff positions to allow new officers coming into Vietnam to occupy line positions and gain combat command experience.

At this point I took my R&R and went to Tokyo, a trip that took 10 days, returning to my new staff job. Sometime later, my former platoon medic stopped by for a visit en route to his own R&R. He filled me in on the details of what had been happening to the platoon since I had left, enjoying the shade of our tent and a cold beer from our refrigerator. The conversation finally got around to Simons, and Danny Small completed the story.

Simons had finally recovered from the thistle in his ass and had come back out to the field. He walked point, pulled his weight, and did all the things that an infantryman needed to do in combat. He was a model soldier, and the rest of the men were starting to lay off calling him a shirker and a straphanger. After three days in the field, orders came from division headquarters to the battalion and company commanders that Simons was to leave Vietnam immediately. The inquiry made by the battalion chaplain had resulted in an official congressional inquiry. Lo and behold, Simons had been telling the truth. His wife was pregnant, and he had been illegally drafted. After less than a week spent in the field, Simons found himself flying back to Tan Son Nhut Airbase, and then back to the World. My medic, one of the few friends that Simons had in the platoon, received a letter from Simons a few days after his return. All was fine; his wife still loved him. They were excited about their new baby and his wife's father, the multimillionaire, was so proud that Simons had served his country in Vietnam that he had given him a job in his company and paid all his outstanding bills. Simons' total time in country: six months; time in the field: three days.

Sometimes the greatest challenge is to believe the things that are hardest to believe.

CHAPTER 26

Walking Point

"Holy shit!" I said to myself, "There's a man coming down the hill." I backpedaled and jumped behind a tree while bringing up my M16, finger tightening on the trigger.

Few men liked walking point. I rotated the task every day, sometimes two or more times a day depending on the terrain and the heat. The point and cover men were in the most dangerous positions. They were also the ones who tripped the booby traps, stepped in punji pits (holes spiked with sharpened bamboo or nails and dipped in excrement) or were immediately taken down in the first volley of an ambush. They walked 25–50m in front of the rest of the platoon, slowly and cautiously, with weapons loaded and selector switches turned to full automatic. They carried their M16s at the ready and could fire within a split second. Men who walked point experienced extreme stress and constant fear. Their lives depended on being alert and fast on the draw. In our AO there were no friendlies. The rule was, "If something moves to your front—you shoot it, and worry about the consequences later."

I was mistrustful of soldiers who were anxious to walk point. These men often were looking to make a kill and establish a reputation. They could be far too aggressive, and their actions ended up risking lives—as well as the life of the cover man who walked a short distance behind. I rarely allowed a man to volunteer to walk point. It was better to rotate the job so that each man took his turn.

The best men to walk point were the ones who had done a lot of deer and bird hunting. They had experience walking quietly through the brush without making noise and without having to constantly look down to see where they were stepping. These men scanned the front, listened for noises, and checked for movement and anything out of the ordinary. It might be some brush that looked a little odd and was being used as camouflage—brush that was a little too brown when compared with the rest of the terrain. It might be an unevenness in the soil that housed a spider hole or punji pit. While these men were incredibly good at walking point, keeping their eyes open and spotting Charlie before he saw them, they were also at greater risk of missing tripwires because their gaze was always to the front and not the ground, so booby traps and trip wires placed right in front of them were a constant danger. Being alert to noises was critical, such as the click of a safety switch. Being alert to no noise was also important. If the birds weren't chirping or monkeys weren't screeching, this could be a sign of danger and possible ambush.

Many of the men I lost were either wounded or killed by booby traps. The most common booby trap was made from our own munitions. It typically consisted of a hand grenade stolen from ARVN or from a US supply depot and used against us. The pin was pulled, and the grenade was inserted inside a C-Ration can and anchored to a bush. The can kept the grenade handle (spoon) depressed. Then a thin green wire (also supplied by the US Army) was attached to the grenade, run across the trail, and tied to another bush on the opposite side. The point man would cautiously walk down the trail looking to the front at 25m intervals. He might not see the thin green wire strung across his path. The man's boot caught the wire and pulled the grenade out of the can. The handle would pop, and the man had five seconds to recognize the sound and react. By the time he started to run and yell "Grenade!" two to three seconds had passed. There might just be enough time to dive for cover if there was some. The kill radius of a hand grenade is 5–10m depending on many factors. If the point man and cover man were very, very lucky, they might only suffer foot and leg wounds from the shrapnel fragments as they dove for cover. If there was cover nearby it might prevent the fragments from hitting vital body parts. However, if the point man did not hear or recognize the ping of the grenade handle popping off he was in big trouble. Sometimes, not realizing it, he stepped over the wire and one of the men following in line would trip the grenade. Booby traps could be quick, quiet, and lethal.

One evening as our entire company was walking in line formation, there was a loud yell of "Grenade!" followed by an explosion and screams coming from the front. Somehow, 10 to 15 men had avoided a "grenade in a can" booby trap. It had finally been tripped by the company commander's RTO. He suffered severe wounds to both legs and was crying out in extreme pain. Our company medic did his best to stop the bleeding and gave the radio operator a shot of morphine. This quieted his screams. I came forward to see what was happening, but there was nothing I could do, and I returned to my position in line. We called in a medevac and were able to get the wounded man back to the battalion aid station in record time. How so many men had walked past and missed the tripwire was beyond me. Some men had simply stepped on or over the wire and pushed it down into the ground. It was just the bad luck of the RTO to have his boot catch the wire and pull the grenade out of the can.

We encountered booby traps that used unexploded 81mm mortar rounds or 105mm artillery shells. These were not practical in jungle terrain and were often used instead on roads to blow up vehicles. They were discovered by engineers who swept the roads around the battalion base camp every day using mine-detecting equipment. When found they were exploded in place. Remote detonated devices or IEDs were not used during the Vietnam War. There were other forms of booby traps employed by the Viet Cong, such as punji pits, full body pits, bamboo whips, tiger traps and mace traps, but my unit only encountered grenades and a few punji pits.

There was always a discussion among the soldiers about whose turn it was to walk point next and when a man had walked point last. Men could not "opt out" of walking point or trade with another soldier. When it was their turn to walk, they walked. Each man ended up with the duty several times a month depending upon the terrain. The only exception was if they had a cold or a foot injury.

As the platoon leader, I always walked fourth or fifth in line; I never walked point. Similarly, my radio operator, platoon sergeant, his radio operator, and our medic never walked point. But for a few days on one occasion, after listening to my men gripe about the job, I started to wonder what it was like to take the front of the line and lead the platoon. I decided that I wanted to find out for myself, and I toyed with the idea of taking a turn.

My platoon had been assigned a typical mission of searching and clearing an area down from the top of a steep hill where our company CP was located. The object was to discover any enemy force in the vicinity. We wanted to prevent them from sneaking up to our perimeter and throwing grenades or satchel charges at us during the night. Each platoon would send a reinforced squad to secure the area surrounding the CP. The maneuver consisted of walking to the base of the hill, turning to the right, skirting one-third of the base of the hill, and then humping back up to the top. The total distance covered was usually about 4–5 klicks, so there was no danger of the patrols contacting one another following this tactic.

While in thick jungle with extreme heat, as usual, the men of the reinforced squad I led on this mission were tired and irritable. I rotated point man and cover man twice because we could not find a trail, and it became necessary to chop our way through some dense jungle. The man cutting the trail could hold out for about 15 minutes before he had to be rotated. The point man and cover man walked close behind the cutter providing cover.

Finally, reaching the bottom of the hill, we took a long break and rested. We were shaded from direct sun, but the heat and humidity were more oppressive than usual. I estimated it was between 110 and 115 degrees. Men were sweating profusely, and everyone was extremely uncomfortable. After an extended rest, we saddled up and continued the walk. After a few hundred meters, we came into a less dense area. The point man stopped abruptly because of the change in terrain. The man cutting trail was retired. We found a small animal trail that seemed to be heading in the direction we wanted to go. This made the walking a bit easier.

After consulting the map, I realized that we had completed our assigned sector of the circle around the base of the hill. It was time to head back up to the company CP with about a half-klick to go. It was then that I decided it was time to walk point. I told my platoon sergeant to come up and take over my position. My platoon sergeant immediately voiced his objection to the idea, saying that the platoon leader was never to walk point. He did not approve of my idea at all.

But I insisted that I wanted to give it a try. We only had another half-kilometer to go, and we were headed back uphill to the CP. We had not encountered any sign of enemy all day. What could go wrong? After a short rest, I grabbed the cover man, and we walked out in front of the platoon by about 50m.

Very soon I became aware of the stress and fear the point man experiences. I was all alone. I had a man about 5m behind me, but there was nothing but jungle in front of me and no security coverage that I was very used to when walking fourth or fifth in line. In my position in line, I could always see men in front of me and my RTO was always within a few feet ready to hand me the handset if I needed to make a call. But now there was no one to my front. I was standing there all alone and vulnerable. I experienced the same feelings that my point men felt. The fear and anxiety washed over me. I felt as if there were hundreds of eyes staring at me all at once. I tried to focus, move cautiously, observe any signs to the front, but found it extremely difficult to get control of my heart rate and control the thoughts running through my mind.

I carried my M16 on full automatic, safety off and at port arms, ready to bring it into a firing position. In fact, I jumped several times hearing the sound of birds and monkeys screeching to my front or side. I tried to walk slowly. In my mind all I wanted to do was climb to the top of that hill and reach the security of the company perimeter. I could not get there fast enough.

For several hundred meters, I dealt with this fear and anxiety not knowing what was in front of me. I alternated between walking too fast and too slow, following that little green trail. The sweat dripped off my face and hands. I repeatedly swabbed my face with the towel wrapped around my neck and dried my hands so that my rifle would not slip.

My cover man hissed at me from time to time, telling me to either move faster or slow down. He was far more experienced at this work than I. I obeyed his instructions and kept climbing uphill. The trail took a sharp turn. I realized that we were getting close to the top of the hill—and the security of the CP. I turned to start a zig zag up a steep slope. It was hard going because I had to look down to make sure I did not slip. I alternated my gaze looking down and then to the front.

So many thoughts flashed through my mind. How easy it would be for a few enemy soldiers to ambush the front of the line and then disappear into the surrounding jungle. I tried to look for tripwires and C-Ration cans, but it was impossible. There were simply too many things to do and remember all at the same time. Something had to be overlooked; tripwires was the item I had to ignore and hope for the best. Later, I realized that this was why so many point men were injured by booby traps. It was extremely difficult to scout to the front and at the same time be alert to something immediately under your nose.

I climbed the steep slope, crisscrossing back and forth to make it easier to gradually move upwards. It was slow going. I was breathing heavily, pushing myself up the hill. I stopped for a minute and took a quick drink from the canteen I kept in my thigh pocket. I pushed on. My hands were so slippery with sweat that I was afraid that I might drop my rifle at any moment. I thought about flipping the safety but decided against it. Occasionally, point men would trip or fall and fire off a burst or pull the trigger by mistake. This would cause everyone to drop and take up firing positions. I had found it annoying when this happened, but now I gained a new respect for what the point man was going through. You always thought the worst when a rifle was fired.

Then, without warning, I heard and saw a man coming down the trail in front of me. He was moving fast and was coming straight toward me. "Holy shit," I said to myself, "There's a man coming down the hill." I backpedaled and jumped behind a tree while bringing up my M16, finger tightening on the trigger. But something told me not to pull the trigger. It was the speed that the man was traveling downhill; perhaps it was his uniform, or his steel helmet with camouflage cover that registered in my brain. In any case the soldier was one of ours and he was just as surprised to see me as I was to see him.

"What the fuck are you doing?" I screamed. "What the fuck are YOU doing?" the man yelled back. I realized that this was another patrol coming down the hill from the base camp conducting reconnaissance for a night ambush. He didn't expect to see me coming up the hill just as I didn't expect to see him coming down.

"I almost shot you! Why didn't you radio that your patrol was coming down?" I screamed at the man. He screamed back: "Why didn't you radio that you were coming up?" I realized that I had been wrong. I should have called the company CP to alert them that my patrol was moving uphill and heading to the CP. I would always do this from my usual position in line, but now my radio operator was 50m behind me. The company commander's radio operator should have radioed that a patrol was coming down, but it was overlooked.

I found out later that this radio communication did take place. My radio operator had received and acknowledged the call, but as I was 50m to his front there was no way to alert me that the other patrol was on its way down the hill.

The other point man and I were both fortunate that day to have our brains instantly register we were both GIs before we pulled the trigger. It could have been a disastrous moment for both of us. To this day I thank God that we recognized each other in that critical second of hesitation.

It was then that realized I did not have the skill to walk point. My platoon sergeant had been right. It had been a dangerous move on my part, and I never tried it again. I did earn some creds within my platoon and in the company as the only officer to ever walk point, but that notoriety was foolishly and dangerously gained. I came away with a new respect and appreciation for my men who walked point—and the courage it took to do so. I realized we placed our lives and security in their hands. It was a formidable responsibility.

I often think about that day and how close I came to pulling the trigger. I remember how scared I was and how I acted. It's a memory and feeling I will never forget.

CHAPTER 27

You Fight It, We Write It

I asked a soldier, "Do you know where the 14th MHD is?" "I think it's about a mile down that road," the soldier responded.

I ended up spending close to seven months in the field. The battalion S-1 remembered that I had been an adjutant with the 82nd Airborne Division when I first met him upon arrival in the unit. He told me he was scheduled to DEROS (Date Estimated to Return from Overseas Service) at about the same time as I was due to come out of the field.

Officers typically tried to take their seven-day R&R at around the six-month mark and be assigned to a staff job upon return. The selection of R&R sites was based on the seniority of days served in Vietnam. If you were in country for six to seven months, you could qualify for Tokyo, Taiwan, Singapore, or Hong Kong. It also depended on the number of R&R slots available to your unit each month as well as the seniority of other soldiers who were applying at the same time. R&R to Hawaii was reserved for married soldiers. Wives would fly to the big island, and they would be able to stay in free temporary military housing and use the post facilities. This would save couples considerable expense that could be used on travel and entertainment. The plum R&R locations for single officers and enlisted were Sydney and Bangkok. A soldier might have to serve 10–11 months to qualify for one of these locations. Australia was preferred due to the availability of "round-eyed women." Bangkok was preferred by troops who wanted to enjoy feminine companionship.

As I passed the seven-month mark, I put in to take my R&R in Tokyo. I was approved to leave in two weeks. Behind the scenes, the S-1 recognized my name and that I was planning to take my R&R in two weeks. He was scheduled to leave in another month. This would be the perfect opportunity for him to recommend me as his replacement and give me a few days of on-the-job training before taking off for my R&R. Then, upon return, I would take over his job.

About 10 days later, my company was on a routine field mission. We were in open terrain with easy helicopter access. I was sitting with my radio operator, medic and platoon sergeant having a smoke while discussing plans for that night's ambush when I was called to come to the company commander's location. I walked over and sat down next to him. I was abruptly informed that a helicopter was inbound with my replacement onboard. The chopper would arrive in 15 minutes. I was to go back to battalion HQ, understudy the S-1, take my R&R, and become the new S-1 upon my return. The CO said: "Go back, pack up and say goodbye to your men." My mouth dropped open as the news sank in… I was leaving the field—permanently.

I jumped into action and ran back to where I had left my platoon sergeant, radio operator and medic. There was just enough time to give 1-5 my maps encased in a heavy, clear plastic map case that I had brought with me from the World. I also gave him my rope and snap links. I heard a chopper coming to our location and smoke was popped marking the spot where it was to land. I said a very quick goodbye to my platoon sergeant, RTOs, and squad leaders. There wasn't time to do more. These were the brothers-in-arms with whom I had spent the last seven months. There was no time for conversation other than quick handshakes, wishing them well and telling them to keep their heads down. The radio squawked telling me to get to the LZ now. The bird was getting ready to land and it did not want to spend any time on the ground. I ran to the LZ at the center of the perimeter where a LOH was coming into land. (A LOH is a small, fast, and highly maneuverable four-passenger helicopter. It is frequently used in tandem with a Cobra to draw enemy fire and pinpoint enemy locations with the Cobra following behind ready to fire rockets and miniguns. I had never ridden in one before.)

As I jumped into the rear seat on the left side of the bird, I saw an officer exiting the chopper on the right. He had on clean, new fatigues; I realized this was my replacement. I said a silent prayer for his safety, buckled myself into the seat and put on the headset. The pilot asked me if I had ever flown in a LOH. I responded that no, this was my first time. He asked if I was leaving the field as he had just brought an FNG officer out to the company CP. I told him, "Yes, today's my last day in the field. I'm taking over as the new S-1." He responded by saying, "Well then, we'll give you a ride you'll never forget."

The LOH bobbed, weaved, and flew high and low. I braced myself in the open doorway and sucked in lots of cold air as the pilots had great fun with the acrobatics. It was fortunate that the flight back to the battalion rear was only about 15 minutes because I came close to losing my cookies on several occasions. We landed at the main airstrip, and I jumped out on rubbery legs. The pilots wished me well and then took off to park their bird.

I made my way to the battalion commander's tent and found the S-1. I let him know I had arrived. He told me to turn in my M16 and equipment to my company headquarters, draw a .45 pistol and a clean uniform, and take a shower. He also told me where to bunk that night and that he would start my training the very next morning. I followed his instructions and enjoyed a luxurious shower, shaved, and savored a hot meal in the mess tent. I even drank a couple of cold beers courtesy of my company's first sergeant.

The next two days were a blur. I was introduced to the S-1's staff and followed the officer around like a puppy dog. I tried not to ask too many questions but concentrated on understanding the fundamentals of how he performed the job. At the end of the first day, I was exhausted and had a splitting headache. I knew this job was going to be challenging, but far better than humping the boonies as a platoon leader. The most difficult part of the work was processing the soldiers who had been KIA or WIA each day, filling out the paperwork and requesting replacements. There was a ton of administrative and logistical requirements. I found myself running to coordinate with the first sergeants for each company. I asked questions and received information needed for the daily mound of reports and paperwork that was required to be filed with division headquarters.

~~~~~~

Letter: 11 October 1968, S-1, 1/5 Cav, 1st Air Cav Division, LZ Nancy, I Corps, Vietnam

The CO sent me to the rear today, never to return! As of the 20th of October, my birthday, when I return from R&R, I shall be the battalion adjutant. Needless to say, I am very happy, both to have such a responsible job and to get out of the field. I truly am lucky. I leave for An Khe, for my R&R on the 6th or 7th. I have a list of things to do and see. I appreciate you sending the brochure about Japan and the suggestions for what to visit.

~~~~~~

On the morning of my second day, I got ready to start my R&R. After taking a shower and putting on a fresh uniform I prepared to fly to the division rear. The S-1 stopped me to ask if I had had any conversation with the 14th MHD about a job. I told him, "No, I don't even know what the 14th MHD is. Do you?" He told me that he didn't know either, but he had received orders that morning instructing me to report to the 14th MHD at division headquarters for an interview. I said that I was planning to replace him as S-1 and had no idea what the interview was about. He advised me to go ahead to the division rear, do the interview and then grab a flight to Bien Hoa in III Corps and take my R&R. I was to let him know my decision after the interview at division headquarters.

Anticipating I was going on R&R, I had packed my khaki uniform, my civilian clothes, some underwear, and my dress boots in a small bag. I also wore a T-shirt and underpants for the first time in six months. This was a big mistake as I was boiling hot and told myself I would take them off the first chance I got.

I jumped on a chopper heading to the division forward at Camp Evans. Twenty minutes later we landed at the airstrip. The division forward base was a sprawling city several miles long that housed more than 12,000 men. There were thousands of tents each wrapped with 4-foot sandbag walls. Roads ran at right angles throughout. The perimeter was surrounded with intense bunker fortifications. As I walked from the landing zone, carrying my small overnight bag, I asked a soldier, "Do you knew where the 14th MHD is located?" "I think it's about a mile down that road," he responded. I asked if he knew what the 14th MHD stood for. He told me he did not. I remained confused and frustrated, not knowing what the 14th MHD stood for and why I was being summoned for an interview.

Walking down a dusty road, sweating profusely wearing both a T-shirt and fatigue shirt, I read the signs in front of each tent. After about a mile's walk, I reached one with a sign that read:

> 14th Military History Detachment
> You Fight It We Write it

I was dumbfounded. I had no idea that such a unit even existed in the army, what they did or why or how I had been contacted for an interview. I walked into the tent and introduced myself to a Specialist 4th Class who was seated at a typewriter. I told him I was there for an interview. The Specialist told me that their captain was at the division briefing but would return soon. I tried to pump the soldier for more information about what the unit did and their activities, but he said that those were questions I needed to ask the captain. I waited. I sweated.

After about 15 minutes the officer in charge (OIC) returned, and I was introduced to Captain Tensey. We shook hands and he asked why I was wearing both a fatigue shirt and a T-shirt. He wondered if that is what I wore in the field. I told him of course not, but that I had worn the T-shirt because I was going on R&R and thought it would be needed. He asked if I would like to take my shirt off and I immediately thanked him and did so. Then he offered me a cold Coke from their refrigerator. A cold Coke was like an offer of gold. I joyfully popped the top on the can. Captain Tensey then pointed out one of several fans in the tent and told me to relax while he explained the mission of the 14th Military History Detachment.

As the captain talked, I stole glances around the tent and noticed that in addition to the fans and refrigerator, there was a small television set. And there were two separate rooms where I could see bunks for the enlisted men as well as the officers. Slowly, I cooled off, drank my Coke, and listened to what he had to say.

Tensey explained that he had gone through the 201 files for every junior officer in the division and I was one of only three officers who had a literature or journalism degree. The job, he explained, involved preparing the division's quarterly "After Action and Lessons Learned Reports," and attending the nightly division briefing. When a significant battle occurred, I might be assigned to visit the unit within a day of the engagement, interview the participants, take photographs, draw maps, and piece together what had happened. Many of these major engagements occurred at night. Under those conditions even the top brass flying overhead in their command-and-control helicopters did not have a clear idea of what was happening on the ground. The 14th MHD's report of the battle was often the first accurate description of what action had taken place, a summary of unit maneuvers, numbers of KIA, WIA, equipment losses and "lessons learned" about both friendly and enemy forces.

After a few questions I told Tensey that I was slated to become the battalion S-1 for my unit. He said that if I wanted to pursue that job it was fine with him, but to consider what my daily life would be like for the next five months if I joined his team. I would be living at the division headquarters (12,000 men) versus the battalion LZ (500 soldiers), a location that was constantly being relocated to support its field units as well as being frequently under attack.

I asked if I could still take my R&R and make my decision upon return, but was told no, I must make my decision then and there. If I accepted the job, I would return to the 14th MHD and begin work there once my R&R was over. I looked around the tent enjoying the "comfortable living quarters," access to hot showers, refrigerator filled with soda and beer and other amenities. I told Captain Tensey that I would accept the job.

In retrospect I concluded the decision may not have been the best one for my future military career, but at that point, I was through slogging through the jungles of Vietnam, engaging in firefights, and dealing with the loss of my men. I was not at all sure I even wanted to make the army my career. The opportunity to reconstruct a battle, interview combatants, write and draw conclusions about friendly and enemy actions—after it was over—sounded much more interesting than keeping track of KIAs, WIAs, submitting daily casualty reports, writing casualty letters and award recommendations for the battalion commander to sign, and handling personnel issues.

We shook hands on the decision, and I was introduced to the other men in the unit: Sergeant Gonzales (aka Speedy), a combat photographer and artist; Sp4 Mooney, a clerk typist; and SP4 Johnson, also a clerk-typist. We chatted for a few more hours. Then I grabbed my bag and headed back to the airfield where I caught an afternoon flight to An Khe in II Corps. I continued to catch another flight to Bien Hoa and from there on to Tokyo.

My R&R flight was uneventful. I flew for over 17 hours and arrived in Tokyo early in the morning bleary-eyed and jet lagged. I had no plans and had no idea where to go or what to do. I linked up with another officer and, as we disembarked, we were approached by a horde of spokespeople offering tours, rides, hotels, and various entertainment opportunities. One man was not overly pushy, so we spoke with him about his tour opportunity, which lasted five of our seven-day R&R. It was the right price and included hotel stays, meals, and tour bus excursions. Also included was a bullet train ride to the ancient city of Kyoto. We would have the last two days free to visit the post exchange and see more Tokyo sights on our own. For lack of any other plans, we signed up and paid our money.

The first event on the tour was dinner that evening at 8 PM followed by a chorus show. We were so exhausted that we crashed on our beds as soon as we got to our hotel room and slept soundly until 7:15 PM at which time we were awakened with a phone call from the tour operator. We were informed that if we didn't come down to catch the tour bus immediately, we would miss dinner and the show. As we had already paid our money, we dragged ourselves out of bed and sleepwalked through the evening's activity.

The next four days flew by packed with tours of palaces and temples, lots of noodles, a karate demonstration and more local entertainment. The bullet train to Kyoto was impressive with train speeds far exceeding 100 mph. Finally, we returned to our hotel in Tokyo and spent two days on our own. We enjoyed a trip to a local spa, personal baths, massages, and dips in both hot and cold pools... all "au naturel." This was followed by cold beer, all for the princely sum of $12.00 plus tip.

I called home and chatted with my parents. My father, an engineer, asked if I could purchase a small engine for a model boat he was building. He gave me the specs. I had no idea how to go about doing this and the hotel concierge was of no help. So, I went to the USO and asked the receptionist if she could help me find a model toy store that might carry the engine. She was Japanese but spoke fluent English. I gave her the name of the engine and she made several phone calls, finally confirming a store that sold the model. She wrote down the address and directions in Japanese.

Soon thereafter, I found myself in a taxi driving erratically through the Tokyo streets. We finally reached the model toy store, and I told the driver to wait for me, but he didn't speak English. Just as soon as I paid him and got out, he was gone. I had been told that people in the store spoke English, but when I walked in this was not the case. After I showed my paper to the staff, a young high-school girl came out from the rear of the store. She was able to translate to the store manager what I wanted to buy.

They did indeed have the engine. I bought it along with other parts which they assured me I needed to go with the engine. They were also nice enough to call me another cab and give the driver directions so I could return to the USO. I spent my last day walking the streets of Tokyo, taking in the sights, and avoiding street hustlers. I took a bus to the military base and was able to visit the post exchange where I ordered a suit and bought a battery-operated radio. I had the suit shipped back to my parents' home so that I would have it when I returned. I ordered it one size larger than my waist size but after a few weeks back in the World, I had to have the pants let out for it to fit. The intense heat of Vietnam and lack of appetite had kept me "lean and mean." Regretfully, I returned to my normal weight after a few months back in the World. I wore the suit a few times, but it never fit very well.

So ended my Tokyo R&R. I enjoyed my time off but unsurprisingly, was not happy to be returning to Vietnam. I knew I was not going to have to endure the daily humping through dangerous jungles, always living on the edge of a possible ambush. I would not regret having to wrap the dead in their ponchos and write letters to their next of kin. I would not miss going out on ambush at night and the anxiety I felt every time I heard a twig snap, or a strange noise. And I certainly would not miss the heat, the sweat, the smell, and the fear. I was going to live in a much safer and more secure location. I would have to endure less than five more months in country before I could return to the World. I colored the spaces on my short-timer calendar getting ever closer to the "sweet spot" at the center of the nude figure's outline.

Despite all that, what encouraged me most and gave me a positive outlook on returning, especially after what I had been through, was the prospect of recording and contributing to the history of the 1st Cav Division's exploits in Vietnam, by writing meaningful and accurate battle accounts.

Boy, was I mistaken!

~~~~~~

Letter: 20 October 1968, A Company, 1/5 Cav, 1st Air Cav Division, Cam Ranh Bay, III Corps, Vietnam

What a fine way to spend your birthday—waiting in an airport! Wouldn't you know it, the moment I returned from Tokyo to VN, we were hit by a typhoon. All planes are grounded, so I sit and wait. One consideration though: I am not out in the field getting soaking wet. I will eventually make it back to Camp Evans. When I return I will assume the Assistant to the Division Historical Officer job. I feel very positive about this new opportunity. I still must return to A Company to pick up my personal belongings, clear out of the battalion, see the CO, and battalion CO for a last good-by. I'll also pick up my mail and leave a change of address.

~~~~~~

CHAPTER 28

The Battle of the Parrot's Beak

"I want you to rewrite the end of the report. Any commander who allows his position to become compromised by the enemy is wrong. Make sure your conclusion makes this statement. And change the damn name of the battle."

Barely catching my breath after return from R&R, I began training at the 14th MHD. Frankly, there was little for me to do in comparison to what I had been used to. I luxuriated in the safety, showers, hot food, and dramatic change of pace from humping the boonies daily. I had gone from an environment of extreme stress and anxiety to no stress at all. There were five of us in the unit initially but soon after my return, one of the SP-4s said his goodbyes and returned to the World.

Letter: 26 October 1968, 14th Military History Detachment, Camp Evans, HHC, 1st Air Cav Division, I Corps, Vietnam

Today, we built a box to put my things in. I finally have a "place to live" with my own desk, a bed and more. I am beginning to get settled and find out where everything is. In addition, I have my first assignment. It is a special report on the LRRPs. My predecessor started the project and when complete, the report will be about 10 pages long.

I am excited about the work and what I am doing. I went back to my company yesterday to pick up my gear and mail. My platoon had been in contact the day before and five men had been wounded including the new platoon leader. He had been shot in both legs, breaking them. It looks as if I got out of the field just in time! I left a package for my platoon sergeant and got out of there fast.

To stay in shape, we took long runs at night when it was cooler along the airfield runway. The Marston mats or perforated steel planking (PSP) (metal plates used to create a runway on which C-130 planes could land) gave bounce to every step.

We took hot showers whenever we wanted, ate hot food, drank cold sodas and beer from our refrigerator. I read paperback novels, watched TV (three English channels), wrote long letters home, and often took afternoon naps. The photographer/artist assigned to our unit, nicknamed "Speedy Gonzalez," was an accomplished cook. He received frequent care packages from home containing cans of tamales, beans, rice, and other Mexican staples. On these occasions, he would cook up a mountain of food on our hot plate and share it with the team. This prompted me to run for my pack of Tums as soon as I finished a meal.

Every evening, promptly at 5 PM, my CO and I would put on clean, starched uniform shirts with full black insignia, strap on our .45 pistols, and put on our steel helmets. We would head for the commanding general's (CG) bunker for the daily briefing. These meetings usually lasted between 45 minutes and an hour unless a significant engagement was brewing. Each of the general's staff officers (G-1, G-2, G-3, and G-4) would stand up, put up whiteboards, maps or paper charts and bring the CG up to date on anything of significance that happened that day. The G-1 officer (personnel), a major, reported on friendly and enemy KIAs, WIAs, accidents and replacements. The G-2 officer (intelligence), also a major, put up a large map marked "Confidential" and reported on confirmed and suspected enemy troop movements within our division's AO as well as overall within Vietnam. The most interesting briefing was usually from the G-3 (operations), a lieutenant colonel. He talked about significant contacts our units had that day, the nature of the contact and the results (i.e. body count). Often there was either no enemy activity or only minor skirmishes. Occasionally, we ambushed small VC units or were ambushed by them. On less frequent occasions, we would encounter a North Vietnamese unit and a significant battle would ensue—sometimes progressing over several days. The G-4 officer (supplies and maintenance), a major, would end the briefing with a report of available aircraft, incoming supplies, and maintenance status of heavy equipment. If the briefing ran long, the G-4's briefing was often postponed. We were allowed to ask questions during the briefing but most often would save them until afterwards to speak one-on-one with the staff officer and to clarify points made.

One of the reasons our contact with the enemy was typically light within I Corps was because the division had such tremendous helicopter support for troop movements and fire support. The enemy had quickly learned that our division could rapidly reinforce an engagement with fresh troops strategically placed to engage and destroy them. Any enemy force having been fired upon by Cobra helicopters and gunships thought twice about fighting American troops during daylight hours.

Thus, my seventh month in country was spent in transition from being a combat platoon leader in the field to a staff officer at the division level. I felt that I had suddenly entered a new world. There would be occasional rocket or mortar attacks and sometimes a couple of the bunker positions would blow a Claymore by mistake or fire off a machine-gun blast, but the daily danger I had faced before was gone.

Our tent was surrounded with waist-high sandbags and a front blast door. It took about three weeks, but I finally started to relax and not dive for cover every time I heard an artillery piece go off. It was during this period that I wrote and published my essay, "The Trail," reproduced at the start of this book. It was published in the 1st Air Cav Division Newspaper as well as *Army Digest*.

I spent time reading all the regulations describing the functions of our unit. We had a filing cabinet full of confidential historical reports on major past engagements written by previous members of the unit. There was a specific format to be followed in each report. This included a description of the terrain, enemy and friendly unit strengths, troop movements during the battle, a synopsis of the battle, report of both friendly and enemy KIAs and WIAs. The most important part of the report format at the end was the "statement of conclusion" concerning what was evaluated to be both positive and negative about the engagement. The reports were accompanied by photographs and maps of the terrain, drawings of enemy and friendly troop movements, photos of equipment destroyed, pictures of captured weapons and photos of enemy KIA if available. A drawing was also included that became the report cover. I learned I needed to be prepared, on a moment's notice, when directed by the G-3, to go to a battle site *after* it was over. I was to interview the combatants, make notes and reconstruct the battle, accompanied by our artist/photographer.

It became clear, especially with battles that occurred at night, that the officers and men directly involved in the contact usually had great difficulty understanding both friendly and enemy troop movements. Certainly, the CG and his staff flying overhead in the command-and-control helicopter (C&C) were even more perplexed. They made judgments and command decisions based on radio traffic and looking at the rifle, machine-gun and mortar fire on the ground. So, it would be my job to interview the officers and men who were still alive or those wounded at the battalion aid station. Then, I would try to piece together what had happened. I was to prepare a report of the battle including photographs, maps, and drawings. If a major enemy contact occurred, our unit would assign a name to the battle and draw a report cover that emphasized the nature of the engagement based on the resources used.

As I reviewed past reports, I silently noted that none of the reports in our files had been written during Captain Tensey's tenure. In time, I would also discover there was a giant gap between what my responsibilities were on paper compared with what was happening in the field. Obtaining a clear picture of a battle and drawing conclusions required a good deal of speculation. Officers' careers often hung in the balance of the outcome of my report. As I had been in the field myself, I was aware and respectful of the challenges that the men on the ground faced during a firefight, especially one that occurred at night.

In addition to the preparation of major battle reports, our unit prepared the Division After Action Report on a quarterly basis. This was commonly referred to as an Operational Readiness Report, Lessons Learned (ORLL). All the battalions in the division were required to contribute to the document. It was our job to review each unit's submission, edit and compile the findings into a division-level document and distribute it. I was informed that preparation of this report was also my primary responsibility. I had 30 days until the next report, so I had time to read past reports and understand the format, purpose and how it was to be organized. Eighteen copies of each report were required, and we had no copying machines. That meant that each report, usually about 30 pages in length, had to be retyped using carbon paper. A typist could only produce six clear copies at a time, so each report had to be typed three times to produce the required number.

About a week into my eighth month in country, the 1st Air Cav Division received orders to move from I Corps to a new division headquarters in III Corps. The new base camp was located about 50 miles northeast of Saigon adjacent to the town of Phuoc Vinh. The base camp had already been constructed and fortified and we would be moving into established quarters. We spent the following week packing all our belongings and materials and disposing of any unnecessary items.

Letter: 27 October 1968, 14th Military History Detachment, Camp Evans, HHC, 1st Air Cav Division, I Corps, Vietnam

The big news should hit the papers soon: The Cav is moving south! The entire division, starting tomorrow, will commence a journey of about 750 miles by air south into III Corps. We will be located near Phuoc Vinh, about 50 miles northeast of Saigon and Bien Hoa in the Iron Triangle. Our AO will be along the Cambodian border and our mission will continue to be to stop infiltration from Cambodia.

The entire division will fly and be shipped down within the next 10 days. It is a big, complicated, confusing operation to move 12,000+ men and all their equipment. My little group is due to start on Wednesday and we have much to pack. Most of our material is secret or confidential so added security measures must be taken. Here I go moving again, just after I got settled in!

It was during this time that I visited the Public Information Office (PIO) located across the road from our tent. They too were cleaning out unnecessary files and photographs just as we were. I discovered a pile of eight-by-ten black and white photographs, as well as some drawings. I was told that these photos and art were duplicates or rejects to be burned. I asked if I could take some. I was told to "help myself."

All our unit's equipment and material were stowed in a Conex container (large metal box). The four of us piled into our jeep and drove it into the belly of a C-130 aircraft for the flight to Bien Hoa Airbase. After landing we drove in convoy from Bien Hoa to Phuoc Vinh. Eventually, we moved into a Quonset hut, sharing space with the Division Chemical Group.

Letter: November 3 1968, 14th Military History Detachment, HHC, 1st Air Cav Division, Phuoc Vinh, III Corps, Vietnam

I was going to start this letter at 9 PM, but I was interrupted by a mortar attack that lasted for the last hour and a half. It always seems that every time I move into a new place I'm met by a hail of mortars!

We arrived at our new base camp in Phuoc Vinh last night at 9 PM. We have moved into temporary quarters until someone decides where to put us. We planned and packed pretty well. There is no electricity yet, but we do have a Coleman lantern. Water is very scarce as there is only one water trailer. We have a couple of water cans so are OK with drinking, but nothing more. About half of the Division has moved down. Things will get more comfortable once everything is in place.

The Division is working the area along the Cambodian border with the 25th Infantry Division to the north and the 1st Infantry Division to the south. Charlie is again a mixture of VC and NVA. Our mission is the same as it was in I Corps: to stop infiltration from Cambodia and to protect Saigon from a major attack similar to the Tet Offensive last May. Intelligence reports which I can access now that I'm at the division level, indicate that the Cav was so effective at inhibiting infiltration in I Corps, that the NVA are now choosing different routes to infiltrate. The Cav concept is so effective that other divisions are starting to convert to it including the 82nd and 101st. They don't have the same number of choppers that we do, or the experience, so the 1st Air is still "Number One in Nam!"

Other divisions follow a strategy of patrolling around their base camps rather than going out to look for Charlie. They have no search & clear/destroy operations, and their body counts are low in comparison. This is the essential difference between the Cav and other divisions. I prefer it this way. It keeps you on your toes and creates confident, aggressive troops with high esprit de corps. Our men think they are better than the rest. They may not be, but they have that mindset, and it spurs them on. Our contacts reflect this aggressiveness and will to win. If we must fight this war, then let us do it wholeheartedly and, as Kennedy said, "With Vigor!"

The peace talks look so bleak. I am convinced we will remain here for a long time yet to come. I may have to come back for a second tour. The big picture at the division level has done wonders for my understanding of our actions. Unfortunately, I shall probably return to the World, pick up a newspaper, look at TV and just become discouraged again that my efforts have been meaningless. It takes a real "personal commitment" to fight this war. I wonder if I still have it.

After a few days, our Conex container arrived; we unloaded and set up shop. Our Quonset hut was surrounded by waist-high sandbags. Captain Tensey, always concerned with personal security, decided we needed to add an extra measure of security and we spent several days putting down two more layers of bags around our building. During a rocket attack it was common to be sprayed with shrapnel that would easily pierce the walls. Several men had been wounded or killed due to direct hits or near misses in the past. Should a rocket or mortar round land directly on the roof of a hut, it was likely that everyone inside would be wounded or killed.

Tensey, a former artillery battery commander, was an expert at building fortifications. He took the additional step of constructing more protection over the top of our bunks. We took wooden 81mm mortar ammo boxes and positioned them at the head and foot of each man's bunk. The boxes were nailed together and filled with sandbags. When the stack got high enough for a man to slip under and sit on the bed without bending his head, two steel bars were placed overhead. Then more ammo boxes, also filled with sandbags, were placed on the bars over the top of the bunk thereby creating a U-shaped cocoon. This contraption protected men lying in their bunks in the event of a direct hit on the roof. It was a lot of work to construct them, but we completed the structures over the beds for each man in our unit.

We took photos of our "bunk protectors" and included this innovation in the next "Lessons Learned Report." The general's staff was so impressed with what we had done that they sent engineers to view our handiwork. These men were instructed to build similar protection for all the soldiers and officers in the general headquarters sleeping quarters. My CO earned some nice kudos for the innovation.

However, Captain Tensey was still not finished with his protections. There was no bunker immediately adjacent to our Quonset hut and this bothered him. He set about cutting a hole through the wall of our building and then constructed a bunker directly outside. In the event of a rocket or mortar attack, we would all drop to the floor and crawl through the hole in the side of the building and into the bunker. We put air mattresses down on the floor of the bunker, and added some flashlights, candles, and C-Rations for good measure. About two weeks after our bunker and overhead bunk protectors were complete, the base camp was the target of a heavy rocket attack. One rocket landed in the road outside our Quonset hut, and one landed on the roof of an adjacent building, wounding several men inside. A piece of shrapnel about the size of a quarter went through the wall of our building, missing my bunk protector by an inch, and embedded itself in the wall about 2 feet from where my head lay. However, I had already hit the floor and crawled into our bunker. It was an important lesson learned and reinforced the fact that no matter how much you prepared and protected yourself you were always vulnerable to attack. This was true even within a heavily fortified base camp.

Letter: 10 November 1968, 14th Military History Detachment, Phuoc Vinh, HHC, 1st Air Cav Division, III Corps, Vietnam

Cpt Tensey has left on R&R, and I am "in command!" He will be gone for two weeks to meet his wife in Hawaii. He is going to send you something for me… a surprise!

We have been building again. We put ammo boxes filled with sandbags over our bunks. It was hard work but good for me. I think I lost a few pounds. We called it "operation super-safe." We placed steel engineering beams on top of columns of ammo boxes at the head and foot of our bunks and created a cocoon to protect against a direct hit to the roof. The commanding general heard about our invention and sent a team to inspect our construction because he wanted the same thing built for him and his staff.

At the start of my ninth month in country, Captain Tensey put me in charge of the unit. He took his R&R and met his wife in Hawaii. After 10 months in country, he had easily qualified to take the trip. During his absence, I attended the daily briefing and kept abreast of the division's activities. As luck would have it, this was exactly the time when the division became embroiled in a major battle near the Cambodian border. The battle lasted three days. Both the CG and the G-3 were constantly flying overhead, deploying resources and firepower against several NVA regiments that had attacked one of our companies. Because both men were directing the battle from their C&C helicopters, the evening briefing was cancelled for several days. Upon their return, an extensive briefing took place at which the main aspects of the past battle were reviewed. One company had suffered so many casualties (24 KIA and 30 WIA), that it could no longer be deployed and had to be pulled off line. At the close of the briefing, the G-3 asked, "Is the representative from the Military History Detachment in the room?" I quickly stood up and responded, "Yes, Sir." I was told to see him after the briefing.

The colonel told me to be prepared to fly out to the battalion headquarters the very next day. I was to write a full report of the engagement. Even though he had been flying overhead during the three-day battle, he did not have a clear picture of exactly what had happened and why the company had suffered so many casualties. I was to have the finished report on his desk in three days. I gulped and walked back to our building, informing Speedy to pack up. We were to prepare for a flight to the battalion headquarters at 6 AM the next morning. He was to bring along both camera and art supplies.

We waited two hours to catch a flight and arrived at around 8:30 AM the next morning. Speedy and I split up. He went to talk with some of the soldiers involved in the contact; I was going to talk with the company commander and the battalion commander. I decided to start with the battalion commander and visited the S-1 to explain my mission. I was under orders from the G-3 to interview the lieutenant colonel, as well as the company commander and any platoon leaders. I was informed that all the platoon leaders had been casualties of the battle and had been evacuated. He told me he would see if the battalion commander had time to speak with me. He returned about 15 minutes later to say I could talk with the company commander and any of the soldiers that remained from the unit. The battalion commander refused to be interviewed.

I was disappointed in this decision and asked if I could speak with the S-3, only to be informed that he also was not available. It became apparent I was going to have a tough time securing any details of the strategy and battle if these important commanders would not speak with me. I informed the S-1 that if I could not come away with sufficient information I would inform the G-3 that I was only permitted to interview the company commander and available soldiers. The S-1 informed me, "Well, that's the way it's going to be. My CO and the S-3 do not wish to be interviewed. It was the G-3 and the CG who were the ones controlling this fight from their C&C choppers. You can interview the company commander, but if the G-3 wants to interview my CO or the S-3, he will have to do it himself."

Keeping in mind that I was only a first lieutenant with little or no authority to influence the situation, I decided not to press the issue further but headed off to meet with the company commander. I found the man in his company CP tent looking exhausted. I took some time to explain my mission. I let him know I was here to try to determine what had happened as accurately as possible. The captain wanted to know if I had had any field experience. I explained I had been a platoon leader with A 1/5. I let him know that my objective was strictly to reconstruct the battle as he remembered it. I promised to relate the story exactly as he told it to me.

We got a couple of Cokes and the captain sat on his bunk with me opposite and began describing the engagement. I scribbled in my notebook as fast as I could, asking questions occasionally, but allowing him to relate what happened during the three-day battle. He told a harrowing tale that started with one of his platoons being ambushed and nearly wiped out during the first night by a superior NVA force. All the men in the platoon had either been killed or wounded. During the day, the survivors gradually straggled back to the company CP where medics treated them. The dead had to be left behind at the ambush site as it was impossible for the men to carry them back. An effort was then made to send in another platoon during the day to bring back the bodies, but they too came under intense enemy fire as soon as they came close to the ambush site. They were forced to retreat to the CP. The second night found both the CG and the G-3 flying overhead giving the company commander instructions as to what to do. Incoming enemy mortar and rocket fire was intense and the CO on the ground determined that it was best to have his men remain in their foxholes so as not to sustain further injury from the bombardment.

I talked to the CO for two hours and began to get a picture confirming the basic facts of the engagement. After retrieving the bodies and receiving some fresh replacements on the third day, the company began fortifying their position. The men dug their foxholes deeper and added overhead cover to protect themselves from shrapnel. The third night was a repeat of the second. Mortars and rockets rained down on the company. Additional casualties were sustained with direct or near hits on their foxholes. On the morning of the fourth day, the dead and wounded were medevaced. So many men had been killed or wounded that the company ceased to be an effective fighting force. Choppers were brought in, and a fresh company took over pursuit of the NVA force that by now had retreated across the Cambodian border. The remains of the beleaguered unit were then extracted.

I again reminded the captain that I was not there to draw conclusions, but only to report the facts of the engagement accurately. The CO revealed that the CG and the G-3 were so intent on directing the battle from overhead that they created mass confusion giving conflicting orders to the men on the ground. They tried to direct both artillery and ARA fire. No sooner had one command been given that another was countermanded. With the loss of his platoon leaders, the CO did not have enough time to brief his men or to radio the artillery and helicopter gunships to adjust fire. In the dark, the enemy was so close that the captain was deathly afraid that rounds would land on top of his men, or gunships would fire within his perimeter. And, all the while, he continued to suffer casualties from the non-stop enemy mortar and rocket attack. In short, it was a total SNAFU and cluster-fuck. The reinforced company that was brought in at first light on the fourth day tried to chase the retreating enemy, but the force had evaporated into the jungle. All the replacements could do was to send out patrols to scout for the enemy. To make matters worse, no enemy bodies were found. There were plenty of blood trails, but the NVA had retreated with their wounded and dead. There was no way to confirm an enemy body count even though the captain knew many had been killed. The captain was left with tremendous losses to his company. Despite trying to protect his men, the unit had ceased to be an effective fighting force and he was responsible. All the KIAs and WIAs were on the American side with no corresponding enemy body count. (It now became clear to me why the CG and G-3 were so concerned about getting an accurate picture of this battle.)

I thanked the captain for his candor and went to find Speedy. He had struck up a friendship with several sergeants who had survived the battle and was busy marking troop movements on his map and making engagement drawings. These soldiers told a story that was the same as the captain's. They had been under constant bombardment from mortars and rockets all through the second and third nights. Even though they had reinforced their foxholes and added overhead cover, the enemy had their positions zeroed in. They continued to fire their mortar and RPG rounds along the perimeter, killing and wounding more men. Clearly these soldiers had experienced the most frightening engagement of their lives.

At the end of the day, I felt I had captured all the information that was available to me given that the battalion commander and S-3 refused to speak with me. I had pages of notes from the company commander and the sergeants who had escaped the turmoil. We jumped onto a logistics helicopter to make our way back to division headquarters.

I spent the next two days reviewing my notes, writing, and rewriting my report. We called the engagement "The Battle of the Angel's Wing." The area where the contact had occurred resembled an angel's wing on the map. I carefully and thoughtfully worked my way through the official report format for the battle while spending considerable time writing my conclusions as diplomatically as possible. According to the soldiers I had been able to interview, they placed the blame for the confusion and loss of the battle squarely on the CG and G-3.

Just as I brought my report to a close, Captain Tensey returned from his R&R. He had enjoyed a marvelous time with his wife—and was sure she would soon report they were expecting a third baby Tensey. Yes, it had been a happy time for him. He was devastated to be returning to Vietnam with one and a half months still to serve. He read my report and was extremely concerned about the conclusions I had drawn from my interviews. He made a trip to visit with the G-3 and asked for some additional time to revise and complete the report. He suggested that this was my first battle report and he wanted time to review it and make sure of its accuracy.

The two of us spent the next two days reviewing and rewriting with a fine-tooth comb. We changed a few words, rewrote a few paragraphs, and softened some of the language. The revised report still placed the blame for the losses and mismanagement of the battle on the shoulders of the over-controlling CG and G-3.

Captain Tensey delivered the report personally and was gone for several hours. When he returned, his uniform was sweat-soaked, and he looked exhausted. He told me that the G-3 had given him the following instructions: "I want you to rewrite the conclusions of the report placing blame on the company commander. Any commander who allows his position to become compromised by the enemy is wrong. Make sure your conclusion makes this statement. And change the damn name of the battle."

"The Battle of the Angel's Wing" then became "The Battle of the Parrot's Beak." (It was a real stretch of the imagination to think that the border line between Vietnam and Cambodia resembled a parrot's beak because it clearly resembled an angel's wing.) But, as instructed, the title was changed, and a new report cover was drawn. I rewrote the conclusion several times placing blame on the company commander for his failure to move his company to a safer location once the first bombardment began and his position had become zeroed in by the enemy.

We delivered the report a second time complete with Speedy's new report cover, maps, photographs, and drawings of enemy movements. An enemy KIA estimate of 323 was also added to the report at the direction of the G-3. I had no idea where this number originated but was simply told to add it to the report and it was accepted. Thus ended my first experience with the research and recording of military history. As far as I was concerned, the report was a complete fabrication. I did as I was ordered, marked the report "Confidential" and distributed copies to various military agencies throughout the United States. (I also kept a copy of my original report and conclusions under the name of "The Battle of the Angel's Wing.")

Letter: 13 November 1968, 14th Military History Detachment, Phuoc Vinh, HHC, 1st Air Cav Division, III Corps, Vietnam

One thing I wish you would do for me. Take about $10 from my account and buy chewing gum, candy, soap, band aids and other small niceties, both medically and nutritionally oriented. Please send them before Christmas as there is an orphanage near the base and I would like to go with a MedCap or Civil Affairs Team and hand them out at Christmas time. The one, two penny kind of candy would probably be best. Any small gift to hand out to the kids will be very welcome and I'll have fun doing it.

At Christmas several of the units in our area banded together to organize a party for a Catholic orphanage outside Phuoc Vinh that had 60 children in need of cake, ice cream and gifts and a visit from Santa. We hosted the children in our mess hall and handed out gifts, making sure that each child received something appropriate. Several of us wrote home asking relatives to reach out to their communities to donate dolls, trucks and toys that would be enjoyed by the children. The boxes of gifts kept arriving well before Christmas and we wrapped them in Christmas paper with a tag indicating what each gift was. Our mess sergeant outdid himself and baked a huge sheet cake and somehow came up with several gallons of ice cream. The event was an absolute zoo with 60 kids screaming in Vietnamese for Santa to come and hand out gifts. A Santa outfit was obtained from somewhere and one of the soldiers dressed up with a huge red bag over his shoulder, arriving in a military police jeep with sirens blasting. The party was a complete success and the children loved it. The look on some of those children's faces is one I shall never forget. We were thanked profusely for our kindness by the nuns who accompanied the children. I had to take a nap when it was over!

As Christmas approached, Bob Hope gave a performance with Ann-Margret and a tremendous cast at numerous stopping points in Vietnam. Long Binh was the closest show to our base in Phuoc Vinh. Attendance was limited to 100 soldiers and names were drawn from a barrel and none of us were so lucky as to be selected. I was able to obtain some fabulous photographs of the performance taken by one of the 1st Cav combat photographers.

About two weeks later, Captain Tensey, now at 11 months in country, received an urgent request from the Red Cross to return home to his family. One of his children was experiencing some intense psychological problems. His bags were packed in a flash, and he left within hours of the notification. He said he would return just as soon as he could get things straightened out at home, but we all knew it was the last we would see of our leader.

Sometime later, I spoke with another lieutenant in the G-1 shop. He told me the real reason Captain Tensey had been pulled out of the field and assigned to the 14th MHD. The man had been responsible for firing several short rounds in which American troops had been wounded. I was told that he had renounced his responsibility as our unit commander. He entrusted me with the writing and preparation of the combat action reports as well as the preparation of the Lessons Learned Reports. Tensey enjoyed attending the daily briefing and rubbing shoulders with the general's staff, but it was clear that they had his number and he knew it. He couldn't get out of Vietnam fast enough.

I always suspected that the urgent call from the Red Cross to return to the US had been prearranged after he met his wife on R&R. We never heard from Captain Tensey again. I don't know if he remained in the army or not. I will always thank him for giving me a very safe place to spend my remaining five months in country and acknowledge that he certainly knew how to construct outstanding personal fortifications for his own safety as well as ours.

***

Letter: 24 November 1968, 14th Military History Detachment, Phuoc Vinh, HHC, 1st Air Cav Division, III Corps, Vietnam

The Cav has been getting hit hard and we are busting Charlie some too. He has mortared Phuoc Vinh every night for the last five days, between two and twenty mortar and rocket rounds. We built a beautiful bunker and feel quite secure. It has a tunnel leading from our building right into it, so you are safe the whole way into the bunker. It has two layers of PSP (iron slabs) and three layers of sandbags on top with 55 gallon barrels filled with sand forming the walls. Even a direct hit wouldn't touch it. It was a real pain building it though and my arms are still sore. My arm is all healed up by the way. It seemed to heal very quickly and there is only a small scar. I am feeling very fit and healthy. Hefting sandbags seems to have that effect on you.

One thing I could really use is a back scrub brush. I have gotten a lasting case of heat rash on my back. The doctor said it was due to the long missions in the field where we could not wash. He gave me a special soap to get the ground in dirt out.

It gets bad at times, like being stuck in the back with 100 needles. The malaria pills have turned my underarms and whites of my eyes a slight shade of yellow, but I am told that goes away a few weeks after you stop taking the "birth control pills!" My feet too are surprisingly in fine shape after all the swamps, rice paddies and monsoons they weathered.

I heard from my RTO who came by on his way to R&R that our CO of A Company had been killed in a fierce engagement. We lost several men from my platoon. I felt bad about the CO. He was a fine officer and I respected him tremendously.

CHAPTER 29

Assistant Defense Counsel

We agreed to the stipulation. That was a big mistake.

Things started to slow down after CPT Tensey left and while we waited for a new CO to be assigned. I was discouraged at the way my battle investigation and report had been handled by the G-3 and lost enthusiasm for wanting to dash out to the field to conduct additional after-action interviews and write up battle reports. Our little band busied ourselves preparing the quarterly ORRLL, contacting each unit in the Cav, bugging them to send us their reports written in the proper format, editing, and retyping the entire document to produce 18 copies. Preparation of the report took several weeks of continuous work, and everyone was ready for a break after we mailed off the last copy on the distribution list.

I commanded the 14th MHD for about six weeks until a judge advocate general (JAG) officer was assigned as the new CO. Then, about two weeks later, an infantry lieutenant who was to be my replacement and had self-identified as a conscientious objector was assigned to the unit. He was a brilliant guy, but somehow had gotten himself assigned to the infantry and shipped to Vietnam. The man was absolutely panicked about the possibility that he would be assigned to a line unit. We assured him he was safe with us and would not be transferred. He was about as safe as any soldier could be in Vietnam, spending the next year preparing the ORRLL report and reporting on battle actions.

Neither the captain nor the lieutenant had any idea of what the mission of the 14th Military History Detachment was, so I proceeded to organize an orientation program for them to ensure, once I left, the unit would be able to fulfill its mission. This did not make me very popular while the orientation program progressed.

With three officers assigned to the unit, one of whom was an attorney, there was little for me to do. I was not surprised therefore to be assigned additional duties. One of these was acting as assistant defense counsel for two upcoming marijuana trials.

The trial concerned two soldiers who were arrested by MPs (Military Police) after a raid on their sleeping quarters. Several men were playing poker sitting on bunks with an empty bunk between them used as the poker table. There were marijuana cigarettes lying on one of the bunks next to two of the men playing cards, but no one was observed actually smoking. The two soldiers adjacent to the cigarettes were arrested and one was charged with possession of an illegal substance and other for use of an illegal substance.

Letter: 29 January 1969, 14th Military History Detachment, Phuoc Vinh, HHC, 1st Air Cav Division, III Corps, Vietnam

Not much more news to tell you about. I have been appointed as the assistant defense counsel for a court martial on 31 January. It won't be much of a job as all the assistant defense counsel does is research, sit, take notes and watch. I am going to be the defense counsel for another trial next month, so I'd better pay close attention to the procedures.

As assistant defense counsel, it was my job was to support the captain assigned as senior defense counsel to defend the first soldier. This captain was a staff officer at a forward base camp, so was not available to do the administrative work needed for the trial and that job fell to me. The first soldier had signed an affidavit stating he did not reside in the quarters that were raided and was only there to play poker. We were able to substantiate that information. The second soldier did reside in the quarters, and the marijuana was on the bunk next to him, but he claimed his bunk was one further away from where he was seated, and the marijuana belonged to another soldier.

I spent some time reading up on the duties of the defense counsel and the requirements for proving that the substance found was in fact marijuana. The prosecution was required to prove the "chain of custody." This meant that they had to prove that the marijuana had been properly secured, marked, and transported to Long Binh for laboratory evaluation and also prove the substance was marijuana. All of the people who were in the chain of transportation and evaluation would be required to testify they had received the marked material, had properly transported it, and analyzed it correctly. There were at least six people in this chain.

I was approached by the prosecution, and they confirmed that the lab in Long Binh tested the cigarettes and certified that the material was marijuana. They asked us to agree to stipulate to the chain of custody rather than require all six men involved in the transport of the material to be present at the trial and testify to the security of the transportation as well as the lab personnel who tested the material. This seemed like a reasonable request to me, and it would speed up the trial. After discussion with the senior defense counsel, we agreed to the stipulation. That was a big mistake.

After interviewing the two soldiers we felt we had a decent circumstantial evidence case for the first soldier being billeted in different quarters. The second soldier's case was going to be more difficult to prove as the material was located on the bunk next to where he was seated.

Letter: 2 February 1969, 14th Military History Detachment, Phuoc Vinh, HHC, 1st Air Cav Division, III Corps, Vietnam

I have been very busy the last several days preparing for two court martials for which I am the Assistant Defense Counsel. They are both complicated trials and everything will hang on the decisions of the court. We can't prove innocence and the prosecution can't definitely prove guilt. The case charges one man with the use of marijuana, the other with possession. Use is very difficult to prove as I have learned, but this case involves a great deal of circumstantial evidence, so it is hard to say one way or the other. It will be a good experience anyway no matter what happens. Both the trial and defense counsels (captains) are located out on forward LZs, so the lieutenants must do most of the work. I hope this doesn't indicate we're to be the principals in the next case although that is the way it usually works.

The judges in a military trial consist of five officers assigned to the special duty. The defense is allowed to excuse one officer for any reason, and we decided to release one of the captains assigned to judge the trial. This left two captains and two first lieutenants as the judges.

After the prosecution presented its case and outlined the facts as previously described, our first soldier took the stand and stated that he lived in a different billet and was there just to play poker. His platoon sergeant was called as a character witness and confirmed that he lived in a different location from where the marijuana was found and that this was a model soldier. The prosecution stated that the defense counsel had stipulated to the chain of custody and presented signed statements to that effect. The trial judges questioned us to assure themselves that the soldier and defense understood what we were stipulating to and that we were giving up the right to require the prosecution to prove the chain of custody. We again agreed to the stipulation.

The panel of judges met for about 15 minutes, returned, and found the soldier not guilty. After a 30-minute break, the second trial began. This time I was the defense counsel. We followed the same procedure as in the first trial. The prosecution presented its case, and we entered our stipulation to the chain of custody into the record. The soldier took the stand and asserted that the marijuana did not belong to him and claimed although the marijuana was next to him his bunk was actually located one away from where he was seated. Again, the judges met for 15 minutes and this time returned with a verdict of guilty.

"Oh my God," exclaimed the soldier. "You guys have screwed me. How could they find the first soldier not guilty and me guilty? What's going to happen to me now?" I tried to console the soldier by saying that his sentence was only going to be for six months. "Six months!" he screamed. "I was supposed to go back to the World next month! I'm fucked!" With that, the MPs put handcuffs on the soldier and led him away.

I sat in my chair, unsure of what had happened or why the panel of judges had found in favor of the first soldier but not the second. The second trial seemed to come down to the location of the material on the bunk next to the second soldier regardless of where he slept and the fact that he did not have a character witness to support him. I felt very bad for the second soldier, but there was nothing I could do to help him.

Letter: 6 February 1969, 14th Military History Detachment, Phuoc Vinh, HHC, 1st Air Cav Division, III Corps, Vietnam.

We had our court martial today. We got a not guilty verdict on the first man, but guilty on the second. I was the defense counsel in the second case. Even though we presented evidence in extenuation and mitigation, the court gave the maximum penalty: six months in jail. I felt very bad for the soldier as we had worked hard to present a good case and I thought we had. I guess the court just couldn't believe our side of the story. It was quite an experience for me, and I learned a number of valuable lessons for the future. I also learned that it's hard to be the defense counsel.

In addition to court martials, I was tasked with the responsibility of investigating a loss from the local post exchange and several surprise inspections of soldiers' billets looking for pornography and contraband. These were always disgusting assignments for me as the soldiers just wanted to read their *Playboy* magazines (not authorized!) and be left alone. I usually just walked through the billets, chatted with the soldiers, found out what units they'd been assigned to in the field and opened their lockers to perform a cursory inspection. These soldiers always appreciated my inspections, but I never seemed to find any pornography or contraband.

I also continued to perform my duties with the 14th Military History Detachment, writing and editing the quarterly ORRLL Report as well as some special projects. Boredom would frequently creep in, and I often missed the action and activity of being assigned to a line unit.

Letter: 2 February 1969, 14th Military History Detachment, Phuoc Vinh, HHC, 1st Air Cav Division, III Corps, Vietnam

It seems to be the time for many projects to come due: the ORRLL is due on the 15th, am three-fourths through the report on Combat Trackers and have just finished my report on "Operation Liberty Canyon."

I still have the Presidential Unit Citation (PUC) to struggle with. It's just as well that I am busy as the days keep moving by faster. I broke into less than 90 days to go just yesterday and now begins the hardest time. I can't say that I have enjoyed much of this tour of duty with the History Detachment. I shall have some pleasurable memories to take back, but as the article you sent me said: "war does change a man," and it has changed me. There are many bad memories too and it will be hard for me to forget and readjust even though I have been away for only a year.

I just hope that my new assignment offers a challenge as well as responsibility. I would like to "stay put" for a while too. Since I've been in the army I've done nothing but move, move, move. Sometimes too the responsibilities have been heavy, perhaps more than I've been capable of coping with. That's good experience, I know, but it's also been stressful. Well, enough philosophizing.

Contact in our area has been extremely light although some of the forward units confiscated large caches of supplies. One had 40,000 lbs of rice and 47,000 rounds of ammunition. If this keeps up Charles will be in a real bind in trying to launch any type of offensive. The Cav found the largest cache of the war a few weeks ago. It contained sixty tons of ammo, supplies and weapons. I think this may have hit the papers back home.

CHAPTER 30

Buying Art Supplies

Walking into the art supply store fully armed, and removing box after box of supplies from his shelves, I'm sure the storekeeper feared for his life.

My 12th month in country had arrived. I was officially a "short timer." "How short are you?" was the common question. "Thirty days and a wake up," was the answer.

Soldiers in the field started to become extremely anxious as they entered their 11th and 12th months. They had survived this long and only had a short while more to go. Many soldiers waited to take their R&R in their 11th or 12th month to have priority on location selection, as well as avoid the jitters of being wounded or killed at the very end of their tour. Others became so nervous toward the end of their tours that they were no longer dependable in the field and had to be removed to administrative duties at base camp. But if there was a need for boots on the ground, these men still had to grunt it out.

It was different for officers because after serving their six to seven months in the field in leadership positions they were sent to staff jobs in the rear. Even for officers, there was a certain degree of nervousness that crept into the back of minds when you became a short timer. Thoughts of going home, back to the World, occupied your mind. Typically, an officer would receive orders transferring him to his next duty station 30 to 60 days prior to DEROS, but I still had not received mine. I was a Regular Army officer and had filled out a "dream sheet" indicating that I wished to be assigned to the West Coast of the US. That would usually mean an assignment to a training command at Fort Lewis, Washington or Fort Ord, California. But as I entered my 12th month, I still had no idea what my next stop would be. I sent several packages home containing some gifts I had bought on the local market and souvenirs I picked up during my tour. I also sent home the decorations I had won in the field, one of which was the Purple Heart I had earned when wounded.

Letter: 2 March 1969, 14th Military History Detachment, Phuoc Vinh, HHC 1st Air Cav Division, III Corps, Vietnam

About the Purple Heart—I didn't tell you about it because I didn't want to worry you. I was only scratched, and it was a long time ago. It's not important and I'll tell you about it when I get home. Please do not ask me anymore about it as it will only make you more worried. With the time getting short, we don't need that, do we? (68 days and counting.)

I was busy orienting our Military History Detachment's new JAG captain and my replacement lieutenant on the regulations and responsibilities of the unit. Things were going smoothly. Both were smart men and learned the routine very quickly. I felt confident that I was leaving the unit in solid hands. I spent a lot of time talking with these two officers, schooling them about the operations of the unit—things I had learned on my own. I even developed some quizzes to make sure that they knew how to handle the daily and quarterly responsibilities. The two officers were annoyed with my incessant briefings and testing, but it was important they were fully prepared to take on the responsibilities of the unit as there were no written procedures. I also wanted to show off how much I had learned and done over the past five months overseeing the unit. (Yes, I was being a smart-ass!)

But at the start of my 12th month, still not having received transfer orders, I visited the G-1's office to inquire about my status. I was informed that an inquiry would be made, but it might take a couple of weeks to get a response. "A couple of weeks," I thought to myself, "I don't have a couple of weeks, I want to know now."

At the same time, our unit artist/photographer voiced a complaint that he did not have sufficient art supplies to do his job. He was down to five tubes of paint, three brushes, a few colored pencils and one pad of paper. He had ordered supplies through channels months ago, but nothing had been received. Because of his superb artistic talents and reputation, Speedy was constantly being called on for drawings and artwork to support various other requests within the division. This included the commanding general who particularly liked his artistic style. I asked my new CO what we could do to get Speedy the supplies he needed. He would soon be out of materials and unable to fulfill any requests.

To his credit, my CO spoke with the G-1 and received permission for Speedy and me to take a three-day trip to Saigon to buy art supplies. While I was there, I could visit Military Assistance Command Vietnam Headquarters (MACV) to inquire about the orders for my next duty station. We were excited with the news of our good fortune. It was going to be our "mini-R&R."

I was told to draw $300 with which to buy art supplies and convert it into Vietnamese piastres. The resulting bundle of bills filled a gallon-size plastic bag which I dutifully placed in the thigh pocket of my jungle fatigues.

The next convoy to Saigon was to leave in two days. We spent the time checking where to stay in Saigon. I was to stay in a temporary duty officer's hotel, and Speedy in a similar facility for NCOs. Speedy took our jeep to the motor pool for an oil change and engine tune-up. We discovered it also needed a brake job. He spent the better part of the day and evening making sure the vehicle was in top shape. We certainly did not want our vehicle to break down on the way to or from Saigon.

We each put some clothes in a small duffel and loaded it into the jeep. Speedy drew M16 ammo; I drew .45 caliber ammo for my pistol. Being in convoy, we were required to have loaded weapons. At 6 AM on the appointed day, we pulled into a convoy consisting of APCs positioned at the front and rear of the convoy, several two and one-half ton trucks en route to pick up supplies for the division, a few flatbed trucks, a command jeep at the front driven by some MPs and our little jeep. I saw we were being positioned at the end of the convoy and that we would be eating dust for the entire 50-mile journey. I approached the command jeep to ask if we could move up in the column. The sergeant took pity on us, and we were moved up.

At around 6:45 AM, the convoy left the gate of our division headquarters to drive through the town of Phuoc Vinh and into the countryside. We were clocking the exorbitant speeds of 15–20 miles per hour—about as fast as the APCs that accompanied us could travel without overheating. This was the first time I had been in a motor vehicle since my arrival in Vietnam. I realized that for the past year I had walked wherever I was going or flown in a helicopter or fixed-wing aircraft. At this speed, it would take several hours to reach our destination. I rode shotgun, held Speedy's M16 in my arms and settled down for a long, slow, and dusty journey. Finally, after two hours of eating exhaust fumes and dust, we moved onto blacktop and began to see road signs for Saigon.

Traveling by military convoy was the only safe method of transportation in South Vietnam. Driving along dirt roads and even highways was dangerous as you were subject to ambush by VC forces or mines planted the day before. A convoy typically consisted of a dozen or more vehicles traveling in column, spaced 25m apart with APCs interspersed to protect the various vehicles: troop carriers, gasoline trucks, recovery vehicles and jeeps like ours.

The convoy slowly moved ahead to finally reach its destination at Bien Hoa around 2 PM. Speedy had consulted the map. He said he had marked the locations of the hotel where I would be staying as well as his own billet. We approached the command vehicle and were given permission to proceed into Saigon. The return convoy would leave at 6 AM in three days. We were told to be there an hour early or we would have to wait three more days for the next convoy. This detail was promptly forgotten as we drove at the extreme speed of 45 mph into the city. We began dodging hundreds of motorbikes, bicyclists, donkey carts, pedicabs, and pedestrians along the way.

I did my best to follow the route outlined on the map, but the streets were very confusing. We ended up taking some wrong turns. Spotting some MPs, we asked for directions. Fortunately, we were close to my hotel and were given instructions on where to go. We arrived at the hotel at 4 PM; Speedy would be taking the jeep to his quarters. At 7 PM we agreed to meet back at my hotel to find a place to eat. Both of us were nervous about traveling the streets of Saigon armed only with an M16 and a .45 pistol. One never knew if a VC would drive by on a motorbike to drop a grenade in the back of your jeep (a common occurrence).

Upon checking into my hotel, I was informed that I would be the officer in charge (OIC) to guard the front of the hotel from 8 PM until 2 AM the next night. I was also told that I should not travel the streets of Saigon at night but go to the Officers' Club located three blocks away to have dinner. I knew that Speedy, an NCO, would not be allowed in the Officers' Club, so I produced an ideal solution. I had a spare set of lieutenant's bars and crossed sabers insignia in my kit. When Speedy showed up for me at 7 PM, I had him remove his sergeant's insignia and put on the bars. He was extremely nervous about doing this, as it was a court-martial offense to impersonate an officer, but we had little choice in the matter if we wanted a nice meal and a few drinks that night. I told him not to worry. The only person he was going to talk with was me; we could sit at a table and avoid any other officers in the club. And that is exactly what we did. We had a few drinks as well as a great steak dinner. But Speedy was so nervous that he did not enjoy himself. He wanted to leave the club just as soon as dinner was over. I agreed, and he returned me to my hotel. He immediately removed the officer's insignia and put his sergeant's insignia back on his collar.

We agreed to meet at my hotel the next morning at 10 AM for some sightseeing. We spent the day driving around seeing monuments, the American Embassy, and other points of interest. We remained vigilant and nervous as we drove, worried that a VC might sneak up at any moment. Neither of us had been around civilians for the entire time we had been in Vietnam. Being around so many people who were riding bicycles and motorbikes on the streets was nerve-racking. We eventually found an open-air restaurant, ate lunch, and calmed down a bit. We walked a couple of blocks looking at shops. I sat in a pedicab so Speedy could take a picture of me. Finally, at about 2 PM, we headed for MACV Headquarters and went through the main gate into a heavily fortified military facility. We relaxed and felt more secure. After getting directions, we parked the jeep at a large building that turned out to be a gymnasium with basketball hoops pulled up in the air on their cables. On the floor of the gym were hundreds of low tables about 2 feet high. The tables supported tray after tray of Fortran punched cards. Each card represented a soldier in Vietnam—some 500,000 cards in all. (Computers in use by the army at this time were Fortran computers that used punch cards as part of their programming.)

I ended up speaking with a captain to explain I was in my 12th month in Vietnam and had not received orders. The captain checked his records. He informed me that my orders had been dispatched to the 1st Cav Headquarters two days ago—the day before our convoy had left for Saigon. I thanked him and asked if he might be able to tell me where I was going to be assigned. The officer sighed. He then escorted me back out to the gymnasium and the trays of punch cards. We walked to the front trays and proceeded in alphabetical order down the line. We moved from As to Bs and from Bs to the BAs... to Bartlett, John; Bartlett, Paul; Bartlett, Ralph; Bartlett, Robin. He pulled out my card and said, "Lieutenant, you are headed for Seattle, Washington." I responded, "That's great, I'll be going to Fort Lewis, Washington. Hey, I used to live in Seattle." The officer responded, "No, it says here you're going to Ft. Wainwright." I said, "Well, I know there's a Ft. Lawton in Seattle and a Ft. Lewis in Washington, but there's no Ft. Wainwright." The officer responded, "The card reads, APO Seattle for the mailing address. We'll have to look it up in my directory."

We returned to the captain's office, and he pulled a thick book off the shelf. We looked through the book which listed all the military bases in the World, arranged alphabetically. We found the listing for Fort Wainwright and found that I had indeed been granted my request for a West Coast assignment. Fort Wainwright was located in Fairbanks, Alaska. I was shocked and heading from 105-degree daily heat to 20 degrees below zero! The captain laughed and said, "Well, it's summertime there now, so the temps will be in the 50s... At least you won't freeze... not for a while anyway."

I returned to Speedy and our jeep to tell him where I had been assigned. He could not stop laughing. Slowly recovering from the shock of learning about my next assignment, I thought to myself, "Well, perhaps it won't be so bad. I do like to hunt and fish and there will be plenty of that. Guess we'll just have to see how it goes."

Letter: 2 March 1969, 14th Military History Detachment, Saigon, MACV Headquarters, III Corps, Vietnam

While in Saigon, I checked in at the MACV Headquarters and found out what my next assignment is going to be. They had already sent my orders to the 1st Air Cav Division over a month ago, so there is no explanation for why I haven't received them. Anyway, hold on to your hat, here it is ... Ft. Wainwright, ALASKA!!! I have been assigned to the 171st Infantry Brigade at the end of the world. I am going from 110 degrees to minus 20! I have a reporting date of 15 June and am authorized 30 days of leave. Needless to say, I am not ecstatic about this assignment. I did talk with a major who was stationed in Fairbanks, and he confirmed most suspicions: it's a rough tour, cold, desolate, and many other adjectives.

It was getting late in the afternoon. We still had not bought the art supplies, our primary mission in coming to Saigon. The concierge of my hotel had given me addresses for five shops that might sell art supplies. We searched for the first store but couldn't find it. After a 15-minute drive, we found the second store, but it did not look like an art store. It was now approaching 5 PM, so Speedy said, "We're out of time and need to go in and see if they have what we need."

Fortunately, as we walked into the store, we found that it was indeed an art supply store. There was shelf upon shelf of paints, brushes, drawing pads and supplies. Speedy begin taking the boxes of supplies that he needed off the shelves. The shopkeeper came out to greet us and was immediately taken aback. Here we were, walking into the art supply store, fully armed and removing box after box of supplies from his shelves. I'm sure the storekeeper feared for his life. He immediately spoke to us rapidly in Vietnamese. I told Speedy to hold up a minute from what he was doing and asked the shopkeeper if he spoke English. He said he did not. He asked if I spoke Vietnamese. I said I did not. Then, on a remote chance, I asked the man in French if he spoke French. He said that he did. I had taken French in high school and college. I was a bit rusty, but we were able to communicate.

The shopkeeper and I carried on a quick conversation, and I assured him in French that we were going to pay for the supplies we were taking off his shelf. He still seemed nervous, so I reached into the thigh pocket of my fatigue pants to pull out the bag filled with piastres (also called dong) and showed it to him. Suddenly, his mood changed. We became best buddies. Speedy knew what he needed. We piled the supplies on the counter while the shopkeeper scribbled a hand-written receipt and put the supplies into cardboard boxes. The total came to just under the $300 that I had been given. We added a couple more items to round out the sale. The shopkeeper was delighted. It was clearly one of the largest sales he had made.

After packing up the supplies, we were invited into the back room to meet the shopkeeper's family and have tea. We sat for a while. I did my best to speak with the man using the French I had not spoken for more than two years. The shopkeeper translated to his family in Vietnamese. We kept the banter up for about a half-hour before we told the man that we had to leave. The man and his family insisted on carrying the boxes of supplies out to our jeep. He thanked us profusely; the entire family waved goodbye as we drove off.

We returned to my hotel. Speedy was to store the boxes at his billet, then planned to meet me the next morning at 6 AM so we could get to Bien Hoa to catch the convoy at 7. That was the night I was required to be OIC at the hotel. This meant I was stationed at the entrance of the hotel along with two MPs to guard the other officers sleeping inside. My shift started at 8 PM; I was to wake up the relief officer at 2 AM. It was an exceptionally long six hours standing behind sandbags at the front of the hotel accompanied by two other soldiers. They clearly did not wish to be there anymore than I did. I tried to engage them in small talk, but they were only interested in being relieved and getting back to their bunks. As I stood at the front of the hotel that night, I realized we were in an incredibly vulnerable position. There were only three of us standing behind two sandbag emplacements on either side of the door. It would have been so easy for a VC to fire an RPG at us or throw a hand grenade. We had cover, but certainly could not have repelled a sustained attack. The enemy had to know that there were officers billeted in the hotel. This made us a prime target.

"Nothing I can do about this," I thought. Thankfully when 2 AM finally rolled around, I went upstairs to wake up the captain who was to relieve me from 2 AM to 6 AM. He was an intelligence officer who wore a signal officer's insignia. I asked about his job. He informed me that he monitored radio traffic of troops in contact to determine if a large force had been engaged. If so, he would often call for airstrikes. I asked if he had ever listened to radio traffic from my unit, A Company, 1/5 Cav. He asked which platoon I led in the field. I told him that I had been the first platoon leader. He responded by saying, "Oh yes, you're Foggy Day 1-6." I was flabbergasted. The man even knew my radio call sign.

I was exhausted after pulling guard duty until 2 AM. I fell asleep immediately, leaving a call to be awakened at 5:30. It seemed as if I had only been asleep for five minutes when I was being shaken by the soldier assigned to wake me. I got up, dressed, grabbed my gear, and went downstairs to meet Speedy at 6 AM. It was 6:15 when I got to the front of the hotel. There was no Speedy in sight. Then 6:30 came and at 6:45, I went to the desk and asked them to call the NCO billet to see if Speedy had left. They could not tell us anything, and there was nothing I could do but to sit and wait. Finally, at 7:15 Speedy arrived. He apologized that there had been a great delay in getting the jeep out of the motor pool as it did not open until 6 AM. Then, he had to transfer all the boxes from his billet to the jeep.

We sped off for Bien Hoa which was a good 30-minute drive from where we were in Saigon. We hoped the convoy had been delayed in leaving—just as it had when we left Phuoc Vinh. We arrived at Bien Hoa only to learn that the convoy had left on time. We missed it. Told that we were required to travel by convoy, we would have to return in three days at 6AM to catch the next one.

As we drove off the base, I looked at Speedy and he looked at me. I said, "Should we drive like hell and see if we can catch the convoy? They have a one-and-a-half hour start on us, but are only traveling at 20 mph. We can catch them, and we can't spend three more days here waiting for the next convoy." Speedy said, "We're in a hopeless situation. The motor pool doesn't open until six, so I'll never be able to get our jeep out in time." So, instead of turning south and heading back to Saigon, we turned north toward Phuoc Vinh and started to drive like hell. Riding shotgun, I loaded a magazine into Speedy's M16 and put a round in the chamber.

We had a map but were not exactly sure of the route to follow. In the convoy, I had not paid close attention to roads. We simply followed the vehicle in front of us. We made excellent time for the first 20 miles on paved road, but then the road ended, and we were on dirt. After a while, we came to a fork in the road. We could not determine whether to go left or right. Choosing the left and driving for about 15 minutes, we finally ended up in a small South Vietnamese hamlet. We had clearly taken the wrong turn. At that very moment, we ran directly into an ARVN unit that was conducting a search and clear operation in the village. Fortunately, there was a US advisor with the ARVNs. He told us to get the hell out of there as there were VC in the area. We turned around and headed back to where we had made the wrong turn.

Both of us were extremely nervous that we would be ambushed at any moment, but luck was with us. We returned to the fork, took the correct turn, and continued to drive well beyond the speed limit, bouncing furiously over ruts and potholes. We didn't care. All we wanted to do was to get back to Phuoc Vinh and the security of our base camp. We spotted a road sign that pointed the way to the town and were relieved to see that we had only 15km to go.

Upon return to the base, we were questioned about why we were not traveling with the convoy. A report was filed with the MPs stating we had not followed proper procedure of driving with the convoy and had taken needless risks. We made excuses but acknowledged we had taken needless risks by returning to the base camp alone.

Of course, we omitted the fact we had taken a wrong turn and had driven into the middle of an ARVN search and clear operation. But Speedy had his art supplies. Printed orders for my next duty station had already arrived at our headquarters while I had been away. Alaska was now in my future.

Letter: 2 March 1969, 14th Military History Detachment, Saigon, Art Store, III Corps, Vietnam

I'm rested now from the trip. It really was exhausting. It's a 50 mile trip to Saigon, and bumpy, dirt road three fourths of the way. You have to drive fast as no stops are allowed in convoy. A jeep isn't the most pleasant vehicle to travel in.

When I got to Saigon we really got lost. We had no map and couldn't find an MP. We drove for an hour and wound up at the Tan Son Nhut AFB. They gave us directions, but we got lost again. Finally, we just started following military vehicles. We would up in IV Corps, the Delta (the Delta was another name for IV Corps, bordering on the southern outskirts of Saigon). We got directions and a map and finally, at 8 PM we got to the hotel which had been converted to a military BOQ. I was so thankful to finally arrive.

The next day, map in hand, we went to the USO and found out where the art stores were. Then came the real search. When we finally found them it was 11:30 and

Saigon closes for three and one-half hours for lunch. We toured the city a bit, went to the Cholon PX, Tan Son Nhut PX, USO and shopped. We went by the President's palace. It's a beautiful building except it's surrounded by barbed wire, fences, guards, tanks, and bunkers. They kind of destroy the atmosphere.

We went back to the art store at 3 PM and spent an hour and a half buying out the store. We spent all the money the army had given me. The owner only spoke French, so we had quite a time. Another Vietnamese came in who spoke English but no French. I got so mixed up that I'd start a sentence in English and finish in French.

We left early the next morning for Bien Hoa and Long Binh (close to one another) to look at their PXs and then back to Phuoc Vinh. (We tore up the road). On the way, we passed the base camps of the 1st Infantry Division and the 82nd Airborne Division at Phu Loi (southeast of Bien Hoa).

All in all, it was a fine trip. There were no incidents in the city or along the way which make it even better. I would have liked to have seen more of the city, especially the floating gardens and the zoo, but it was too dangerous to go traveling all over. I never did feel safe in the city. Americans must walk in pairs and be armed at all times. I felt nervous all the time and kept jerking around looking at people. An open jeep isn't the safest thing and those darn motor bikes are so close you can touch the riders. I guess I'm a little too cautious, but I've had very little contact with the people, only the enemy, and you can't tell them apart.

Welcome Home

In the dim light of the terminal, I saw two people and a dog standing behind the fence overlooking the airfield. I thought to myself: "Those have to be my parents."

One of the unusual things about Vietnam, compared with previous American wars, was the length of the tour of duty. It was only one year—365 days. This was a good thing for troop morale. Soldiers thought to themselves, "Hey, I can survive for 365 days." When you subtracted time spent on in-country processing, travel, R&Rs, and pulling base camp security, soldiers spent less than 10 months humping the boonies. And, realistically, 10 soldiers worked in the rear in support roles for every field soldier. Therefore, only about 30 percent of American troops in Vietnam saw actual line combat duty.

The negative aspect of a one-year tour policy was that it tended to make you cautious of taking risks. This statement is tempered by the unit one served in. Aggressiveness and risk-taking were hugely different from one unit to the next and from one commander to the next. But in the 1st Cav, there was a general caution about not taking unnecessary risks. There were many commanders who were extremely aggressive and wanted to mix it up with NVA and VC forces. They looked for every opportunity to find the enemy and generate body count. The average GI and most small-unit leaders (squad leaders, platoon sergeants and platoon leaders) quickly learned the importance of safety first before aggressiveness. Why take a risk with your own life and the lives of the men you were responsible for when you only had a few months left to serve? This is not to say that American troops were afraid to engage the enemy. My soldiers were fierce fighters when they became engaged. But in my unit, there was an attitude of caution both on my part and on the part of many small-unit leaders throughout the division. Smart tactics dictated that we make every attempt to fully deploy our superior firepower, artillery, and helicopter gunships before involving ourselves in a close-in firefight. Furthermore, 1968 was a period of extreme questioning about the war—for all soldiers, up and down the chain of command. Soldiers had begun to question why we were in Vietnam and what we were accomplishing. Frustration mounted over the "hands tied behind our back" strategy that prevented us from following Charlie into his base camps in Cambodia, Laos, or North Vietnam.

Awareness of serious war protests at home began to filter in as new replacements came into units. (We received little or no news about protests except through letters from home.)

Letter: 2 April 1969, 14th Military History Detachment, Phuoc Vinh, HHC, 1st Air Cav Division, III Corps, Vietnam

The other night Charlie had a field day with 122mm rockets and 57mm recoilless rifles. He put about 30 rounds into our camp and wounded 12. He fires only a few rounds at a time thereby making spotting by helicopter difficult. It's also harassing to be diving into our bunker every 15 minutes.

Recent intelligence reports indicate that Charles is preparing for his fourth major offensive and it's supposed to come in January directed at Saigon. The object is to bolster their position in the Paris Peace talks. Our kills have increased measurably since the 24th with an average of 40 to 75 per day. Charlie's combative ability has grown too. We have captured radar, radio monitor equipment and larger more sophisticated weapons (122mm rockets, 4.2 inch mortars and recoilless rifles). He even launched an ambush on APCs with some land mines, but he has not fared very well in these attacks (casualties are five to one). But he is becoming much more daring.

The VC and the NVA were intelligent fighting forces. They recognized they would always be outgunned and lose in any daylight firefight. They had to pick their battles carefully in order not to sustain heavy losses. This typically meant night ambushes and guerilla attacks on patrolling units with mortars, automatic weapons, and RPGs. There were also strategic, well-choreographed propaganda offensives like the Tet and Mini-Tet offensives of 1968. The NVA kept their fighting units small. They would only mass when there was a significant opportunity to catch American or ARVN units by surprise and deliver a decisive blow. Then they would strike viciously, inflicting as much damage as possible within a brief period. Once their objective was accomplished, they would break into small groups and scatter back across the Cambodian or Laotian borders, areas where we could not pursue. This reality created extreme frustration for American troops. We were fighting with our hands tied behind our backs.

Letter: 7 April 1969, 14th Military History Detachment, Phuoc Vinh, HHC, 1st Air Cav Division, III Corps, Vietnam

I have saved a number of photographs from the PIO that have appeared in our Cav newspaper. There are scenes I have personally seen or areas I've been in. There's even one of me crossing a stream with my map in my mouth!

The other night Charles broke his three-week non-firing record and dropped in 8–10 rounds. One fell across the road from our Quonset hut. I can assure you that my reaction time is still super quick. It took me two seconds to be in the bunker after the first round hit!

I've begun work on two new reports: Scout Dog Teams and Combat Trackers. I will let you know when I go out to the field to interview the principals. (It will be a forward base camp, not "in the field.")

Given this philosophy, as DEROS drew near, soldiers became squirrely and even more cautious about taking risks. Not wishing to take any chances, I personally slept in our bunker for the last week before leaving our base camp.

In 1968, tragically, 16,592 Americans were killed in Vietnam and 87,388 wounded. Public opinion about the war changed and the nightly news showed color pictures of those who died that day. This was the year when South Vietnamese General Nguyen Ngoc Loan executed a Viet Cong operative in front of the media, an image that has been widely published. Walter Cronkite, considered to be the "voice of the American public," called for an honorable exit from Vietnam. He thought the war had been lost. However, with access only to controlled military news sources, American soldiers knew less than Americans back home about what was going on in Vietnam. Still the growing dissatisfaction with the war gradually became apparent to soldiers and officers in country. The thought in the back of our minds was: "Why should I risk my life for a war we cannot win and has no meaning?"

When I finally received my printed orders at the end of April 1969, I was instructed to report to the DEROS Center in Bien Hoa for a departure date between May 9 and 14. The departure date was a window based upon the number of troops scheduled for return to the States, as well as the availability of flights incoming and outgoing. At the time, President Johnson had established a cap of 549,500 American troops in country. The logistics people were constantly juggling the strength figures so as not to exceed that magic number. I had arrived in country on May 9, 1968. The date, May 9, 1969, was the last square to be colored in on my short-timer calendar.

On May 6, after sleeping in the bunker next to our building for the past week, I asked my CO if I could leave for Bien Hoa to spend my remaining days waiting for my flight back. This was two days before my earliest potential departure date. I told him I wanted to visit the PX (post exchange), eat some hamburgers and French fries, sit in an air-conditioned Officers' Club and drink cold beer. He consented, and I was given permission to leave the next day. My unit threw a party for me that night; the cook made a farewell cake for our party. It was a bittersweet celebration. I would be leaving the next day, but the rest of the men were locked in to serve many more months. I was headed for my next duty station in Alaska while most of the rest of the men would be headed back to civilian life. We knew our paths would not cross again.

After celebrating way too much, I spent my last night in our bunker and awoke, hung-over and with a splitting headache around 7 AM. I immediately got ready, put on a clean uniform, and packed a small overnight bag of my possessions, silently recalling the huge duffel bag I had originally brought into Vietnam.

I made a call to the airfield and learned I could catch a flight that morning at 9:30. It was now 9:00; and I would need to be there within 15 minutes to get a seat. Checking with my CO, I was given the OK to leave. I shook hands all around and said a quick goodbye to the other officers and men. Then Sergeant Speedy drove me to the airfield. Of course, the flight was delayed. I sat around the terminal for an hour until it was ready. As I was getting ready to board, Speedy drove up a second time and ran into the terminal. He presented me with a plaque saying they had wanted to give it to me the previous night, but it had not been ready. He had driven into the town of Phuoc Vinh after dropping me off to see if he could pick up the plaque and get it to me before departure. I opened the box and read the inscription:

HHC, 1st Air Cav Division (Airmobile)
The Officers and Men of the 14th Military History Detachment
Bid the orally fulminating, intellectual neophyte
1st Lieutenant Robin Bartlett
A Fond Adieu
Bill, Jim, Speedy and Phil

I thanked Speedy for delivering the gift and told him to thank the other members of the unit on my behalf. I asked him to remind the staff that while it was true I had been "orally fulminating," I was certainly not an "intellectual neophyte." I told him to say to the other officers that there would come a day when they would thank me for the orientation I had put them through. They would know the answers to the questions being asked of them by the G-3 or CG. We hugged and wished each other the best. I boarded the plane headed for Bien Hoa.

I did indeed spend the next two days, May 7 and May 8, enjoying the air-conditioned PX and Officers' Club, binging on junk food, eating popcorn, and watching movies. There were thousands of officers, NCOs, and soldiers at the DEROS Center waiting for flights. I estimated that it would take several days before my turn to head for the airfield.

I joined several other officers for a trip into the neighboring town to enjoy a native Vietnamese meal with some cold beer. I remember eating some delicious meat along with rice and drinking local Vietnamese beer. The meat might have been dog or cat for all I knew, but at that point I really didn't care. I thoroughly enjoyed myself, returning to my bunk at around 8 PM. Upon my return, there was a piece of paper on my bunk stating that I was scheduled to leave the next morning, May 9, on a flight departing at 8 AM, exactly one year to the day. I was ecstatic. (Author's note: my wife's birthday is on May 9 and my youngest son was also born on May 9. I have played 5/9 in every possible betting combination but have yet to win anything.)

At 6 AM the next day, I put on my khaki uniform and boarded a big, beautiful jet airliner. While in Vietnam I had never encountered a Donut Dollie, a female nurse or attended the Bob Hope or any other show. So, the American flight attendants were the first "round-eyed" females I had seen in a year, and several of them were incredibly attractive. I was fortunate to capture the bulkhead window seat next to the door.

As the door closed, you could hear a pin drop throughout the plane. No one spoke as the engines fired up and the plane taxied to the end of the runway. The moment the wheels left the tarmac, there was a tremendous roar with men cheering, shaking hands, and slapping one another on the back. A few minutes later, there was a similar cheer when the pilot announced we had cleared Vietnamese airspace. The feelings of happiness and relief were momentous. The anxiety seemed to flow out of us no matter what job we had performed or where we had been assigned.

One of the flight attendants caught my eye. I decided I would impress her by estimating the number of steps she took during the flight delivering meals and responding to the passenger's requests. I made several estimates as to the length of her stride, the frequency of her trips, the length of the cabin, and the number of trips she made up and down. I calculated it on a napkin and gave it to her. It came to about 8 miles of walking. She thanked me for the estimate, but thought my calculations were a bit on the short side—hers were closer to 10 miles. She showed no further interest in me or my calculations, and I soon fell asleep.

After receiving orders, I had written to my parents indicating I would catch a flight back to Travis AFB in California sometime between May 7 and May 14. There was no way for me to know exactly what day I would return. After landing, I would be bussed to Oakland Army Terminal. I would call them then and we would decide whether I would take the bus to Oakland or if they would drive up and pick me up for the return trip to our home in Monterey.

Following a 17-hour flight with a short stopover at Eielson AFB in Alaska to refuel, we landed at Travis AFB in California. It was 11 PM. There was another momentous cheer as our wheels touched down. As we taxied close to the terminal, I peered out the window of the jet. In the dim light of the terminal, I saw two people and a dog standing behind a fence overlooking the airfield. I thought to myself: "Those have to be my parents."

The field grade officers (majors and above) disembarked first. Then the rest of us proceeded down the steps to the tarmac. When I reached the bottom, I bent down and kissed the ground. I was so happy to be back in the US.

I walked over to the fence and, sure enough, my parents were standing there. As all of us were dressed the same it wasn't until I was right in front of my mother that she recognized me. We kissed right through the fence, and I briefly held her hand. Our dog, Farouk, a French poodle, took one sniff, recognized me, whimpered, and jumped on the fence to try to lick my hand.

The last step was to have my bag inspected for contraband by an officer in the terminal. I was a bit nervous about this as I wanted a souvenir to bring back from Vietnam. I had taken a hand grenade, removed the blasting cap, exploded it in a 55-gallon drum of water, and retrieved the inert handle. Then, I took a hacksaw and sawed the hand grenade in half. I had these pieces in my bag. Of course, the inspecting officer saw them immediately. But he also saw that the blasting cap had been exploded and the grenade was in two pieces. It was no longer dangerous, so he let me go after my explanation that I wanted to have a souvenir for my desk. I later superglued the halves of the grenade together. The grenade sat on my desk in Alaska for many months until it was stolen.

I told the officer in charge I had received orders transferring me to my next duty station and would not need transportation to Oakland Army Terminal. He noted my name. I walked outside the terminal for a reunion with my parents.

"How did you know what flight I was scheduled to take?" I asked. As my father was a retired Air Force colonel, he had been able to get a copy of the manifest of all incoming flights from Vietnam for the period. While individual soldier names were not listed, he could tell which flights were Army and coming from Bien Hoa. My parents met *every* incoming flight starting on May 7, at all hours of the day and night.

We went to the officers' hotel located at Travis AFB. My parents were exhausted after meeting flights coming in early that morning. I was too keyed up to sleep and my body clock was in a different time zone. I spent hours watching the first live color TV I had seen with different shows and many channels.

The next day we drove down Highway 101 to my parents' home in Monterey. My father drove at about 65 mph. In the passenger seat, that speed and the highway freaked me out as the fastest I had traveled for the past year had been 45 mph.

I was aware that many soldiers threw away their uniforms as soon as they returned to the US. They were not welcomed home and if recognized as soldiers, were often harassed. For many soldiers there were no parades, no celebrations and certainly no congratulations for what we had been through. I was very fortunate not to experience this treatment. I lived at home in a secluded area away from any large cities. My parents were aware of how the tide of American opinion had changed and kept me removed from it. I was still in the Army and invited a small group of close friends and classmates and relatives to a welcome home party at the Officers' Club at the

Presidio of San Francisco. It was a lovely evening and I thanked all for writing to me and supporting me while in Vietnam.

I spent a final week buying uniforms and getting my personal gear and car ready to survive the Alaskan winters. I needed a dipstick heater, a circulating water pump heater and a battery blanket installed prior to shipping my car from Seattle to Anchorage, Alaska. After 10 days, I said farewell to my parents again and headed for my next adventure.

~~~~~~

Letter: 14 April 1969, 14th Military History Detachment, Phuoc Vinh, HHC 1st Air Cav Division, III Corps, Vietnam

I just returned from a two-day trip to Bien Hoa and Long Binh, to a historian's conference and to get information for an investigation of the combat loss of merchandise at the PX (a special duty I've been assigned to research and write up.)

As I'll be arriving home in less than a month, I wanted to mention a few things about my plans for when I get back. First, please do not plan any dinners, appointments, dates, or days for me. You must realize that this experience in VN has changed me a great deal. I am by no means the same person as when I left home. At present, my mind is a jumble of confused facts, ideas, shattered dreams, hopes and many other things. I am going to need some "peace and quiet" for a while and time to adjust to a new environment, both physically and mentally. My ideals and ideas about most subjects have changed; many have taken a 180 degree turn. I want to face decisions at my own speed, on my own terms and when I want to face them. So please attempt to take it easy on me for the first few days and let me make the approaches for divulging information, plans and arrangements. You must do this for me, otherwise I am going to become more confused and frustrated than I already am.

What I am saying then is to go ahead and plan your affairs but let me work out my problems by myself. I shall need your help and advice, but don't rush me for the first several days. I am going to be in a "difficult to handle and communicate with" state for some time after I return. I must attempt to settle many questions in my mind and outside pressure may only aggravate me. I have been accustomed to a life which is only one step away from that of an animal and in some cases much worse than that, so please, be patient and understanding. I know that you already know these things, but I want to emphasize them as the first several days can really "make or break me." Please try to work with me as it is going to be a difficult time.

I have had to kill a number of the enemy soldiers over here and have risked my life a number of times. This was not a pleasant task. These risks and dangers often well up inside me and there is no escape from the fears and frustrations. My temper is easily excited, and I shall need some time to get a good grip on myself. I may also be a bit "gross" as I have had to commonly use a lot of strong language. This too will pass in time and as soon as I can make the adjustment. Again, please go slow with me and be patient. It's very important and you must do this for both our benefits.

I don't know much more about my assignment at this time. I spoke with some others who have been assigned there, was told the fishing and hunting are great. I'm looking forward to that. I can expect to be in Alaska for 18 to 24 months and then will probably return to VN for a second tour. I assume that I shall be doing some cold weather training and perhaps training in rescue and ski tactics. In any case it's likely to be cold and hard.

Reading this letter today, I can see the eventual shift in my attitude from when I first went over to how I was feeling upon my return to a somewhat normal military life. I didn't know it at the time, but I had begun to experience PTSD in its formative stages. I lived with it for many years after returning and still live with it today.

CHAPTER 32

Butterfly Coincidences

Was this a butterfly coincidence? Perhaps… but perhaps not.

On the day I arrived at my duty station in Fairbanks, Alaska, in May 1969, I was still a first lieutenant. I was interviewed by the brigade commander, a full colonel. He took one look at my ribbons and personnel file, and called in his S-1 who was a captain, asking: "When is Lieutenant Bartlett due to be promoted to captain?" "He will be promoted next month," the S-1 replied. The colonel then told me: "Well, Lieutenant Bartlett, we're going to send you down to your battalion as a captain and start things off right." He had the S-1 take the bars off his uniform and pinned them on me. Bingo, after two years of service I was a captain! By comparison, it took my father eight years to be promoted to captain and my brother four. Here you could see the impact of the Vietnam years on officer promotions. Captains were in high demand in 1969. There were very few of them in the US, as most were leading companies in Vietnam.

On arrival at my battalion, my CO placed me in charge of the headquarters and headquarters company (HHC). This company consisted of 240 men, 75 track and wheeled vehicles including jeeps, ambulances, two and one-half ton trucks, heavy duty recovery vehicles and more. I was required to sign for $25 million dollars' worth of equipment. At 23 years of age, I was in over my head, unprepared and untrained to take on this assignment. Ultimately, my performance suffered.

Vehicle maintenance was not my forte. Our track and wheeled vehicles were old and in desperate need of repair parts. We could not get them through the normal supply chain as Vietnam received priority over all other requests. We were constantly redlining our vehicles (i.e. they were taken out of service). When my battalion went out on maneuvers, we would lose 60 percent of our vehicles within the first 5 miles due to overheating and parts failure.

Early in my tenure as the HHC company commander, I had all my soldiers lay out their vehicles for inspection at the motor pool. As I proceeded down the line of vehicles to be inspected, I saw that one of the ambulances had a big red tag on the front. I asked the soldier responsible for the vehicle what was wrong with it. This soldier was from the deep south of the US. He responded, saying: "It's da hon, sir." Not understanding, I asked him again. His reply was the same: "It's da hon, sir." Still not understanding, I told him to show me what was wrong. With a quizzical look on his face, the soldier opened the door to the vehicle and pressed on the horn, repeating: "It's da hon, sir, da hon!" Totally embarrassed, I walked on down the line continuing my inspection.

My strengths have always been in writing and administration. After a year in this position, I was transferred to the S-1 job at battalion headquarters. This was a role I knew how to do very well, and my performance improved dramatically.

There wasn't much to do in Alaska. In the winter months, it was unbelievably cold and dark for 20 hours a day. It never got brighter than twilight. Wives got "cabin fever" from being cooped up in their sparse quarters, husbands away from early morning until late at night, nothing to do and nowhere to go except the post exchange, commissary, and the movies. Births, alcoholism, and divorces were frequent occurrences among officers and NCOs. Parties were thrown every week at the Officers' Club to try to create some diversion and generate camaraderie. I lived in a BOQ consisting of two rooms connected by a bathroom, equipped with a refrigerator, hotplate, TV, and stereo. I worked six days a week, rising at 6 AM and usually working until 8 PM. I came home, ate a TV dinner, crashed into bed, and started it all over again the next morning. Winter temperatures of minus 20, 30 and even 40 degrees were common. I plugged my car into an electrical socket located in front of every parking space. This heated the battery blanket and dipstick heater and ran the circulating water heater. If you forgot to plug in, you could count on your car freezing solid and having to be towed to a warming garage to thaw out. This cost several hundred dollars, so it was something you never failed to do.

The town of Fairbanks consisted of a lot of bars and not much else. There was one great little restaurant serving pancakes, steak, and eggs for brunch for $8.00; several officers went there every Sunday morning. There was one movie theater showing one new movie each week. We had three or four TV channels, and the national news was flown up on tape each night to be broadcast the next day. Hunting and fishing were plentiful during the summer months and something I thoroughly enjoyed. Unfortunately, I was always so busy trying to keep our vehicles running that it was rare to be able to take even a few days off to rest or go hunting or fishing.

Finally, after a year of constant vehicle maintenance, someone in the upper echelons realized that we were wasting too much time trying to keep worn-out vehicles running. We were instructed to pack up all our vehicles and ship them on trains to the California National Guard. Then, suddenly, our unit went from being mechanized to a light infantry battalion. As we approached the winter months, everyone had to learn to ski and use snowshoes. We learned how to survive in extreme cold weather and practiced guerilla warfare tactics. The mission of our brigade was to prevent the

Russians from crossing the Bering Strait should they ever be so foolish as to launch an attack against the US. We only had about 2,000 men in our two battalions for the mission, so our joke was that if the Russians ever decided to attack, we would fire one shot, turn tail, and run for the hills.

After two years in Alaska, I received orders transferring me to attend the Career Course at Ft. Benning, Georgia. I was happy to be leaving the cold climate and dreary existence. I would not miss Alaska. I packed up my few belongings in a couple of suitcases, sold my car and ordered a brand-new gold Dodge Charger to be delivered in care of my college classmate's address in New Jersey. I planned to spend a few days with him before driving down to Georgia. I then jumped on the first available flight back to the lower 48.

After picking up the new car in New Jersey, I took a quick trip to Washington DC, stopping off at the Office of Personnel Operations (OPO). I wanted to receive some counseling and find out what the army had planned for me after attending the career course. I was in for a real surprise.

Part of my surprise had to do with butterfly coincidences. Butterflies have always been a significant symbol in my life. It all started when I was eight years old and spent two weeks of my summer vacation visiting my grandfather in Sacramento, California. My hobby was catching butterflies and I met a little girl named Mitzi who asked if she could use my butterfly net. I let her use it for a while, then told her she needed to get her father to make her one. She did and we caught butterflies for several weeks together that summer before my father moved on to his next duty station in Virginia.

Fast forward 10 years. I was a freshman at college. I received a call from someone named Mitzi Kramer who asked if I remembered her. I said I did not, and she responded by saying "Do you remember when you were eight years old and caught butterflies one summer while visiting your grandfather in Sacramento? I'm the girl who helped you catch butterflies." It turned out that her aunt knew my aunt and names and phone numbers were passed between relatives and resulted in the phone call.

Once the connection was made, we became fast friends. We occasionally shared butterfly experiences but didn't think too much about it. Then some amazing butterfly events started to happen. There was one occasion in Vietnam when trying to save a wounded soldier I saw three butterflies fly past me just as I fired a final star cluster in hopes that a medevac helicopter could find me in three-canopy jungle. I noted the butterflies, fired the star cluster, the chopper saw me, came in, dropped a jungle penetrator, picked up the wounded man, and saved his life. Was this a butterfly coincidence? Perhaps… but perhaps not.

When I visited the Office of Personnel Operations in Washington, I met with a major who I was told was my advisor. His branch of service was armor. I thought it very strange that an armor officer would be counseling an infantry officer.

Furthermore, this major had no combat experience. The man spent only a few minutes reviewing my records and then said: "Captain Bartlett, I see that you've done exceptionally well in your career so far. You've earned the Bronze Star for Valor, the Air Medal and two Purple Hearts. You are in the top five percent of your class. We have a wonderful career path programmed for you. We are going to send you to the Career Course, then to the Monterey Language Institute where they will teach you to speak Vietnamese. Then we will send you back to Vietnam for your second tour as a Vietnamese Unit Advisor."

My mouth dropped. I knew something about Vietnamese Unit Advisors, and their extremely short life expectancy. It was one of the most dangerous jobs an American officer could have, and I had absolutely no desire to become one. I told the armor major that what I wanted to do was to be assigned to Germany as a military attaché. The major's response was: "Well, this is what we have you programmed for. We can talk about that assignment *after* you come back from your second tour in Vietnam."

My reply: "The war in Vietnam is winding down and I have no desire to go back, especially as a Vietnamese Unit Advisor."

The major's response: "Well, this is what we have you programmed for." I responded saying that I did not want to be programmed. I had already earned two Purple Hearts and did not wish to earn another. The major stated for the third time that this was what the army had me programmed for.

I told him: "Well, then un-program me because the Career Course is voluntary, and I want to un-volunteer for it. This is not how I wish to spend my career. I have served four years of active duty and my active military service obligation is complete. I will resign and join the Army Reserve to complete my six-year obligation."

The major came back, saying: "Well, you have accepted orders transferring you from Alaska to Georgia, and therefore you are obligated for an additional year of service. You have been back in the US for 24 months. So, if you refuse to go to the Career Course, we have no alternative but to reassign you to Vietnam… *right now.* Take the weekend and think it over."

In a daze, I climbed back into my car and headed back to my college classmate's home in New Jersey. Here, in the space of less than an hour, my entire future, my dreams, and my military career had been thrown into chaos. I was extremely upset, in crisis, alone and not sure or clear what to do. My life had just been turned upside down by an officer who I felt had no appreciation for what I had already been through and the kind of career and future I wanted to have in the army. I was very sure of one thing however: I did not want to return to Vietnam and especially not as a Vietnamese Unit Advisor. After four years of dedicated military service, I was despondent that the military was going to treat me this way.

It was raining ridiculously hard as I drove into New Jersey and headed up the turnpike. The wipers could barely keep up with the downpour. There were huge puddles along the highway. I was feeling miserable but had the good sense to say to myself that it would be smart to get off the highway until the rain subsided. I pulled into a rest stop. In those days, Howard Johnson's owned the franchise at the rest stops along the turnpike. Because of the rain, all the parking spaces at the front of the building were taken. I was feeling miserable, and I really didn't care if I got wet. So, I parked in the second row, stepped out into the rain, and was instantly soaked. I slammed the door to my car and headed for the Ho Jo's—just as in the famous Humphrey Bogart movie, *Casablanca*. I was pissed at the way I had been treated by the armor major and the role the army had "programmed me" for. I banged open the door to the Ho Jo's and stopped dead in my tracks. There in front of me was a giant glass panel of pressed butterflies. Suddenly, I knew this was a sign that everything was going to be OK. Was this a butterfly coincidence? Perhaps... but perhaps not.

Returning to OPO the following Monday, I again met with the same major and told him that I refused to be programmed by the army. "Go ahead and reassign me to Vietnam right now, but before I leave this office, I want my resignation on file for one year from today's date." I put everything on the line.

With that declaration, the major left and went to huddle with two other majors. After a 10-minute conference, he returned and told me: "Well, the army has spent all this money to move you and your family from Alaska to Georgia. We will go ahead and reassign you to the Infantry School at Ft. Benning and you can be an instructor or something. If you change your mind, we can reprogram you for the Career Course and subsequent assignment to Vietnam."

His response showed me just how much this officer had studied my file. I was not married and had no family. Everything I owned fit in the trunk and back seat of my car. But, for once, I kept my mouth shut and accepted this decision. Soon, I was back on the road headed for Georgia and to an assignment which served to direct my future civilian career.

I was subsequently assigned to the Leadership Department of the Infantry School. Selected as a member of a special team, I worked to develop a required course of instruction that was implemented throughout the army worldwide called "Leadership for Professionals." The course consisted of a book of readings, overhead transparencies, and an instructor's manual. An officer and a sergeant from every infantry unit in the US were ordered to come to Ft. Benning for instruction in the course. These soldiers then taught the course to every officer and NCO in the army. It was a gratifying experience to help create leadership training that was implemented army-wide, and it led to the start of my civilian publishing career.

I left the army in 1973 and went to work as a sales representative for Prentice-Hall Publishing Company in Santa Monica, California, calling on college professors and promoting the company's college textbooks. There were times when I missed aspects of my military experience, but overall, I felt I had made the right decision. The army was not the right career for me. I was bothered by the tremendous time and material waste, training and retraining for possible events that seemed to be fabricated to keep soldiers occupied, and by the ability of the army to transfer you after only one or two years in one location with little regard to personal preferences or demonstrated abilities.

After two years as a textbook sales representative in California, I was promoted to the Prentice-Hall headquarters as the Assistant to the National Sales Manager in New Jersey. I stopped by to visit Mitzi on the way to my new job.

It was September, cool in Sacramento—sweater weather. In the late afternoon, as the sun was starting to go down, we decided to take a walk. I suggested that we walk over to my grandfather's house and return to the place where our relationship had begun. Amazingly, as we stood in front of my grandfather's house, talking and reliving old memories, two monarch butterflies flew in front of us. Monarch butterflies are usually in hibernation at that time of year. What were the chances that two butterflies would fly in front of us at the moment we were standing in front of my grandfather's house? Was this a butterfly coincidence? Perhaps ... but perhaps not.

Mitzi and I remain close friends to this day. On some of the most unexpected occasions, butterflies have been known to flutter in front of both of us out of nowhere. It has always been a sign of hopeful things to come ... coincidences perhaps, but their significance is hard to ignore in my life.

CHAPTER 33

Attributions

"Two Simple Words"

After years working in various sales and marketing positions and becoming familiar with the book publishing industry, I decided to write about my combat experiences in Vietnam. I had become close friends with Louis Cannizzaro, the president of a small communications company who designed advertisements for some of the book promotion work I was doing. I showed him the photographs and art pieces I brought back from Vietnam, and he read my essay, "The Trail." Lou was extremely impressed with my photographs, art, and story. He felt it needed to be memorialized in a video. We spent a great deal of time organizing the shots and preparing to record the audio. We found a young man who had the right voice and enlisted him to do the narration. The result is a YouTube video called "The Trail by Robin Bartlett." Even though many years have passed, this video remains as fresh and informative today as it was when we first recorded it. (See www.RobinBartlettAuthor.com)

Most of the photographs I brought back from Vietnam were taken by unknown combat photographers assigned to the Public Information Office of the 1st Cav Division. The same is true of the combat art which was part of a book proposal that was rejected by the top brass because the subject, "Men Killed in Combat," was felt to be too dark to be published into a book. Consequently, the art and photos were trashed and scheduled to be burned. I rescued them along with several hundred black-and-white and color photographs. None of the names of the photographers or the artist are known. I have been concerned about not being able to give credit to these men. I knew that the photos and artwork had been created by combat photographers and artists assigned to the 1st Air Cav Division and was thus in the public domain. Even so, I would have liked to acknowledge their contributions to my video.

These photographs and art pieces have survived two lost and found experiences. I first rescued them when the 1st Air Cav Division relocated from Camp Evans in I Corps to Phuoc Vinh in III Corps. I kept the photographs and art pieces in three binders and ultimately decided to donate them to the Vietnam Art Museum located in Chicago. I was told that an exhibit would be arranged and the photos and art displayed, but after several months of not hearing from them, I contacted the museum to find out what had happened to my donation. I learned that the museum had been temporarily closed. After a personal visit to the facility the photographs and art pieces were found and rescued for a second time.

Sometime after the video was created, I was asked to make a presentation to the New York/New Jersey Chapter of the 1st Cav Division. I showed my video and answered questions about my tour of duty. There were 50 men in the room and when it was over the room was silent for several minutes. I was afraid that my presentation had totally bombed. But then one veteran said that he had not heard such moving words or seen such an emotional video since his own tour. Other soldiers followed suit. My video and story had touched them and spoke to them with words and images that resonated with their own experiences. I was praised for my production by the collective audience.

One of the veterans who attended the presentation was the VA representative for the State of New Jersey. He spent some time looking through the original art and photographs that I brought to the meeting. He told me that he thought he recognized the artist who had created the book proposal and would put me in touch with him. The VA rep told me that this veteran lived in southern New Jersey but was dying from cancer caused by Agent Orange. He might not be able to contact me because he had little time left. The rep took my name and contact information, but I did not hear anything further and completely forgot about the exchange.

Many weeks later, I was driving my son to the University of Scranton. My cell phone rang. I answered the call and heard a voice say, "This is Ronald Jacobs and I understand you have used some of my artwork in a video you produced." We chatted briefly and I told him how he could view my video online. He told me that he would look at it and call me back to confirm if it was his art that I had used. I pulled into a rest stop and waited nervously for his return call. I was concerned that I had used this man's art without permission and might be in copyright violation.

Jacobs called back 15 minutes later and the first words he said to me were, "I am so pleased you used my artwork in your video. Thank you for honoring me. Your video is amazing, and I'm so proud to be a part of it." We chatted and he shared some of his personal story. He ended the call again thanking me for being a part of my project. I got his address and promised to send him a DVD of "The Trail."

As we ended the conversation, his parting words were: "Welcome Home, Brother!" I was so struck by these words that my eyes filled with tears and a lump formed in my throat. I could not speak. I mumbled goodbye and ended the call. It was the first time someone had said those words to me since returning from Vietnam.

Since then, I have learned that the most important words anyone can say to a Vietnam veteran are "Welcome Home!" Those code words will strike a chord with Vietnam vets and demonstrate that you know and understand the significance of their service far more than the common acknowledgement, "Thank You for Your Service."

Consider these words by Robert Flournoy, who was assigned as an FO from the 1/21st Artillery and attached to A Company, 2/8th Cav, 1st Cav Division, from his Facebook post, *Reflections of an Artillery Forward Observer with an Air Cav Rifle Company*:

> I find it awkward when someone says, "thank you for your service". I usually mumble some thanks back, and with averted eyes, move on. These words almost always come from people who did not serve, and while respectfully rendered, they make me squirm a little bit. I do not know why. But a "welcome home" salutation is a universal greeting almost always from a fellow veteran. I smile and return the thanks with those same two words. Welcome home are bonding words that have grown over the years from aging vets who, when looking back, remembered coming home from Vietnam so long ago with a bewildering, sudden, thud.
>
> Many of us arrived in Oakland 12 hours after leaving a fire base, some after walking point on a patrol, still wearing the red dirt of that duty, and were on the streets in civies a few hours later with some travel pay to make their way back to Ohio, Alabama, or New Jersey. And when the hugs and tears of our families were done with, we would look around us, somewhat bewildered, with a head full of "what now"? Ensuing nights filled the mind with sounds of popping flares, the hammering of an M-60, the constant boom of artillery and the whop whop whop of Hueys coming and going, left us dazed and confused to have left all that behind so suddenly. Many of us sank into silence, most tried to explain our experience to uncomprehending parents, and spouses, and so many sought the solace of fellow vets at the local VFW or Legion Hall, usually accompanied by liquor which too frequently led to loud, aggressive behavior. And how many of us wanted to go back? Back to the jungle, to the fire bases that we hated, but where likeminded men with singular purpose treated us like brothers, silent respect and understanding hanging over us like a warm blanket. Our home comings were, all too frequently, the beginnings of frustration and despair.
>
> Yet, most just moved on, putting it all behind. But, however we all might have handled the home coming, there was never a welcome home feeling from our country much less the people who never served. We didn't look for it, expect it, or even think about it. It was a non-issue. So, Vietnam vets became an obscurity in the landscape of America, an awkward presence that most vets acknowledged with their own silence. But, decades later, when old ghosts started creeping out of their closets, and the wisdom of age made its way into their reflections, combat veterans from the Vietnam war began remembering their experiences in softer toned colors, instead of the garish bright reds and oranges that they brought home with them. A kind gentleness emerged as they sought out their brothers from long ago. The greeting "welcome home" emerged not as a resentful "we never got a proper welcome", but simply as a soft nod of the head to those who made it back so long ago. Two simple words that belong exclusively to them and their kin, brothers who know as only they can know. Those men own those words, another right shoulder patch seen only by those who also wear one there.

Please try it: next time you meet a Vietnam vet try saying these two simple words and watch the reaction. These words summarize the pain so many Vietnam vets lived through and dedication and sacrifice we made.

To all my Vietnam Veteran Brothers: "Welcome Home!"

CHAPTER 34

A Boots on the Ground Point of View

Rarely a day goes by when I am not reminded of something about that war.

What was it like to be a grunt (infantryman) in Vietnam? Consider these two posts from soldiers from A Company, 508 Infantry, 82nd Airborne Division in country 1968–9:

> It wasn't just contact with the enemy but having to endure the elements. Flesh eating ants, the deadly snakes, scorpions, rats the size of cats—just to name a few of the things we hated. Not to mention the dislike for us by civilians back home. Booby traps that were crude but very effective. Running out of water and having to drink from bomb craters and rivers. (Excerpted from Facebook Group post of A Company, 508th Infantry, 82nd Airborne, Vietnam 68–69, 4/14/15.)

> This is what 45 days in the bush looks like. No showers, no clean clothes, pulling ambush at night while sleeping a few hours. Eating C-rations out of a small can, (most of the time cold). Learning to live on a few hours of sleep a day. Every day is the same. Searching for the enemy, and when you find him, it turns into a moment of sheer terror. When it's over, you get the wounded and KIAs on a medevac helicopter and continue your mission. Then it's more of the same. Carrying a hundred-pound rucksack in a hundred-degree heat—almost everyday someone would pass out due to exhaustion. (Excerpted from Facebook Group post of A Co, 508th Infantry, 82nd Airborne, Vietnam 68–69, 7/19/19.)

Because of my role as a platoon leader in combat, I've always had a "boots on the ground point of view" of the war (0 feet, not 50,000). Even though I was an officer, I got just as dirty, smelled just as bad, endured the same heat, ate the same food, carried the same load, and faced the same fears as the men I led humping the trail. As an officer, I was also a grunt (infantryman), just as they were, but with one essential difference: I was their leader, responsible for their safety, and sometimes had to make life-and-death decisions in split seconds. I carried this burden then, and still do to this day. I have relived many of the decisions I made—especially the ones that caused men to be wounded or to lose their lives. The last helicopter leaving Vietnam was not the end of the war. The radiation from my experiences lingers in me as it does in so many Vietnam vets. For me and for many, the war is still not over.

There is something called the Vietnam Syndrome. It became a popular term during the Reagan Administration in the 1970s. Politically, the term is used to describe America's reluctance to commit soldiers to overseas combat. In person, the syndrome is characterized in soldiers by recurring nightmares, depression, anxiety and sometimes even rage. For many returning soldiers it has resulted in suicide, aggressive behavior, drug dependence and homelessness. I recall snippets of my Vietnam experience almost on a daily basis—while brushing my teeth, having a conversation with a friend, and especially in day and night dreams. If someone calls out to me in the middle of the night, I can be awake and alert in seconds. I have cautioned family members only to touch me on the foot when asleep, as I can rise abruptly in reaction to their touch. I've gotten much better with these wounds, both psychological and physical. (I once had a sonogram and the clinician who read the results asked what the small, fingernail-like fragments were in my groin. I informed her they were leftover shrapnel pieces that had not been removed and had become embedded in me. A few have even worked their way to the surface.)

My military training was the best that the army had to offer. They taught me to be aggressive, fearless, and how to kill. I learned that if ambushed, the best way to survive was to quickly analyze the situation, try to discover a weak avenue and attack the enemy *viciously*. Under the circumstances, this was usually the only way to survive. While this training provided tremendous self-confidence and knowledge of small-unit tactics it did nothing to prepare me for the reality of killing the enemy, the loss of my men's lives or my own near-death experience. This preparation became a double-edged sword, straddling the line between accomplishing the mission I had been assigned and not taking unnecessary risks with the lives of my men or my own. It was often a heavy burden for a 22-year-old to carry.

I trusted, naively, that the senior officers and generals commanding me, and the politicians back home, knew more about the war than I did. I believed they were more aware of the big picture and made intelligent decisions about the strategies and combat orders they gave. I believed their decisions and combat plans were based on sound judgment and reasonable intelligence and did not place men in harm's way unnecessarily. They knew what was best for me, a first lieutenant, leading 28–32 men humping the trail. Some did, but it often seemed that as you went higher in the chain of command the concern for the soldiers grew less and less. We lost the war and we lost Vietnam, and veterans have paid the price because of it. Some may not like that the Vietnam Veterans' flag is black, but it seems very appropriate to me as do the black granite walls of the Vietnam War Memorial in Washington, DC. It is commonly called "The Wall That Heals," and those words say it all for me.

Adrian Lewis in his article "Vietnam War POWs and MIAs," commented that the words at the bottom of our flag read "You Are Not Forgotten." They have real meaning to Vietnam vets and especially the families who suffered for years trying to learn the fate of their loved ones listed as Missing in Action. In 1973, the original missing number was 2,646. Seven hundred and twenty-nine were repatriated after the signing of the Paris Peace Accords which included 687 POWs held in North Vietnamese prisons. An additional 55 soldiers and seven civilians were officially reported as "died in captivity" by the North Vietnamese government. This left more than 1,800 that officially remain missing in action. It has been extremely difficult to account for these lost souls. The US was unable to search North Vietnamese battlefields where pilots and crews were lost. We also could not search prisons and cemeteries in North Vietnam. An unknown number of Americans may also have been transported to China and the USSR. South Vietnam is densely covered with jungle and the geography of the terrain and climate have made it almost impossible to recover remains of downed aviators and MIAs lost in battle. (Statistics excerpted from "POWs and MIAs: You Have Not Been Forgotten," by Carl Asszony, Guest Columnist, Veterans Affairs, *The Record*, September 2021)

As the war progressed beyond its height in 1969, it became clear that many senior officers, generals, and politicians were now focused on protecting their careers, pleasing their superiors, earning medals, and scoring body count figures to benefit their personal standing. Generals and politicians selected bombing targets and made life-and-death battle decisions from tens of thousands of miles away—often based on fuzzy intelligence. Some politicians may have personally benefited from PACS and lobbyists by continuing to vote for and support the war machinery and military supplies shipped in to support the US and South Vietnamese forces.

The United States believed it learned important lessons from Vietnam about imposing our democracy on a foreign country, but this tragedy has been repeated in subsequent conflicts such as the "never-ending war" in Afghanistan. We have not learned from history. While fewer American lives were lost in Afghanistan, the similarities are apparent. Billions of dollars were wasted on equipment, training, bribes and supplies with no clear military or political objective. This was followed by years of winning terrain, destroying infrastructure, losing it, regaining it, and resulting in more American casualties and civilian collateral damage.

In 1971, as the war progressed toward conclusion, soldiers and civilians alike became disenchanted with our role in Vietnam. The tide of civilian support had turned. A Harris Poll in March 1971 cited the statistic that most Americans now believed the Vietnam War was "morally wrong." The American press cited cases of military carelessness and extreme drug addiction by soldiers. The Pentagon Papers were released and stirred controversy about the truthfulness of our leaders responsible for directing the war. Veterans threw their medals over the White House fence and Lieutenant William Calley was convicted for his role in the My Lai massacre. A dramatic increase in "fragging" was reported by the Pentagon. There were also reports of soldiers going out on "ghost patrols" (playing it safe and failing to follow the prescribed route of the patrol). There were even cases where soldiers refused to carry out missions suspected to be unnecessarily dangerous—especially those who were within 60 days of DEROS.

The peace talks with Hanoi continued to drag on. Nixon refused to accept the moniker of being the first American president to lose a war and pressed for "Peace with Honor," thereby continuing the folly. Finally, in his State of the Union address in 1974, after the POWs had been returned the year before, he is quoted as saying: "all our troops have returned from Southeast Asia—and they have returned with honor." In truth, no soldier wanted to be the last man to die for a lost cause, or "die for a tie" as was the common phrase. The same tide of negativism in the US also impacted soldiers engaged in fighting the war. The unrest on American streets was carried across the sea to the soldiers in the field as replacements brought stories of what was happening back in the World. Soldiers in the field received no news briefs. They had to rely on only one source, the *Stars and Stripes* military newspaper, and letters from home. These troops gradually grew to understand that our politicians and senior leaders had lied and continued to mismanage the war. They determined to survive their tours and not take unnecessary risks. They questioned what was worth fighting for and what was not. It was true that some soldiers and small units questioned and disobeyed combat orders especially when it appeared to them that these decisions placed them at unnecessary risk. To their valiant credit however, these same soldiers always remained committed to doing whatever was necessary to save wounded and recover KIAs on the ground or from downed helicopters.

Having been raised in a military family, served as a platoon leader in Vietnam, and spent six years in "service to my country," I have been extremely sensitive to the lack of awareness about my war. This is not only true for young people but from my own generation.

It is a sad state, and I don't see much of a difference for those vets who served in more recent engagements as well as the "never-ending war" we have recently concluded. I wonder if recognition of service is a lost cause. I do not disparage what happened to this country on 9/11, but those events have commanded more public attention, ceremonies, physical memorials, and TV documentaries than many of the wars this country has fought. This may be because it happened on home turf and impacted so many civilian and public servant lives rather than soldiers who were "obligated to die for their country."

Speaking in broad terms, my belief is that so many Americans today have become completely focused on their own welfare as well as unaware and uneducated about history and totally divorced from anything military. Many can't distinguish or even recognize the major wars that have caused so many more deaths than 9/11. Vietnam is rapidly becoming a dream of the past similar to Korea, World War II, and World War I. In their article, *The Downside of High Trust in the Military,* September 16, 2021, Jessica Blankshain and Max Margulies state: "When the public is almost totally insulated from the human and financial costs of war, it has no reason to care. Call this 'when the military is at war, Americans are at the mall' theory."

The true meaning of recognition celebrations such as Vietnam Veterans Day, Memorial Day, Veterans Day, and POW/MIA Recognition Day (and even Labor Day) is not understood and has degenerated into major sales opportunity days for retailers. Ask any teenager and many adults about the difference between Memorial Day and Veterans Day and see what they say.

In the 50-plus years since my tour, like many Vietnam vets, I have buried my experiences and turned my back on it all. I hid my military service believing that we had lost the war, and everyone hates a loser. To this day I believe that all that I did, all that I volunteered for, my entire time in Vietnam and the military was wasted. I didn't realize it upon my return, but I suffered from PTSD and went through several stages: shock, abandonment, depression, hardening of emotion and finally assumption of an uncaring and apolitical attitude. It may have been a bit easier for me upon my return to the World because I remained in the military for several years following my tour. I continued to "drink the military Kool-Aid." While my true feelings about the war remained unspoken, I continue to have tremendous respect for all veterans and their service. My family always spoke of us as being "in the service to our country." I was raised in a military family. My grandfather, father, and brother all attended West Point. I went through the ROTC program. We all served as officers and took "service to our country" as a sacred oath and obligation. It was a three-generation commitment to our country and something that was highly respected when I was young… but not so much today. It was a different mindset then, and many Americans simply don't understand it.

Like me, so many Vietnam vets today are bitter about how they were treated returning home. They have hidden their military service from those who thought they were responsible for losing the war. Many have suffered frustration seeking health services from some poorly run VA hospitals. There has been a general lack of adequate psychological care and benefit counseling even to this day. Compounding the tragedy, our military and government have failed to recognize the deadly impact that dumping 20 million gallons of Agent Orange throughout South Vietnam has had on the lives of the thousands of men who dispensed it, walked through it, and breathed in the deadly dust, as well as the Vietnamese people who live with the aftermath to this day.

Today, rarely a day that goes by when I am not reminded of something about that war. I continue to exhibit a high level of self-confidence. I'm often fearless when facing a stressful situation—something that can be both good and bad. Sometimes my experiences, so foreign to my peers, have caused me to be unsympathetic to friends, family, and colleagues. I know I have suffered from people thinking I am unfeeling and uncaring. And there are times when anger has overwhelmed me, and my ability to remain in control in an adversarial situation is diminished.

In my heart and in my life the Vietnam War is not and never will be a positive experience. It damaged me and so many of my veteran brothers in so many ways, even to this day. I will never forgive my military and political leaders for the lies and deception that caused so many of my brothers to be wounded or die. Our "Band of Brothers" is a virtual association of veterans. Popularized by the book and miniseries of the same name, the concept reflects the bond we all share and the oath we took to serve and defend our country and the Constitution against all enemies, both foreign and domestic. For most of us, this was a sacred oath and something we took seriously. Many shed their blood or gave their lives for that cause. Shakespeare's *Henry V* said it best in 1599:

> We few, we happy few
> We band of Brothers,
> For he today that sheds
> His blood with me
> Shall be my Brother

I started this book many years ago to tell some combat stories and events that I thought were unusual. Some of my experiences were gut-wrenching and horrific, some humorous and unbelievable. I hope I have accomplished that goal and that you, my reader, will take away some of the same feelings and understanding of my experience, keeping in mind that the story I've told is from the ground level, face to face with the enemy. It's a small-unit leader's "boots on the ground" point of view.

Glossary and Abbreviations
of Military Terms

AFB – Air Force Base

Agency man – CIA operative

Agent Orange – herbicide mixture used to kill vegetation, containing a dangerous chemical contaminant called dioxin. Used extensively by the US military from 1962 to 1975. Named for the orange band around the storage barrel. Veterans who may have been exposed to Agent Orange have suffered from Type II diabetes, ischemic heart disease, Parkinson's disease, neuropathy, and a large list of cancers

Airborne Course – training to be a paratrooper, 4 weeks

Air Cav – Air Cavalry

Airmobile – entire unit fully equipped with sufficient helicopters to conduct heliborne or combat assaults. Capable of being carried or lifted by helicopter

AK – Avtomat Kalashnikov, AK-47 rifle invented by Mikhail Kalashnikov

AO – Area of Operations (also Agent Orange)

APC – Armored Personnel Carrier

APO – Army Post Office

ARA – Aerial Rocket Artillery

Arty – Artillery

ARVN – Army of the Republic of Vietnam, South Vietnamese Army. Formed in 1955; surrendered to the North Vietnamese Army in 1975.

AWOL – absent without leave

Basic – basic military training, 13 weeks

Blasting cap – device used with C4 and det cord in demolitions

BN – battalion, made up of four infantry companies, one combat support company with mortars and a reconnaissance platoon, and a headquarters company that provides staff, logistics, transportation, communications, and medical support to the companies

BN CO – battalion commander, usually a lieutenant colonel

Booby trap – most often a hand grenade with pin pulled, placed in a C-Ration can and attached to a trip wire, also punji stakes and various other similar devices

BOQ – bachelor officers' quarters

Brigade – commanded by a brigadier general or colonel and composed of two or more subordinate units, such as regiments or battalions

Bronze Star – award for meritorious service

Bronze Star with V – fourth highest award for valorous service

C-130 – large, fixed-wing aircraft used to carry heavy loads and troops

C4 – plastic explosive blocks used for demolitions

C&C helicopter – command and control helicopter used by the commander directing the battle from above

CA – combat assault (Charlie Alpha). An offensive action conducted by infantry units using helicopters. The Huey helicopter (UH-1 Iroquois) was the primary helicopter used in assaults

Cadence caller – a soldier who runs adjacent to a formation and helps keep the unit in step

Camp Evans – the base camp named after Marine Lance Corporal Paul Evans, KIA in 1966 when Marines occupied the base from 1966 to 1967. Located 24km northwest of Hue on Highway 1

Cav – cavalry, members of the 1st Cavalry Division

CG – commanding general

Chain of custody – the secure handling of substance from discovery location to laboratory evaluation and then to trial

Claymore mine – 700 steel balls propelled by C4 explosive with a range of 50m

CO – commanding officer. The senior leader in an infantry company, battalion, or brigade. The division also has a commander with the title commanding general (CG). Company commanders are usually captains (CPT); battalions are commanded by lieutenant colonels (LTC); and brigades are commanded by colonels (COL)

COL – colonel, officer grade 0-6

Company commander – The most important person in an infantry company. Responsible for deploying his platoons and squads, engaging firepower to defeat enemy force. With assistance of his Forward Observer (FO) and RTO, he had the ability to command division's artillery, attack helicopters and USAF or Marine close air support

CONEX container – secure metal container designed to transport equipment and supplies

Cover man – the soldier who walks second in line and protects the point man

CP – command post

CPT – captain, officer grade 0-3. Serve as company commanders or staff officers at battalion and brigade level

C-Rations – Cs or C-Rats; 12 meals of various types in a case

CS gas – ortho-chlorobenzalmalononitrile. Tear gas with nauseating agent added

CSM – command sergeant major, senior enlisted grade E-9

CSR – combat stress reduction

Danger close – term used when calling in mortar, artillery, or air support to alert those who are firing that friendly troops are in close proximity to the intended enemy target (200m for artillery, 600m for jet fighters)

Defilade – a depression in the earth

DEROS – date estimated to return from overseas service

Det cord – detonation cord used in demolitions

DiDi Mao – Vietnamese for "go quickly"

DMG – distinguished military graduate from ROTC

DMZ – Demilitarized Zone

Dong – Vietnamese currency, also called piastres

DP – dismount point

DSC – Distinguished Service Cross, the second highest award for valorous service

E-5 – sergeant responsible for a squad

E-6 – sergeant responsible for a platoon

E-7 – first sergeant responsible for a company

E-8 – sergeant major responsible for a battalion

EOD – explosive ordinance disposal

First lieutenant – 1 Lt, officer grade 02

First sergeant – 1 SG, senior enlisted position in a company, enlisted grade E-8. Manages the company's rear area including administrative, supplies and accountability of weapons and equipment

Flechette – 1-inch steel darts fired by multiple types of devices, from a 40mm grenade launcher to a 105mm howitzer

FNG – Fucking New Guy

FO – forward observer. A second or first lieutenant attached from an artillery unit to an infantry company. Under direction of the company commander, provides coordination and control of artillery fires, attack helicopter and close air support to infantry unit

FOB – forward operations base

Foggy Day 1-6 – call sign for 1st platoon leader of A Company, 1/5 Cav, 1st Air Cav Division

Foggy Day 1-6 Romeo – Call sign for the RTO for the 1st platoon leader of A Company, 1/5 Cav, 1st Air Cav Division

Fortran – general-purpose programming language using punch cards to create programs

Fragging – dropping a grenade with or without pin pulled into an officer's or NCO's sleeping quarters to warn against excessively aggressive attitude

Friendly fire incident – event in which US or allied soldiers were killed or wounded by their own fire while on a combat operation

FSB – Fire Support Base or Firebase. Located on mountain tops or other locations where artillery could support infantry operations. Base was large enough for an artillery battery and one or two helipads. Defensive perimeter was provided by an infantry company

G-1, G-2, G-3, G-4 – general staff. Same as the S-1, S-2, S-3, and S-4 but at the division level

GI – government issue

Grenadier – soldier who fires a 40mm grenade launcher

Grid coordinates – six digits used to identify specific locations to the nearest 100m on military map

H&I – Harassment and interdiction – artillery fire at night designed to intersect crossroads and possible enemy targets

HE – high-explosive artillery round

Heat tab – combustible tablet designed to heat C-Rations or a drink

HHC – headquarters and headquarters company

HQ – headquarters

Huey – Bell UH-1 Iroquois helicopter, commonly referred to as a Huey, workhorse of Vietnam

Hump – to carry a heavy load on your back

I Corps – The northernmost division of South Vietnam. The country was divided into four corps zones. Each was occupied by a South Vietnamese Army Corps. I Corps was bounded by the Demilitarized Zone (DMZ) in the north that divides North and South Vietnam. Laos is on the west and the China Sea on the east. Major cities in I Corps were Hue, Quang Tri, Quang Ngai, Danang, Chu Lai and Tam Ky. I Corps had more US battle casualties than any other, especially in 1969. II Corps, to the south, was commonly known as the central highlands. III Corps encompassed the area around Saigon (Ho Chi Minh City), Bien Hoa, Long Binh, and Tay Ninh to the western border with Cambodia. IV Corps was called the Delta

IED – Improvised Explosive Device

Instant NCO – 90-day training course to promote soldiers to noncommissioned grade. Also called "Shake and Bake"

IOBC – Infantry Officer Basic Course, six weeks

Jerry cans – metal canisters containing 5 gallons of water

Jungle fatigues – uniform worn by soldiers in Vietnam

Jungle penetrator – cable lowered from a helicopter with a seat designed to extract soldiers in deep jungle

KIA – Killed in Action

Km – kilometer, klick. Military distances are measured in kilometers and meters. Military maps are divided into 1km grid squares. One kilometer is equal to .6 miles. A meter is roughly equal to 1.1 yards. *See* Maps

LBE – load-bearing equipment

Leg – a soldier who is not airborne qualified

Log bird – a logistics and supply helicopter, usually a Huey, used to deliver supplies to units at fire support bases or in the field

LOH – Light Observation Helicopter, OH-6 Cayuse

LP – listening post

LRRP – Long Range Reconnaissance Patrol

LRRP Rations/MREs – Meals Ready to Eat. Mix with water in a pouch. Lightweight and easy to carry

LT – lieutenant, officer grade 0-1 or 0-2

LTC – lieutenant colonel, officer grade 0-5

LZ – landing zone. Combat assaults always had one or more LZs designated as the point where combat units were inserted on the battlefield. If an enemy was encountered on the LZ, it was called a "hot" or "red" LZ. A "cold" or "green" LZ meant there was no enemy contact on landing

M16 – standard military issue rifle during the Vietnam War, capable of firing semiautomatic or full automatic

M79 grenade launcher – single shot weapon, similar to a sawed-off shotgun; fires a variety of 40mm projectiles

MACV – Military Assistance Command Vietnam

MAJ – major, officer grade 0-4

Maps – military maps used in Vietnam for combat operations were scales 1:50,000. 1cm on the map equals .5km on the ground. Map grid squares were 1,000m or 1km on each side

Medal of Honor – highest military award for valor

Medevac – medical evacuation, extraction of wounded soldiers by helicopter

Medic – no position in an infantry unit was more important than the company or platoon medic. The medic's MOS (military occupational specialty) was 91B. Medics were trained in advanced life-saving skills and carried basic medical supplies to treat soldiers who were WIA

Memorial Day – commemorates all men and women who have died in US military service, celebrated last Monday in May

MHD – Military History Detachment

MIA – Missing in Action. US military members missing in combat were designated as missing in action. This term applies when the whereabouts of a soldier on the battlefield cannot be determined

Mission – infantry unit operations were guided and controlled by brief but clear mission statements which were part of an operations order. The mission statement includes what the unit is to do or accomplish and its purpose in performing the mission. A complete mission statement includes who, what, when, where, why and how

MOS – military occupational specialty. Each officer and enlisted soldier has an MOS. An infantry company had the following for enlisted soldiers: 11B Infantryman (11 Bravo or 11 Bush); 11C, Indirect Fire Infantryman (81mm and 4.2-inch mortars); some infantry soldiers had the 90mm Recoilless Rifle Gunner. 91 B Medical Corpsman (medic) were attached to infantry platoons and companies from the medical platoon in the battalion headquarters company. Officers in infantry companies were either 71542 (airborne qualified) or 1542. Officers with Special Forces qualifications were 31542. The Artillery forward observer was 13A for officers and 13F for enlisted

MP – Military Police

MPC – Military Payment Certificates, also called scrip

MRE – Meals Ready to Eat – *see* LRRP rations

NCO – non-commissioned officer. They include the four ranks and pay grades: Sergeant E-5, staff sergeant E-6, Sergeant First Class E-7 and first Sergeant E-8. NCOs obtain their rank by promotion within the enlisted ranks for meritorious performance and/or time in grade

NDP – night defensive position. Infantry units in the field would assume a defensive position at dusk which was generally circular, providing 360-degree security against enemy attack

NVA – North Vietnamese Army soldiers. The primary combat forces in the Vietnam War. NVA infiltrated from North Vietnam through various routes in Laos and Cambodia. They were generally well-trained and well-equipped, and courageous fighters in infantry operations

Oak Leaf Cluster – given for second award of a medal

OD – olive drab color

OIC – officer in charge

OP – observation post

Operations order – these orders were used to assign a new mission to an infantry unit. The order has a standard format that gives the Situation (friendly and enemy), its Mission (what the unit is to do), Execution (concept of the operation including coordinating instructions), Service Support (supply, transportation, medical and other administrative matters), Command and Signal (chain of command and communications). Written orders were given orally or in a brief written form called a fragmentary (frag) order. Warning orders were short orders giving advance notice to units to prepare for an upcoming new mission

OPO – Office of Personnel Operations

ORRLL – Operations Readiness Report, Lessons Learned

Piastres – Vietnamese currency, also called the dong, carryover from the French occupation

PIO – Public Information Office

Platoon – there were three infantry platoons and a weapons platoon in the typical infantry company. Three infantry platoons each had three infantry squads. Each squad was authorized a staff sergeant squad leader and 10 soldiers. But in Vietnam they were led by sergeants E-5, one grade lower, and had about eight soldiers assigned in the field (before casualties). Infantry squads were further divided into fire teams each led by another junior sergeant or sometimes a specialist or even an experienced Private First Class. Platoons carried one M-60 machine gun and one M-79 grenadier. The infantry platoon was led by a lieutenant platoon leader with a platoon sergeant as second in the chain of command. Each had a radio-telephone operator (RTO) who carried an AN/PRC-25 radio. A medic was normally attached to each platoon if available. The weapons platoon was equipped with three 81mm mortars and two 90mm recoilless rifles but carried only one mortar in the field

Platoon leader – a first or second lieutenant in charge of a 30- to 40-man unit

Platoon sergeant – second in command of a 30- to 40-man unit. Platoon sergeants with the rank of sergeant first class (SFC) are the most experienced infantry soldier in the infantry platoon. They serve under the platoon leader and may act as platoon leader if the position is vacant

Point man – an experienced soldier who walks in front of an infantry squad, platoon, or patrol. He has primary responsibility for providing frontal security by detecting the enemy's presence, booby traps, or other hazardous situations. Point men are usually skilled navigators and are closely followed by a cover man who provides additional security for the point man

POW – prisoner of war

POW/MIA Recognition Day – observed on the third Friday in September, honors those who are still missing in action

PRC-25 (Prick-25) – portable radio communications

Psyops – psychological operations

PT – physical training

PTSD – post-traumatic stress disorder. Experienced by soldiers after combat event who continue to have disturbing thoughts and feelings that last long after the incident is over. Some may relive the events through flashbacks and nightmares. In some cases, these memories may cause sadness, fear, or anger

Purple Heart – Military decoration for wounds suffered in combat

Pyrotechnics – also called star clusters. Rockets in a can; shoots 200 feet into the air and bursts or illuminates the area

PX – post exchange

QRF – Quick Reaction Force

Quonset hut – oblong prefabricated building with metal roof

R&R – rest and relaxation

RA – Regular Army

Ranger School – small-unit combat training, 12 weeks

Reconnaissance by fire – firing artillery shells into a suspected enemy position prior to entering

Reconnaissance in force – A combat mission assigned to infantry units in which the intention is to locate and engage enemy forces. Previously such missions were called "search and destroy" missions, but that term was dropped for political reasons

Regiment – similar to a brigade, commanded by a colonel and divided into several companies, squadrons, or batteries and often into two battalions

Repo Depo – Replacement Depot located in Long Binh, Vietnam

ROTC – Reserve Officer Training Corps

RPG – rocket-propelled grenade

RTO – radio telephone operator. RTOs had the vital role at the company and platoon level in an infantry company. They were usually experienced combat soldiers who had a basic understanding of infantry operations and could communicate clearly during enemy contact. Most carried the PRC-25. There were four RTOs at the company level. One RTO was responsible for the company command radio net which included the company's platoons. A second RTO carried the radio for the battalion command net which communicated with the battalion tactical operations center (TOC). A third RTO operated on the battalion logistics radio net and was responsible for supplies, medevacs, and administrative radio traffic. A fourth RTO supported the artillery forward observer and operated on the battalion's fire direction net. In an infantry platoon there were two RTOs, one for the platoon leader and one for the platoon sergeant. On occasion, squads were assigned the PRC-25 when operating independently on a combat patrol or ambush

RVN – Republic of Vietnam (South Vietnam)

S-1 – The adjutant or personnel officer of a unit responsible for personnel and morale

S-2 – The intelligence officer of a unit

S-3 – The operations officer of a unit

S-4 – The logistics officer of a unit

Sapper – enemy soldier who penetrates the perimeter carrying explosives in a satchel and attempts to blow up something important

Saturation ambushing – ambushing technique that places reinforced squads at intervals along a trail. Designed to achieve maximum kill ratio

Scrip – see MPC

SEAL – Navy: Sea, Air and Land

SFC – sergeant first class, senior enlisted grade E-7. Platoon sergeants in infantry platoons are authorized the SFC rank. Most infantry companies in 1969 were short SFCs

SGM – sergeant major, senior enlisted grade E-9

SGT – sergeant, enlisted grade E-5. The lowest non-commissioned officer rank in an infantry company. Due to shortages, they often led a squad rather than an infantry fire team. Infantry squads usually had two fire teams

Short-timer calendar – picture of a nude female divided into various units. Soldiers would color in one unit each day. Many versions existed

Silver Star – third highest award for valorous action

Sitrep – situation report. A report usually made on a periodic basis by subordinate units to their higher headquarters. Sitreps may also be called in as needed or required to report on combat actions or other battlefield events, activities, or circumstances

SNAFU – Situation Normal, All Fucked Up

SP4 – specialist 4th class, enlisted grade E-4. A rank between PFC and SGT, designating a soldier who had become proficient in his military occupational specialty

Squad – there are usually three infantry squads in an infantry platoon. An infantry squad is authorized 10 soldiers assigned, but due to casualties, leave, sickness or other assigned duties most infantry squads in the field averaged six to eight infantry soldiers. Infantry squads are authorized a staff sergeant E-6 squad leader but often were often led by sergeants E-5, or sometimes SP-4

Squad leader – usually a sergeant E-5 responsible for a 10- to 12-man unit. Squad leaders in infantry platoons have the closest relationship with squad members and have the most influence on the squad's effectiveness in combat

SOP – standard operating procedure

Squelch – white noise coming from a radio

SSG – staff sergeant, the rank E-6 immediately above SGT. SSGs lead infantry squads. They may be called upon to fill platoon sergeant or even platoon leader position

Star cluster – see pyrotechnics

Stick – a line of paratroopers getting ready to jump from an aircraft

Straphanger – soldier who works in the rear areas, often a short-timer

Tet – Vietnamese lunar New Year, late January or early February

The World – back in the USA

Tiger Team – Special Operations teams conducting clandestine activities

TOC – tactical operations center. The TOC is the command post of a battalion or brigade. Officers and NCOs from the brigade or battalion staff operate the TOC. The TOC is managed by the S-3 operations officer, who at battalion level is usually a major. The battalion TOC maintains communications with the battalion's companies and with the brigade TOC. Battle reports and situation reports from the companies come into the TOC, which maintains and updates status of combat operations and keeps the brigade TOC informed of all developments

USAF – United States Air Force

USARV – United States Army Vietnam

VA – US Department of Veterans Affairs

VC – Viet Cong, guerilla soldiers, commonly called Charlie. Organized into two groups: main force units and irregular forces (guerilla fighters). Irregular forces were not well equipped or trained and provided support to the NVA and VC main force units. They were used to harass, ambush, and set booby traps

Veterans Day – originally known as Armistice Day, observed on November 11, honoring military veterans of the US Armed Forces discharged under honorable conditions

Vietnam Veterans Day – observed on March 29, the date of the departure of the last American troops from Vietnam

VT – variable timed artillery round, explodes overhead of enemy

Welcome Home – what you should always say to a Vietnam vet

WIA – Wounded in Action

XO – executive officer of a unit

US and Enemy Weapons

US weapons

AH-1G Huey Cobra – The army's attack helicopter in Vietnam. Arming of the Cobra was flexible. Two nose turrets held a 7.62 minigun with 8,000 rounds and the other held a 40mm grenade launcher with 400 rounds. Four rocket pods each held 19 x 70mm rockets with two pods mounted under each wing.

F4-Phantom – A US Air Force, Navy, or Marine two-seat, twin-engine long-range, supersonic jet interceptor and fighter bomber. When used in close air support for ground forces, it was equipped with 500 lbs. Carried bombs, napalm, and a 20mm cannon with a rate of fire of 6,000 rounds per minute.

8-inch howitzer – A self-propelled, indirect fire support weapon weighing 28.2 tons and manned by a crew of 13, the weapon had a maximum rate of fire of three rounds per two minutes and sustained rate of one round per two minutes. The HE round had a maximum kill radius of 80m and a maximum range of 23km. Also fired a controlled fragmentation round containing 108 bomblets that air burst over enemy positions. This devastating round was nicknamed a "Firecracker" round because of the sound it made when all 108 bomblets rapidly exploded over the target. Similar versions were also available for the 105mm and 155mm howitzers.

81mm mortar – A high-angle, smooth-bore, indirect fire weapon. Max range of 4,500m. Could also fire night illumination rounds.

105mm howitzer – This howitzer was the artillery's most prevalent indirect fire weapon in Vietnam. Found at every firebase supporting infantry units in the field, it was easily moved by helicopter. Six M102s made up an artillery battery. The maximum range was 7.1 miles or just over 11km. The barrel is 7ft, 7 in. A typical crew could fire 10 rounds in a minute or a sustained rate of three rounds per minute. Had a kill radius of 30m per round. A crew of eight was authorized, but the howitzer could be operated with fewer if required

155mm howitzer – A turreted self-propelled, indirect fire support weapon. Weight 27.5 tons. Manned by a crew of four, the M109 had a maximum rate of fire of four rounds per minute and a sustained rate of one rpm. The HE round had a kill radius of 50m and a maximum effective range of 18km.

175mm gun – A self-propelled, direct-fire support weapon weighing 28 tons. Manned by a crew of 13, the M107 had a maximum rate of fire of one round per minute and a sustained rate of one round per two minutes. The HE round had a kill radius of 80m. Maximum effective range is 40km. Because of the high chamber pressure and heat to achieve maximum range, the barrels would wear out and be replaced after only 300 rounds

Claymore mine – A directional anti-personnel mine with an effective range of 50m, containing 700 ball bearings. It was packed with 1.5 lbs of C4 explosives. These mines were especially valuable in ambushes and night defensive positions. An infantry platoon would carry 15 to 20 mines

Colored smoke grenade – This 19 oz grenade was used as a ground-to-ground or ground-to-air signaling device, a target or landing zone marking device, or a screening device for unit movements. It came in four colors: red, green, yellow, and violet

Fragmentation hand grenades (Frags) – Used to supplement small arms fire against the enemy in close combat. Round in shape (similar to a baseball) and at 14 oz, it contained 6.5 oz of high explosive with a 4- to 5-second delay fuse. It had a kill radius of 5m and a casualty radius of 15m. The M67 was a newer version and included an additional safety clip

M16 rifle – The basic infantry rifle adapted from the Armalite AR-15 for the military. The M16 was a shoulder-fired, gas-operated, lightweight rifle that uses a 20-round box magazine and had a maximum effective range of 400m. It could be fired on semi-automatic or automatic using a selector switch. In fully automatic mode, the weapon could fire a magazine load of 20 rounds in less than 2.5 seconds

M60 machine gun – The most important weapon in an infantry platoon. Each platoon had one M60. The gun fired a 7.62mm round and was belt-fed, gas-operated, and air-cooled with an effective range of 1,100m. Rate of fire was approximately 600 rounds per minute. Weight 23 lbs unloaded

M72 light antitank weapon (LAW) – An 8 lb., 24.8-inch, one-shot, shoulder-fired 66mm anti-tank rocket with an effective range of 200m. Also used against enemy bunkers

M79 grenade launcher – A single-shot, shoulder-fired, break-open to reload weapon, capable of firing a 40mm grenade to an effective range of 350m. Commonly called "the Thumper" because of its distinctive sound, the M79 could fire several types of rounds: high explosive (HE), night illumination, anti-personnel flechette (steel darts), and buckshot. The launcher was 29 inches in length and weighed 6 lbs empty. The 40mm HE round weighed about .5 lbs and was 4 inches long. The grenade launcher was the second most important weapon in the infantry platoon. A grenadier carried a variety of ammunition types in a knee-length vest

Enemy weapons

.51 cal heavy machine gun – This 55 lb gun was used extensively in both a ground and anti-aircraft role with great effectiveness. It was capable of 600–700 rpm and had a maximum effective range of 1,500m against air targets or 2,000m for ground targets

7.62 light machine gun – This light Russian machine gun was a standard and deadly weapon for both the NVA and VC. It fired 7.62mm rounds at 650–750 rpm to an effective range of 1,000m. It could be fired handheld or on a bipod. Ammunition was fed via a 100-round cylindrical drum mounted on the underside of the gun or belt fed. At 14.5 lbs it was 10 pounds lighter than the US M60 machine gun

7.62mm rifle – The rifle was manufactured as semi-automatic with a non-removable magazine fed by a 10-round stripper clip. Some rifles were later modified to fire full automatic and have removable magazines. The Chinese also made a version called the "Type 56." Both were used in Vietnam

60mm mortar – A Chinese-made smooth bore indirect fire weapon. It was a copy of the American M2. The Type 31's assembled weight was 44 lbs. It fired a 3 lb round to a maximum range of 1,500m, a shorter range than the American M2 due to the shorter firing tube. It had a blast radius of 20–25m

82mm mortar – A Chinese indirect fire weapon widely used in Vietnam by the NVA. It weighed 123 lbs assembled and fired an 8.2 lb shell to a maximum range of 3,000m with a kill radius of 30m

122mm rocket – The rocket had a range of 11km. Its length was 6.2 ft and weight 102 lbs with an explosive warhead that was 86 percent TNT. It was used as heavy artillery by the NVA along with 120mm mortars

AK-47 rifle – Designed in the Soviet Union, this assault rifle fires a 7.62x39mm round either semi or fully automatic. The rifle's weight fully loaded with a 30-round magazine is 8.5 lbs. The rifle was shoulder-fired and gas-operated with a muzzle velocity of 2350 FPS

RPG (Rocket-propelled grenade launcher) – A portable, shoulder-fired anti-tank weapon. The launcher with its rocket weighed just over 10 lbs. An 82mm rocket was inserted in the muzzle and protruded from the launcher. With an effective firing range of 150m using an iron sight, 3–4 rounds per minute could be fired against US ground forces or landing helicopters

Author's Military Awards, Decorations, Assignments and Timeline

Awards and decorations

Combat Infantryman's Badge, Ranger Tab, Paratrooper Wings, Combat Air Assault Badge, Bronze Star with V Device and Oak Leaf Cluster, Purple Heart with Oak Leaf Cluster, Air Medal, Army Commendation Medal with V Device and Oak Leaf Cluster, National Defense Service Medal, RVN Service Medal, Vietnamese Cross of Gallantry, RVN Defense Medal, VN Campaign Medal, Tet Offensive Campaign Medal, Presidential Unit Citation Medal, Valorous Unit Citation Medal

Unit assignments

1st Battalion 325 Infantry, 82nd Airborne Division, 1967–8, Ft. Bragg, NC
1st Battalion 5 Infantry, 1st Air Cav Division, 1968–9, I & III Corps, Vietnam
171st Infantry Brigade, 1969–71, Ft. Wainwright, AK
US Army Infantry School, 1971–3, Ft. Benning, GA

Timeline

June 11, 1967	Graduated from Claremont McKenna College, Claremont, CA
June 17, 1967	Reported to A Co, 1/325 Infantry, 82nd Airborne Division, Ft. Bragg, NC
July 11, 1967	Started Airborne Course, Ft. Benning, GA (3 weeks)
August 1, 1967	Started Infantry Officer Basic, Ft. Benning, GA (5 weeks)
September 5, 1967	Started Ranger Course, Ft. Benning, GA (12 weeks, was recycled)
November 14, 1967	Returned to 82nd Airborne Division, assigned as S-1, 1/325 Infantry
May 9, 1968	Departed for Vietnam from Travis AFB, CA
May 12, 1968	Assigned to 1st Air Cav Division, Long Binh Repo Center, III Corps, Vietnam

May 13, 1968	Arrived at Division Rear, An Khe, 1st Air Cav Div., II Corps, Vietnam
May 20, 1968	Arrived at Division Forward, Camp Evans, 1st Air Cav Div., I Corps, Vietnam
June 10, 1968	Joined A Co, 1/5 Cav, 1st Air Cav Division, LZ Jane, I Corps, Vietnam
October 21, 1968	Returned from R&R to 14th Military History Detachment, HHC, 1st Air Cav Div., Camp Evans, I Corps, Vietnam
Nov 3, 1968	1st Air Cav Division relocated to Phuoc Vinh, III Corps, Vietnam
Nov 10, 1968	Prepared report on the Battle of the Parrot's Beak,14th Military History Detachment, HHC, 1st Air Cav Div., Phuoc Vinh, III Corps, Vietnam
Dec 27, 1968	Christmas party for orphans at 14th Military History Detachment, HHC, 1st Air Cav Div., Phuoc Vinh, III Corps, Vietnam
February 6, 1969	Trial as Assistant Defense Counsel, HHC, 1st Air Cav Div., Phuoc Vinh, III Corps, Vietnam
March 2, 1969	Trip to Saigon to buy art supplies and obtain orders
May 9, 1969	Returned to Travis AFB in CA from Long Binh, III Corps, Vietnam and took leave at parents' home in Pebble Beach, CA
June 3, 1969	Reported to 171 Infantry Brigade, Ft. Wainwright, Alaska; promoted to captain
June 8, 1971	Reported to Leadership Department, US Army Infantry School, Ft. Benning, GA after meeting at Office of Personnel Operations in DC
June 11, 1973	Resigned commission in Army and went to work for Prentice-Hall Publishing Company in Santa Monica, CA

Bibliography

Books

Banks, Herbert (Editor). *1st Cavalry Division*. Paducah: Turner Publishing Company, 2002.

Coleman, J. D (Editor). *The 1st Air Cavalry Division: Vietnam, August 1965 to December 1969*. San Francisco: 1st Cavalry Division (Airmobile), 1970.

Dougan, Clark and Weiss, Stephen. *The American Experience in Vietnam*. New York: W. W. Norton & Company, 1988.

Henri, Raymond. *Vietnam Combat Art*. New York: Cavanagh & Cavanagh, 1968.

Lopes, Sal. *The Wall: Images and Offerings from the Vietnam Veterans Memorial*. New York: Collins Publishers, Inc., 1987.

Morgan, Lauren (Editor). "The Wall: 25th Anniversary Commemorative." Newtown: Boston Publishing Company (2007).

Phillips, Jeffrey and Gregory, Robyn. *America's First Team in the Gulf*. Dallas: Taylor Publishing Company, 1992.

Scruggs, Jan. *A Legacy of Service*. Washington, DC: Vietnam Veterans Memorial Fund, 2014.

Sinaiko, Eve, (Editor). *Vietnam: Reflexes and Reflections*. New York: Harry N. Abrams, Inc, 1998.

Wallis, Timothy. *Ordinary Heroes*. Zionsville: Sweet Pea Press, 2000.

Ward, Geoffrey and Burns, Ken. *The Vietnam War: An Intimate History*. New York: Alfred A. Knopf, 2017.

Other sources

Bartlett, Robin. "The Trail." *Army Digest Magazine* (April 1969), p.3, https://books.google.com/books?id=JusfAQAAMAAJ&pg=RA2-PA60&lpg=RA2-PA60&dq=Army+Digest+the+Trail+by+Robin+Bartlett&source=bl&ots=pgN4a6BNmD&sig=ACfU3U1IgRM4 nJq9pBzN0Rr6LSSNdQvG6Q&hl=en&sa=X&ved=2ahUKEwiG0c3oqMr5AhVeFmIAHfJUA ZUQ6AF6BAgiEAM#v=onepage&q=Army%20Digest%20the%20Trail%20by%20Robin% 20Bartlett&f=false

Flournoy, Robert. "Reflections of an Artillery Forward Observer with an Air Cav Rifle Company." (February 25 2022), p. 205. https://www.facebook.com/groups/Vietnam17tharty/permalink/ 2796533487159011/

Kramer, Al (Editor). "Vietnam: The Shadow War." Palo Alto: N-F Photo Publications (1967).

Lewis, Adrian. "Vietnam War POWs and MIAs." Encyclopedia Britannica, Inc, (April 28 2016), p. 207, https://www.britannica.com/topic/Vietnam-War-Pows-and-MIAs-2051428.

The Air Cavalry Division. Volume 1, Number 2, Tokyo: Dai Nippon Printing Co., Ltd. (July 1968)

"Tour 365: For Soldiers Going Home." APO San Francisco: USARV Information Office (Mid-Year, 1969) p. 57.

Excerpt: Arca, Paul (Paul@paularca.com), "It wasn't just contact with the enemy..." A Company 1/508 Infantry 82nd Airborne Vietnam 1968–9, Facebook.com, 4/14/15, p. 206. https://www.facebook.com/Aco1508inf82ndAirborneVietnam6869/posts/1650500581751970.

Excerpt: Arca, Paul (Paul@paularca.com), "This is what 45 days in the field looks like..." A Company 1/508 Infantry 82nd Airborne Vietnam 1968–9, Facebook.com, 4/14/15, p. 206. https ://www.facebook.com/Aco1508inf82ndAirborneVietnam6869/posts/1650500581751970.

For additional references and information please visit www.RobinBartlettAuthor.com

Resources

50th Anniversary of the Vietnam War Commemoration

https://www.vietnamwar50th.com/
Across the Nation, Americans are uniting to thank and honor Vietnam veterans and their families for their service and sacrifice. This is the main focus of The United States of America Vietnam War Commemoration—a national 50th anniversary commemoration,

Gold Star Organizations and Family Related Topics

American Gold Star Mothers (AGSM)
https://www.goldstarmoms.com/
An organization to connect and support Gold Star Mothers & Families

Tragedy Assistance Program for Survivors (TAPS)
https://www.taps.org/
Caring for the families of fallen heroes

Gold Star Children
https://goldstarchildren.org/
Organization that raises awareness about American children survivors whose mothers or fathers were killed while serving in the United States military

National Gold Star Family Registry
https://www.goldstarfamilyregistry.com/
Comprehensive database of the United States' fallen soldiers

Gold Star Wives of America, Inc.
https://www.goldstarwives.org/
Preserve and enhance benefits to surviving United States military spouses and their children

Honor and Remember
https://honorandremember.org/
To perpetually recognize the sacrifice of America's fallen military service members and their families

Military Families United
http://www.militaryfamiliesunited.org/
National coalition of Blue Star, Gold Star, next of kin, veterans, and patriotic
American families to honor the fallen, support those who fight, and serve their families

No Greater Love Foundation
https://nglfoundation.org/
Provide the nation's military and their families with opportunities to recover from the stress and physical
hardships of protecting and serving America

Sons & Daughters in Touch (SDIT)
https://sdit.org/
All-volunteer, national support organization committed to uniting the Gold Star sons and daughters
of American servicemen who were killed, or who remain missing, as a result of the Vietnam War

Gary Sinise Foundation
https://www.garysinisefoundation.org/
Serves the nation by honoring our defenders, veterans, first responders, their families and those in need

Wounded Warrior Project
https://www.woundedwarriorproject.org/
Honors and empowers wounded warriors

Prisoner of War/Missing in Action (POW/MIA)

Joint POW/MIA Accounting Command (JPAC)
https//www.dppa.mil
Conducts global search, recovery, and laboratory operations to identify unaccounted-for Americans
from past conflicts

National League of POW/MIA Families
https://www.pow-miafamilies.org/
Account as fully as possible for American Prisoners-of-War and Missing-in-Action, as well as other
US personnel still unaccounted-for from the Vietnam War and wars and conflicts further past, thus
ending the uncertainty of their families

Rolling Thunder
http://rollingthundermotorcyclerally.com/
Educate, facilitate, and never forget by means of a demonstration for service members that were
abandoned after the Vietnam War

Run for the Wall (RFTW)
https://rftw.us/
Annual motorcycle ride from California to Washington, DC

Defense POW MIA Accounting Agency
https://www.dpaa.mil/
Provide the fullest possible accounting of our missing personnel to their families and the nation

PeaceTreesVietnam.org
https://www.peacetreesvietnam.org/
Removing dangerous explosives, returning land to safe use, promoting peace and cultivating a brighter
future for the children and families of Vietnam

Mines Advisory Group Vietnam
https://www.maginternational.org
Reduce the risk of landmines and unexploded bombs and release land to support socio-economic development

Vietnam War Memorials

Vietnam Women's Memorial
http://www.vietnamwomensmemorial.org
Honors the women who risked their lives to serve their country

Vietnam Veterans Memorial Fund
https://www.vvmf.org/
Never forget those who served and sacrificed in the Vietnam War

Vietnam Memorial Traveling Wall
https://www.travelingwall.us/
3/5 scale reminder of the great sacrifices made during the Vietnam War. Purpose to help heal and rekindle friendships and to allow people the opportunity to visit loved ones in their hometown who otherwise may not be able to make the trip to Washington

The Virtual Wall
http://www.virtualwall.org/
Brings the Vietnam Veterans Memorial to one's home to help remember the sacrifices of the fallen and their families

Vietnam Veterans Memorial Fund Registry
https://registry.vvmf.org/
Enables veterans across the world to locate fellow Vietnam Veterans and of course, connect their stories with those who made the ultimate sacrifice

Vietnam Veterans Memorial Fund In Memory Program
https://www.vvmf.org/In-Memory-Program/
Honors those who died from Agent Orange and Vietnam War related causes after return

US Department of Veterans Affairs

https://www.va.gov/contact-us/
Access a wide range of services offered by the Veterans Administration

Veterans Organizations

The American Legion
https://www.legion.org/
To enhance the well-being of America's veterans, their families, our military, and our communities by our devotion to mutual helpfulness

Disabled American Veterans (DAV)
https://www.dav.org/
Empowering veterans to lead high-quality lives with respect and dignity

Military Order of the Purple Heart (MOPH)
https://www.purpleheart.org/
To foster an environment of goodwill and camaraderie among combat wounded veterans, promote patriotism, support necessary legislative initiatives, and most importantly, provide service to all veterans and their families

Paralyzed Veterans of America
https://pva.org/
PVA will use its expertise to be the leading advocate for quality health care for members, research and education, benefits and civil rights that maximize independence

Veterans of Foreign Wars (VFW)
https://vfw.org/
Foster camaraderie among United States veterans of overseas conflicts. To serve our veterans, the military, and our communities. To advocate on behalf of all veterans

Vietnam Veterans of America (VVA)
https://vva.org/
Promote and support the full range of issues important to Vietnam veterans, create a new identity for this generation of veterans, and change public perception of Vietnam veterans

Vietnam Helicopter Pilots Association (VHPA)
https://www.vhpa.org/
Enhance and accredit the cohesiveness, esprit de corps, and traditions of valor of rotary wing aircrews that flew in Southeast Asia during the Vietnam Era

1st Cavalry Division Association (1CDA)
https://1cda.org/
Mission: to preserve old friendships and conduct periodic reunions

82d Airborne Association
https://www.82ndairborneassociation.org/
To further develop the bond between current and past airborne forces of the US military

VN Dog Handlers Association
https://www.vdha.us/
Unite veteran war dog handlers and honor the memory of their war dog partners

15th Medical Battalion Association
https://15thmedbnassociation.org/
Promotes goodwill and brotherhood among our membership, their families, all veterans, and military men and women presently serving in the United States of America

Vietnam War Podcasts

Cherries Writer Vietnam
https://cherrieswriter.com
See what war is like and how it affects our warriors

Echoes of the Vietnam War (VVMF)
https://www.vvmf.org/Echoes/
Even after 50 years, the impact of the Vietnam War echoes across generations. Hear stories of service and sacrifice from people who are affected

The American War Podcast
https://www.washingtonpost.com/podcasts/the-american-war/
A podcast guide to "The Vietnam War," the new documentary from Ken Burns and Lynn Novick

Napalm in the Morning
https://soundcloud.com/user-607552064-959869054
The Vietnam war through film

Warriors In Their Own Words/First Person Stories
https://evergreenpodcasts.com

Tracking Our History/Francis Remkiewicz
https://podcasts.apple.com/us/podcast/tracking-our-history
First person war stories

Digital and Print Media

Vietnam
https://shop.historynet.com/products/vietnam
Firsthand accounts of firefights

Army Digest
https://ship.historynet.com
Official US Army publication

Stars & Stripes
https://www.stripes.com/
Provide first-hand reporting from bases around the world

Redstone Rocket
https://www.theredstonerocket.com/site/
Official installation newspaper for the US Army Garrison—Redstone Arsenal located in Huntsville, Ala

Saber
https://1cda.org/saber-newspaper/
Association Newspaper of the 1st Cavalry Division

Paraglide
https://82ndairborneassociation.org/paraglide.html
Association newspaper of the 82d Airborne Division

Vietnam Veterans of America Magazine
https://vva.org/category/arts-of-war/magazines/
Association Magazine

Military Journals

Military Review
https://www.armyupress.army.mil

Joint Force Quarterly
https://ndupress.ndu.edu/jfq/

US Army War College Quarterly: *Parameters*
https://press.armywarcollege.edu/parameters/

Army History
https://history.army.mil/army/history/

Army Sustainment
https://www.army.mil/armysustainment/

Army Magazine AUSA
https://www.ausa.org/publications/army-magazine

On Point: The Journal of Army History
https://armyhistory.org/on-point/

Military History Quarterly
https://historynet.com/magazine/military-history-quarterly

Infantry Magazine
https://www.benning.army.mil/infantry/magazine

Proceedings: US Naval Institute
https://www.usni.org/magazines/proceedings

Primary Source Information

Vietnam War National Archives
https://www.archives.gov/research/vietnam-war
Photographs, textual, and other records from the National Archives related to Vietnam diplomacy, in country, the home front, and post-conflict events

The Virtual Vietnam Archive and Sam Johnson Archive at Texas Tech University
https://www.vietnam.ttu.edu/virtualarchive/
Huge archive of mostly personal items from the war, including documents, photographs, slides, negatives, oral histories, artifacts, moving images, sound recordings

Vietnam Veterans History Project: Vietnam War
https//www.loc.gov/classroom-materials/veterans-the-veterans-history-project/
Personal accounts, photos, letters, and recordings of American veterans of the Vietnam War

Antiwar and Radical History Project
https://depts.washington.edu/antiwar/photosdocs.shtml
Hundreds of photographs and documents cataloguing the history of protest and activism against war–particularly, the Vietnam War–among students, soldiers, and citizens

Recommended Vietnam Reference Books

Caputo, Philip. *A Rumor of War: The Classic Vietnam Memoir* (40th Anniversary Edition). New York: Picador, 2017.
Danziger, Jeff. *Lieutenant Dangerous: a Vietnam War Memoir.* Hanover: Steelfourth Press, 2021.
Downs, Frederick Jr. *The Killing Zone: My Life in the Vietnam War.* Reissue edition. New York: W. W. Norton & Company, 2007.
French, Albert. *Patches of Fire: A Story of War and Redemption.* New York, 1998.
Halberstam, David. *The Best and the Brightest.* New York: Ballantine Books, 1993.
Henderson Gary. *Memoirs of a Grunt: On the Ground in Vietnam 68/69.* Knoxville: Independently Published, 2020.
Herr, Michael. *Dispatches.* New York: Vintage, 1991.
Kovic, Ron. *Born on the Fourth of July.* New York: Akashic Books, 2016.
Maraness, David. *They Marched into Sunlight.* New York: Simon & Schuster, 2004.
Mason, Robert. *Chickenhawk.* New York: Penguin Books, 2005.
Milligan, Benjamin. *By Water Beneath the Walls: The Rise of the Navy Seals.* New York: Bantam, 2021.
McCullough, Timothy. *Mongoose Bravo Vietnam.* Vancouver: Storyteller Books, 2019.
O'Brien, Tim. *If I Die in a Combat Zone,* New York: Crown, 1999.
Patterson, James & Eversmann, Matt. *Walk in My Combat Boots.* New York: Grand Central Publishing, 2022.
Puller, Lewis. *Fortunate Son.* New York: Grove Press, 2000.
Sheehan, Neil. *A Bright Shining Lie.* New York: Vintage, 1989.
Turse, Nick. *Kill Anything That Moves.* New York: Picador, 2013.
Vietnam War Bibliography
http://edmoise.sites.clemson.edu/bibliography.html
A compilation of hundreds of books, articles, and dissertations by Edwin Moise, professor of history at Clemson University
Wallace, Wallace. *Bloods: Black Veterans of the Vietnam War.* Novato: Presidio Press, 1985.
Wolff, Tobias. *In Pharaoh's Army.* New York: Vintage, 1995.
Yuzuk, David and Yuzuk, Neil. *Giant Killer.* Traverse City: Mission Point Press, 2020.

Index

References to images are in *italics*.

Abrams, Gen Creighton 32, 105
Aerial Rocket Artillery (ARA) 3
Afghanistan xv, 231
Agent Orange (AO) 133, 134, 233
Airborne course 14–16
aircraft, US 26
  C-130 14
  see also helicopters
Alaska *see* Ft. Wainwright
ambushes 6, 27–30, 91–5, 142–5; *see also*
  saturation ambushing
American Civil War xiii, 55
An Khe 8, 44–9, 88–9, 169
Ann-Margret 195–6
Army of the Republic of Vietnam (ARVN)
  xvii, 120, 147
art supplies 204–5, 208
Article 15 punishment 165, 166, 167
artillery support 107–9
artworks 226–7
ARVN *see* Army of the Republic of Vietnam
assistant defense counsel 198–202
autorotation 119, 121–3

base camp 73, 74–5, 128
Bien Hoa 42–4, 214–16
Blankshain, Jessica 232–3
blocking force missions 120–1
booby traps 120–1, 173–4
boonies *see* jungle terrain
"buddy ratings" 20
butterflies 67–8, 222, 224, 225

C-Rations 7, 23, 45, 64, 65, 72
  and heating 90–1
cadences 14–15

call signs 2
Calley, Lt William xviii, 231
Cam Ranh Bay 9
Cambodia xviii, xix, 146, 213
Camp Evans 45–9, 180–1
Cannizzaro, Louis 226
Career Course 222, 223
caution 212–13
CG *see* Westmoreland, Gen William
Charlie Alpha (CA) assaults 4–7, 55–6,
  101–2
China 231
"Choi Hoi" leaflets 80, *83*, *85–6*
Christmas 195–6
CIA 21, 147
civilians 60, 73, 87
Claymore mines 7, 47, 86, 90, 91–5, 142–4
code books 66, 101, 108–9
confidence tests 22, 25, 30
court martials 60, 61, 198–201
cover men 61, 63, 74, 77, 78–9
Crane, Stephen: *The Red Badge of Courage* xi
Cronkite, Walter xviii, 214
CS gas 150–1, 152–4

Dahlonega (GA) 19, 20, 23–5
death cards xxi, 7
Deerling, S/Sgt John 51–2
Demilitarized Zone (DMZ) 55, 61, 76, 133
DEROS (Date Estimated to Return from
  Overseas Service) 203, 214–19
Dickens, Charles: *A Christmas Carol* xiv
door gunners 4, 102, 113, 117, 118, 119

Eglin (FL) 19, 20, 25–32
equipment 44–5, 50–2, 64

Explosive Ordinance Disposal Team (EOD) 58, 120–1

field missions 128–32
fire missions 57–8
firebases 129–31
firefights 3, 6, 157–63
Flournoy, Robert 228
FNGs (Fucking New Guys) 2–3, 74–5
food see C-Rations; Long Range Reconnaissance Patrol
fragging 60, 231
Ft. Benning (GA) 13–18, 19–23, 222, 224
Ft. Bragg (NC) 10–13, 33
Ft. Wainwright (AK) 207, 220–2

gas masks 150–1, 152–4
Gentry, Sgt Maj Neal R. 32
Gonzales, Sgt Speedy 182, 186, 191, 195, 215
and Saigon 204–6, 207–11
grenadiers 64, 79
guerrilla warfare 6
Gulf of Tonkin 55, 80, 155

Hackworth, Col David 146
Hastings, Lt Dennis 39, 43
Hawaii 40
headquarters and headquarters company (HHC) 220–2
heat stroke 15, 61, 64, 96, 137
helicopters 3, 73, 116–19
and autorotation 121–3
Cobra gunship 46–7, 107
and landing zones 63
see also Charlie Alpha assaults; medevacs
Ho Chi Minh Trail 55, 76, 167–9
Holocaust xiv
hooches 69
Hope, Bob 195–6
Hue xvii, xviii

Infantry Officer Basic Course (IOBC) 13–14, 16–18
intelligence 101, 146, 151
Iraq xv

Jacobs, Ronald 227
Johnson, Lyndon B. xvii, 80, 214

Johnson, Specialist 2, 3, 4
Jump School 13–14, 15–16
jungle terrain 61–70, 76–8

Kennedy, Robert F. xviii
killed in action (KIA) xvii, xxi, 157–61, 214
and memorials 9
and MHD 186, 187, 192–5
and Roberts 6, 7–8
King, Dr. Martin Luther xviii
Kit Carson Scouts 80, 147
Kramer, Mitzi 67–8, 222, 225

landing zone (LZ) 4–5, 101–2, 111–15, 117
Laos xviii, xix, 61, 146–8, 213; see also Ho Chi Minh Trail
latrines 75
Lee, Lt Col Robert E. 55
leg cramps 138–40
Lewis, Adrian: "Vietnam War POWs and MIAs" 230
listening posts (LPs) 129–30
Loan, Gen Nguyen Ngoc xviii, 214
Long Binh 195–6, 199
Long Range Reconnaissance Patrol (LRRP) 97, 146

machine gunners 64, 79
malaria 73
maps:
American unit locations 54
corps areas, South Vietnam 53
Margulies, Max 232–3
marijuana see pot smoking
medevacs 66–8, 137, 139–40
medical supplies 69
Military History Detachment (MHD) 180–2, 185–97, 201–2, 204
military payment certificates (MPCs) 73, 87–9
mines see Claymore mines
Mini-Tet Offensives xvii, 48
Miranda 35, 36–8
missing in action (MIA) 230–1
monsoons 72, 76, 142–5
mortar platoons 56–9, 72–3
mountain training 23–5
My Lai massacre xviii–xix, 231
Myers, Charles xiii

NCOs (non-commissioned officers) 3, 13, 19
night firefights 157–63
Nixon, Richard 80, 232
North Vietnam xvii, xix, 146, 231
North Vietnamese Army (NVA) xvii, 144–4,
    213
    and prisoners 151
    and surrender leaflets *84–5*
    see also Kit Carson Scouts

Oberdorfer, Don xviii
Office of Personnel Operations (OPO) 222–3,
    224
Operational Readiness Report, Lessons Learned
    (ORLL) 187–8, 190, 198, 201–2

parachute jumps 14, 15–16, 26, 35, 37–8
Paris Peace Accords 231
"Parrot's Beak, Battle of the" 192–5
parties 35, 36
Patton, Gen George xiii
pay officers 87–9
photographs 226–7
Phuoc Vinh 188–90, 195–6
point men 6, 62, 63–4, 74, 77–9, 172–7
point shooting 22–3
Post Traumatic Stress Disorder (PTSD) xiii–xiv,
    xv, 218–19, 230, 233
pot smoking 60–1, 71, 198–201
Prentice-Hall Publishing Company 224–5
Presidential Unit Citations 55
prisoners of war (POWs) 230–1, 232
protests xviii, xix, 213
Psyops 80
PTSD *see* Post Traumatic Stress Disorder
Purple Heart 203–4

Quang Tri xvii, 49–52
quick reaction force (QRF) 110–15

radio telephone operators (RTOs) 62, 93, 99,
    113–15
rain *see* monsoons
Ranger School 16, 17, 19–32
rappelling 24
reconnaissance by fire 61, 102–4
Replacement Depot (Repo Depo) 41, 42–4
"Report of Survey" 12–13

Roberts, Sgt Ron 2, 3, 4, 5–9
ropes 124–5, 126–7
Ross, Lt 70
R&R 178, 182–4

S-1 (personnel officer) 33–5, 38, 179–80
Saigon xvii, 204–11
salt tablets 15, 45, 73, 137, 138, 140
San Francisco 39–40, 217–18
sapper teams 48
saturation ambushing 96–100
scrip *see* military payment certificates (MPCs)
SEALs (Sea, Air, and Land) 21
search and destroy operations 61–70, 80,
    125–6
"short-timer calendar" xix, *xx*
showers 74–5
shrapnel 158–6
Simons, Pvt Peter 165–71
sky cranes 3
slope running 124–5
Small, Danny 65, 66, 67, 70, 171
smoke canisters 113, 117
snipers 65
Sons and Daughters in Touch (SDIT) 9
South Vietnam xvii–xviii, *53*; *see also* Army of
    the Republic of Vietnam (ARVN)
Soviet Union 231
stream crossing 125–7
supplies 116–17
swamps 26–7, 30–1
Syria xv

Tan Son Nhut Airbase 41–2
tear gas 150–1, 152–4
teeth 131–2, 166–7
Tensey, Capt 181–2, 187, 190–1, 194, 196
Terhune, SP4 5–7
Tet Offensive xvii–xviii, 3
Thomas, Sgt 65, 66–8, 70, 71
Tiger Teams 146–8
Tokyo 182–4
tracers 134–6
"Trail, The" (Bartlett) xi–xii, xxi, xxii, 187,
    226
Travis AFB 39, 40, 216–17
turn-in leaflets 80, *81–2*
typhoons 97

unexploded bombs 70
United States of America (USA) xvii–xix, 214, 230–3
US Army:
    1st Air Cav Dvn xxii, 2–3, 44–9, 226–8
    82nd Airborne Dvn xix, 10–13, 33–8
    101st Airborne Dvnx xix, 38
    1st Btn, 5th Cav Rgt 49–52, 55–9

veterans xiv, xv, xviii–xix, 9, 227–34
Viet Cong (VC) xvii, 77
    and ambushes 94–5, 97–100
    and booby traps 120
    and Camp Evans 48
    and Charlie Alpha assaults 5, 6
    and face to face 78–80, 86
    and hideouts 155–6
    and prisoners xviii
    and tactics 213
    and Tan Son Nhut Airbase 41
Vietnam Syndrome 230
Vietnam Veterans War Memorial xvii, xxi
Vietnam War xiv–xv, 230–4

Vietnamese Unit Advisors 223
Villard, Dr. Erik xvii

walking point 172–7
water 72, 73, 74–5, 116, 135–6
    and resupply 137–8
weaponry, US 1, 3, 47, 245–6
    and FNGs 74
    and losses 125–6
    M14 rifle 1, 21–2
    M16 rifle 1, 23, 65, 78–9
    M79 grenade launcher 133–4, 135
    see also Claymore mines
weaponry, Vietnamese 1, 247
    AK-47 1, 65
West Point 13–14, 21, 23
Westmoreland, Gen William 104–5
Wilson, Woodrow xiii
World War I xiii
World War II xiii
wounded in action (WIA) xvii, 186, 187, 192–5, 214

YouTube 226